The Modernist Impulse
in American
Protestantism

WILLIAM R. HUTCHISON

The Modernist Impulse in American Protestantism

Harvard University Press
Cambridge, Massachusetts
and London, England   1976

Library of Congress Cataloging in Publication Data

Hutchison, William R.
    The modernist impulse in American Protestantism.

    Bibliography: p.
    Includes index.
    1. Modernism.   I. Title.
BT82.H87   273′.9   75-20190
ISBN 0-674-58058-3

To Ralph Henry Gabriel

Preface

This study began as an effort to trace the development of Protestant liberalism in the United States through the decades immediately following the heyday of New England transcendentalism—that is, from the 1860s to the end of the century. I was led, however, by my own increasing interest in the religious uses of the idea of progress, to reach back into the earlier part of the nineteenth century and, even more, to press forward through the first quarter of the twentieth. At the same time, as I looked into and behind the progressivist ideology of American liberals, I came to understand the inseparability of that progressivism from a larger theological construct that by the early twentieth century was being identified as modernism. My investigation from that point on, though subjected to minor changes of direction, remained centrally concerned with the modernist impulse that constituted either one important force or the single most important one (I think it was the latter) informing and shaping Protestant liberalism over a period of about 120 years.

My attitudes toward modernism, like the definition of my subject, have altered within a fairly stable frame of questions and predispositions. An author, though in some ways least qualified to warn of his or her biases, usually is well advised to make the attempt and then let readers judge for themselves how much to take personal orientation into account. I would suggest, first of all, that this book rests on affirmative assumptions both about the value of intellectual history and about the importance and force of religious ideas. More specifically, it presupposes the continuing need for a type of intellectual history that traces the development and fortunes of particular ideas over long spans of time—even though this usually means that the equally important demand for thorough treatment of an idea's social dimensions must be met in separate, more time-concentrated studies.

Within the context of that understanding of intellectual history and its validity, I recognize biases that are more individual, or at least are more likely to be controverted. One of these consists in a supposition that religious ideas are as likely as their secular counterparts to operate with some autonomy, that religious thought is only partially reducible to social experience or explained by it. Another, and perhaps the really salient bias to recognize in connection with the present study, is a greater personal sympathy for liberal than for conservative forms of religious expression.

While the latter affinity is one of long standing, this is the area in which I recognize some considerable change. My respect for Protestant liberals has increased substantially during the period in which I have investigated their movement and thought. One hopes that such shifts or intensifications of attitude proceed mainly from accumulating knowledge of the documents and data. But they also undoubtedly happen because the scholar is engaged in so many other conversations while he or she converses with the historical figures under direct scrutiny. I believe I undertook an earlier study of transcendentalism, and began this one, under substantial corrective influence from the views of human nature and religion that came to my generation through Niebuhrian neo-orthodoxy. This later study is doubtless affected by a lessened enthusiasm for the neo-orthodox positions, and commensurately by a willingness to listen to what even the more ardently progressive or humanistic spokesmen for an older liberalism were trying to say.

Most persons profoundly concerned about religious questions, whether they are in some ordinary sense "believers," or like the present writer are unconventional in belief, value a religious movement or position both for its prophetic strength and for its capacity to foster the greatest possible integrity of expression. Few, among those who are willing to make evaluative judgments at all, would knowingly sacrifice or minimize either of those criteria. But just as many critics of liberalism saw it striving for purity of expression at too great a sacrifice of prophetic or proclamatory power, many onetime enthusiasts for neo-orthodoxy came eventually to feel that this form of realism, while exhilaratingly countercultural, too frequently encouraged one to speak less than the simple truth about one's religious and moral beliefs.

St. Paul's and Reinhold Niebuhr's bold assurance that we all could be deceivers in literal statement, yet true in symbolic reference, held immense appeal for a generation (roughly between 1930 and 1960) undergoing sharp reaction against what seemed a lack of all boldness in liberal thought. And few persons, even in the changed climate of Protestant thinking that has followed neo-orthodoxy, would be such positivists as utterly to deny (what the liberal Horace Bushnell also argued in the 1840s) that the truest language must, because it is language, be deceiving. In the longer run, nonetheless, the brave neo-orthodox prescriptions for an effective religious realism became, for me at least, less convincing than the much-scorned liberal alternatives. That shift in personal views has doubtless affected, as well as grown out of, my analysis of a movement that struggled toward maximum candor both in the use of religious language and in dealing with the riddle of religion's cultural involvement.

Having tried to expose my point of view, I must make a start at acknowledging debts. My wife's wisdom and support have been so important that I can hope to do minimal justice to them only by mentioning her contribution first. Students in a number of seminars in American or comparative cultural history offered straightforward criticism and highly stimulating ideas, and willingly explored byways they knew might be cul-de-sacs. Among research assistants at several universities who helped in large and smaller ways, I must especially thank John Kuehl, Charles McCormick, Lars Hoffman, James Tyrrell, Gene Sessions, Ernest Kurtz, Dennis Voskuil, Edith Waldvogel, and Grant Wacker. Carol Quigley, Trudy Brand, and Barbara Davis typed the manuscript and labored over the bibliographies and charts that we hoped would reduce the labor of later investigators.

In planning illustrations for this volume, an assistant and I combed archives, biographies, and family collections for pictures that would represent figures in the book during the appropriate years or decades of their lives and that might also offer more insight into personality than the most formal studio portraiture often conveys. The first objective proved easier to realize than the second, and sometimes thwarted the second: the illustrations, therefore, while nearly all timely, are predominantly formal. Since we received many more interesting photographs, casual and formal, than we have been able to publish, the Andover-Harvard Library of the Harvard Divinity School will retain copies of the unused pictures for the benefit of investigators who may wish to see or use them.

For research support I am grateful to officials of the Guggenheim Foundation, the American Philosophical Society, the Charles Warren Center, the American Association of Theological Schools, the American University, the University of Wisconsin, and the Harvard Divinity School. The editors of the *American Historical Review, American Quarterly, Church History, Harvard Theological Review*, and the *Journal of American History* have permitted me to use material first published, in different form, in their pages (see Bibliography). Harvard University Press has allowed me to republish substantial portions of the chapter I contributed to John K. Fairbank, ed., *The Missionary Enterprise in China and America* (Cambridge, Mass., 1974. Copyright © 1974 by the President and Fellows of Harvard College). Friends in the historical and American studies fields who kindly read, and probably too kindly criticized, parts or all of the manuscript are H. Shelton Smith, Sydney Ahlstrom, Ernest Sandeen, George Marsden, Martin Marty, Conrad Wright, and Michael T. Gilmore. My debt to Ralph H. Gabriel, onetime colleague and perennial teacher and friend, is emphasized in the book's dedication.

W. R. H.

Cambridge, Massachusetts

Contents

Illustrations

The Modernist Impulse
in American
Protestantism

NOTE ON CITATIONS

Items listed in the alphabetized Bibliography at the end of this book will be cited in the footnotes by short titles only. In those cases, full publishing data do not appear with the first reference to the item in the text.

Introduction: Faith and Force Enough

> Whatever else I may repent of, therefore, let it be
> reckoned neither among my sins nor follies
> that I once had faith and force enough to
> form generous hopes of the world's destiny.
>
> COVERDALE, IN HAWTHORNE'S
> *Blithedale Romance*

Hawthorne's romantic reformers and their nine-teenth- or early twentieth-century successors have been granted, at best, a partial immunity from charges of sin and folly. To those who experienced the middle decades of the twentieth century, the earlier widespread confidence in some form of earthly Kingdom seemed nearly inexcusable. In immediate historical retrospect such faith appeared not merely mistaken, but debilitating and even demonic. Great wars and ruinous depressions might have been averted—so this argument ran—had the ascendant social philosophies of the preceding decades been less fatuous in their hopes for human society.

In recent years, nonetheless, certain forms of liberalism and humanism have been viewed with new tolerance, and characteristic liberal attitudes have been revived. In religious thought, for example, the conception of God as immanent or indwelling has regained much of its former strength; and theology has resumed the critique of religious language that liberals pursued. In social thought generally, though both radical left and radical right retain their perennial objections to liberalism, the current generation seems to have outlived an earlier sharp resentment at having been, as we thought, hoodwinked and humiliated by our society's experience with humanistic optimism. Alternative systems of thought, moreover, such as political realism or religious neo-orthodoxy, now seem as flawed in their own ways as the progressive idealism they sought to displace.

In any renewed scrutiny of the liberal tradition, expressions within American Protestantism deserve close attention. In this book I have tried to trace not the entire history of Protestant liberalism but rather the development and demise of a cluster of liberal ideas that usually was called—after a prominent Roman Catholic example—Protestant modernism.

Modernism, like fundamentalism and most other -isms, was understood and defined in varying (though usually not contradictory) ways, and I do not present my own definition as the only one possible. I have found, however, that when "modernism" finally became a common term in the early part of this century, it generally meant three things: first and most visibly, it meant the conscious, intended adaptation of religious ideas to modern culture. The popular or journalistic definition tended to stop there, or to move directly from there to a functional explanation of modernism as the direct opposite and negation of biblical literalism. But for the Protestant theologians, preachers, and teachers who either championed or opposed the idea of cultural adaptation, two further and deeper notions were important. One was the idea that God is immanent in human cultural development and revealed through it. The other was a belief that human society is moving toward realization (even though it may never attain the reality) of the Kingdom of God.

This cluster of beliefs—in adaptation, cultural immanentism, and a religiously-based progressivism—has been my principal concern. Since I consider the modernist impulse, as thus defined, to have been central to the liberal movement—at least from the 1870s to the 1930s—and not just one force among many, I have been led into discussions of biblical, creedal, institutional, philosophical, social, and other components of liberalism that strike me as having been most affected by the modernist convictions. But I would not want to claim that I have dealt with any one of these related liberal themes in truly systematic fashion. Most of them deserve either separate consideration or treatment within a more comprehensive history of the liberal movement than I am able to offer.

Protestant liberalism, even more notoriously than its modernist formulation, has been difficult to capture in any agreed description. So again a working definition is in order.

The American Protestant liberalism referred to in this study was a movement first identified and rendered self-conscious at the opening of the nineteenth century. A number of its themes had, to be sure, made inroads in American culture and intellectual life before that time. Modifications of the more rigorous doctrines concerning God's sovereignty, human wickedness, and the exclusiveness of Christian revelation could claim long indirect pedigrees in Christian history and more immediate instigations in the Arian, Arminian, and rationalist currents of the eighteenth century. But in America it was the Unitarians of the first half of the nineteenth century who fused such modifications into an organized movement. Unitarianism remained small as a denomination but performed disproportionately large service as a vehicle and testing-ground for liberal religious ideas.

In the late nineteenth century, when a considerable portion of the most dynamic Unitarianism was moving "beyond Christianity," or moving outside of specifically religious institutions, the larger Protestant denominations became rapidly infiltrated by liberal ideas much like those of the earlier movement. This was true especially in the Congregational, Episcopal, Methodist, Baptist, Disciples, and Presbyterian churches; and particularly in their northern and western components. Though no exact measurement is possible, one might be safe in estimating that by 1920 liberal ideas had become accepted and respectable in more than a third of the pulpits of American Protestantism and in at least half the educational, journalistic, social, and literary or theological expressions of Protestant church life.[1]

The most characteristic attitudes, by that time, could be readily identified. Liberalism emphasized the immanence of God in

---

[1] The conservative *Ministers' Monthly*, in a poll of theological seminaries in 1923, found that forty considered themselves liberal, thirty-three orthodox; eighteen were noncommital. In the *Monthly*'s view, which no doubt must be corrected somewhat for alarmism and excessively narrow definitions, 500 out of 800

nature and human nature. It tended, in consequence, toward a general humanistic optimism. It made much of a universal religious sentiment—or, increasingly, of the variegated forms of religious experience—that lay behind the institutions, scriptures, and creeds of particular religions and that preceded such formal expressions in order of importance. It valued good works, conceived in either individual or more collective terms, over professions and confessions. Among the traditional doctrines of Christianity, the most important and controlling for liberalism was the Incarnation, which signified and ratified the actual presence of God in humanity.

In order to understand what was distinctive about the modernist impulse that flourished within this larger liberal context, one must recognize that liberalization could—and until the later years of the nineteenth century generally did—proceed without conscious reference to modernity. Occasionally, in fact, it took forms that involved considerable hostility to modern culture. Liberals could rest the case for theological change upon direct appeals to scripture, or rely upon a universal and essentially timeless reason, or appeal to intuition; and in all these cases the accompanying attitude toward contemporary culture, toward modernity, was almost as likely to be negative as it was to be affirming or celebratory.

One no doubt can speak of an unconscious or unintended modernism; of tacit accommodations, especially within liberal or reformist Christianity, to the thought and culture of particular eras. Both the adherents and the opponents of modernism occasionally used the term "modernist" in that way—the first when they were anxious about historical precedents and justification, the second when laying the blame for modernist heresies upon a particular tradition. Modernists like Shailer Mathews muddied the waters with claims that Jesus, Paul, and certain Old Testament prophets had been modernists; while their assailants often felt free to extend the rubric to embrace Luther, or Wesley, or some other reformer not of the writer's denomination who had somehow

---

Chicago Protestant ministers were unsound, "practically every one" of the denominational publishing houses was liberal, and liberals controlled the ecclesiastical machinery in nearly all the leading denominations. *Ministers' Monthly*, 2 (September 1923), 5-6; (October 1923), 3-5.

got into the wrong pew. Even when this was done, however, it was commonly recognized that the nineteenth- and twentieth-century phenomenon, in its clear intentionality, was something different. William Lawrence Wood made the appropriate distinction in an article of the 1930s:

Not until the nineteenth century was the attempt made consciously (one might say self-consciously) to do what often before had been done quite naively, to re-express the gospel in terms of the then-modern thought. Then for the first time the modernist became aware that he was a modernist.[2]

The great German theologian Friedrich Schleiermacher, in this as in many other respects the father of modern Protestant theology, had embodied and articulated the new attitude toward culture. A latter-day antagonist (but also admirer), the Swiss theologian Karl Barth, argued that Schleiermacher had been the first personality in Protestant history in whom one could perceive a fully conscious alignment between theology and the wider intellectual life. "He took part in the philosophy, science, politics, social life and art of his time," Barth observed, "as the man who was responsible in all these fields." Not that Schleiermacher could have claimed exclusive credit for having attained to this degree of catholicity; the "personal union" between theology and culture that he "so wonderfully fulfilled," Barth suggested, was possible only "beyond Rousseau's outbreaks, beyond Lessing's struggles, beyond Kant's critique, in the time which found it possible to take Hegel's synthetic philosophy as its sign." Schleiermacher nonetheless excelled and pioneered "in realizing the possibility of the theologian's being at the same time entirely a modern man, with a good, and not with a divided conscience."[3]

As one who explicated as well as embodied the argument for religious-cultural accommodation, Schleiermacher spoke most influentially in his *Speeches to the Cultured Despisers of*

---

[2]William Lawrence Wood, reviewing Walter Lowrie's *Our Concern for the Theology of Crisis*, in *Anglican Theological Review*, 15 (April 1933), 168. For a particularly lucid sorting-out of the differences between a conscious and an unconscious or muted affirmation of the world, see John Tonkin, *The Church and the Secular Order in Reformation Thought* (New York, Columbia University Press, 1971), pp. 164-168.

[3]Barth, *Protestant Thought*, pp. 314-315.

Religion (1799). Here he proposed that the cultured person can scarcely despise what is most essential in religion without rejecting what is natural to him or to her as a human being. Conversely, as Schleiermacher insisted elsewhere, it is futile and self-destructive for Christianity or any other religious faith to harbor disdain for culture, which in principle is no more non-religious or alien than that which calls itself religion.[4] Culture and religion are related, he contended, not as parent and child, nor as antagonists, but as joint heirs and products of the religious sentiment that constitutes human apprehension of God. "Accommodation," therefore, involves no capitulation of one entity to another, but rather the proper submissiveness of the concretized forms of each before a common and commanding spiritual reality.

Schleiermacher and his school in Germany actively pursued the task of reconstructing theology on these presuppositions; and the rationale for doing so was provocatively restated by Ernst Troeltsch in the early twentieth century.[5] But conscious or explicit modernism, a frank adaptationism based on a belief in the interpenetration of religion and culture, prospered especially in an American context. Protestant liberals everywhere in the Western world appeared to be acting, and constructing theologies, on the basis of a belief that God is present and active in the great forward movements of human culture; but the American liberal movement exceeded others in the explicitness with which such beliefs were rendered.

Even British liberalism, which most resembled that of the Americans in this respect, remained notably more theoretical than the American form and more subdued in its overt humanistic enthusiasms. Within the corpus of British theological liberalism in the late nineteenth century, very few writings dealt extensively or centrally with the questions of human nature and progress that pervaded so much of the American literature. Not many voiced candid appeals for cultural adaptation. British writers who did treat such questions either tended to be sharply restrained in their

---

[4] See, in particular, the two open letters of 1829 to Friedrich Lücke, in Schleier-macher, *Sämmtliche Werke*, II, 575-653.

[5] Benjamin A. Reist, *Toward a Theology of Involvement: The Thought of Ernst Troeltsch* (Philadelphia, Westminster Press, 1966), pp. 156-168.

celebration of the divine leadings in contemporary culture, or else—as in the case of the ebullient Canon Fremantle—were read far more in the United States than in Great Britain.[6]

To view modernism as a frank explication of certain liberal principles and methods—as a preaching of much that liberalism at large practiced—is to throw doubt on a common way of categorizing different types of liberal. During a generation or more of recent scholarship it was common to assume that the difference between "modernists" and "evangelical liberals" was a difference of starting points and of fundamental loyalties. An "evangelical liberal" was alleged to have been a religious thinker who made the Christian revelation normative and then merely interpreted it in the light of modern knowledge. A "modernistic liberal," on the other hand, was said to have been someone who had made modern science his criterion and then, in a kind of afterthought, retained what he could of the Christian tradition.[7]

---

[6]See Hutchison, "Americanness of the Social Gospel." German-American and perhaps other bilateral comparisons must be made before we shall be able to speak more confidently about the peculiarities or even archtypicality of American liberalism and modernism. Though the greater practicality and human-centeredness of American religious thought have usually been taken for granted, the question merits tough comparative study. Ernst Benz, in stressing the pioneering nature of Anglo-American, and particularly American, excursions into evolutionary theology, has forcefully presented one starting point. See his *Evolution and Christian Hope: Man's Concept of the Future from the Early Fathers to Teilhard de Chardin*, trans. Heinz G. Frank (Garden City, Doubleday and Co., 1966), pp. 143-167. See also Marty, *Modern Schism*. More extensive comparative treatment may be anticipated in the forthcoming second volume (post-1870) of Claude Welch's *Protestant Thought in the Nineteenth Century*.

For Canon William Fremantle's analysis of the indifference of Englishmen and the positive response of Americans to his *The World as the Subject of Redemption*, see his preface to the second edition.

[7]Kenneth Cauthen defined "evangelical liberals" as persons "who stood squarely within the Christian tradition and accepted as normative for their thinking what they understood to be the essence of historical Christianity." "Modernistic liberals," however, were "basically determined in their thinking by a twentieth-century outlook," and "had no real sense of continuing in the line of the historic faith." Cauthen, *Impact of Religious Liberalism*, pp. 27, 29.

Cauthen's book, produced in 1962, is the most substantial recent treatment of liberal theology. Earlier volumes by participants—John W. Buckham's *Progressive Religious Thought in America* (1919) and Frank Hugh Foster's *Modern Movement in American Theology* (1939)—employed a method of person-by-person theological description similar to Cauthen's, but offered a greater sense of development over time. Other useful appraisals are *The Andover Liberals*, by Daniel Day Williams (1941); *Liberal Theology*, edited by David Roberts and

Such a differentiation made sense as embodying an opinion about the theological consequences of varying modes of liberal advocacy; it was not very helpful in clarifying what liberals themselves had intended. Few, if any, Protestant liberals—modernistic or otherwise—denied normative status to Christ and to the Christian tradition. As Shailer Mathews of the University of Chicago wrote in *The Faith of Modernism*, "Modernists as a class are evangelical Christians . . . They accept Jesus Christ as the revelation of a savior God . . . [Their] religious starting point is the inherited orthodoxy."[8]

That expresses the intention. Whether one or another modernist succeeded, according to a given standard of judgment, in his attempt to find and express the real meaning of Christianity is a legitimate question; but it is a different question and not one to be begged at the beginning of a historical analysis.

The deeper difficulty in any sharply drawn distinction between liberals who built on revelation and those who allegedly began with science or culture was that it could not deal with the liberals' crucial contention that this distinction is, from the start, largely invalid. The antinomies that such a system of classification presupposes—between sacred and secular, between a starting point in revelation and a starting point in reason or in science—were precisely what proponents of this movement, for good or ill, sought to minimize. When the "new theology" of the liberals, as early as the 1880s, was accused of secularizing Christianity, Theodore Munger offered a typical response: "The New Theology," he said, "does indeed regard with question the line often drawn between the sacred and the secular,—a line not to be found in Jewish or Christian Scriptures, nor in man's nature."[9]

The religious liberalism of this period, in other words—especially in its modernist expressions and especially in the United States—represented a vivid pursuit of the apologetic effort ordained by the school of Schleiermacher. This was, in the end,

---

Henry P. Van Dusen (1942); and Lloyd Averill's *American Theology in the Liberal Tradition* (1967). See also William R. Hutchison, ed., *American Protestant Thought: The Liberal Era* (1968).

[8]Mathews, *Faith of Modernism*, pp. 34-35.

[9]Munger, *Freedom of Faith*, p. 32.

less an effort to adjust religion to culture than an attempted renunciation of the long-standing and singular commitment in Western thought to what seemed an artificial disjunction between these two supposed entities.[10] Often enough, liberals fell into a more usual pattern of discourse and spoke of adjustments that a reified religion must make to modernity, or that secular thought and its institutions should make to Christianity. Nearly always, however, they took at least the first step away from such ways of thinking: they ordinarily refused to make automatic moral distinctions between church and world, or even between the religious and the secular. Culture, in liberal discussions, might still sound "out there," but it no longer sounded alien.

The first two chapters of this book trace the uncertain development of the main modernist themes before 1875—first in various branchings of the Unitarian movement, then in the thought of the Congregationalist theologian Horace Bushnell and the liberal Presbyterianism of Chicago. The two chapters following are concerned with different phases in the establishing of liberalism as a major force within American Protestantism: one phase in which a "new theology," mainly in the 1880s, expanded Bushnell's theory of individual regeneration into a theory about the regeneration of culture; another in which, about a decade later, liberals were concerned to preserve the special claims of Christianity within a schema that, like the natural religion of other eras, found God revealed in many places besides Holy Writ. The next phase of liberal development, discussed in the fifth chapter, saw notable attempts to apply modernist attitudes within a society that was increasingly perceived as entering a period of crisis, and within a church that allegedly had to be refurbished if modernist hopes were to stand a chance of fulfillment.

As both social crisis and the sense of the church's inadequacies

---

[10]Wilfred Cantwell Smith discusses and deplores the Western dichotomizing tendency in *The Meaning and Truth of Religion* (New York, The Macmillan Co., 1962): "Men throughout history and throughout the world have been able to *be* religious without the assistance of a special term, without the intellectual analysis that the term implies." "There are . . . relatively few languages into which one can translate the word 'religion' . . . outside Western civilization" (pp. 19, 18).

became more desperate during the first third of the twentieth century, the most fundamental assumptions of modernism were called into question. A concerted external attack upon these assumptions, together with a serious questioning from within the liberal movement, began before World War I, and the sixth chapter describes such questioning. The war then sharpened issues bearing upon human nature and progress, and the entire liberal scheme of religion came under pressure from postwar fundamentalism, from naturalism and secular humanism, and after 1930 from the type of "crisis theology" commonly in this country called neo-orthodoxy.

Liberalism through all of this not only survived but fought back with a good deal of resourcefulness. On some points, such as the brief for nonliteral interpretation of the Bible, liberals gave virtually no ground. (Neo-orthodoxy, at least, rarely asked that they do so.) On others, such as the conscious adaptation to culture and the stress upon divine-human continuities, the older rhetoric became decidedly unfashionable even for a time among some who continued to call themselves liberals. Yet neither the rhetoric nor the convictions behind it seem to have been truly or thoroughly renounced; so that when the so-called radical theologians of the 1960s demanded honest-to-God language and a new look at secularity, they were to some extent continuing the discussions of the liberal era. These later radical spokesmen also uttered new, previously unthinkable thoughts; and in such matters as the finiteness of religious language they clearly built upon neo-orthodox convictions at least as much as upon those of the liberal movement. But over large areas of discourse the newer Protestant theologies of the "turbulent Sixties"[11] were turning up the volume on a liberal broadcast that had never really gone off the air.

As this may imply, the long-lasting and the more transient elements in modernism form a whole spectrum, not a simple polarity.

------

[11]Ahlstrom, *Religious History of the American People*, pp. 1079-1096. W. Warren Wagar emphasizes the more persistent elements of the nineteenth-century belief in progress, and their reassertion particularly after 1960, in *Good Tidings*, pp. 243 and 239-349 passim.

At the positive end of this scale of permanence, the attempt—however tinged with ambivalence—to renounce long-standing categories of "religious" and "secular" probably constitutes the most important claim that modernism makes as a movement reaching beyond the needs and illusions of the time in which it flourished. At the other end is humanistic optimism; modernism's cultural hope and progressive cultural immanentism appear not to have been restored even during recent decades of withdrawal from neo-orthodoxy.[12] It still seems reasonable, as it did to Walter Lippmann in the 1950s, to view nineteenth-century confidence about an earthly Kingdom as "a daydream during a spell of exceptionally fine weather."[13] For the people of the Western world, at least, such dreams may have been permanently dispelled.

The present volume, so far as it attempts to make a point as well as understand a historic position, argues that Protestant modernism deserves to be known both for its transient and for its more permanent qualities—that it can be seen and appreciated as a relic of peculiar times, yet also as a contribution to debates of persistent and very current importance within American religion and the Western culture.

---

[12]The work of Teilhard de Chardin, despite orthodox critics who have thought otherwise, did not represent full return to nineteenth-century patterns of cultural optimism. See Benz, *Evolution and Christian Hope*, on this point (pp. 226-229) and, more generally, on the interplay between perennial and more transitory strains in nineteenth- and twentieth-century theologies of hope. See also Jacob Viner's discussion of the rise of "optimistic providentialism." Viner, *The Role of Providence in the Social Order: An Essay in Intellectual History*, The Jayne Lectures for 1966 (Philadelphia, American Philosophical Society, 1972), pp. 1-26.

[13]Walter Lippman, *Essays in the Public Philosophy* (Boston, Little, Brown and Co., 1955), p. 10. Sidney Mead, some two decades later, viewed this phenomenon with similar poignancy but with greater appreciation for what the optative mood may have produced: "Of course the ideal 'Republic' dreamed by the Founders never existed in actuality . . . It was a vision, an artist-people's creative idea that imbued them with the Energy to strive—and with considerable success —to incarnate it in actuality." "American History as a Tragic Drama," *Journal of Religion*, 52 (October 1972), 359.

The Unitarian Movement and "the Spirit of the Age"

> The life of the time appoints the creed of the time
> and modifies the establishment of the time.
> OCTAVIUS B. FROTHINGHAM, 1873

David Swing, a celebrated Presbyterian preacher in the last third of the nineteenth century, was fond of suggesting to his Chicago audiences that "we are . . . all more than willing to give our hearts to the spirit of our own times." He proposed, repeatedly and eloquently, that the doctrines of the church be submitted to transformation by this same modern spirit. Because of such utterances, Swing in 1874 was tried for heresy.[1]

At that same time in the East a leader of the radical wing of Unitarianism was being called old-fashioned for expressing views much like Swing's. Octavius B. Frothingham's *Religion of Humanity*, published in 1873, began with declarations that "the interior spirit of any age is the spirit of God," and that the life of the time must therefore appoint the creed of the time. Frothingham went on to describe at length and in detail what the new creed would be. His whole proposal—from the introductory effusions about spirit through what he thought were tough, "naturalistic" revisions of old Christian doctrines—seemed dreamy and reactionary to certain of his colleagues in religious radicalism. The scientific theist Francis Abbot acknowledged that Frothingham's book could charm many readers, "like a

---

[1]Swing, *Sermons*, p. 85.

lovely landscape seen through ever-shifting and dissolving mists." But it would scarcely serve, Abbot thought, as a guidebook to one who simply wants to find his way to the next town."[2]

To see in such occurrences a symbolic passing-of-the-torch from Unitarian to evangelical liberals is not to use too extravagant a metaphor. These were not isolated events. Both of them—Frothingham's publication and Swing's trial—achieved national celebrity.[3] And because Swing won his case, his ordeal and triumph served to announce the existence not only of liberalism but of a modernist version thereof within the great body of American evangelical Protestantism.

Though that infusion derived from many sources, none had been more powerful nor more clearly influential than the nineteenth-century Unitarianism to which Frothingham's work provided one culmination. Unitarians, in their role as pathbreakers for a wider liberalism, had never been unequivocal celebrants of the modern. But the Unitarian movement, in its successive rationalistic, romantic, and scientific stages, had provided far and away the most potent ground for the growth of a rationale justifying religious adaptation to culture.

Channing Unitarianism: "Humble, yet unfaltering hope"

In Protestant thought, as a recent writer has remarked, the eighteenth century lasted somewhat longer in America than in Europe.[4] Theological conversation in New England, both among the followers of Jonathan Edwards and between Edwardseans and liberals, continued during the early nineteenth century to be centered upon the issues raised by eighteenth-century rationalism. Preachers and theologians persisted, that is, in

---

[2]Frothingham, *Religion of Humanity*, pp. 7-8; Francis Ellingwood Abbot, review of *The Religion of Humanity* in *Index*, 4 (March 15, 1873), 131. A recent collaborative history of the Unitarian movement in the United States is C. Conrad Wright, ed., *A Stream of Light.*

[3]Henry May is justified, I think, in calling *The Religion of Humanity* "the principal manifesto of advanced religious thinkers in the postwar decade." May, *Protestant Churches*, p. 81. Swing's views, his trial, and his importance in the seventies are treated at length in the second chapter of this book.

[4]Welch, *Protestant Thought*, pp. 108-109, 127.

arguing the relative weight to be given to reason and to the literal word of scripture in assessing particular points of inherited Calvinist doctrine. They rarely referred in any but the most abstract terms to the visibility of the work of the Holy Spirit in modern thought or current human progress. The modernist question, in other words, was seldom explicitly raised.

For many of the early liberals, this was not a matter of aversion to modernity—to which they might show sympathy in other contexts—but a question of the theologian or preacher sticking to his last. Scripture, for liberals as well as for the orthodox, remained the preeminent source and criterion for religious truth. To be sure, the more advanced thought of the eighteenth century had added (or restored) a God-given, timeless reason as a mighty criterion. But the notion that modernity itself might convey religious meanings was, among most of those advocating theological change, simply an idea whose time had not come.

Rationalistic liberalism was likely to exhibit at least two kinds of inhibition against anything resembling a modernist formula for religious change. One of these was an equivocal or even hostile attitude toward modernity. The other was a negative rather than constructive or reconstructive outlook upon the institutions or doctrines that a religious modernist would seek to reform. Thomas Jefferson, though an enthusiast for "the progress of science in all its branches," was sufficiently troubled about "the perils of metaphysics" to doubt the usefulness even of modern philosophy in the work of restoring the pure message of Jesus. Greek philosophy had distorted that message, with disastrous results, and little better was to be expected from the work of the metaphysicians and other formalists in these latter days. At the same time, and for some of the same reasons, Jefferson placed little stock in the reform of Christian doctrine or of institutional Christianity. He would "as soon think of writing for the reformation of Bedlam," he told Charles Clay, "as of the world of religious sects . . . I consider reformation and redress as desperate, and abandon them to the Quixotism of more enthusiastic minds." The office of reason was essentially negative—a work of defoliation—in relation to systems and institutions. This was so whether one spoke of the ecclesiastical and philosophical systems that had subverted humanity and reason in the past or of the structures that some considered the glory of contemporary human society.[5]

Neither Jefferson nor other rationalistic liberals were fully consistent in their expressions on these points; yet Jeffersonian liberalism promoted an influential pattern of thought that constituted virtually a denial of the possibility of religious modernism. Instead of an affirmative use of the secular culture in the reform of religion, rationalistic liberalism commonly promoted a severe skepticism about their usefulness to each other. Rationalists with more than the Jeffersonians' faith in modernity were likely to be even less sanguine about the reform—as opposed to the extirpation—of current religious institutions and theologies. Theodore Parker, the great Unitarian radical of mid-century, would declare with characteristic passion that "the new literature of our time, the new science of our time, the new philanthropy of our time, have no relation to the popular theology, but that of hate and warfare."[6]

Yet from the beginning, from as far back as the proto-Unitarian days of Jefferson and Thomas Paine, a rather different tradition also found expression within rationalistic liberalism. The same enthusiasm for essential religious values that animated Jefferson and Parker could issue in more affirmative attitudes both toward modern institutions and toward the reform of Christianity.

Among the deists who reached an American audience, for example, Thomas Paine was one whose view of the relations between religion and culture often, and in important ways, sounded more like Schleiermacher's version of Enlightenment thinking than like Jefferson's. Paine's *Age of Reason* was a book that for millions too frightened to read it made his name a byword for irreligion; but the author's professed purpose was to avert

---

[5]Thomas Jefferson to Elbridge Gerry, January 26, 1799, *The Writings of Thomas Jefferson*, Andrew Lipscomb and Albert Bergh, eds. (Washington, D.C., Thomas Jefferson Memorial Association, 1905), X, 78; Thomas Jefferson to Charles Clay, January 29, 1815, ibid., XIV, 232, 234. For the Jeffersonian distrust of metaphysics, see Daniel Boorstin, *The Lost World of Thomas Jefferson* (New York, Henry Holt and Co., 1948), pp. 128-139.

[6]Parker, *Sermons of Theism*, p. 131.

the threatened destruction of religion and theology. The French Revolution, he said, with its necessarily destructive impact upon all "compulsive systems," had created an imminent danger that "in the general wreck of superstition, of false systems of government, and false theology," men would lose sight "of morality, of humanity, and of the theology that is true." Though deism, with its remote "clockmaker" God, often seemed the ultimate transcendent-ism, Paine's thought veered toward immanentist conceptions of the continuing presence and agency of God in nature and culture. Under the pressure of his own hostility to the church's constricted definition of revelation, Paine was led to insist upon the common origins of religion and the sciences—not, indeed, in what romantics were calling religious feeling or the sense of dependence, but in "the power and wisdom of God."

Such depictions of the workings of divine power and wisdom bespoke at least incipient cultural immanentism. Paine, for example, chided the Christian theologians for insufficient belief in God's pervasive action throughout his creation. The crowning apostasy had been the church's attempt to depreciate the sciences as mere "human invention." That practice had originated, he contended, with obscurantists who had feared the effects of scientific discoveries upon their own dogmatic fabrications, and who therefore had sought to depict science as the work of the devil. The "true theology" could be restored only by the overthrow of all such attempts to depict God and his creation as alien to each other.[7]

Among New England Unitarians, a similarly affirmative method, now applied to a more specific form of religion than Paine had cared to reform or defend, began to show itself in the 1820s as the first battles against the Edwardsean theology came to an end. Appeals to the twin authorities of scripture and reason did not disappear from Unitarian polemics, certainly not in this early generation, but they came to be supplemented by wider and bolder appeals to the spirit of the age—a tutelary authority

---

[7] *The Theological Works of Thomas Paine* (Chicago, M. A. Donohue and Co., n.d.), pp. 5, 35, 43.

perceived as a projection of individual reason, yet increasingly spoken of as something palpable and identifiable in itself.

The preaching and lecturing of William Ellery Channing, minister of Federal Street Church in Boston and the most influential of the first-generation spokesmen, began especially to develop such an emphasis. "The Demands of the Age on the Ministry," an ordination sermon that Channing preached in 1824, started with a simple plea, similar to that of earlier Channing discourses, that ministers must do their cultural homework. "Religion," he asserted, "must be dispensed by men who at least keep pace with the intellect of the age in which they live."[8] And Channing acknowledged that the liberal preacher must continue to busy himself with the negative work of purging theology and the church of cherished corruptions.[9] But the bulk of this discourse was given over to an attempt to define the leading intellectual and social imperatives of the age and to state their implications for religious reform.

Religion, Channing said, had always been required somehow to come to terms with the wider thought of its time. But the present age was making unprecedented demands, simply because its peculiar illumination was a more spiritual and generally superior one than that of previous ages. The new element was society's recognition of mind, in place of bodily strength or military prowess, as the arbiter of society and as "sovereign of the world."[10]

Among the resulting demands placed upon religion, the foremost was a demand for engagement. Channing expressed satisfaction with religion's current emergence "from the cell of the monk, and the school of the verbal disputant, into life and society." He appeared, in fact, to be anxious to do penance for his own participation, however necessary that had been, in the rationalistic disputations of the early Unitarian controversy. Seeking to minimize the claims made for a negative or destructive use of reason, he warned liberals not to suppose that the recently

---

[8]Channing, *Works*, III, 138.
[9]Ibid., 149-153.
[10]Ibid., 141.

achieved modifications in doctrine had come about because of the devastating logic of Unitarian polemicists. "All these changes are owing, not to theological controversy so much as to the general progress of the human mind."[11]

In the same vein, Channing saw the age as demanding a fervor and sense of immediacy in religion which he thought (fourteen years before Emerson's Divinity School remarks to the same effect) had been inadequately represented up to then in Unitarian liberalism. Religion, he said, must be presented in more exciting form; it must concentrate upon affirming rather than denying; and it must become more inward, must concern itself less with mechanical proofs or confessions and more with the testimony of the spirit.

Excitement and inwardness, which at first might seem antithetical, were linked by Channing's explanation of what he meant by excitement. "Religion," he said, must not be presented "in the dry, pedantic divisions of a scholastic theology . . . No; it must come from the soul in the language of earnest conviction and strong feeling." Persons of religious sensitivity, he added somewhat ominously, "will not now be trifled with." If Unitarianism proved unexciting, then it would, "and still more, it ought, to fall." For in that case it would not suit "the spirit of our times."[12]

Characteristically, Channing's admiring reference at this point to the spirit of the age was balanced by an equivalent or perhaps stronger sign of reliance upon "the essential and abiding spirit of human nature."[13] Despite his conviction about the superior illumination of the current age, he remained cautious on both theoretical and empirical grounds. Like Theodore Parker a generation later—but with more skepticism than Parker would express about modernity—he advised teachers of Christianity to separate "what is of universal and everlasting application, from the local and the temporary."[14]

The moral actualities of the age, as distinct from its aspirations,

[11]Ibid., 144, 154.
[12]Ibid., 146-154.
[13]Ibid., 147.
[14]Ibid., 153.

were not entirely reassuring. Improvement was a fact, and moral optimism was a need and requirement to which the preacher must respond. But Channing warned against "romantic anticipations." He called his society corrupt, "not because I consider it as falling below the purity of past times, but because it is obviously and grossly defective, when measured by the Christian standard."[15] His discourse on "The Present Age," given just a year before his death in 1842, left expectations for the future of civilization wrapped in mystery:

As yet . . . we are encompassed with darkness. The issues of our time how obscure! The future into which it opens who of us can foresee? To the Father of all Ages I commit this future with humble, yet courageous and unfaltering hope.[16]

Even Channing Unitarianism expressed the modernist synthesis only in rudimentary form. Partly because Unitarians felt they had solved doctrinal issues for the present, and were weary of discussing them, the doctrinal implications of attentiveness to the spirit of the age were offered as general admonitions about method more than as prescriptions about content. Yet Channing and his generation had constructed some parts of the modernist mold. The original rationalistic critique of orthodoxy had served to clear the ground for the more positive theology that developed in the 1820s. And Channing's later search for cultural sources of religious affirmation—a search provoked partly by stirring times and partly, no doubt, by a realignment of Channing's method with the demands of an affirming temperament—advanced the notion that contemporary culture might be called upon to guide theological reform.

Transcendentalism: The Times and the Eternities

Transcendentalist or romantic Unitarianism in some ways was even less friendly to modernity than the rationalism of the elders had been. Henry David Thoreau was not atypical in reacting adversely to railroads and similar products of the modernizing

---

[15]Ibid., 155-159.
[16]Ibid., VI, 181-182.

spirit. Nor was Thoreau unique in perceiving the spirit of the age as something that supported slavery and unjust wars—as something, therefore, that the individual was bound to resist.[17]

More broadly, the romantic mode of thought, bolstered by philosophical idealism, lent itself readily to a minimizing of modern culture, or at least to a principled neutrality toward the claims of the modern. The past and its traditions might not be controlling, and in American religious romanticism they almost never were;[18] but in romantic or idealist theory, modern culture could not be controlling either. Past and present were equally under judgment; and if this judgment was now construed, in a transcendentalized Christianity, as issuing from the spiritual laws or from a humanized Christ rather than from the edicts of a stern Jehovah, it still could issue in sharp rejections of modernity.

Ralph Waldo Emerson's "Lecture on the Times," given in 1841, depicted the times as "the masquerade of the Eternities," and treated the traditional and the modern as almost equally culpable in their offenses against the moral laws that govern the universe. Similarly, the Divinity School Address of 1838, Emerson's most notable exposition of ideas on religious reform, took a stance quite above any dependence upon models either past or present. What Emerson called historical Christianity was unmistakably the villain of this piece, but the corrective did not lie in accommodation to any part of modern culture. The values of the culture, Emerson said, simply would not suffice: "We easily come up to the standard of goodness in society." The arts offered little guidance, he said, and learning was not an ultimate. "The compositions we call wiser and wisest" were superior only by "little shades and gradations of intelligence." "The orators, the poets, the commanders encroach on us only . . . by our allowance and hom-

---

[17]Henry David Thoreau, "Walden," *The Writings of Henry David Thoreau* (Boston, Houghton, Mifflin, and Co., 1894), II, 181-186; "Civil Disobedience," *Writings*, X, 131-170. Paul Boller presents a brief, but well-informed and perceptive, interpretation of Transcendentalist philosophy and social attitudes in *American Transcendentalism*.

[18]There are important, if partial, exceptions such as the theological movement led within the German Reformed church by John W. Nevin and Philip Schaff. See James H. Nichols, *Romanticism in American Theology: Nevin and Schaff at Mercersburg* (Chicago, University of Chicago Press, 1961).

age." The remedy for the ills of religion, in his view, lay no more in modern times than in any other epoch of human culture. On the contrary, the remedy was timeless: "first, soul, and second, soul, and evermore, soul." The deformities of religion would be corrected only by a faith like Christ's in the infinitude of man.[19]

Those who do seek to learn from contemporary culture, Emerson insisted, must discern the reality behind the masquerade. "Only so far as *that* shines through them are these times or any times worth consideration." The New Teacher whom Emerson called for would refuse to accept his culture sheerly on its own recommendation. He would distinguish the real from the unreal, the permanent from the transient, in contemporary science and art as much as in Christianity. New revelations in culture would receive perhaps equivalent respect, but certainly not greater respect than new promptings of the individual soul. The New Teacher would "see the identity of the law of gravitation with purity of heart," and would teach "that the Ought, that Duty, is one thing with Science, with Beauty, and with Joy."[20]

Emersonian religious reform, therefore, even though it was phrased in what one interpreter has called the "optative mood,"[21] could at best accord only secondary or derivative importance to the genius and insights of a given age of history. Culture received its authority from a moral order that held a veto power over culture's real or apparent directives, much as scriptural revelation in traditional Calvinist thought had retained a corrective authority over reason and throughout the sphere of secondary causation.

Yet transcendentalism, even in its more ethereal and individualistic forms, did help to lay a foundation for more cordial attitudes toward the spirit of the age. The aforementioned optative temper demanded appropriate expression. In any juxtaposing of the unconditioned and the historically conditioned, the latter came off second best; but when it came time to choose between the historical

---

[19]*Emerson's Complete Works* (Boston, Houghton, Mifflin, and Co., 1883-1893), I, 247, 144-145, 147, 142.

[20]Ibid., pp. 275, 148.

[21]F. O. Matthiessen, *American Renaissance: Art and Expression in the Age of Emerson and Whitman* (New York, Oxford University Press, 1941), pp. 3-75.

realities of the past and those of the present—to support the Party
of Memory or the Party of Hope—Emerson was prepared to forego
his abstract neutrality. The need of the moment, in fact, as the
champions of intuition set themselves against the claims of
particular past revelations, was a recognition that "the sun shines
also for us"; and Emerson's cultivation of the optative mood
clearly involved turning a sympathetic ear to the promptings
of the contemporary culture. "Let it not be recorded in our own
memories," Emerson admonished in 1841, "that in this moment of
the Eternity, when we who were named by our names flitted across
the light, we were afraid of any fact." He then added a proto-
modernist gloss upon his earlier definition of the scholar as Man
Thinking: "What is the scholar, what is the man *for*, but for
hospitality to every new thought of his time?"[22]

This propensity, whenever the chips were down, to opt for the
present and future rather than for the past would be less important
had it been merely a posing of rhetorical questions. In fact, however, the transcendentalists were the central contributors in their
own time to the actual work of making modern thought available
to religion. They occupied themselves in transmitting and translating German philosophical idealism for American use; and were
enormously important in promoting biblical criticism and the
study of world religions. At both a theorizing and a practical level,
therefore, the transcendentalist movement contributed, almost in
spite of itself, to an emerging modernist outlook.

The central achievement in this respect was their success in
turning the flank of an antiphilosophical thrust that had been
powerful in both liberalism and evangelicalism at the beginning
of the nineteenth century. This is one area in which William
Ellery Channing stands as something more than a mere precursor
of the transcendentalist movement. Channing, along with the
trinitarian James Marsh, demanded rapprochement specifically
between religion and philosophy. Again rejecting the negative
rationalism that had been so prominent in his own generation,
Channing in the 1820s deplored current tendencies to eschew

---

[22]Emerson, *Works*, I, 275-276.

philosophy except insofar as it opened a way back to the "pure religion of Jesus." The fashion, he said, was to pretend reliance on mere common sense, and to suppose that one can thus restore the naked truth of Christianity. This was nonsense, Channing declared: "There is no such thing as naked truth, at least as far as moral subjects are concerned." Some contend, he remarked mockingly, "that Christianity has an intrinsic glory, a native beauty, which no art or talent of man can heighten." Yet everyone knows, or should know, that the diffusion and power of any body of truth depend upon its being organized systematically and in fullest awareness of its connections with other known facts.[23]

At the end of the twenties, James Marsh, then president of the University of Vermont, voiced the same protest in the context of a plea for a particular philosophical movement. In his celebrated introductory essay for the first American edition of Samuel T. Coleridge's *Aids to Reflection,* Marsh ridiculed those scholars who were objecting to Coleridge's kind of post-Kantian metaphysics as "too deep for them." That objection, he said, was either a disingenuous way of hinting that these particular depths are not worth exploring, "which is more than the objector knows," or else just a confession that the scholar for all his professed love of truth prefers to "sleep after dinner."

Like Channing, Marsh excoriated the current prejudice "against the introduction of philosophy, in any form, in the discussion of theological subjects." Terms like "metaphysics" and "rational," he remarked, had acquired newly pejorative meanings, so that a philosophical view of religion had come to be defined as a view not only at variance with the Bible but at war with it. Under the illusion that they were escaping metaphysics, writers were prone to insist that they were guided solely by common sense and the laws of interpretation. "But I would like to know," Marsh retorted, "how a man comes by any common sense in relation to the movements and laws of his intellectual and moral being without metaphysics." What, he asked, would be the common sense of a Hottentot on subjects of this sort? He con-

---

[23]Channing, *Works,* III, 142, 141.

cluded that it is "nearly, if not quite, impossible for any man entirely to separate his philosophical views of the human mind from his reflections on religious subjects."[24]

The Religion of Humanity and the "Deeper Return" to Christian Doctrine

Along with future-mindedness and the championing of philosophy, a third contribution of the romantic theologians to modernism lay in their insistence upon the immanence of God.in nature and human nature. Here again the modernist implications in a romantic principle were by no means clear or inevitable. Immanentism became a vehicle of the modernist impulse for the somewhat accidental reason that one line of Unitarian thinkers— with considerable assistance from current popular enthusiasms— interpreted immanence to mean God's indwelling, not simply in nature or the individual, but in humanity. The resulting reverence for humanity, which might have remained simply a mystique, led instead to very concrete investigations of the human religious sentiment in its varied expressions. And for some Unitarians the next, perhaps paradoxical, step was a renewed appreciation of Christian doctrine, which they now approached as one—and not the least valid—of these varied forms. The result, in the work of O. B. Frothingham, Cyrus Bartol, and others, was enough like the emerging Presbyterian or Congregationalist liberalism to explain why puzzled Unitarian colleagues suspected these men of being reactionaries and apostates to the Unitarian cause.

The first important statements of the romantic religion of humanity[25] were voiced early in the century by Orestes Brown-

---

[24]Marsh, "Preliminary Essay," pp. xv-xvi, xxii. The Marsh papers, at the University of Vermont and elsewhere, have recently become more accessible, and new glosses on his work and importance are appearing. For the theology, see McGiffert, "James Marsh," pp. 437-458. John J. Duffy provides a brief biography in the handsomely produced *Coleridge's American Disciples.*

[25]It is almost unnecessary to use the adjective "romantic" here because the nonromantic or positivistic form of this faith had little impact in America before the Civil War. See Richmond Laurin Hawkins, *Positivism in the United States (1853-1861)* (Cambridge, Mass., Harvard University Press, 1938), p. 3. But, as the following discussion will show, an empirical strain was also evident from the beginning in the American religion of humanity; and this countertendency, if not the cultus of Auguste Comte, could make substantial claims by the 1880s.

son, whose successive reappropriations of tradition had led him by the 1830s from freethought to Unitarianism and would propel him thereafter into the Roman Catholic Church. Brownson in 1836 inaugurated his Society for Christian Union and Progress, in Boston, with a sermon on "The Wants of the Times." In this he announced a working principle, for his organization and for Christianity, which he said had been integral to the message of Saint Paul but had subsequently been ignored by the church: namely, that Christian spokesmen must constantly adjust the gospel to the demands of their age and community. American and Jacksonian conditions, Brownson said, were unprecedented and "demand what I have called a new Dispensation of Christianity, a dispensation in perfect harmony with the new order of things which has sprung into existence." Specifically, the times required a freer theology and a more democratic church polity than even the most liberal groups were offering.[26]

In a lengthier manifesto that same year, called *New Views of Christianity, Society, and the Church*, Brownson expanded both upon his indictment of the churches and upon his description of the new Christian dispensation that was needed. In doing so he deepened the paean of praise for his own times. He interpreted the entire history of Christianity up to the present as a conflict between the excessive spirituality of Roman Catholicism on one hand and Protestant materialism on the other. Now, at long last, the agelong antinomy was being overcome: specifically, the doctrine of the Atonement (or At-one-ment) was being recognized in its true, previously obscured meaning—"that all things are essentially holy."[27]

While Brownson praised ecstatically nearly every tendency of the times, he was especially impressed by evidence that people as well as principles were now coming together. "At-one-ment" was being realized, for example, in new contacts between the West and the Orient. By philosophical and commercial exchange, Brownson said, East and West were being "thrown together into the crucible." At the same time, the West, and America in particu-

---

[26]Brownson, *Wants of the Times*, pp. 5-6 et passim.
[27]Brownson, *New Views*, pp. 13-16, 96.

lar, was experiencing a burgeoning of voluntary associations, which Brownson saw as further expressions of faith in humanity. "All over Christendom," he observed, "men seem mad for associations . . . And—what deserves to be remarked—all these associations, various as they are, really propose in every instance a great and glorious end . . . There is a more than human power at the bottom of them. They come from God, from a divine inspiration given to the people to build the new Church and realize the Atonement." Finally, synthesizing and presiding over all the rest, the so-called "eclectic philosophy" of the Frenchman Victor Cousin had made its providential and reconciling appearance.[28]

Brownson's enthusiasm for a duly sanctified and spiritualized present seemed strong enough to sweep all before it. If a timeless "intuition" should try to stand in its path—if it were said, for example, that a true transcendentalist could never regard "the inspiration of the people" as different today from what it has always been—then, it appeared, intuitionism would simply be overwhelmed by the obvious fact of contemporary human progress. But Brownson, for all his intensity, was too careful a thinker to let it go at that. He valued Cousin's eclecticism precisely because it harmonized conflicting principles and obviated the need for any one of these principles to conquer another. With the aid of the eclectic philosophy one not only could reconcile matter and spirit, Protestant and Catholic, West and East; one could also, by direct analogy, reconcile intuitionist and more inductive approaches to the problem of knowledge.[29]

Brownson's eclecticism and emphasis on reconciliation made him peculiarly the prophet of a religion of humanity that despite its romantic emphasis would strive increasingly to accommodate science and scientific method.[30] The religion-of-humanity formu-

---

[28]Ibid., pp. 85-90. For a comment on Brownson's interpretation of the Atonement as "At-one-ment," see an unsigned review of *New Views* in *Western Messenger*, 3 (February 1837), 531.

[29]*New Views*, pp. 91-92.

[30]Theodore Parker similarly combined—or perhaps alternated between—intuition and induction, and the historians have been impatient with him for doing so. (For references to the literature, see Hutchison, *Transcendentalist Ministers*, pp. 101-105.) Parker's choice of the term "absolute religion" in place of "religion

la, from Brownson's time to Frothingham's, provided a convenient way of erecting a bridge between epistemological principles. Religion could be seen as fundamentally a matter of intuition, of a universal "religious sentiment"; yet the proof of this assertion could be made to depend more or less heavily upon scientific demonstration. Just what one should do if intuition and scientific demonstration pointed to opposing conclusions was a question that the enthusiasts of this faith rarely confronted. In the absence of such confrontation, the formula proved enormously serviceable to a generation of liberals hovering in the uncertain area between older romantic enthusiasms and newer scientific ones.

For Brownson himself, the mystical sense of divine-human identity predominated over the call for scientific demonstration. He did repeatedly declare himself in favor of an experimental approach. He complained, for example, that "every sect labors to conform human nature to its own creed" instead of "studying human nature, ascertaining its elements and its wants, and seeking to conform to them." But he could just as readily retreat to *a priori* assumptions. The churches would fail in warping human nature to dogma, he said, because human nature essentially will not warp; it will not be changed in any way. "Its laws are permanent and universal . . . Be they good or bad, we must accept them, we must submit to them and do the best we can with them."

Fortunately—here Brownson's enthusiasm for humanity reaches its transcendental height—"human nature is well made, its laws are just and holy, its elements are true and divine." The symbolic function of Jesus, the God-Man, is to teach mankind "to find Divinity in Humanity, and Humanity in Divinity. By presenting us God and Man united in one person, [the Christ symbol] shows us that both are holy." Brownson called W. E. Channing's sermon on "Likeness to God" "the most remarkable since the Sermon on the Mount"; but that famous discourse, easily read as an encour-

of humanity" for his ideal system is indicative of tendencies toward abstraction and rationalism that distinguish Parker from those who showed attachment to a mystique of humanity. Parker's influence on virtually all of them was nonetheless very marked.

agement to transcendental individualism, had become in Brownson's interpretation the charter for a distinctly collective interpretation of human infinitude.[31]

Highly ethereal transcendentalists who were similarly collective in their thinking—the young William Henry Channing is the leading example[32]—proceeded in the 1840s to expand this mystical interpretation of the spirit of the times and its demands upon religion. And in the 1850s the romantic formulation received important support from Henry James the Elder, in whose writings an ebullient sense of divine humanity provided the benchmark for the reform of Christianity and the extirpation of "ecclesiasticism."[33] But the same decades brought experiences in Western life and scholarship that provoked new respect for science and empirical method—respect that tended to undercut more mystical ways of conceiving human solidarity. The religion of humanity was both abetted and altered in the 1850s by what a modern writer calls the "intense national bonfire of faith in progress."[34] As Americans cheered Louis Kossuth, Commodore Perry, or Cyrus Field; as, according to their several tastes, they crusaded against slavery or claimed a Caribbean manifest destiny, hymns to the spirit of the age increasingly came through as celebrations more of the age than of spirit.

Early work in comparative religion, together with several massive studies of universal civilization, were seen as offering empirical support to the growing sense of human unity. "Every year brings new knowledge of the religions of the world," Thomas Wentworth Higginson reported in 1855, "and every step in knowledge brings out the sympathy between them." The generation of the 1850s saw some of the first competent analyses of exotic religions in the early essays of Max Müller. Readers of the Unitarian *Christian Examiner* were exposed to reliable accounts

---

[31]*New Views*, pp. 68-69, 94-95. For a discussion of the widening of this particular disparity between Channing's views and Brownson's, see Hutchison, *Transcendentalist Ministers*, pp. 160-165.

[32]Ibid., pp. 169-178.

[33]See Henry James, *Lectures and Miscellanies* (New York, Redfield, 1852); *The Church of Christ not an Ecclesiasticism: A Letter of Remonstrance to a Member of the soi-disant New Church* (New York, Redfield, 1854).

[34]Schneider, *American Philosophy*, p. 133.

of Comte's systematization of knowledge (along with Comte's positivistic version of the religion of humanity) and of Baron Humboldt's weighty reports on the nature of the universe. Americans could read Harriet Martineau's compendium of Comte (1853), volume one of Buckle's *History of Civilization* (1857), and Frederick D. Maurice's *Religions of the World in their Relations to Christianity* (1854). The transcendentalists James Freeman Clarke, Samuel Johnson, and T. W. Higginson were preparing pioneer studies in comparative religion.[35]

Many liberals such as James Freeman Clarke who promoted these new interests had regularly shown a lingering sympathy for traditional Christian and Calvinist doctrines and probably should not be represented as returning to these sympathies by way of the religion of humanity. But several other Unitarians do reflect such a pattern of return, or at least of sharpened Christian-radical dialectic. One of the most interesting is Cyrus A. Bartol, who was pastor of the West Church in Boston from 1837 until 1889.

Bartol's habit of attaching himself to radical causes and then apparently drawing back from them struck some contemporaries as merely erratic. Yet he was perhaps the most conscientious and consistent devotee of spiritual religion to come out of the transcendentalist movement. Frothingham was enough like him to recognize Bartol as "the model Transcendentalist"—almost the only one, he said, who had truly kept the faith. From the earliest days of transcendentalism to the last active days of the radical Free Religious Association at the end of the century, Bartol opposed what he thought were roughly equivalent rationalisms in the Unitarian right and left. He expressed this opposition not by standing placidly between the two extremes but by moving back and forth between them as hope and disappointment dictated.[36]

The "hardness and dryness" of a literalistic Unitarianism

---

[35]Higginson, *Writings*, VII, 320; *Examiner*, 50 (March 1851), 174-202, and 48 (January 1850), 53-88. The essays later collected in Max Müller's *Chips from a German Workshop* (1867-1875) were first published during the 1850s. Maurice's *Religions of the World* had appeared in three English editions before the first American edition of 1854. Clarke's *Ten Great Religions* appeared 1871-1883; Johnson's *Oriental Religions*, 1872-1877.

[36]Frothingham, *Transcendentalism*, pp. 342-343; Hutchison, "To Heaven in a Swing," pp. 275-295.

repelled Bartol and made him a transcendentalist in the 1830s. And he denounced its apparent reemergence in the new Unitarian denominationalism and creedalism of mid-century. But "the other extreme of free thinking, endless speculation, and well-nigh savage independence and solitary vagrancy of religious manners" displeased him just as much. He deplored some ideas and actions of his friend Theodore Parker; and in the pretensions of many other liberals he could see only pseudospirituality and self-indulgence. "We are devoured with conceit," he complained, "in some of its specimens incredible."[37]

When the Unitarian regulars, embarrassed by Parker, began in the mid-fifties to issue their statements of common belief and to tighten denominational structures, Bartol at first went along, then reacted strongly. He thus became for a time, if not an ally of Parker, at least a co-belligerent. At this point he found new value in the protests of Henry James, Sr., against ecclesiasticism. With the help of James's mystical conception of the human race as itself the true Church of Christ, he now became specifically a devotee of the religion of humanity. Bartol also at this time resumed a lapsed personal relationship with Emerson and requested a copy of the latter's crucial but still unpublished anti-ecclesiastical sermon on the Lord's Supper. "The day of sect is done!" Bartol warned his denominationally minded friend Henry Bellows in 1855; "the day of humanity is at hand."[38]

A few years later, Bartol's thinly disguised rebuttal to a powerful, institutionally minded sermon by Bellows on "The Suspense of Faith" committed him more firmly to the antidenominational position and to the religion of humanity.[39] Yet he was equally unrelenting in his dissent from Parker's iconoclastic way of using science and the tools of scholarship. In a memorial discourse after the radical preacher's death, Bartol remarked sadly that the Parker who could ridicule Catholics for identifying a wafer with the Body of Christ had been missing the point:

---

[37]Bartol, *Christian Body and Form*, p. 2; Bartol, review of Wilhelm DeWette's *Theodore: Or, the Skeptic's Conversion*, in *Christian Examiner*, 31 (January 1842), 371.

[38]Quoted in Hutchison, "To Heaven in a Swing," pp. 284-285.

[39]Bartol, *Word of the Spirit*.

He had not faculty to penetrate the purport or appraise the contents of a religious tradition . . . He had not imagination, simple reverence, and holy wonder, to admit the marvels at which the scientific understanding balks . . . He tore off the veil of error, but brightened not the countenance of truth . . . We reflect, at his sepulchre and over his page, on the vain magnificence of every plan to make out of abstract intellectual axioms a religion for the human race.[40]

Bartol passed through the cycle again in the 1860s and 1870s. He aided in the formation of the Free Religious Association but, never able to adjust to the views of the scientific faction within the association, became more disaffected as that faction gained in influence.[41] When Francis Abbot, the intellectual leader of the scientific theists, proposed that the world must await the verdict of science upon religious questions, Bartol filled his two most notable books with the answers of an essentially unrepentant transcendentalist.

Abbot and his followers among the free religionists were by this time granting science a degree of recognition that even Parker had withheld. To Abbot, the final answers to "the religious questions that have burned themselves deep into the heart of the race" were not, as Parker had always thought, written upon that same heart primordially; they must come from "him," Abbot insisted, that is from a new *deus ex machina* named Science. The faith in God and immortality to which Parker had clung as a matter of *a priori* knowledge was to be weighed on the scales held by this personified authority. "A whole world," Abbot said, "waits to hear . . . his final verdict."[42]

The mistake in all this, Bartol wrote in *Radical Problems*, is "to make the everlasting things subjects of argument instead of sight . . . Wait awhile, says the investigator, and we may tell you if God exists and you are immortal. But God is no conclusion. A Deity deduced from phenomena were finite as they, and nothing worth."[43] And two years later, in another intuitionist volume hopefully entitled *The Rising Faith*, Bartol was still objecting to one side—the inductive-negative side—of the Parkerite teaching as

[40]Bartol, *Discourse on Parker*, pp. 16, 22, 27.
[41]Hutchison, "To Heaven in a Swing," pp. 286-293.
[42]Abbot, "Intuitional and Scientific Schools," p. 114.
[43]Bartol, *Radical Problems*, pp. 83-84.

he stated his objections to the Free Religious Association. "Free Religion has its mission," he allowed,

It gives us criticism, it adds to our scholarship, it has great ability and the virtue of sincerity, it vindicates liberty, it is conscientious and humane. But it frees rather than feeds us. We cannot live on negations . . . My religious nature is not nourished by this literature . . . I cannot get out of the refuse and ash-heap of the objector's laboratory, from whose crucial experiment the vital principle has escaped.[44]

Half a century of the liberal movement in New England had, from Bartol's point of view, turned the pale negations of orthodox Unitarianism into the even paler ones of the Free Religious Association. He was forced to agree that, despite similarities of aim and of heritage linking the intuitional and scientific schools, there was now, as Abbot had said, "a deep and apparently bridge-less chasm" separating them. Abbot himself retained a narrowly defined place for intuition; a reader is surprised to find him speaking of such things as faith, deductive logic, and the moral law. But as a matter of conscious intention he had laid all of these things, together with God and immortality, open to experimental proof or disproof.[45] Bartol spoke for those who had decided Abbot not only was going too far but also was moving in the wrong direction.

What would the right direction be? Not back to orthodoxy, surely; and Bartol himself saw that science could not now be ignored to the extent that Emersonian transcendentalism had ignored it. The clue to an answer lay in Bartol's complaint that Parker had lacked the ability "to penetrate the purport or appraise the contents of a religious tradition." Somehow science and modernity must be welcomed and allowed to affect the tradition without proscribing the equivalent rights of the religious imagination as it expresses itself in the present and as it has spoken in the past. The spirit of the age cannot be, or be made to seem, inimical to the spirit that is constant in all ages; and the true modernist, in that sense at least, must be a reverent traditionalist.

One might argue that Bartol, the longtime friend and intellectual

---

[44]Bartol, *Rising Faith*, pp. 376-377.
[45]Abbot, "Intuitional and Scientific Schools," pp. 113 et passim.

confidant of the Congregational liberal Horace Bushnell,[46] came closer than Octavius Frothingham did to prefiguring the most fundamental attitudes of American Protestant modernism; and also that in direct and indirect ways Bartol may have exerted more influence upon mainline Protestantism. Frothingham, however, offered a sharper rendition of the double thrust of the modernist impulse. His *Religion of Humanity*, published while this Brahmin radical was leader of the Independent Liberal Church of New York City, professed nearly unqualified cordiality toward the spirit of the age even in its most scientistic aspect; yet it also turned with unprecedented concern to the detailed reworking of Christian doctrine.

Frothingham's opening plea for the principle of adaptation was unquestionably strong. Men and institutions, he wrote, must move with the "providential current" of their age. It is not up to mere mortals "to remould the age, to recast it, to regenerate it, to cross it or struggle with it." What the religious thinker must do is penetrate the meaning of the age, "enter into its temper, sympathize with its hopes, blend with its endeavors, helping it by helping its development and saving it by fostering the best elements of its growth." Since the interior spirit of any age is the spirit of God, no religion can resist that spirit and still be a living faith. No church can be strong unless allied with it.[47]

But as soon as Frothingham began explaining what he meant by terms like "nature," "science," and "chemistry," it became plain that he himself had not left transcendentalism behind. Though he had become convinced, far more than Bartol had, that

---

[46]Tragically for scholarship in American religious thought, the Bushnell-Bartol correspondence, which extended over thirty years, has not been found, although some of it is published in Mary Cheney's life of her father: Cheney, *Life and Letters of Bushnell*. Bartol's papers are thought to have been destroyed by fire. Descendants of the two men, in any case, think no papers will be located. Howell Cheney to author, May 25, 1956; Dr. George M. Bartol to author, May 2, 1961.

[47]Frothingham, *Religion of Humanity*, pp. 7-8. Cf. Pope Paul VI, reconvening Vatican Council II in September 1963: "The Church looks at the world with profound understanding, with sincere admiration and with the sincere intention not of conquering it, but of serving it, not of despising it, but of appreciating it, not of condemning it, but of strengthening it and saving it." Quoted in Carter, *Spiritual Crisis*, p. 109.

Octavius B. Frothingham

science supplied the voice of God in contemporary culture, his view of science remained highly spiritualized. He wrote in Abbotean vein of chemistry as the great prophet of the new dispensation. But Frothingham's personified sciences were Coleridgean prophets, who had fed on honey-dew and drunk the milk of Paradise. Chemistry, which rudely "pulverizes the solid substances of the earth," also "resolves establishments into ideas, and behind the bodiless thought feels the movement of that Universal Mind whose action men call the Holy Spirit."[48]

Similarly, though Frothingham took "naturalism" to be the key concept of the age, he avoided the most common usage of that term. His naturalism, instead, reflected Emerson's view of nature as the bodying forth of the eternal, together with a homespun "faith in natural powers." He chided Horace Bushnell for attempting in *Nature and the Supernatural* to keep open a "little overgrown postern-gate for the lurking Deity"; yet he himself left other gates ajar, in transcendentalist fashion, by divinizing the natural man and the human race. To Frothingham, the triumph of naturalism meant the prevalence in the modern world "of a subtle and a deep conviction that the spirit of God has its workings *in and through human nature.*" It meant recognition of "the inspiration of the moral sentiments, the divine character of the heart's affections, the heavenly illumination of the reason, [and] the truth of the soul's intuitions of spiritual things."[49] In everyday life, naturalism in medicine dictated a minimum of meddling with the recuperative powers of the body. In education it entailed a recognition of internal laws of development that must be allowed to express themselves in each individual. In social science it implied "free competition, free trade, free government, free action of the people in their own affairs." In the discipline of personal character, it called for "a deep faith in the soul's power to take care of itself."[50]

---

[48]*Religion of Humanity*, p. 8. Frothingham's indebtedness, direct and indirect, to Hegel is discussed by Loyd Easton, *Hegel's First American Followers*, pp. 134-135.

[49]*Religion of Humanity*, pp. 8, 13, 15.

[50]Ibid., pp. 8-10.

Such projections could be rather easily set down by Frothingham's critics on either side as one more vague effort to bolster transcendentalism with pseudoscience. But the bulk of the volume was concerned with more specific applications of this naturalism to Christian doctrines. Critics of radicalism had been asking, Frothingham said, for constructive ideas, for "the plan of our edifice."[51] He now offered such a plan, and it turned out that the doctrines of the religion of humanity were substantially the teachings of the Old and New Testaments refurbished in accord with the naturalistic spirit of the age.

The doctrine of God resulting from such an investigation, Frothingham wrote, posits a hidden deity, one too great for human knowledge. Every seeker, whatever the religious context, "brings back the same report . . . 'There are footprints, but He that made them could not be found.'" This conception of an unsearchable God, he claimed, far from being too vague to be effectual, "inspires will and braces endeavor and makes glorious the dream of possibility . . . The assurance that He is there gives us perfect confidence."[52]

The Bible of humanity must of course be an eclectic one, combining writings of all faiths and times, canonical and otherwise. Frothingham retained the idea, or at least the terminology, of revelation; the unknowability of God and his self-revelation must both be accepted as logical necessities. "God must reveal himself . . . He cannot remain concealed . . . Thus the universe is the embodied thought of the Creator. It is God's frozen breath." Since only the poet or the religious genius, however, can read the message of God in the physical universe, human beings have also required "a spoken voice, an articulate word, a revelation to the ear, a message to the average mind"; and therefore each race that has risen above savagery has had its bible, the written revelation of God to that race.[53]

Jesus in the religion of humanity becomes the representative of the real Christ, which is mankind itself. "Nothing less than all

---

[51]Ibid., p. 32.
[52]Ibid., pp. 44, 55.
[53]Ibid., pp. 56, 60.

the humanity there is in the race," Frothingham asserted, "meets the conditions of a doctrine of incarnation . . . To try to crowd the attributes of the theological Christ into the personality of the historical Jesus, is to plant a whole forest in a porcelain vase." Traditional interpretations of the purpose of Jesus' life and death had been similarly narrow. If the life offered a moral example, this was not because Jesus induced people to emulate him, but because he showed them how to turn from themselves to the true Christ, to humanity. If his spiritual triumph over death offered the promise of immortality, this was a promise not that the individual would continue beyond the grave but only that "the human element in mankind" would persist within the context of the natural immortality of the race.[54]

As such revisions suggest, Frothingham placed himself frankly "beyond Christianity." On the crucial point, his denial of finality to the Christian religion, he set himself apart from Christian liberals both within and outside of Unitarianism; and Frothingham was far more willing than Bartol was to be identified with the Free Religious Association. The similarity of his method, and even of his results, to those of a professedly Christian liberalism became especially clear, however, when Frothingham turned to what one might have thought would be a negative discussion of the errors of orthodoxy.

Rarely since the beginnings of the Unitarian Controversy in New England had a professing radical found so much good in the traditional doctrines. "We believe," Frothingham began, "that all error embodies a soul of truth. Even the most hideous beliefs owe their hold on mankind not to misanthropy but to their success in giving to the spirit of truth a temporary form."[55] The much-ridiculed doctrine of the Trinity had been an attempt "to state the belief that God was in the world and at the same time out of it, that the universe was divine, but did not exhaust the divine."

The Father represented the infinite, endless, unexhausted, inexhaustible capacities of Deity. The Son represented the organized and organizing

---

[54]Ibid., pp. 89-90, 100, cf. 233-264.
[55]Ibid., p. 319.

power that expended itself in creation. The Spirit represented the continuous movement of power, the ceaseless intercourse, the perpetual action and reaction between the two.

"Call it a rude device," Frothingham continued, "but no better has yet been discovered by theology."[56]

Unitarians also believe the deity of Christ to be an erroneous idea, he wrote, yet this error, too, contains a deep truth. Early Christians felt, "as devout minds feel now, that there was a point where the divine and the human met and mingled," and the doctrine of Christ's deity provided the majestic, if misleading, language for expressing that insight. Similarly, the stories of Eden and the Fall were efforts to put into words the vision of a perfect manhood; ancient men felt no warrant to anticipate a glorious earthly future, so they pictured in the Edenic myth an ideal past. As for the doctrine of a total depravity occasioned by Adam's sin, it was indeed horrible; but did that mean that its originators were "cynics and misanthropes"?

That can hardly be. They must have had something in their minds that struggled for voice. What was it, but the fact that man is limited, constrained, incapable, imbecile, that he cannot at the moment do what he would, cannot break his bonds, restrain his passions, eradicate his vices, put away his infirmities, lift off the burden of his social evils, make himself and the world in an instant just what they should be?[57]

As for the related idea of a transmission of Adam's guilt to his posterity: What was that but the plain truth that men of one generation do have an inheritance from the generations that have gone before, "and that this inheritance is largely one of pain, weakness, and sorrow"? The doctrine of election is a monument to "the effort of sincere minds to get some light on the most mysterious questions" of human existence, the questions of chance and fate. Having failed, as men still are failing, to dig the heart out of the mystery ("We are unable to explain these things; we cannot account for them scientifically"), they "bowed their own hearts beneath it . . . Finding the fact unmanageable, they just col-

---

[56]Ibid., p. 320.
[57]Ibid., pp. 320-325.

lected the whole shocking mass of facts together, and flung it upon the broad shoulders of the upholder of the universe."[58] And finally, though early Christian theology did concoct something terrible in the idea of an eternal punishment of the wicked, that scarcely proves that those ancient men were "more heartless or cruel than the best of us." What it shows, rather, is that the circumstances of their world and society made them *"more deeply impressed with the hatefulness of guilt than we are,"* and that "they were more in the habit than we are of measuring guilt by supreme standards."[59]

The Unitarian Vanguard

Frothingham, though one of the more prolific and interesting figures in nineteenth-century liberal history, claims no place in the front rank of American Protestant thinkers. But his *Religion of Humanity* stood at an important crossroads. If the author seemed, in the apparent antinomies that bothered critics, to be giving the inquiring intellectual traveler inconclusive advice about which road to take, surely in that respect he resembled many of humanity's more provocative philosophic guides. The free religionists, together with humanists yet unborn, could thank pioneers like Frothingham and Bartol for entrusting religion to "the interior spirit of the age." Christian modernists, on the other hand, could follow the examples these guides themselves had set, and could put the spirit of the age to work not to destroy the tradition but to understand and transform it. The Congregationalist George A. Gordon, in *The Christ of To-day* (1895)—an important statement of the New Theology—emphasized this second line of indebtedness. Gordon recalled that once the necessary critical work of the Unitarians had been accomplished, some of them had begun the "meditation of a deeper return to the past"—a return not to orthodoxy but rather to "the essential and eternal truth hidden in the old creeds."[60]

For the main body of Unitarianism itself, which by the 1890s

---

[58]Ibid., pp. 325, 327, 329.
[59]Ibid., p. 331, emphasis Frothingham's.
[60]Gordon, *Christ of To-day*, pp. 143-144.

was officially divesting itself of commitments to the primacy of
Christianity, Protestant modernism was, clearly enough, the road
not taken. But that circumstance in no way weakens the usual
depiction of Unitarianism as the cutting edge for signal developments in American Protestant theology. Among the freedoms that
Unitarians had gained for themselves, one that stood out im-
pressively in the historical record was the freedom to pioneer
intellectually; in particular, to take note of new philosophical
and scientific ideas, or new departures in literature, and to apply
them with relatively few inhibitions to theology. Like other
pioneering, this often had been crude and tentative. But in opening religion to philosophical idealism and later to scientific
method, in broadening the subject matter of preaching, in allevi-
ating the astounding American provincialism about world
religions, the nineteenth-century Unitarians had made incalculable contributions.[61] As pioneers of a modernist synthesis, they
had trafficked with complexity and doubt as often as with plain
affirmations of modernity; but even in this respect they were true
precursors of the liberal movement that was to broaden out
through much of American Protestantism.

---

[61]See J. W. Brown, *Rise of Biblical Criticism*; Buell, "Unitarian Movement,"
pp. 166-190; *Literary Transcendentalism*, pp. 23-39; and Howe, *Unitarian Conscience*, especially pp. 174-204. On "provincialism" consult Ahlstrom, *American
Protestant Encounter*.

The Evangelical Groundwork

The local gospel was compelled to become a
mode of virtue, rather than a jumble of doctrines.

DAVID SWING, ca. 1873

Historians of religion have usually located the
first stirrings of the so-called New Theology, or
late-nineteenth-century surge of liberal thought,
in the New England Congregationalism of the
years after 1875.[1] While such a depiction has merit, it also undoubtedly owes something to traditional preoccupation with New
England, together with long-standing reliance on the most accessible literary record. It would be wrong, in any case, to suppose
that liberal and modernist ideas had gained no hearing at all
within the evangelical churches, and no hearing outside New
England, during the years when they were being developed among
the Unitarians. Swing, the Presbyterian liberal, managed in the
1870s to find a substantial Western audience—and also to gain the
support or tolerance of his clerical colleagues—for an adaptationism that seemed an evangelical version of Frothingham's. While
it is not easy, before that time, to find explicit modernism in the
Presbyterian or other major Protestant denominations, it seems
clear that the accused heretic won his case in 1874 because by then
some kind of groundwork had been laid, both in formal theology
and in popular thought, within the evangelical bodies.

---

[1]See, for example, Buckham's *Progressive Religious Thought in America*,
which is subtitled *A Survey of the Enlarging Pilgrim Faith*; also Foster, *Modern
Movement*, pp. 14-15.

Horace Bushnell

Formal evangelicalism at its most wildly modernistic had not advanced, by the 1870s, beyond the "progressive orthodoxy" that from mid-century onward had been associated with the name of Horace Bushnell.[2] Preaching and popular thought, however, as the responses to the Swing Trial indicated, in some outposts of the evangelical world were moving well ahead of the theologians.

Horace Bushnell: Immanentism and Doctrine

W. H. Auden, in a brilliantly succinct and truthful use of hyperbole, wrote that when William Butler Yeats passed from life to death "he became his admirers." Seminal and inspiring leaders do achieve reembodiment, particularly in the immediately following generation and often in ways that are oddly perilous to their own reputations. Jeremy Bentham would have retained a presence in all the discussions of the Utilitarians even if his clothed skeleton had not been preserved at University College; and there is a sense, an entirely unsentimental one, in which prophets like William Ellery Channing or Horace Bushnell must be seen as active participants in successor movements with which they could not fully have sympathized. Epigoni, much to the inconvenience of scholars who must debate whether Marx was a Marxist and Channing a transcendentalist, do tend to internalize the master's principles and spirit—so much so that they scarcely realize how misleading it may be for them constantly to invoke his name.[3]

Horace Bushnell, the Hartford preacher and theologian who died in 1876, retained in this way a remarkable presence both in the Social Gospel of the late nineteenth century and in Protestant modernism. The adaptationism even of his immediate successors in the liberal movement would have shocked him; yet no one else had done so much to lay the foundation of their cultural im-

---

[2] Such contemporaries as Edwards Park of the Congregationalist Andover Seminary or Henry Boynton Smith and Albert Barnes among the New School Presbyterians adopted positions very near to Bushnell's, and exerted a similar, if lesser, influence upon the next generation. See Marsden, *Evangelical Mind*, pp. 142-181; Vanderpool, "Andover Conservatives"; and Stoever, "Henry Boynton Smith," pp. 69-89.

[3] To quote Auden further, "The words of a dead man/Are modified in the guts of the living." "In Memory of W. B. Yeats."

manentism, and it is not strange that his name and ideas were never far from their consciousness.

In his attitudes toward modernity, Bushnell had been very much the evangelical counterpart of Emerson. He had stood with the Emersonian transcendentalists in stressing God's indwelling and humanity's direct intuitive access to the divine. Like them he had voiced a creative protest against both the old orthodoxy and the rationalistic or "sensationalist"[4] forms of liberalism. In dealing with science and modernity he had expressed, in the terms of a higher and more serious christology, both the hesitations of the transcendentalists about modernity and their half-willing concessions to it.

Bushnell and the English romantic theologian Frederick D. Maurice have sometimes been pictured as jointly resistant to the idea of "synthesizing Christian faith with culture or some prevalent system of thought."[5] Yet Maurice cared enough about the relations of science and religion—a subject "which all my circumstances and occupations have compelled me to consider"— to address the matter directly in 1863;[6] and Bushnell did the same on several occasions, most notably in an article on "Science and Religion" published in 1868.[7] In such writings the romantic theologians showed themselves to be very much interested in synthesis; it is simply that their interest seemed less a sincere consultation of science than a benign religious imperialism. Their cordiality toward science and modernity was ultimately the cordiality of the spider's invitation to the fly.

Bushnell's attitude, which seems to have remained fundamentally the same throughout his career as a theologian, was first of all that religion and science must regard each other with mutual respect, since each has its own integrity, and since ultimately they

---

[4]That is, relying for religious knowledge upon the testimony of the ordinary senses.

[5]Welch, *Protestant Thought*, p. 242.

[6]Frederick D. Maurice, *The Claims of the Bible and of Science: Correspondence Between a Layman and the Rev. F. D. Maurice on Some Questions Arising Out of the Controversy Respecting the Pentateuch* (London, Macmillan and Co., 1863), pp. 15 et passim.

[7]*Putnam's Magazine*, 1 (March 1868), 265-275.

are in harmony. Just as nature and the supernatural constitute "the one system of God,"[8] so the instruments of their apprehension—reason and faith—are part of one great continuum. Science and religion ought not to be at odds.

But religion was to make its accommodation with science, in the end, by enveloping it, by bringing every proven scientific finding within the total system of God's will, where Bushnell was sure all true science naturally belonged. Christianity, as he insisted in a famous essay of 1848, does not come into the world "armed against all other knowledge, to destroy it." But it does claim a right

to possess and appropriate and melt into unity with itself, all other truth; for whatever truth there is in the universe belongs to the Lord of Christianity, and holds a real consistency, both with him and it. Therefore Christianity must open its bosom . . . and gather to its poles all particles of knowledge and science, as the loadstone gathers the particles of iron.[9]

Many later liberals, despite acknowledged indebtedness to the romantic generation of liberal evangelicals, found it hard to forgive them for constructing a formula that the younger men saw as depending upon ignorance of science or else upon a kind of deviousness. In either case, according to Frank Hugh Foster, the liberals of mid-century had been superb representatives of "the old apology." They could not address the post-Darwinian age because despite their actual survival into the 1870s they "did not live in" that age. Foster suggested that Henry Boynton Smith, Bushnell's nearest soulmate among the Presbyterians, had thought Darwinism unimportant because he had missed its point. "That an age of *exact observation of facts*, such as had never been known, had been ushered in, and that all reasoning was to take on new forms in consequence, had entirely escaped him."[10]

---

[8]Bushnell adopted this phraseology for the title of his most comprehensive work, *Nature and the Supernatural, as Together Constituting the One System of God* (1858).

[9]"Dogma and Spirit," *God in Christ*, pp. 313-314.

[10]Frank Hugh Foster, *A Genetic History of the New England Theology* (New York, Russell and Russell, 1963, originally published 1907), pp. 447-448. Cf. Stoever, "Henry Boynton Smith": "the philosophers were to be met and defeated

Bushnell, though he too rejected what he knew of Darwinism, and though he stood by his assertion of the ultimate "rights" of the Christian system, did at length offer concessions to science that implied discomfiture with his own basic formula. Even in the discourse of 1848, he used a governmental metaphor which, if followed at all precisely, qualified his more imperialistic conceptions. "Regarding the realm of reason, and the realm of faith, as our two Houses of Assembly," he said, "we are to consider nothing as enacted into a law, which has not been able to pass both houses."[11] And in 1868, with the claims of Darwinian scientism in full view, he granted further concessions by discriminating among different degrees of scientific certitude.

Bushnell placed the Darwinian hypotheses low on the scale of certitudes; they had not been "proven," and Bushnell was sure they would not be. Similarly, naturalistic theories of spontaneous generation were not estimable alternatives to the biblical explanation of creation; there was less evidence for them than for a belief in conscious divine action. But other scientific findings such as those relating to an alleged pre-Adamic human being were, he thought, more substantial and must be considered partially proven. Still other conclusions, from those of Copernicus to those of the geologist Sir Charles Lyell, deserved outright assent, and called for changes in religious forms of expression.[12]

Thus, while Bushnell never became explicitly an enthusiast for the spirit of the age as a reliable guide to theological change, he did approach a modernist position when forced to deal with the concrete actuality of science. To be sure, the final eloquence of his 1868 article went into a plea that religion and science must stand their ground, merely listening respectfully to each other. But Bushnell at this point also offered considerable warrant for the modernist extrapolations that another generation would construct from his position. "Religion," he asserted, "must consent to be

---

on their own ground (though for all of Smith's rhetoric, it was orthodox ground) . . . His work . . . like that of his German teachers, was dominated by the interests of a particular strain of Christian piety" (pp. 88, 89).
    [11]"Dogma and Spirit," p. 316.
    [12]"Science and Religion," pp. 268-272.

configured to all true points of science." Having the Bible on hand to convert the world, "it must, in a different sense, be converted to the world. And it can never stop being thus converted, till science stops discovery. It must seek to put itself in harmony with every sort of truth, else it cannot be true itself."[13]

In Bushnell's case, as in that of Maurice, discussions of adjustment to science form a minute part of the corpus, and it would be distorting to suggest that such discussions bulk large among the contributions to a modernist impulse. More important Bushnellian legacies were those conveyed in his "Dissertation on Language,"[14] and in *Christian Nurture*. The first, which asserted that the language of the creeds is poetical and not literal, helped establish the foundation for a modernism that would claim to be conserving the doctrines of Christianity rather than superceding them. The second by its environmental approach to religious nurture bolstered a growing confidence in the redemptive potentialities in the realm that had been known and feared as "the world."

These were the foundations. But Bushnell also offered laboratory examples of the kind of doctrinal revision his theories demanded and expedited. He particularly, in *God in Christ* and its sequels, restated the doctrine of the Trinity and the customary assertions concerning the person and work of Christ. But his revisions nearly ran the gamut, if not of the Christian system, at least of those segments that had been disputed actively in American theology since Jonathan Edwards.

This determination seriously to revise doctrines, rather than dissolve them in an intuitionist faith in direct access to God, constitutes in itself a signal contribution to later modernism. Here the foundation document is the aforementioned "Dogma and Spirit," an essay that gives less space to Bushnell's responses to science than to his insistence that doctrines (though not dogmas) are the essential vehicles of mediation between traditional faith and contemporary thought.[15]

---

[13]Ibid., pp. 273-274, 272.

[14]"Preliminary Dissertation on the Nature of Language, as Related to Thought and Spirit," *God in Christ*, pp. 9-97.

[15]*God in Christ*, pp. 310-317.

To Bushnell's conservative critics, of course, a championing of doctrine could not be reassuring if particular doctrines had been "spiritualized" beyond recognition. From the critics' point of view Bushnell was, like the twentieth-century military commander, destroying villages in order to save them. And just here lies the heart of the dispute between any form of modernism and its most sophisticated opponents: Was a mediating theologian like Bushnell Christianizing the romantic movement, or was he destroying Christianity?—giving transcendentalism a higher christology, or reducing the Incarnation to mere immanence? Bushnell's work could be seen either as the emancipation of theology or as the head and front of a great offense. Either way, though, he had done more than any other single person to create the possibility in America of a professedly Christian modernism.

The Poetic Evangelicalism of David Swing

Washington Gladden, the famous Social Gospel leader, devoted three of the chapters in his autobiography to certain great public events of the early 1870s. The first of these chapters dealt with the Tweed Ring. The next was divided between Horace Greeley's presidential campaign and the Credit Mobilier scandal. The third treated the David Swing Trial of 1874.[16]

Swing, one of the half-dozen most prominent preachers in America during the last third of the nineteenth century, is now less well remembered even by historians of religion than is Henry Ward Beecher or Phillips Brooks. Whether that contrast is just, or whether it results from overattention to the eastern seaboard, Swing and his heresy trial were of signal importance in announcing and augmenting the presence of modernist ideas within the evangelical churches. Swing himself, both as a Presbyterian before 1874 and as an independent for twenty years thereafter, preached to several thousand people each week, and his sermons were regularly published. His trial for heresy not only was the most spectacular in the decade of the seventies;[17] it seemed, at least

---

[16]Gladden, *Recollections*, pp. 197-231.

[17]The Crawford Toy "trial" in Louisville (1879) is the closest competitor. It gained substantially less national attention. Pope A. Duncan, "Crawford Howell Toy: Heresy at Louisville," Shriver, ed., *American Religious Heretics*, pp. 56-88.

to Presbyterians and Congregationalists, the most startling event of that kind in nearly half a century—since the trials of Albert Barnes and Lyman Beecher in the early 1830s.

From the historian's point of view, Swing as a religious thinker qualifies as the first modernist among prominent evangelicals, or at the least shares that position with Henry Ward Beecher. The controversy in which he became embroiled, moreover, proved to be an especially revealing herald and preparation for the New Theology. Extending widely in time and space, it forced many people to articulate latent beliefs, and provoked an uncommon sounding of opinion at several levels of society and the clerical profession.

Swing, forty-four when heresy charges were brought against him, had become pastor of Fourth Presbyterian Church (then called Westminster Church) in 1866, following several years as a professor of classics at Miami University in Ohio. A mild and diffident man, he had doubted his own ability to preach to a large urban congregation. Friends urging the Chicago job upon him had finally resorted to implying that he was about to be purged at Miami; and even after initial success in Chicago he had taken up the study of law to hedge what he assumed was an uncertain future.[18]

His drawing power remained something of a mystery to himself and to others. After he had moved, as an independent, to Central Music Hall on State Street, the Chicago *Inter-Ocean* remarked that

Swing's continued success excites surprise. The churchgoing element in America is easily enamoured of oratory . . . [Henry Ward Beecher] issued his words of instruction and love from lips which quivered with magnetic fire, while [Swing] utters everything in that same woe-begone, nasal whine which can be heard nowhere on earth but in Music Hall . . . Added to a personal presence singularly unattractive—a face, the lower half of, which suggests frozen sensuousness, while the upper half indicates anxious thought—and a physique without form, is the elocutionary manner of a country undertaker inviting the cousins of the corpse to take the last look. And yet he holds and sways three thousand people every Sunday.

---

[18]Newton, *Swing*, pp. 56-57.

David Swing in 1875

Swing, asked to explain this, replied wryly that he found it un-accountable, and could only guess that he had acquired that many friends since coming to Chicago.[19]

An age that had known the monotone lecturing of an Emerson, and been moved by orators as ungainly as Lincoln, should perhaps have had no difficulty in explaining Swing. It had always been possible, despite some reports to the contrary, to find American popular audiences concerned more for matter than for manner. And Swing's partisans thought that he had more to say than the stirring "princes of the pulpit" with whom he was compared. The editor of the Boston *Herald* observed that "if Mr. Beecher has taken the American sermon out of its conventional methods and taught the preachers freedom, Swing has taught them . . . how to make the sermon as inclusive in its range and as constructive in its methods as is the large, free life through which we are passing." Swing, this admirer suggested, was almost the only leading man of the American pulpit who knew what to say to thoughtful people in a time of painful religious transition.[20]

This ability to talk the language of doubters, however, gradually brought the liberal preacher into conflict with more orthodox spirits who detected on Swing's side of the conversation a clear erosion of the Westminster standards, the written creed of Presby-terianism. Swing and his supporters responded that, erosion or not, the theology in question stood well within the tradition of evangelical Christianity, and within the boundaries agreed upon in a recent reconciliation between New- and Old-School Presby-terians.[21] In a statement offered at his trial, Swing affirmed his belief in "the inspiration of the Holy Scriptures, the Trinity, the divinity of Christ, the office of Christ as a mediator . . . conver-sion by God's spirit, man's natural sinfulness, and the final separation of the righteous and wicked."[22] And he preached these

---

[19]Ibid., pp. 242-243, 176.

[20]Ibid., pp. 138-139.

[21]The background in Presbyterianism and the personal characteristics of the chief actors in this trial are discussed in some detail in Hutchison, "Disapproval of Chicago," pp. 30-47.

[22]Johnson, *Swing Trial,* p. 20.

tenets, if not with literal incisiveness, still with a fervor that derived from religious experience of a deeply emotional kind. Unlike most liberal leaders of succeeding decades, Swing in his youth had gone through a strongly marked conversion. His biographer, Joseph Fort Newton, reports that for days after this episode, which occurred at a Methodist revival meeting, the young man had "felt as if he were walking on air, upheld by tides of ecstasy"; and that always thereafter, "though his gifts were of another kind," though he had little enough affinity with Bible-thumping evangelism, "he was a lover of evangelical fervor and a believer in its cleansing and exalting efficacy." It was typical both of Swing's humor and of his religiosity that when a young clerical admirer reported failure to reach his own congregation with any of the current intellectual topics or literary devices, Swing replied in two words: "Try religion."[23]

Yet from a strictly orthodox point of view, Swing's religion was unsatisfactory. The first and most frustrating problem was the poetic form in which it was presented. The editors of the *Dial* remarked at the time of Swing's death that in his sermons dogma, "which most theologians offer to their public in solid lumps, had gone completely into solution."[24] The solvent was compounded of personal spirituality, which in itself could appear dangerous to a severe biblical literalist, and of cultural relativism, which was a good deal more suspect.

The crux of Swing's deviation from orthodoxy lay in his insistence that all religious expressions are dependent upon the culture within which they are formulated, and that they cannot be understood apart from that culture. Negatively, this meant that scriptures, doctrines, and creeds are of less than absolute validity, and that parts of all of them must be discounted. On the positive side, because Swing believed in progress, it meant that new religious expressions could be found that would improve upon

---

[23]Newton, *Swing*, pp. 35-36, 176. Swing, besides having experienced dramatic conversion, was also atypical among liberal leaders in having been reared in a western, rural, and relatively impoverished setting. His upbringing and Christian training, however, conformed to the pattern of tolerance and lack of repression found in the personal histories of most of the liberals. Ibid., pp. 35-40.

[24]*Dial*, 17 (October 16, 1894), 217.

older ones. One would not need to do away with doctrines altogether; the need, rather, was for adaptation. And because human
culture itself showed steady improvement, it was possible to urge
doctrinal adaptation not just grudgingly, as a necessity, but with
enthusiasm and confidence.[25]

In a context of cultural relativism, the "inspiration of the
Scriptures" signified a "divine assistance given to man," not a
guarantee that inspired human authors would infallibly write the
words and thoughts of God. Only God is perfect, Swing argued;
men and their utterances are not. The Bible therefore contains
many wrong and terrible things, such as the psalmist's plea to
Jehovah to destroy the enemy and his widow and his fatherless
children. Swing thought such passages could only be excused, if
they could be excused at all, as battle cries in a necessary war for
the principle of monotheism.

But creedal expressions were even more questionable than
scriptural ones. Creeds at their best reminded Swing of Louis
Kossuth's constitution. The great Hungarian patriot had toured
America with a marvelous document in his hand, issuing bonds
in the name of a nation that never became. Similarly, said Swing,
the creed of the church "has been read long and loud at all crossroads, but I will leave it for you all to answer . . . whether we
have the state or only a good constitution for one in some far-off
futurity."[26]

A corollary to this view of creeds as mere ground plans was
Swing's emphasis upon a doctrine of works. To make salvation
dependent upon "faith in Christ," Swing asserted, is all very well;
but how can one claim faith in Christ and then ignore what Christ
taught? And Christ taught the doctrine of good works in every
speech that he uttered. The church that condescends to make a
real place for the importance of good works, the preacher added
sardonically, merely gives Jesus his due. "To the teachings of

---

[25]This is the setting of Swing's remark, quoted in part at the opening of the
previous chapter, that "we are . . . all more than willing to give our hearts to
the spirit of our own times, and would not for any gold go back to the age of
terrorism in politics, in domestic life, and in Christianity." Swing, *Sermons*, p. 85.

[26]Ibid., pp. 94-99, 90.

Calvin and Luther," he said, "it adds the teachings of the Saviour as an important supplement."[27]

Swing recognized that some people were apprehensive about the possible emergence, from such an emphasis on works, of a religion of "mere morality." But in view of the then-notorious Credit Mobilier scandals, in which Christian businessmen and politicians had perpetrated or permitted the cheating of the public, he judged such apprehensions to be premature. "I see no tendency on the part of public men," he told his congregation, "to base their soul's salvation on good works . . . Upon all the horizon we cannot behold any encroachment of this evil." On the contrary, "there are thousands of Christians who are getting their salvation by faith and their fortunes by rascality."[28]

Professions and confessions therefore must prove themselves in action. Swing viewed creedal statements very much as William James viewed absolutes—they are valuable to the degree that they get you around among particulars. Doctrines that do not help one to navigate the moral exigencies of human life are worse than useless, and debate over them is, Swing thought, "a dim battle in a doubtful land."[29] It followed, as he remarked some years before his own heresy trial, that heresy hunters are "the most useless and forlorn men who have lived since the world began . . . living for a certain assemblage of words just as the miser lives for his labeled bags of gold." Upon hearing a new idea, they will not open their souls to consider it, but rather will mutter with Shylock, "It is not so stated in the bond."[30]

Swing in the early 1870s believed the days of the forlorn heresy hunters were over. Trials were occurring "nowhere in orthodox denominations." This was not for lack of important deviations from orthodoxy. Such a lack, Swing claimed, would never deter a professional heresy hunter. It was rather because the whole notion of heresy had become irrelevant. There is something unreal, he argued, about putting a man on trial for saying what the best

---

[27]Ibid., pp. 103, 106.
[28]Ibid., pp. 103-104, 107.
[29]Newton, *Swing*, p. 18.
[30]Swing, *Sermons*, p. 33.

thought of his time holds to be true; and the deviations of his own time were, he thought, "universal rather than individual. If they were the new departures of one man there would be trial and discord, but they are the modifications of a whole generation."[31]

So there were to be no more heresy trials, just as, in the view of this benign and hopeful man, there were going to be no more wars. Swing had, seemingly, a poignant sense of evil. He spoke of "the world's confessed wickedness" and of its "universal and inborn depravity," and meant every word of it. The minimizing of human sin he called "the ultimate sloth . . . surrender . . . death. Evermore the Cross of Christ rises up to refute" those who make light of human evil. Yet this same man, noting the signs of progress all about him in the later nineteenth century, believed there were some follies that human societies would never again descend to. War, for instance; and xenophobic nationalism. He averred that the *Marseillaise* was as out of date as the vengeful 109th Psalm, and remarked that the old, rarely sung, American patriotic song about a "star-spangled banner" was as dead as the old feelings of Anglophobia of which it was a sad reminder. "No heart remains so warlike," he asserted, as to sing either of those martial lays.[32]

Dogmatists and warmakers alike had been put out of business by an age that actively disdained their services. In thus denouncing those who divide the garment of Christ, Swing stood in a venerable antiformalist tradition; the "forlorn men" who seek out heresy had often been accused of bringing dissension and destruction. But Swing, like Channing before him, was sure the church faced an unprecedented cultural situation. In this place, in this century, more than anywhere or ever in the past, an institution that closed its mind was courting disaster. In the American democracy, people had rejected the theologies natural to more confined societies and more tyrannized cultures. God could no longer be a despot; men and women must be known as free agents; and mysteries such as predestination and reprobation could have no interest for those

---

[31]Ibid., p. 20.
[32]Ibid., p. 46; Newton, *Swing*, p. 248; Swing, *Sermons*, pp. 98-99.

who were daily concerned with "the acceptance and enjoyment of facts." At the same time, America's vastness and diversity had necessitated and produced human understanding. In the midst of all this, it was unthinkable that the church should not adjust. "It is impossible for the state to be engaged making us brothers and the church to be engaged making us enemies and strangers. One or the other effort must abandon the field." There could be no doubt which must give way. "The church bows justly to the spirit of the republic."[33]

Swing's sense of the influence of environment, of the genius of place, focused more specifically on the prairies and cities of the American Midwest. His sermons regularly employed images of stifling confinement when he referred to theological conservatives, metaphors of space and expansion when he praised religious liberality. The trouble with creeds, said Swing in one of the sermons that provoked the trial, is that they try to cage up the manifold glory of God "in the phrases of a few men at some given time and place." That, he complained, is like plucking a few flowers "from the vast prairie between Lake Michigan and the Missouri."[34]

The Chicago preacher's life and rhetoric constituted striking support for a later historian's observation that "the bounties of the virgin space" in the American West helped people confront all traditional institutions "with tolerance, with amusement, with anger, with impatience, but never with submissiveness."[35] In the case of Swing the connection between place and doctrine was quite consciously proposed:

It appears that, not only in Arabian dream but in reality, there is a genius of each place holding an invisible wand that touches every heart. A Quaker influence presides over Philadelphia; a Calvinistic Hercules holds Pittsburg in great subjection; and thus onward until

---

[33]Swing, *Sermons*, pp. 15-19.

[34]Ibid., p. 10.

[35]Mead, "The American People: Their Space, Time, and Religion," *Lively Experiment*, p. 7. Cf. Gay Wilson Allen, "The Influence of Space on the American Imagination," in Clarence F. Gohdes, ed., *Essays on American Literature in Honor of Jay B. Hubbell* (Durham, Duke University Press, 1967), pp. 329-342; Tony Tanner, "Notes for a Comparison between American and European Romanticism," *Journal of American Studies*, 2 (April 1968), 83-103.

each city may be seen to lie under a powerful enchantment peculiar to itself. *Chicago is an attempt at evangelism.* All the details of the creeds between Jerusalem and Geneva seem forgotten . . . The local gospel was compelled to become a mode of virtue, rather than a jumble of doctrines.[36]

Against the background of Swing's fervent evangelicalism and sense of human wrongdoing, such revelling in the possibilities of a particular time, place, and culture expressed not an unlimited belief in human powers but rather a faith in radical regeneration. "The world's greatest *fact* being its degradation," Swing asserted, "its greatest *want* is to be expressed by the word 'recreation,' or 'reborn.'" The church would be useful, he contended, in proportion to the depth of its realization "that men must 'be born again'—not hereafter, but in these passing days."[37]

Swing in fact based the argument for religious adaptation in large measure upon the need to combat the "great vices" of the age. Creedal religion, in this area as in others, had failed the pragmatic test. "The world has tried external doctrines to the extreme limit," he said, yet vices flourish and "laugh at the puny arm of religion." What is necessary is "a Christianity of life which shall plead for all reforms," which shall lift the multitude "not to our long theology, but to such a life of spirituality and purity and moral grandeur as is spread out before them in that golden page of Bethlehem."[38]

Turning to the church's foreign policy, Swing set forth a theme that was destined to wind its way for sixty years through the complex relations between liberalism and the missionary movement. That theme was the simple but controversial proposal that Christianity go before the world as a way of living rather than as a dogma. Again Swing was somewhat too sanguine about the progress of liberalism. He thought the change had already come about. One hundred years of the missionary movement having taught hard lessons, he saw no future probability "that any missionary gold will be exhausted upon any indoctrination of the heathen world in denominational ideas." There would be, he

---

[36]Quoted in Newton, *Swing*, p. 59.
[37]Swing, *Sermons*, pp. 46, 48, 50.
[38]Ibid., pp. 92-93.

thought, "little disposition to inculcate abroad doctrines which are rapidly dying by our own firesides." We hide our dividing dogmas when we meet foreigners because "we fear their smile of unbelief or derision."[39]

If Christianity could not be spread as a dogma, it could grow and spread both as a life and as a civilization. All the ages since Christ have attempted to spread their religion, Swing admitted, but "our age alone is the fortunate one that has come anywhere near reading aright the religion of Christ," and therefore is the first age that can hope successfully to promote Christianity as a civilization. Rightly read, the religion of Christ is "an action rather than a philosophy"; its genius is "that of *outgoing* love, a love which grows by going and dies in any confinement." If it could be preached on that assumption, "legislators and statesmen would begin their careers by a study of Christ as a teacher and an impulse," and the outreach and example of Christianity would then be not a matter of clerical missionaries but of a Christianized civilization.[40]

The Liberal Victory in Chicago

Swing, since he lived only until 1894, was not forced to watch the commitment of some of America's Christian resources to imperialism; he never suffered disillusionment in his hopes for the ending of warfare and similar human follies. But in the matter of heresy trials, the awakening came swiftly. In the summer of 1873, Francis Patton, a young professor and editor recently brought to Chicago from Princeton,[41] began a series of attacks, first upon Washington Gladden, religious editor of the *Independent*, and then, by the early months of 1874, upon David Swing.

---

[39]Ibid., p. 43.

[40]Swing, *Truths for Today*, pp. 208-212.

[41]Patton, twenty-nine years of age, had served briefly in a Brooklyn pastorate. His Princeton mentors, in response to requests from Chicago conservatives, had recommended him for the chair in Didactic and Polemical Theology that had been established at the Presbyterian Theological Seminary of the Northwest by Cyrus McCormick. See W. T. Hutchinson, *Cyrus Hall McCormick*, II (New York, The Century Co., 1935), 250-253; and G. M. Harper, "Francis Landey Patton," *DAB*, XIV, 315.

Gladden, who was to become one of the foremost leaders of the Protestant Social Gospel, had published a series of articles complaining that "outmoded" and "immoral" doctrines were still being taught in some pulpits and seminaries. The sin of Adam was still being imputed to his descendants, Gladden asserted, and some Calvinists were continuing to preach the terrible doctrine of infant damnation that had aroused such indignation in the earlier nineteenth century.

The young liberal received two kinds of adverse reaction to these articles. One set of critics denied indignantly that such ideas were still taught, and demanded proof (which Gladden supplied). Francis Patton and others, however, admitted that the indicted doctrines were current, and vigorously assailed Gladden for being disrespectful of them. Gladden in New York City received the same kind of local support, at this point, that Swing would later enjoy in Chicago. He was able to assert that nothing the *Independent* had published for many years had "drawn forth such a chorus of unanimous approval." But in the national press, his detractors kept up the attack all through July and August of 1873.[42]

In the fall of 1873, public attention was diverted by the more exciting spectacle of the Evangelical Alliance and the Free Religious Association both holding their meetings in New York (much to the disadvantage of the free religionists). In December Patton was busy arguing with Henry Ward Beecher's *Christian Union* over the question whether Octavius Frothingham was or was not an advocate of free love. And early in 1874 the focus shifted to the Midwest when, as Gladden wrote, "Professor Patton found a heretic nearer home."

On every side, Patton's battle with Swing was perceived as a continuation of his fight with Gladden. The young Princetonian, in his newspaper (the *Interior*) and elsewhere, had been commenting upon Swing's preaching for nearly two years; and apparently he had been compiling a concordance of the heresies contained therein. But the appearance of Swing's book, *Truths*

---

[42]Gladden, *Recollections*, pp. 223-225; *Independent*, 25 (July 3 and August 7, 1873); editorials and editorial notes in all issues through October 23.

for Today, confirmed that the liberal preacher's popularity was mounting despite the *Interior*'s efforts to contain and counteract it. Patton at that point reached his fateful decision to give Swing his undivided attention.[43]

Patton's prospect of convicting Swing seemed dubious from the start. The Chicago *Tribune*, shortly before the hearings began, quipped that "the theological market may be quoted as fairly active, with brisk inquiries as to futures"; but on April 13th, when Patton presented his charges, futures were clarified with almost indecent rapidity. The first charge held that Swing had not been faithful in maintaining the truths of the Gospel; the second, that the accused did not sincerely receive and preach the Presbyterian Confession of Faith. Of the twenty-eight specifications offered in support of these charges, many attacked the vagueness of Swing's preaching; so when the Judicial Committee of the Presbytery turned things around and complained about the vagueness of Patton's specifications, the young prosecutor must have known he was in trouble. Patton went to work and made his specifications more specific, whereupon the Presbytery agreed to try the case; but the Moderator made a point of reminding Patton that, according to Presbyterian law, "if he failed to prove the charges he must himself be censured as a slanderer of the gospel ministry in proportion to the malignancy or rashness that shall appear in the prosecution."[44]

In retrospect one sees that Patton would have been well advised at this point to drop about two-thirds of his specifications. Eight or ten of them caught Swing in actual disparagements of Presbyterian doctrines, or at least offered prima facie evidence of important omissions. But Patton could not resist retaining twenty other charges that imputed guilt-by-association or that called upon sheerly circumstantial or inferential evidence. Patton complained, for example, that Swing had shown too much admiration for John Stuart Mill; that he had helped the Unitarians dedicate a chapel; and that he had phrased many traditional doctrines so

---

[43]*Christian Union*, 8 (December 24, 1873); Gladden, *Recollections*, p. 225; Newton, *Swing*, p. 95.

[44]Newton, *Swing*, p. 80; *Swing Trial*, pp. 4-16.

freely or poetically that they could be accepted by Christian Unitarians like James Freeman Clarke. As brush strokes in the portrait of a man at odds with a creed, these bits of evidence had meaning; as technical specifications they were inept. A venerable Episcopal minister in Chicago suggested that Patton in effect was asking the poetic Swing to use Pattonian language, and added that this was like asking a mountain stream to sound like a coffee mill. To meet Patton's standards of precise doctrinal statement, another minister remarked, Jesus himself would have had to be clearer on a number of points.[45]

The decision to launch an attack upon Swing, who was as respected by his ministerial colleagues as he was beloved by his congregation, seems so ill-advised that one begins to wonder whether the allegedly brilliant Patton was also quixotic. Yet this would be too hasty a judgment. Patton not only thought he was right; he thought he had a chance to win.

"Winning," so far as Patton was concerned, did not mean simply gaining a favorable verdict in the Chicago Presbytery. That was important to him. But other and wider arenas were available, and from Patton's point of view even more important. Just as Swing spoke for the liberality of Chicago Presbyterianism and, beyond that, for a self-conscious western freedom, Patton was defending something more and deeper than the prestige of Princeton. The basic issue, as he and his backers saw it, was that of doctrinal integrity: if you profess a creed, you should either stand by it in detail or else renounce it. Those creedalists whom Swing (like Theodore Parker before him) was wont to picture as forlorn, crabbed creatures, the Princeton men saw as strong and clear-eyed champions of a faith that meant exactly (or almost exactly) what it said. To the objection that the doctrine of eternal punishment is unpalatable to modern Christians, Patton's quite typical retort was that "I cannot help it if that is a doctrine which is unpleasant to the feelings. It is in the Confession of Faith."[46]

---

[45]Newton, *Swing*, p. 98; *Swing Trial*, p. 137.
[46]*Swing Trial*, p. 71.

*Francis Patton as a professor at the Theological Seminary
of the Northwest*

In the attachment of each of these antagonists to diverging formulations of evangelical Christianity, and to the communities or constituencies that embodied them, elements of personal ambition, of loyalty, and of disinterested conviction are rather thoroughly intermixed. It would not be possible to argue that Patton was singularly actuated by a desire for the applause of Princeton, tempting though it is thus to explain his persistence in a lost cause. The more apt and ultimately more revealing picture would instead show both Patton and Swing dependent in decisive ways upon the approbation of their respective communities of belief and interest. Patton could persist in a doomed prosecution because he felt confident of the support of another community, quite different from the one that surrounded and beset him in Chicago. Swing, on the other hand, could hold to his convictions "with amusement and impatience" because of the approbation of a community—Chicago Presbyterianism and its public— that on the whole cared as little as he did for the good opinion of eastern dogmatists. Patton, therefore, should not be explained as a fanatic. He was far from that. He may have known, deeply, that he could not win in Chicago; but he could also be fairly sure that Swing would not win in the arena of national Presbyterianism.

Swing's defense against Patton's charges centered in his well-known conviction that creeds are human expressions and necessarily imperfect. He asserted that human society and culture change so rapidly that creeds cannot keep up with them. The church cannot call a Westminster Assembly every ten years, any more than a state can rewrite its laws every ten years. Therefore, he said, in the political realm we necessarily treat certain legislative acts as dead letters; and unless we wish to encourage dishonesty in the pulpit we must allow Christian ministers to omit, or even to denounce, some of the language of the creeds. Swing pointed out, correctly, that there were certain creedal doctrines— infant damnation, for instance—that Patton himself did not preach. Turning to his colleagues at the time, Swing submitted that "not one of you, my brethren, has preached the dark theology of Jonathan Edwards in your whole life. Nothing could induce you to preach it, and yet it is written down in your creed in dreadful plainness."[47]

This, as already suggested, was the heart of the matter. Swing also defended himself against the various imputations of guilt-by-association, arguing that an evangelical minister could not refuse to associate with professing Christian Unitarians unless he could suppose that they are "outcasts from God." The Unitarians' understanding of scripture might be incorrect, but that could not mean that Dr. Hodge of Princeton is to go to Heaven and Dr. Peabody of Harvard to Hell. "Paradise," Swing remarked, "is not to be a reward of scholarship."[48] But having had their fun with these elusive charges, the Swing men returned to the substantive issue, which was whether a church should have a stated creed and then allow its ministers to depart from it at historically cardinal points.

During a trial that extended, sporadically, over a month's time and that required 300 double-columned pages to record, Patton was gradually led to give up his misty endeavor to prove that Swing was not preaching "evangelical Christianity"; and to take his stand, instead, on the almost irrefutable position that Swing was not preaching the Westminster Confession. When he had heard all of Swing's answers and the arguments of the defense counsel, Patton said, he remained convinced that Swing

does not believe in the plenary inspiration of the Scriptures, as that doctrine is taught in the Confession of Faith; that he does not believe in the doctrine of Justification by Faith, as it is taught in the Confession of Faith; that he does not believe in the doctrine of the Trinity as it is formulated in our standards; that he does not believe in one or more of the five points of Calvinism. I say that David Swing does not believe the doctrines of the Confession of Faith.

If the Chicago Presbytery, Patton continued, wished to confirm Swing's standing as a minister in spite of his clear "slipping away" from the standards of the church, "they may do so and take the responsibility." But, he warned grandiloquently,

---

[47]Ibid., pp. 16-19.
[48]Ibid., p. 17.

the magnitude of this case arises out of the fact that it is a typical case
. . . In settling it, you do give your own judgment, whether the Presbyterian Church has a creed, or whether broad churchism without limit is
to be the policy of the future . . . Let me say that you have the eyes of
the Presbyterian Church upon you today . . . and the Presbyterian
Church expects every man to do his duty.[49]

When, following this summation, the floor was opened for
debate, a number of the pro-Swing presbyters gave their speaking
time to Dr. Robert W. Patterson, a venerable New School leader.
In an attempt to deal with the question whether creeds are not
meant to be adhered to, Patterson took the line that it is both
necessary to have statements of common belief, and essential to
allow latitude in their interpretation. Once the requirement of
word-for-word acceptance is dropped, there is no alternative to
allowing Professor Swing the same freedom you allow Professor
Patton. The prosecutor, Patterson said, had listed certain theories
such as that of "general atonement" which are allowable even
though they contradict nonessential points in the Westminster
Confession. Patton must permit others to omit or contradict points
which *they* consider nonessential.[50]

But who shall decide what is essential? Is every man to be his
own Westminster Assembly? Patterson's answer, again bowing
to inevitability, was that the Confession is whatever the General
Assembly—the highest legislative and judicatory body in Presbyterianism—says it is. "The church must judge, and has judged,
how far a man may depart from the letter of the Confession and
still sincerely adopt it as containing the Scriptural system." The
General Assembly had rendered such a judgment, in effect, when it
sanctioned the theology of the New School. Unless Swing could
be shown—and Patterson thought he had not been—to hold views
inconsistent with New School theology, no Presbyterian body
could consistently eject him.[51]

Others among Swing's defenders found it hard to maintain
presbyterial dignity as they expressed their dislike for what the

---

[49]Ibid., pp. 184-186.
[50]Ibid., p. 199.
[51]Ibid.

young prosecutor had done. Dr. Arthur Swazey charged Patton
with theological fanaticism. David Swing had lived and worked
among these ministers for years, he said, without their finding
any censurable fault in him. And then "a stranger comes in here,
and for reasons that are largely partisan, invites us to denounce
him . . . I will not trust myself to fix the epithets upon this
whole transaction, which justice . . . might require." The Rev.
J. B. McClure, with little attempt at euphemism, spoke of Patton's
charges as lies, and as "largely impelled by the spirit of jealousy."
The Rev. J. H. Trowbridge likened Patton's own preaching to a
body with its skeletal system, instead of its flesh, on the outside;
and he asserted that he, and others generally considered orthodox,
would simply be unable to remain in the ministry if forced to
preach Patton's line of doctrine.[52]

In the evening of a second long day of these speeches, the Rev.
J. T. Mathews reflected what must have been a general feeling
that the defeat of Patton was becoming a rout and a humiliation.
It was no longer possible to speak soberly of Swing's heresy,
Mathews said, because it had dwindled until it was no longer
visible to the naked eye. He thought Patton in coming to Chicago
had found Mark Twain's "splendid hunting ground," where a
man could hunt for weeks without finding a thing. Patton's
trouble, Mathews said, was that he was looking for the wrong kind
of game. He would enjoy better success if he would stop worrying
about "heresies of the head," and concentrate on those of the heart.
The latter, he said, were rife in the Presbyterian Church, many of
whose ministers "are prouder of their theology than they have
reason to be of their virtue," many of whose most ornamental
figures "tithe out their mint and anise and cumin of systematic
theology, so as not to fall short by a scruple, and yet forget the
weightier matters of the law, justice, and mercy, and truth."
Mathews said he only wished his vote could bring one hundred
David Swings into Presbyterian pulpits.[53]

The final defense of Swing from the floor was offered by William

---

[52]Ibid., pp. 225-256, 238-239, 246-247.
[53]Ibid., pp. 249-250.

Beecher, a Congregationalist and the eldest son of the man whose trial in the thirties had been considered—by liberals at least—the last of its kind. Asked if he wished to speak, he retorted: "Did you ever know a Beecher that had a chance to speak that didn't?" He thought it would be "impossible, according to Christian rule, or according to Presbyterian rule, to convict the brother on any one of the charges or specifications." Beecher added a pun about the defendant swinging clear of the charges which, while excusable only on the grounds of advanced age, did illustrate the amusement that lurked just beneath the surface of most of the defense arguments.[54]

Speakers on the other side, by contrast, found it inappropriate and probably difficult to speak lightly of any of the matters under consideration. The ablest of all the prosecution arguments was given by Dr. L. J. Halsey, the later historian of McCormick Seminary, who documented the united church's commitment to the Westminster standards and who deplored the practice of subscribing to a creed and denouncing it at the same time. Then, wisely eschewing Patton's scatter-shot approach, Halsey focused on three "essential" Presbyterian beliefs for which Swing had steadily shown hostility: the "supreme divinity" of Christ (Halsey himself would not say "deity"); the sovereignty of God as expressed in election and predestination; and justification by faith. All of these, as Halsey said, were important in distinguishing Presbyterianism from other forms of Christian belief. If the church wished to change its standards, it was competent to do so. Meanwhile, it was improper to try to distinguish, as Swing was doing, between a "church historic" that is defined by its creeds and a "church actual" that is not. Such a distinction really means keeping or discarding doctrines according to individual whims and the fashions of the times:

It is perfectly manifest that we could not stand for an hour on such a basis as that. But the moment you say we can, then your appeal is to public opinion and not to the law and testimony of God—to uncertain and fickle voices of popular feeling, and not to our ancient symbols;

---

[54]Ibid., p. 275.

and you are governed in your judgment by the outside world rather than by the Church of Christ.[55]

Halsey not only questioned the propriety of adjusting theology to the spirit of the time, but also doubted whether Swing had correctly estimated that spirit. Had the "church actual" moved so far from the "church historic" as Swing asserted? Halsey was sure it had not. "Are we ready to merge all denominations into one, and sink all differences out of view, and all adherence to the symbols of the past? The time has not come, Mr. Moderator, when the church is ready for that." So Swing, when he told people that certain doctrines were "dying around our own firesides," in Halsey's view was just misrepresenting the church and the public. Many Chicagoans, he said, because of Swing's kind of preaching had indeed come to believe "that the Confession of Faith is an obsolete system . . . It has gone out from the secular press and been spread all over the country that it is a rotten platform." But neither the official church nor most of its membership, he thought, were prepared to accept such a verdict.[56]

The State of the "Church Actual"

The Presbytery's verdict in the case immediately before it favored David Swing—or perhaps rebuked Patton—by a vote of 48 to 13. Liberals everywhere were encouraged. Yet whether or not such a result bespoke readiness in the churches, and in the "popular mind," for Swing's kind of liberalism remained a serious and very practical question.

Swing's own actions after the trial could be interpreted as conflicting with his expressed confidence about the changes already wrought in Presbyterianism. In May of 1874 he resigned from the Presbyterian ministry rather than undergo the processes of appeal that Patton was promising to instigate. His letter of resignation indicated both visceral distaste for battle, and objective doubt whether the battle was worth fighting:

---

[55]Ibid., pp. 215, 211.
[56]Ibid., pp. 218-219, 211.

The desire has daily increased to terminate relations which not only confer no happiness upon me, but confer power upon another to arraign me, from time to time, on some dead dogma, or over the middle of a sentence, or over some Sabellian or Mohammedan word . . . It would be only a mania for war to the knife that would induce any one to carry to [the Synod and the General Assembly] a debate so radical, so sudden and so clouded by personal friendships and animosities. What the church needs now is peace.[57]

What David Swing needed was peace; there was no doubt about that. But his friends, having come this far with him, could not agree that peace was the greatest need of the church. To them the dogmatists and heresy hunters, whom Swing liked to picture as negligible in number and force, seemed formidable and dangerous. With Henry Ward Beecher's reputation under a cloud because charges of adultery had been brought against him, a man of Swing's caliber was needed to lead the liberal forces. "His reputation is unblemished," Gladden argued. "The Presbyterian Church would not have ventured to expel such a man from its communion, and when the decision affirming his good standing had been proclaimed there would have been 'light all round' the sky."[58]

But probably Gladden was mistaken. Between 1874 and 1903, all attempts to revise the standards of the Presbyterian Church failed utterly, and the few changes accepted in 1903 were regarded by nearly all parties as nugatory. Swing in the 1890s conceded, though with his usual bittersweet melding of despair and hope, that Halsey had been right about the unreadiness of his own church. Presbyterian moderates at this later time were proposing in all seriousness that the objections to the church's creed might be stilled by a footnote expressing the mercy of God. "The Mercy of God in a footnote!" Swing exclaimed. "The Sermon on the Mount might also be added as an appendix! Logic will follow that church until it has nothing left but its Christ, and then for the first time in its history it will be rich!"[59]

When one looks beyond official actions of the Presbyterian and other churches, however, it becomes apparent that a considerable

---

[57]Newton, *Swing*, pp. 108-109.
[58]*Independent*, 26 (May 28, 1874).
[59]Loetscher, *Broadening Church*, pp. 39-89; Newton, *Swing*, p. 252.

groundwork had been laid, by the middle seventies, for the quiet, elliptical liberalism of the Chicago preachers, and consequently for the coming New Theology throughout Protestantism.

Since there could be little suspense about the outcome of the Swing trial, the intensive coverage offered in the national press suggests, at the least, a popular readiness to enjoy the hazing of a Princeton dogmatist. Washington Gladden noted with astonishment that the Chicago daily papers were carrying verbatim transcripts, and that the religious newspapers of all denominations were covering the trial. A newspaper alliance operating out of Chicago furnished regular reports which were taken up in the secular press generally.[60]

More indicative of advanced public sentiment, however, was the degree of support for Swing in the religious press. Next to Joseph Medill's excoriations of Patton in the Chicago *Tribune*,[61] the most impassioned public championing of Swing in the public prints appeared in the *Independent* and the *Christian Union*. Such advocacy perhaps was not surprising in papers that essentially represented the Congregationalism of the Northeast. Yet it is worth noting that the *Independent*, from the end of the Civil War until the later 1870s, held an almost undisputed place as the country's leading religious journal. It had reached the high point of its circulation (75,000) in 1870. It enjoyed more advertising patronage than any secular newspaper, and three times as much as the nearest competitor among religious journals. The *Christian Union*, though already injured by Henry Ward Beecher's difficulties, was scarcely less influential. Both were markedly literary and political in content and were read widely beyond Congregational or ecclesiastical circles.[62]

Among the scores of religious newspapers, many no doubt tried to report the level facts, colored only by the sort of pleasure at Presbyterian discomfiture that required no slanting of the news toward either disputant.[63] But Gladden, who monitored the entire

[60]*Independent*, 26 (May 28, 1874); Gladden, *Recollections*, p. 226.
[61]Newton, *Swing*, pp. 80, 100.
[62]Mott, *American Magazines*, pp. 11, 372, 375.
[63]See, for example, the Chicago *Advance* (Congregationalist), September 11, 1873 to July 30, 1874.

religious press, came up for air on June 4th and reported a "pleas-
ing variety of opinions," some fourteen of which he gave as
instances. He had found marked sympathy for Swing all through
the Methodist and Unitarian papers. The same was true for the
Congregationalists and the Broad Church Episcopalians, and in
the one Presbyterian organ of clearly liberal sympathies, the New
York *Evangelist.*

Gladden seemed anxious to show that the other Presbyterian
papers, along with such hard-line Calvinist organs as the *Baptist
Standard,* were solidly against Swing; but his own returns showed
that some of them were as ambivalent as the Chicago ministers
themselves. Neither the *Observer* nor the *Herald and Presbyter,*
for example, cared for Swing's theology, but the first called Patton's charges unconvincing and the editor of the second said that
he himself, if unlucky enough to be caught in Chicago in May,
would have cast his final vote for Swing.

Such conclusions may have reflected annoyance with a fellow
conservative for bungling the job, but they also involved a recognition that evangelical liberal preaching of Swing's kind simply
could not be outlawed. Conservative papers displayed little conviction that Swing's heresies were of the kind "which could be
proved to the conviction of the accused." Patton, it seemed, had
bungled not just in his way of framing the charges, but in bringing
them in the first place.[64]

The venerable *North American Review* made a similar point
from its more secular perspective. Charles E. Grinnell, a theologically trained Boston lawyer, pointed out that the evangelical
churches were going to have to deal with a new kind of liberalism
which, he implied, would not be so vulnerable as those they were
accustomed to. Swing's preaching might not sound much like
Westminster, but "the fundamental state of mind" was Calvinistic.

He is not a Unitarian. His case is another sign that the passionate
rebellion of the last generation against Orthodoxy is now giving way to
mild and gradual transitions within Orthodoxy. Among the ministers of
most, if not of all, the Protestant churches there are now men who are

---

[64]*Independent,* 26 (June 4, 1874).

young enough never to have felt much oppression in theology or morals, who are learned enough to appreciate their new opportunity, and who have sufficient character to use their freedom as it is needed in our mixed communities.

The writer placed Swing well up in the leadership of this new generation. Though clearly a liberal himself, Grinnell minimized Henry Ward Beecher's liberalism as an expression of "popular theological flippancy," and he criticized Robert Collyer, a celebrated Chicago Unitarian preacher, for the "vanity and levity" of his manner since his rise to prominence. Both Swing's scholarly training and his conduct during the trial gave reason to hope, Grinnell thought, "that he will still keep his head now that his well-deserved local influence has been forced so suddenly into a national reputation."[65]

In July the leading quarterlies of the Southern and Northern Presbyterians both reviewed *Truths for Today*. The *Southern Presbyterian Review* had nothing good to say about Swing except that his type of religious emotionalism was preferable to that of "the rude laboring classes of our Southern region." But the notice in the (Northern) *Presbyterian Quarterly* was mixed—or, better, schizoid. In the interest of Presbyterian unity, the journal had appointed as joint editors Lyman Atwater, of the Old School, and Henry Boynton Smith, the leading theologian of the New School. Atwater wrote a long and scathing review of *Truths for Today*. But this was accompanied by a reprinted editorial from the liberal *Evangelist*, and this in turn was bracketed by approving comments which almost certainly were written by Smith. The two entries were somewhat distinct in function—Atwater's concerned the book, Smith's the trial—and both were polite enough that one does not picture the editors at each others' throats. Yet these items, set together without explanation, expressed the awkwardness of the whole gallant attempt to repair the fissure in Presbyterianism.[66]

Another discussion that provided some perspective on the

---

[65]*North American Review*, 119 (July 1874), 215-216.
[66]*Southern Presbyterian Review*, 25 (July 1874), 428; *Presbyterian Quarterly and Princeton Review*, 3 (July 1874), 512-532.

public temper was one that arose, during the trial, between Swing and the popular anticleric Robert Ingersoll. Ingersoll in a Chicago lecture rang the changes on each of Patton's specifications against Swing. He expressed horror that a minister could be tried on such charges in "this city of pluck and progress," and, misreading the local situation entirely, castigated a Presbytery whose members he assumed would convict the accused—who would in fact have happily warmed themselves, he said, at the burning of Servetus. Ingersoll pictured Swing as a dove among vultures.[67]

The dove in question, knowing better, dissociated himself from these aspersions on his Presbyterial colleagues, and preached two characteristically irenic, acute sermons on "The Good and the Bad in the Addresses of Robert Ingersoll." Admitting obvious agreements between Ingersoll and himself, and asserting that society could get nowhere without its iconoclasts, Swing yet insisted that Ingersoll was a clever critic rather than a great orator— able to lampoon the age but unable to inspire it. Ingersoll was not even a genuine skeptic, Swing said, because profound skepticism issues in pathos, not in ridicule.

More than this, Ingersoll was tiresome, according to Swing, because he was out of date. His speeches were interminable tirades against people and ideas too old or foolish to merit so much attention—a pitiful little group of literalists and Popes and monks, together with painted gods and absurd heavens that were, Swing said, caricatures of the pictures ordinary people carry in their heads. To spend so much invective on these things, as he later put it, was like training heavy artillery on a choir of mosquitoes. If one could imagine all the Pattons of this world on a desert island (an appealing idea to Swing at the time when he advanced it), and could suppose the Ingersoll estates to stand by prior right on the same plot of ground, then Ingersoll's alarm would begin to sound eloquent.

But when we remember how imaginary are those Calvinists and their island, and what a vast world there is that does not desire to enforce

---

[67]Ingersoll, "Heretics and Heresies," *Works*, 12 vols. (New York, 1900) I, 233, 247, and 231-247 passim; Newton, *Swing*, p. 126.

religion, and that would not disturb the fireside of even the most bold infidel, then the basis of his eloquence disappears, and his speeches become only the anger of one who has had bad dreams about his fellow man.[68]

Swing never relinquished this oversanguine trust that dogmatism was falling of its own weight, that it scarcely needed to be battered down by the efforts of liberal assailants. Even if such trust stemmed partly from a mere distaste for battle; if, as Newton acknowledged, the Chicago preacher simply "was not of the stuff of which reformers are made"; still it was probably very well that Swing declined to spend the rest of his life planning assaults on the General Assembly. What he did instead was to establish his independent church; and when Central Music Hall was constructed for him (just as Music Hall, Boston, had been constructed for Theodore Parker many years before), his services and church schools were enabled to reach an imposing 5,000 to 7,000 people per week. Through his printed sermons he reached many more.[69]

With Swing keeping his promises in that fashion, theological dispute and ecclesiastical politics could be left to the young Gladdens of the East; and to midwestern modernists, at the new University of Chicago especially, whose way would be made easier by Swing's experience of the mid-seventies and his effectiveness thereafter.

The methods of intellectual history, even when supplemented with attempts to measure the diffusion of ideas and the attentiveness or indifference of ordinary people, are likely to thrust minority, relatively elite expressions into too bold relief. So one should acknowledge that "modernism," as of 1875, had not yet become either a common term or a fully self-conscious ideology. A few Frothinghams in Unitarianism, the fewer Swings in the evangelical bodies, could not constitute a movement. But the component

---

[68]Newton, *Swing*, pp. 126-128, 148-149.

[69]Swing preached twice each week, usually to a total of 2,000 to 3,000 people. Sunday School attendance numbered about 4,000. Newton, *Swing*, p. 243. The main auditorium at Central Music Hall held just under 2,000. John Moses and Joseph Kirkland, *History of Chicago* (Chicago, Munsell and Co., 1895), II, 574.

ideas had been articulated, and under the catalyzing pressures of the Swing affair—the first great controversy of the New Theology —had even been shaped into something like a program. To the dual respect for contemporary culture and quintessential traditions that flowered in later Unitarianism, liberal evangelicals had added their own explanations of God's immanent nature and their own proposals for identifying irreducible and empowering truths within the "jumble of doctrine." Self-consciousness as a modernist movement lay some years in the future, but the foundations had been laid for the definition, in the eighties, of a New Theology in which the modernist impulse would be a major force.

The New Theology and the Wider Christian Nurture

"The New Theology does indeed regard with question the line often drawn between the sacred and the secular . . . a line that, by its distinction, ignores the very process by which the kingdoms of this world are becoming the kingdom of the Lord Jesus Christ."

THEODORE T. MUNGER, 1883

In the East, despite Gladden's active relation to the Swing affair, the stirrings of new thought and controversy were not apparent, outside of Unitarianism, before the later seventies. Evolutionary theory and the Higher Criticism by then had been working powerfully under the surface for twenty years and more. Popular preachers such as Henry Ward Beecher and Phillips Brooks had been regularly dispensing a liberal evangelicalism, with Swing-like omissions, for which in due time they would be taken to task by the conservatives. But controversial views had not yet been brought, or forced, into the public forum. Gladden later recalled that as late as 1875, though Massachusetts Congregational ministers were aware of the newest biblical scholarship, and were both shaken and convinced by it, "there was still great timidity in admitting so much in the hearing of the public."[1]

---

[1] Gladden, *Recollections*, p. 260. Gladden suggests that New England Congregational ministers were hesitant to speak out partly because the new biblical criticism had been so much identified with New England Unitarianism, and especially with the name of Theodore Parker. Hesitancy in this line may also have borne a direct relation to the extent of one's knowledge of the Higher Criticism. Those who knew most were likely to be most awed by the implications for popular religious life, and also most aware of the probability that the scientific evidence was not all in. Carl E. Hatch makes this point in *The Charles A. Briggs Heresy Trial: Prologue to Twentieth-Century Liberal Protestantism* (New York, Exposition Press, 1969), pp. 13-41.

Shortly after that, according to Gladden, those attuned to the noises and silences of the theological forest could hear "the sound of a going in the tops of the trees." The first stirrings occurred in 1877, when Congregational conservatives blocked the installation of a young liberal named James F. Merriam at Indian Orchard, Massachusetts, and tried unsuccessfully to prevent that of Theodore Munger at North Adams. In the same year, Newman Smyth, a young, and clearly vigorous, Maine Congregationalist serving a Presbyterian church in Quincy, Illinois, published the first of three books in which, within a four-year period, he would set forth most of the themes of the New Theology.[2]

The tempo of controversy then quickened considerably, both in Congregationalism and in the other Protestant bodies. The installation episodes of 1877 gave place to a larger-scale Congregational dispute when the Board of Visitors of Andover Seminary, in the early 1880s, refused to confirm the appointment of Newman Smyth to the Abbot Chair of Christian Theology. At about the same time, an active controversy arose in the Presbyterian Church between the biblical scholar Charles A. Briggs of Union Seminary and his more conservative brethren at Princeton; while the Episcopalians fought over the biblical views of R. Heber Newton. Among the Baptists, Professor Crawford Toy in 1879 was allowed to resign from the Southern Baptist Theological Seminary at Louisville in a dispute over the higher criticism; and Newton Seminary in Massachusetts, also Baptist, was stirred by controversy three years later. In 1889, the Disciples of Christ expelled their "first modernist," R. L. Cave, from the denomination. The climax, though by no means the termination, of the controversies of the New Theology came in the early 1890s with challenges to the appointment of Phillips Brooks as Bishop of Massachusetts and with the trial of Charles A. Briggs, probably the best known heresy trial in American religious history.[3]

---

[2]Gladden, *Recollections*, pp. 262-266. Gladden's evocative "sound of a going" quotation seems actually to be a paraphrase—and improvement—of a line from George MacDonald's "Somnium Mystici": "That instant, through the branches overhead/Sounds of a going went." The three Newman Smyth books were *The Religious Feeling, Old Faiths in New Light*, and *The Orthodox Theology of To-day.*

[3]For the Andover dispute see Tucker, *My Generation*, chap. 7; and Williams,

Besides Gladden, Briggs, Newman Smyth, Brooks, and Beecher, the leading eastern figures of the eighties were Alexander V. G. Allen, of the Episcopal Theological School in Cambridge; Theodore Munger, pastor in New Haven; George Harris, who assumed the chair at Andover that had been denied to Newman Smyth; and William Jewett Tucker and Egbert Smyth, both of the Andover faculty. All of these men except Beecher (born 1813) had been born between 1829 (E. Smyth) and 1844 (Harris). Most had been raised in middle-class New England families and educated in New England colleges. Nearly all were either Congregationalist or, like Brooks and Allen, linked to the Congregational tradition by family ties and education. Unlike the liberals who came to prominence after 1890, most of these men had not pursued graduate studies beyond theological seminary; and only Briggs and the Smyths had studied abroad. Notably lacking from their backgrounds were conversion experiences of an even conventionally emotional or precipitate kind, or experiences of sharp reaction against a repressive home or church environment; only Allen, and to a lesser extent Beecher, could be said to have made his way into the New Theology by means of an agonized repudiation of the faith in which he had been reared.[4]

As these patterns of personal history may suggest, the New Theologians were men of irenic temper and of mediating personality. The acerbity of Charles A. Briggs stood out as an exception; otherwise, the individual variations—the especially commanding presence of Brooks or Tucker, the political skill and activism of Newman Smyth, the literary flair of Munger, the wit

---

Andover Liberals. Briggs and his opponents in the 1880s are best treated in Loetscher, *Broadening Church,* chap. 4; the Heber Newton dispute in Manross, *Episcopal Church,* pp. 311-312; the Toy case in Pope A. Duncan, "Crawford Howell Toy: Heresy at Louisville," in Shriver, ed., *American Religious Heretics,* pp. 56-88. For the Newton Seminary dispute, see George R. Hovey, *Alvah Hovey: His Life and Letters* (Philadelphia, The Judson Press, 1928), pp. 167-169; for the Cave controversy, Garrison and De Groot, *Disciples of Christ,* pp. 386-392. Raymond W. Albright discusses the opposition to Brooks in *Focus on Infinity,* pp. 361-373. For Briggs in the 1890s see Hatch, *Briggs Trial,* passim.

[4]The group biographical statements in this chapter are drawn from data compiled for these and approximately 150 other liberals. Hutchison, "Cultural Strain," pp. 386-411, summarized this information.

of Allen or Gordon, the reserve of Gladden—seemed all to operate within a similarly mild personality type. The fact that eight of the ten survived their seventieth birthdays, and that four survived their eightieth, may indeed say something about relatively happy lives and even dispositions.

The dominating theme of the New Theology, God's presence in the world and in human culture, could not be articulated, to be sure, without negative commentary upon earlier ways of thinking. Conceptions of God and the world as, in one degree or another, alien to each other had been for centuries a part of the common mental and linguistic equipment, particularly in a Calvinistic culture; and such conceptions could not simply be set aside by a few majority votes or exercises of rational persuasion.

Yet persuasion rather than polemic clearly was the preferred method of the New Theologians. Brooks, years before his own run-in with the Anglican conservatives, had told his notebook that "local heresies are little things and the mind is weakly empty that fills itself with care for them."[5] Charles Grinnell had been right in identifying Swing with a whole generation for whom "passionate rebellion . . . against Orthodoxy" had given way to "gradual transitions within Orthodoxy;"[6] most of the liberals would have joined Swing, if they could, in withdrawal from all argumentation. The tirades of Beecher, the oldest of the eastern liberals, against "spiritual barbarism" and "hideous doctrines" made him seem a voice from the past, an avuncular, slightly embarrassing coworker for those who dominated the movement of the eighties.[7]

In general, these men preferred to assume that the old issues with Calvinism and bibliolatry were now beyond argument, and that they could go on to something more constructive. Briggs remained embroiled in a denomination in which such issues could not be avoided; and Beecher insisted that discredited notions of

---

[5]Albright, *Focus on Infinity*, p. 368.
[6]See above, p. 71.
[7]William McLoughlin is essentially right, I think, in seeing Beecher as belonging to mid-century American culture—though Beecher's very real participation in post-Civil War liberalism should not be minimized. See McLoughlin, *Beecher*.

original sin were still the official working theories of the churches. But the others refused to accord that much standing to the old theology. Newman Smyth thought that what he and Briggs called "orthodoxism," really was unworthy of extended refutation. "I do not . . . feel called upon to answer old objections, often urged, against the Latin or Calvinistic theology. I am to speak simply for what I regard as the orthodox theology of to-day."[8]

In this penchant for the affirmative, the liberals seemed to be seeking not only to persuade their immediate audience about the fulfillment of God's promises in history, but also, somehow, to help inject a new self-esteem into the human historical consciousness and into the mind of the new scientific culture. Human civilization, quite definitely including those parts of it reached by Christianity, was as yet unsaved. Conversion was still in order. But the sovereignty of God and Lordship of Christ meant, for the New Theology, that the world stood in the relatively hopeful and grace-filled condition of the child in Bushnell's scheme of Christian nurture. The world, long slandered as the devil's realm, must now "never know [itself] as being otherwise"[9] than Christian.

European Sources and Examples

Though ideas of cultural immanentism and a wider Christian nurture seemed especially indebted to Bushnell's theology, they also drew upon overseas sources, many of which Bushnell himself had relied upon. For most liberals of the eighties, steeped in older Germanic traditions but not generally conversant with current German scholarship, the most powerful and immediate influences from abroad were the writings and sermons of two Englishmen: Frederick Denison Maurice and Frederick Robertson. At a moment when the chief problem for the New Englanders seemed to be homiletics, rather than criticism or even apologetics, these two English liberals provided the electrifying words. "I had immediately broken away," Munger wrote later, "from the already yielding theology, and the question was—What should I

---

[8]Beecher, "Progress of Thought," pp. 114-115; Smyth, *Orthodox Theology*, p. 40.

[9]Bushnell, *Christian Nurture*, p. 10.

preach?"[10] Maurice and Robertson, along with Bushnell, had formulated the most appealing answers to that question.

Maurice, the primary theologian of the English Broad Church movement (though he rejected, for himself, that and all party identifications), had not entirely escaped the necessity of engaging in negative polemics. He had been involved in severe controversies over "eternal punishment" and the nature of revelation; and his central theological affirmation, the Lordship of Christ, had entailed depreciation of theologies that seemed to Maurice to be conceding lordship to the devil. Yet the prevailing mood of Maurice's thought was affirmative, catholic, expansive. Preceding conceptions of the creation, of predestination, of Christ's work of justification, of the meaning in creeds, of miracles, had all been not so much wrong, in his view, as small and cramping.

In Maurice one finds a spaciousness of conception that both resonates with David Swing's ideas and suggests that one should avoid giving too much credit to the American prairies for inducing them. The point about the sixth day of creation, said Maurice, is the creating of mankind, not the creation of the man Adam. God's purpose in election, moreover, is inclusive rather than exclusive, and human justification comes not from a mere belief or rhetorical statement that Christ is head of the human race, but rather from the fact of this headship. "The condemnation of every man" is that he will not own the truth that "man, as man, is the child of God. He does not need to become a child of God, he needs only to recognize that he already is such." In the same way, miracles for Maurice were manifestations and not violations of divine order. Even the term "religion" was suspect, as it has been for more recent Christian thinkers, because it seemed to encourage too small and too humanly limited a conception of God. The Bible was to be seen as a revelation of God, not of "religion."[11]

Frederick W. Robertson, the Brighton preacher who died in

---

[10]Bacon, *Munger*, p. 118.

[11]C. F. G. Masterman, *Frederick Denison Maurice* (London, A. R. Mowbray and Co., 1907), pp. 115-133; Alec R. Vidler, *Witness to the Light: F. D. Maurice's Message for To-day* (New York, Charles Scribner's Sons, 1948), pp. 171-176, 35, 29-41, et passim. The quotation appears in *Presbyterian and Reformed Review*, 2 (July 1891), 481. For an excellent account of Maurice's personal struggle to attain and hold this view of human nature, see Brose, *Maurice*, pp. 52-76.

1853 at the age of thirty-seven, became known to Americans only through a *Life and Letters* and through the posthumous publication of several volumes of sermons and addresses. Although his impact seems to have been less sustained than that of either Bushnell or Maurice, it was unquestionably powerful. Its homiletic emphasis coincided with the special, quite pastoral tone of the early New Theology.

Since Munger, the New Haven minister, is connected especially with Bushnell—as disciple, biographer, and early interpreter— his testimony to Robertson's comparable importance is striking. "If I were asked today," Munger wrote in 1906, "what is the most important thing in theology for a preacher, young or old, to know, I would answer: 'The six principles of Robertson's thought.'"[12] The reference was to a summation of aims and convictions that the Brighton pastor had offered in a sermon of 1853:

First. The establishment of positive truth, instead of the negative destruction of error. Secondly. That truth is made up of two opposite propositions, and not found in a *via media* between the two. Thirdly. That spiritual truth is discerned by the spirit, instead of intellectually in propositions; and, therefore, Truth should be taught suggestively, not dogmatically. Fourthly. That belief in the Human character of Christ's Humanity must be antecedent to belief in His Divine origin. Fifthly. That Christianity, as its teachers should, works from the inward to the outward, and not *vice versa*. Sixthly. The soul of goodness in things evil.[13]

The best and most analytic of the liberal autobiographers, William Jewett Tucker, identified Robertson's special contribution as a sense of "reality" which became one keynote of the New Theology. Reality here meant what terms like realism, functionalism, or sincerity have always meant for young persons of moral passion appalled by formalism and by the inapplicability of old solutions to new problems. Robertson himself, put off and disgusted by the "unreality" of the Tractarian controversy in the English church, had worked his way through a season of the darkest skepticism:

It is an awful hour—let him who has passed through it say how awful— when this life has lost its meaning, and seems shrivelled into a span; when the grave appears to be the end of all, human goodness nothing

---

[12]Bacon, *Munger*, p. 118.
[13]Robertson. *Life and Letters*. II. 160-161.

but a name, and the sky above this universe a dead expanse, black with the void from which God himself has disappeared.[14]

Robertson had emerged from this experience with a theology centering in the Person of Christ and embodying a high estimate of human beings as children of God. He summed up the meaning of Christianity in a statement that linked him to Bushnell and especially to Maurice: "This, then, is the Christian revelation— man is God's child and the sin of man consists in perpetually living as if it were false."[15]

This was realism, in Tucker's estimation, because it eschewed formalism and based all religious action upon a steady working faith in human nature. Such faith, though sometimes based upon mere naiveté or humanistic hubris, could also arise, Tucker explained, from a serious acceptance of the Incarnation, of the reality of God's presence in the world. Since the New Theology rested on an Incarnational base, he had not, he said, "been afraid of what may have seemed to others an overestimation of men."[16]

Tucker tried to outline the exact role Robertson had played in the New England theological situation. The liberalizing of the Edwardsean theology between 1750 and 1850, he reported, had created "an unmistakeable feeling of satisfaction"; but the resulting system—as taught at Andover, for example—had been too neat, too pat, "quite too near the finished article." Neo-Edwardseans, much like the Boston Unitarians Henry Adams remembered, had solved the universe; and by mid-century the real human emotions of conflict with doubt, of "baffled but determined demand for personal assurance and personal possession, were not conspicuously in evidence." The theological atmosphere in this period, Tucker wrote, had not been "highly charged with intellectual or moral passion."[17]

Into this situation, one more of inanition than of the spiritual anguish Robertson himself had experienced, had come the "unique and timely influence" of Robertson's candor and clarity. What Robertson conveyed to the seminarians of the fifties and sixties was that it was going to be possible after all to think

---

[14]Quoted in Tucker, *My Generation*, p. 60.
[15]Ibid., p. 61.
[16]Ibid., p. 62.
[17]Ibid., pp. 58, 61-62.

well of God, think well of humanity, and yet preach a Christianity that would stimulate and save.

One further name needs to be mentioned. Among the liberal leaders who had studied abroad, and less directly among others, an outstanding influence was Isaac A. Dorner of Berlin.[18] Dorner is of special importance for several reasons. Though only Briggs and Newman Smyth knew him at first hand, these two men were quite central, respectively, to the Biblical studies of the era and to the theological adjustments that were made to Darwinism and its concomitants. Secondly, Dorner, like Robertson, filled very special needs of the moment, and filled them by means of a positive theology that focused upon the Person of Christ. Finally, it was Dorner who introduced into American theological discussion, through Newman Smyth, the startling and controversial possibility of a second chance, after death, for those who had not attained salvation in this life.

Dorner, in the eyes of his American admirers, represented the best of German theological speculation. He was the mediating theologian who had, they thought, most effectively held the citadel of Christian faith against the skepticism that had long infected European thought and that now loomed in a Darwinian context in America. He seemed not only to have mediated between religion and science, but also to have mounted a dual offensive against two current, and to them quite unsatisfactory, ways of vindicating the Christian religion. H. E. G. Paulus of Heidelberg had proposed to salvage something from Christianity by offering natural explanations for all the allegedly supernatural events in the Bible. David Friedrich Strauss, sometime tutor at Tübingen, had countered Paulus by construing the Gospels as teaching genuine truths by means of mythical and allegorical symbolization. Dorner's major effort, which extended in time from a set of articles in 1835 to a major work on the doctrine of the Person of Christ in 1856, rejected both modes of defense and insisted that Christianity must stand or fall on belief

---

[18]The *Congregationalist*, 35, reviewing seven expositions of the New Theology on June 7, 1883, remarked that "behind all these, shining with more or less of dimness through all, stands Dr. Dorner's *Glaubenslehre*."

in Christ as the one "in whom the perfect personal union of the divine and human appeared historically." To Dorner this meant that "neither a merely historical nor a merely ideal and metaphysical significance belongs to Christ, but rather that both are absolutely one in His perfect Person."[19]

Dorner's emphasis on the Person of Christ made his teachings harmonious with those of Maurice and Robertson, as did his speculations about the future state and his relatively conservative views of biblical inspiration.[20] The noticeable divergence in Dorner's thought, and in that of his American disciples, from the English patterns just described, lay in Dorner's preoccupation with scientific legitimation. Bushnell, Maurice, and Robertson were not centrally concerned about such legitimation. But Dorner insisted that his conception of Christ was scientifically verifiable. He rejected with impatience the idea that theologians should forego what some were calling the "vain and empty" project of verifying Christian truth scientifically. The data of faith, he argued, stand on an equal footing with those of natural science.

But faith, in a fairly traditional sense, had both the first and the last word in Dorner's system of evidences. Though he made Christian experience subject to empirical verification, still "the faith through which Christian experience is gained . . . must precede scientific knowledge and demonstration." Dorner is paraphrased by Newman Smyth as holding that "Christianity can be read scientifically only in its own pure light."[21] Even the men of this generation who grasped the mediations of Dorner with a special eagerness would come eventually to find such condescension toward science inadequate, and would seek to remedy the defects in Dorner's scheme with more sophisticated definitions of religious experience. From the beginning, indeed, Smyth and Briggs resisted Dorner's tendency, whenever the path of rational

---

[19]Smyth, *Dorner*, pp. 22-23; Dorner, *Person of Christ*, pp. vi, ix. For Dorner's position in German apologetics, see Pfleiderer, *Theology Since Kant*, pp. 211-219.

[20]For Dorner in relation to biblical criticism, ibid., p. 161. For Maurice, see Vidler, *Witness to the Light*, pp. 149-176.

[21]Smyth, *Dorner*, pp. 7, 11-12.

apologetics became difficult, to fall back upon orthodox views of biblical inspiration and infallibility.[22]

Yet the Americans did follow Dorner closely at one point after another—for example in viewing the Incarnation as something that would have occurred whether or not man had sinned, in seeing miracles as believable because of the total character of Christ, and in raising questions about final condemnation in the future state. Behind all such points of attraction in Dorner lay the assertion that was of paramount importance to the Americans: the assertion of the fundamentally ethical—the "Christian" —personality of God.

For Congregational liberals in the 1880s, as for Unitarians in the 1820s, the real issue, underlying more technical questions about God's nature, was that of God's morality and ultimately his credibility. Secondary matters of eschatology came to the fore in the late nineteenth century, as Newman Smyth pointed out in 1883, because earlier secondary issues such as the technical form of the Trinity and the freedom or dependency of the human will had been settled, and this very resolution had created new problems. The acceptance of free will had been especially important in this respect, since a theology that has decided that point must (assuming a continuing insistence on a morally credible deity) face the question whether the God who allows some human beings to choose salvation would damn those who have had no opportunity to choose.[23]

Under an older New England dispensation, Bostonians theoretically had stood in the same danger of damnation as Chinese or Maoris. But when theological theory had launched forth upon the seas of voluntarism it had left the unfortunate heathen marooned. Presumably those who had not heard of Christianity were also oblivious to this latest twist in New England theology, and felt no deprivation. But the liberals felt it on their behalf; if Christian theology was offering a new deal to humanity in the

---

[22]Williams, *Andover Liberals*, pp. 92-93. For Smyth on biblical inspiration see his *Old Faiths in New Light*, pp. 33-37. For his caution about total endorsement of Dorner, see his *Dorner*, pp. 22, 32.

[23]Ibid., pp. 27, 30-37.

nineteenth century—and liberals were clear that it was—then all of humanity would have to be dealt in. Thus the Americans valued Dorner both because he seemed to have vindicated, *contra* Strauss, the objective reality of Christ and the Gospel events, and because he delinented an ethical, caring, morally credible deity who offered the chance of salvation to all persons and not merely to a fortunate *cognoscenti*.

In these explosive matters of eschatology, Dorner's American influence merely supplemented that of Bushnell and the English churchmen. But Germanic emphases also led to actual variations within the patterns of the New Theology. In Smyth, for example, one finds an insistence upon being scientific, and proving Christianity scientific, that is productive even of a certain awkwardness and overargument in his apologetic writings. And Charles Briggs, knowing what he did about Germanic biblical research, was not remotely able to stand, with Maurice, "calm amid the storm" over higher criticism.[24] Smyth was more laconic than Briggs, yet the writings and influence of both men carried a note of insistent and anxious modernism that is quite unlike their colleagues' more serene brand of reliance upon ultimate harmonies.

Religion and Science: New Grounds for Dialogue

At the deepest level, the New Theologians' attitudes toward science did nonetheless derive from Maurice and Bushnell, and before them from Schleiermacher's insistence upon the common origins of religion and other cultural expressions in the primordial sense of dependence. The younger liberals, as just suggested, did not entirely abandon arguments that subsumed scientific knowledge in an ultimate harmony. Newman Smyth's first book, *The Religious Feeling*, proclaimed that "the ideas gained primarily through the feeling of absolute dependence are the conditions of all ordered, or scientific knowledge."[25] When asked to define justifications for such ventures as foreign missions, they remained

---

[24]Vidler, *Witness to the Light*, p. 151.
[25]*Religious Feeling*, p. 107.

capable of championing at least the benign imperialism implied by conceptions of Christ as Lord of History.

Yet the New Theologians were more troubled than Bushnell's generation had been when such an outlook resulted in cordial invitations to science to serve as iron filings on the Christian magnet.[26] The younger liberals displayed a growing sense of the inadequacy of Bushnell's or Dorner's conception of scientific verification. Unlike Henry Boynton Smith (who had been instrumental in introducing Schleiermacher to the American evangelicals), Newman Smyth sought specifically to adapt Schleiermacher's thought to the new era by recognizing and meeting the scientific demand for demonstration. He complained in 1877 that the disciples and admirers of Schleiermacher had nowhere provided, either in German or in English, a work in which the arguments for the primacy of the religious feeling were thought out "with sufficient reference to modern scientific theories of man's origin and history."[27]

Smyth, though an outspoken crusader, was also known for a "consummate adroitness" that would have served him well as a politician had he not become a minister. Perhaps it was this trait that enabled some conservative reviewers of *The Religious Feeling* to interpret the young liberal's emphasis on religious intuition as a rejection of evolutionary theory.[28] That such a rejection did not, in his mind, logically follow, Smyth's next two books demonstrated rather fully. It is true, on the other hand, that Smyth was more concerned with scientific verification than with evolutionary theory as such. He spoke of his own thought

---

[26]One important application of this generation's receptivity to science and empirical method has received systematic treatment in Henry Warner Bowden's *Church History in the Age of Science.*

[27]Ibid., p. vi. Smyth admitted a possible exception in the "excellent, but voluminous" writings of Hermann Ulrici, theistic philosopher of Halle. For Henry B. Smith's championing of Schleiermacher, see his posthumously published *Faith and Philosophy*, especially pp. 35-39.

[28]See, for example, *Presbyterian Quarterly and Princeton Review*, 6 (October 1877), 759-760. Smyth did approach the Darwinian theory cautiously, not because it might not be true, but because if true it was a half-truth. *Old Faiths*, pp. 383-384. The characterization of Smyth is from an obituary in the *Congregationalist*, 110 (January 22, 1925), 111.

as having arisen by "a process of natural selection, in an American mind, from the German idealism, and the English positivism"; but his positivism was somewhat more evident than the theory of natural selection from which he took this and other metaphors. There was, at any rate, in Smyth's work a serious effort, much like that of Theodore Parker several decades before, to document scientifically the claims made for religious intuition.[29]

Smyth at some points insisted that science assume the burden of proof. Unless science and logic could show the unreasonableness of belief in God or of the belief in a purposeful universe, he said, then the evidence of the universal religious feeling must be accepted.

Can any reasoning eradicate this upspringing religious faith from human nature, or even for any length of time arrest its growth? Can reason dig beneath it, and uproot it? Does it remain indestructible under the strongest tests of our logic? Then it is self-proved . . . If the reason cannot disprove it, it remains, like our consciousness of existence, like our sense of the external world, a rational faith.[30]

But Smyth's verifications were also of the affirmative sort. He recited the experimental evidence—among all peoples, in all ages and religions—for the universality and strength of the religious sentiment.[31] To the objection that all of this might be evidence merely of subjective realities, and not of objective ones, Smyth's general response was that specifically religious inferences from experience are not markedly different in that regard from those we allow ourselves in other areas of knowledge.[32]

Christianity could "adapt" to science without fear of self-betrayal partly because of what Smyth called "the scientific tendency of the Bible." In one revealing chapter of *Old Faiths in New Light* (1879) he presented most of the arguments that by the 1890s were to become common coin in the transactions between

[29]*Religious Feeling*, p. v. The interest of Parker, Orestes Brownson, and others in scientific verification is discussed in Hutchison, *Transcendentalist Ministers*, pp. 102-105, 153.

[30]*Religious Feeling*, pp. 159-160.

[31]Ibid., pp. 29-105.

[32]Ibid., pp. 15-21, 106-119.

science-conscious Christian apologists and their public. The Bible is scientific in approach, said Smyth, because it breaks with animism, polytheism, and superstition. The miracles it records, while not all acceptable or explicable to the modern intelligence, have served to impress men with the supreme power of God and thus with the reality of one all-pervading law. The biblical writers are "scientific" also in the accuracy of their observations of nature, and in their freedom from extravagance and animistic superstition. The much-maligned first chapter of Genesis, he pointed out, does at least depict God as creating the sun, instead of presenting the sun as itself a god.[33]

Smyth's argument for the scientific modernity of the Old Testament reached a climax in his discovery that the biblical authors had taught evolution. He expressed some indignation that writers like John William Draper (whose *History of the Conflict between Science and Religion* had appeared three years earlier) were acting so churlish about recognizing Moses as the scientist he was. If a scientific or secular writer in 1700, Smyth wrote, had hit upon the Genesis six-day metaphor as a device for teaching the idea of evolution, he would be venerated by Tyndall and Huxley as a thinker of the first magnitude. If the first chapter of Genesis were some newly discovered remnant of Arabic literature, he said, "Dr. Draper would have exulted in it as a scientific trophy, and have found some way to show that religion suppressed it."[34]

"Adaptation" to science and culture is therefore, according to Smyth, warranted by the nature of religion and the history of Judeo-Christianity. It was the attitude of hostility to this process, the New Theologians thought, and not the process itself that was unnatural and productive of hypocrisy. John P. Gulliver, first incumbent of Andover's Stone Professorship of the Relations of Christianity to the Secular Sciences, delivered an inaugural lecture in 1880 that seconded Smyth's claims about the scientific verifiability of religious experience, and that added its own emphasis upon the inevitable cultural relativism of religious thought and institutions. Because of periodic unwillingness to

---

[33]*Old Faiths in New Light,* pp. 138-150.
[34]Ibid., pp. 171-172.

recognize the fact of relativism, Gulliver argued, Christianity had been burdened with theological and scientific ideas that had then become difficult to discard. Only the extraordinary power of Christianity "as *a life* and *a law* and *a refuge* and *a hope*," he suggested, could explain its survival despite the "unhallowed alliances with wooing philosophies and sciences, [that] have drawn deserved discredit upon the reputation of Christianity as a system of scientific truth."[35]

Charles A. Briggs, more forcefully than either Smyth or Gulliver, sought to advance from the Bushnellian position that theology and science are harmonious, to the supplementary statement that theology is itself a science. Exegetical theology, that which has to do, in Briggs's words, with "the sacred Scriptures, their origin, history, character, exposition, doctrines, and rules of life," is not only fundamental to all the other branches of theology; it is a science whose premises and materials are as clear as those of any other. Its results, which touch man's salvation and everlasting welfare, are "vastly more important than [those of] all other sciences combined."[36]

Exegetical theology could not, however, maintain such a position, Briggs contended, by any sort of prescriptive or imperial right. Its place as "the royal, yes, the divine science" would be recognized "only in so far as theology as a whole is true to the spirit and character of its fundamental discipline, is open-eyed for all truth, courts investigation and criticism of its own materials and methods, and does not assume a false position of dogmatism and traditional prejudice, or attempt to tyrannize over the other sciences in their earnest researches after the truth." The primary scientific task of exegetical theology, Briggs wrote, is to determine what the biblical writers, given all the known circumstances of their time and culture, really were saying. What they were saying can then be applied in the circumstances of our time.[37]

Here Briggs took the further step of insisting that the theology

---

[35]Gulliver, *Christianity and Science*, pp. 20, 19.

[36]Briggs, *Biblical Study*, pp. 10, 15-16. For the development of American biblical scholarship up to Briggs's time, consult J. W. Brown, *Rise of Biblical Criticism*.

[37]Ibid., p. 16.

that is truly scientific, and that is recognized fully as a science, will actually be freer of untoward cultural entanglements than a theology that takes a haughty attitude toward contemporary thought. "Systematic theology," he wrote, "will not satisfy the demands of the age if she appear in the worn-out armor or antiquated costume of former generations. She must beat out for herself a new suit of armor from Biblical material which is ever new." The Bible is "ever new," never to be captured once-for-all in any creed (or by any science) both because our perceptions and questions change and because our knowledge of the civilizations that produced the Bible is constantly growing.

Experience shows us that no body of divinity can answer more than its generation. Every catechism and confession of faith will in time become obsolete and powerless, remaining as historical monuments and symbols, as the worn and tattered banners that our veterans or honored sires have carried victoriously through the campaigns of the past—but not suited entirely for their descendants. Each age has its own peculiar work and needs, and it is not too much to say, that not even the Bible could devote itself to the entire satisfaction of the wants of any particular age, without thereby sacrificing its value as the book for all ages. It is sufficient that the Bible gives us the *material* for all ages, and leaves to man the noble task of shaping the material so as to suit the wants of his own time.

Each age has "its own providential problems to solve." It goes to scripture for their solution, "looking from the point of view of its own immediate and peculiar necessities."[38]

The interpreter of Briggs must marvel at the ingenuity he exercised in proving his heterodoxies not only orthodox, but perfectly obvious to all thinking persons; and must marvel also at the ingenuity, if not deviousness, he imputed to God and to Jesus. Briggs agreed with Archbishop Whately that God had refrained from presenting in the Bible a complete system of theology, and had instead arranged that the church in each era should have only so much of the truth as it needs. Correspondingly, God had decided, for the purpose of revelation, to make use of the various languages of humanity instead of creating a "holy language"; and Jesus, even though he knew better, refrained from

[38]Ibid., pp. 11, 36-37, 367.

disabusing his contemporaries of some of their wrong notions, for example in the field of cosmology. God had wished to approach mankind familiarly, in linguistic and other forms that they could readily understand. Jesus had accommodated himself to the culture and prejudices of his day—though not in the sense of being himself taken in by them.[39]

Failure to recognize the substantially human and culturally conditioned nature of religious expression leads, Briggs thought, to a dangerous proof-texting way of using the Bible, and beyond that to larger dogmatic rigidities. Conservatives, in other words, stood accused in Briggs's indictment of practicing a culture-religion that was the more pernicious for its obliviousness to its cultural conditioning. All users of the Bible must beware lest "in transferring the thought to new conditions and circumstances, there be an insensible assimilation first of its form and then of its content to these conditions and circumstances, and it become so transformed as to lose its biblical character and become a tradition of man." The literalist's proof-texting method ignores this danger; his attempted absolutizing of the text ends instead in drowning the eternal message, along with its transient forms, in the seas of relativity. Thus in the longer run creedal dogmatisms are, lo and behold, the unfortunate result of an undue subservience to culture.

What one must do, Briggs advised, is to distinguish clearly among three authorities: the Bible, the creeds or symbols derived from it, and—least as well as last—tradition. The Bible is "the sole *infallible* norm," Briggs contended. The creed or symbol is a banner for a particular religious body, binding upon those who adhere to that body. But tradition "demands at the most our respect, and reverence, and careful consideration, and the presumption in its favor."[40]

Briggs's biblical radicalism was so thoroughly expressed in this influential volume of 1882 that it is misleading to picture him, as some scholars have done, holding his fire until 1891, when an address on "The Authority of Holy Scripture" provoked heresy

---

[39]Ibid., pp. 36, 76, 185-187.
[40]Ibid., pp. 6, 98-99.

proceedings against him.[41] He did seem, however, to take ever greater delight, as the decade of the eighties passed, in snatching from the hands of the conservative opposition all those arguments which they had thought were uncontestedly theirs. *Biblical Study* depicted the Higher Criticism and the New Theology as the true defenders of the Bible. In *Whither?*, the study of the Westminster Confession that Briggs published in 1889, he portrayed the liberals as the real champions of the Westminster standards, and remarked with solemn magnanimity that the Hodges of Princeton probably ought not to be excluded from the church even though their perversion of the Confession might justify such action. In the same book he expanded upon a distinction Newman Smyth had drawn between orthodoxism and orthodoxy, and claimed the latter title, definitively and invidiously, for a theology open to "new light" from God's word. Both in *Whither?* and in the address of 1891 he resorted to highly charged language about removing theological rubbish from the temple of Christianity; about the "fallacies and follies" of those who oppose the Higher Criticism; and about the "Bibliolatry" that insists upon treating the Bible as a magical object instead of what it is—"paper, print, and binding." The growing, and probably quite calculated, vehemence with which Briggs reiterated his position after 1882 is illuminated by a typically military statement of intent that appears in the famous Inaugural of 1891: "We have undermined the breastworks of traditionalism; let us blow them to atoms. We have forced our way through the obstructions; let us remove them from the face of the earth, that no man hereafter may be kept from the Bible." So far as Briggs was concerned, liberalism stood at Armageddon and genial talk was passé.[42]

---

[41]Briggs, *Authority of Holy Scripture*. Hatch, in *Briggs Trial*, pp. 24-29, makes such an error. It is probable, however, that Briggs himself was responsible for distortions on this point. He indulged in more than a little messianism about his own role. Though only two years Newman Smyth's senior, he cautioned the latter, in about 1881, not to publish too much "until he and Professor Hitchcock [Roswell D., professor of church history at Union] could prepare the church for it." Smyth, *Recollections and Reflections*, p. 101.

[42]*Whither?* pp. ix-x, 6-22, 21; *Authority of Holy Scripture*, pp. 33, 30, 41. Smyth had defined orthodox*ism* distinctly in 1881: "the dogmatic stagnation and

Doctrinal Revision and Cultural Conversion

Almost as if to reassure the public that not all liberals were as wild-eyed as Briggs, Theodore Munger, in the year following the appearance of *Biblical Study*, published a book of essays that aimed to define just what the New Theology was about, and that offered a very different picture of the way in which fundamental changes occur in religious thought. Instead of banners and barricades and cataclysm, Munger in *The Freedom of Faith* wrote of the subtle processes by which new truths work their way into human consciousness.

Munger, fifty-three at this time, was perhaps the most literary and literate of the New Theologians—a sermonizer of "chaste and flexible diction." He had also, after a pattern quite common among the liberals, been exposed in his own upbringing to conscientious doubt in a devoutly religious context: his father, a farmer and physician, had left off studying for the ministry because he could not profess assurance of his own election.[43]

The son now offered his elucidations of the New Theology for the benefit of ordinary believers who had been left bewildered, even if relieved, by the loss of traditional doctrines; and who felt additional bewilderment as various liberals offered replacements. The complicating factor, Munger suggested, was that the New Theology proposed the revision of an older system rather than the wholesale scuttling or exploding of that system. An analyst of the movement could not without distortion picture a neat dichotomy between generations or factions, because much of the conflict between old and new was going on within individual minds.[44]

Yet Munger thought the New Theology could be defined; and in the best-known essay in this collection—one rightly remembered as a manifesto of the movement, he argued that it differentiated itself clearly from its predecessors at a half dozen points. The New Theology, he contended, stood for a "larger and broader"

---

ecclesiastical abuse of orthodoxy . . . an orthodoxy which has ceased to grow . . . a crust of dogma kept over from another century." *Orthodox Theology*, p. viii.

[43]"Theodore T. Munger," *National Cyclopaedia of American Biography* (New York, James T. White & Co., 1898), I, 533; Bacon, *Munger*, p. 4.

[44]Munger, *Freedom of Faith*, pp. 7-10.

Theodore Munger in 1885

use of reason in religion. It offered a "natural" interpretation of the Bible, one that sees scripture as the work of writers who were inspired but were also limited by the conceptions of their own times. It sought to replace the "excessive individuality" of the old theology "by a truer view of the solidarity of the race." While not willing to reduce the spiritual to material terms or merge theology in natural science, the newer thinking nonetheless refused to recognize any fundamental antagonism between the kingdoms of faith and of natural law. It moreover directed attention to human beings in all the relations and circumstances of their lives, not merely to the abstract persons defined by the propositions of Calvinist logic. And finally, Munger said that the New Theology saw the need, in the area of eschatology, for a restatement that would place more emphasis upon God's persistence in seeking and saving, and less upon his zeal in exacting punishment.[45]

Munger showed a certain impatience or embarrassment in dealing with currently disputed questions in eschatology. Are the unredeemed punished eternally? Is there a second chance or "probation" in the afterlife? It matters little, he answered, whether one speaks of one or two or more probations, since the real point is the timeless dimension of God's action. Eternity, he argued, echoing Maurice, is not wholly a time-word, as the discussion of eternal punishment often seemed to assume. It is, rather, a word of moral and spiritual significance. "It has little to do with time, but rather has to do with things that are above time."[46]

In his discussion of the liberals' "wider study of man," Munger betrayed no similar frustration with current theological discussions. His exuberance at this point, and the richness of his argument, showed where the deepest concerns of the New Theologians were centered. Munger characterized the views of human nature in the old theology as lifeless, coldly logical, and often irrelevant. He asserted that in dealing with the real problems of real people the pulpit was ahead of theology, and literature was ahead of both. The key to this new realism, he suggested, was "the ethical habit

---

[45]Ibid., pp. 11-44.
[46]Ibid., p. 36.

of thought," the tendency to render all spiritual facts and processes, including the nature of God, in moral as opposed to "magical" terms.

Munger took "the wider study of man" as his point of departure for responses to two charges commonly brought against the New Theology: its lack of system and its tendency to "secularize" theology. The liberals, Munger said, did not disparage system; they simply refused to make system an end in itself. They disapproved, for example, of the tendency among system-mongers to manufacture or overextend doctrines chiefly to permit the survival of other doctrines.

As for secularization, the New Theology, Munger said, did disparage the drawing of a line between the sacred and the secular. Such a division is unscriptural and unnatural, and "by its distinction ignores the very process by which the kingdoms of this world are becoming the kingdom of our Lord Jesus Christ." If secularization were to mean adopting the spirit and methods and morality of the unredeemed world, if it meant failing "to distinguish between good and evil," then the New Theology would not be interested in secularization. What the movement sought to do, instead, was "to recognize in the composition and on-going of human society a divine revelation and process."[47]

With respect to traditional doctrines, the task of the New Theology, like that of its predecessors since the first ages of Christianity, was to state in contemporary terminology the spiritual truths perpetually suggested and validated by experience. Munger explained that the New Theologians, preeminently conscious of the divine indwelling and divine righteousness as facts of experience, affirmed God's sovereignty but refused to consider this the cornerstone of the Christian system. The Incarnation remained a physical event, but the physical reality was overshadowed by a spiritual one, namely "the entrance into the world through a person of a moulding and redeeming force in humanity." The idea of resurrection as a reinstitution of the physical body, which had arisen from the necessities of debate in the early

---

[47]Ibid., pp. 28-35.

church, required replacement; but resurrection as a continuation, in some unknown new form, of the human spirit and personality was credible and a fully legitimized use of traditional terminology. The ideas of Atonement, Judgment, Justification by Faith, Regeneration, and Sanctification all could be vindicated in similar fashion.[48]

Along with their common approach to doctrinal revision, and their considerable agreement about specific doctrines—both of which Munger had reported accurately—the new liberals for the most part shared a pastoral, conversionist attitude toward contemporary culture that especially marked their central message as a broadening of Bushnell's.[49] The New Theology found "the age" neither frightening nor completely convincing, but rather a ripe and likely prospect for regeneration.

Once again Beecher provides counterpoint. More concerned than his colleagues were to excoriate older theologies, he was also less cautious in his expectations about human progress. In an article for the *North American Review* in the summer of 1882 he typically complained of the "hideous" doctrines of Calvinism, and at the same time expressed the kind of ebullience that made Beecher the appropriate clerical person to greet Herbert Spencer, spokesman par excellence for optimistic evolutionism, during the latter's American tour of the same year. With regard both to the American role in cosmic development and to the role of religion, Beecher's optimism, however, considerably outran Spencer's. "In no other period or nation," he wrote, "has religion been such an inspiration to whatever is humane, liberal, and generous; to whatever is pure, true, and just; to whatever is genial, sympathetic, and chivalrous in public spirit; to whatever is brave, heroic, and refulgent in just war, or indulgent and fruitful in honorable peace." Among Americans, "riches have taken the place of poverty; with riches have come art, knowledge, variety in social life, innocent pleasures interlacing life's daily burdens; civil liberty has brought duties and occupa-

---

[48]Ibid., pp. 9-10, 300, and 295-313 passim.

[49]For suggesting the pastoral analogy for Munger's attitude toward contemporary culture (and also for Frothingham's), I am indebted to Gary S. Cross, a member of my Harvard research seminar in spring 1971.

tion to all . . . The brotherhood of the human family is recognized as never before."[50]

Most of Beecher's fellow liberals, by contrast, thought that even the signs of the coming Kingdom were problematic, to say nothing of its fulfillments. But they did believe it had been given to the nineteenth century to comprehend, more fully than any preceding age, what the doctrines of Christianity really meant. As the editors of the *Andover Review* put it,

The church has always proclaimed that "God is love," but there can be no question that in thought and life this truth has a far more commanding influence today than ever before. Christian faith has always accepted the Incarnation, but it cannot be doubted that enlarged views of the contents of this fact have been gained through centuries of earnest discussion and even bitter controversy, or that it is now more amply interpreted than was possible to earlier thought . . . The church of to-day has a fuller knowledge of the purpose of God respecting the expansion of Christianity, a better conception of the dispensation of the Spirit and of the relation of Christianity to human history, than it was possible to communicate to the early church . . . To doubt that a progress thus provided for, pledged, and realized is possible also in our own time is a symptom of unbelief, not the sign of a Christian's faith.[51]

A. V. G. Allen agreed that the nineteenth century had offered Christianity its great opportunity for fulfillment. Ancient as was the immanentism that he thought was central to Christianity, still its reintroduction in the conditions of the nineteenth century had constituted a new ·revelation. This revelation had come, moreover (as was fitting for a doctrine of immanence), through no sudden rending of the veil but "through the natural processes of human thought, research, and experience." The truth of the divine indwelling had been revealed to this age through the physical sciences, through the rise of the historical spirit, through the historical and grammatical reassessment of scriptural meanings, through the Kantian philosophy, and not least through the democratic, or at least nonarbitrary, expectations people in

---

[50]Beecher, "Progress of Thought," pp. 108, 114, 101-102. See also his *Statement Before The Congregational Association*, pp. 1-5. The testimonial banquet for Spencer and Beecher's part in it are mentioned in Hofstadter, *Social Darwinism*, pp. 48-49.

[51]Smyth and others, *Progressive Orthodoxy*, pp. 8-9.

advanced societies were bound to hold about the divine government. The nineteenth century had been the age of Schleiermacher and Wordsworth and Coleridge partly because of the genius of each of those men, but also because this had been an age that was ready for them just as the fourth century had been ready for Augustine. The theology of Schleiermacher, Allen thought, if it had been presented "in some other period of the church's history, might have left no impression and been soon forgotten . . . It is a theology which has grown out of the conditions of modern thought."[52]

If the times demanded particular changes in theology, so did the place and the circumstances in which ordinary people found themselves. Beecher, taking up Allen's stress upon the conditions for receptivity in a given culture, criticized what he saw as a common tendency to laud "original thinkers" and to undervalue the common people who "form an atmosphere, a public sentiment, around investigators," who "give power and practical use to the dry products of the inquiring brain." Theology is forced to change, in large part, because those who build sermons upon outworn doctrines find themselves speaking to the empty air.[53]

The Andover editors, academicians and effete easterners though they may have been, professed to agree. "The necessity of adjusting Christianity to life," they wrote, "is most keenly felt where population is rapidly increasing and constantly changing." Preachers in the West, they said, faced with the need quickly to build the structures of church, school, and family, and often with "hearers who are familiar with scientific treatises and the latest phases of skeptical thought," need sound, practical theological equipment. The professors, to be sure, thought that frontier religion needed help from that careful theological thinking which men in eastern seminaries had the time and perspective to pursue. They nonetheless saw the impetus to theological rethinking as coming in considerable degree from the West, and thought theology would be foolish to ignore the needs thus expressed.[54]

---

[52]A. V. G. Allen, "Theological Renaissance," pp. 280-281; *Continuity of Christian Thought,* pp. 397-407.
[53]Beecher, "Progress of Thought," 105-106.
[54]Smyth and others, "Christianity and Its Modern Competitors," pp. 513-514.

Briggs placed the argument for the inevitability of change upon broader geographic ground. The churches, he said, had adapted to the American environment as a whole in their forms of government and in matters of practical religious life, but remained "over-conservative in matters of doctrine and worship." The latter were derived from "historical circumstances that have long past [sic] and that are no longer appropriate to the circumstances of a new age and a new continent." Before long, Briggs thought, practical Christianity would overwhelm traditionalism, reducing the latter to "those old banners and battle-flags, with which it seems necessary that the denominations should parade once in a while."[55]

Adjustments in theology were therefore both necessary and inevitable. But this was not to say that Christianity had been placed in the position of choosing between extinction and an abject compromise with an alien culture. The demands rising from the people in the pews, from the scientific laboratory, from the everyday practice of political life in a democracy, came not from an alien or even external source, but from what George Harris called the "devout Zeitgeist":

There is a religious spirit of the age from which we may not separate ourselves, a devout Zeitgeist in faith as well as in culture, art and science, which we feel if we cannot describe. While it is not a standard, it is an influence which must not be ignored.[56]

"The church is rapidly learning," the Andover editors added in 1887, "that many of the social and secular conditions of the present time are providential arrangements in the use of which the kingdom of God can be advanced."[57]

What then was still needed, despite all this progress and despite the acceptance of adaptation as a fact of theological life? One answer lay in Tucker's concept of "reality." Congregations were asking preachers to show an even greater sincerity, to make "the spoken word correspond to the actual idea in the mind." And the preachers were passing the word to theology: "Say what you mean."

---

[55]Briggs, *Whither?* pp. 260-261.
[56]Harris, "Rational and Spiritual Verification," p. 471.
[57]Smyth and others, "Christianity and Its Modern Competitors," p. 402.

Theology, moreover, must explain itself not only when dropping old formulas, but when retaining them: "There is responsibility in holding as well as in changing theological forms."[58]

The other, far more stupendous, business still unfinished was the definitive conversion of culture. Smyth saw accommodation running both ways: if human religious perceptions are indeed facts, as he held they were, then scientific theories, for example, that ignore these facts will themselves require revision—will need to undergo "adaptation."[59] Even the theory of a "devout Zeitgeist," which would seem to reflect fundamental satisfaction with the way things were going in contemporary society, left room not only for recognition of regressive and recalcitrant elements, but also for asserting that the dominant Zeitgeist itself was lacking in some essential elements.

The spirit and imperatives of the age might be laudable and still stand in need of deepening and sanctification. Munger's essay, in *The Freedom of Faith*, describing the New Theology was followed by a more profound chapter on "The Reception of New Truth" in which the author distinguished between what the age most wanted and what it most needed. The current age, he said, if simply left to its own devices, would put a premium on breadth of knowledge and experience, to the detriment of height or depth. Ralph Waldo Emerson had begun a critique of an earlier age by calling it "retrospective"; Munger in effect called his own era panoramic in its vision. Such a widening of view, he warned, tends to keep along the level of the earth. It "grows wise over matter and force, pierces to the centre in its search, weighs and measures all it finds, creeps but never soars, deeming the heights above to be empty." This, he said, "is the direction knowledge is now taking."

The turning to this way of thinking from an opposite one is never final; Munger suggested it is cyclical. "There are ages of faith and ages of doubt." And as the cyclical terminology might suggest, the succession of emphases is guided by Providence. That

[58]Tucker, "The Contemporary Pulpit and Its Influence upon Theology," *Andover Review*, 3 (January 1885), 8-9.

[59]Smyth, *Religious Feeling*, pp. 15-16. See also Tucker, "Contemporary Pulpit," p. 7.

the gaze of men should for a time be diverted from the heavens is "for some wise end." It is the result of "a divine and guiding inspiration." The only danger, Munger said, "is lest the tendency become excessive, and we forget to look upward in our eagerness to see what is about us."[60]

The spirit of such an age is not wrong; it is incomplete. And Munger drew an analogy between the process by which the spirit of an age is completed and that by which the individual appropriates and comes to a full understanding of "new truth." In both cases, there is first a process of broadening, of gradual acquisition of knowledge; and then comes the sudden attainment of understanding or spiritual insight. The age that has been thrusting outward in knowledge will suddenly look and thrust upward. The individual who has been acquiring knowledge finds himself suddenly in possession of meaning as well. In each case, the suddenness of the experience of illumination may be misleading. Munger, very much in the Bushnellian tradition, thought that American evangelicalism had been misled, by infatuation with cataclysmic experiences of conversion, into serious depreciation of the processes of education and socialization that precede conversion.

Bushnell had always insisted that his emphasis upon gradual development left a solid place for the experience of dramatic conversion, and that he was not denying the importance of revivalism so long as it was kept to that place.[61] Munger concurred, and extended the analysis from individual to cultural conversion. At either level, the two modes of the reception of new truth—gradual and instantaneous—are compatible because they represent two methods of revelation. Their duality arises from the twofold nature of truth and "the twofold nature of man as spirit and mind." "I gain knowledge slowly," Munger wrote, but "I gain the meaning of knowledge instantly; it is a revelation of the Spirit that acts when knowledge has done its work." A man thinks, he said, "studies, undergoes life, gropes now in dark ways, or stands still,

[60]Munger, *Freedom of Faith*, pp. 50-53; Ralph Waldo Emerson, *Works*, I, 1.
[61]*Christian Nurture* (1861 edition), pp. 59-60.

in despair of truth; but finding this intolerable, presses on, and at last . . . the heavens open to his willing eyes, and in one swift glance he sees the meaning of all he has known, and feels the breath of the descending Spirit." Similarly, in the life of human society "there were ages of civil and ethical training, of progress and lapse and recovery and growth, but the meaning of it flashed upon the consciousness of the world in a day."[62] The current age, the age of the late nineteenth century, was teachable because God was in it, just as God is in the individual. And the age was learning. But the moment of comprehensive insight had not yet arrived; fulfillment was still a matter of hope and, in the longest view, of confident expectation.

The Awakening of an Opposition

The very patent yearnings on the part of this and other generations of kindly liberals for reasonably complete victories unaccompanied by controversy or unpleasantness can be regarded either as disingenuous or as a laudable impatience with nonessentials. In either case, the hope of avoiding divisions was poignant and ironic. It resembled the determined irenicism of the many antisectarian and antidenominational movements throughout history that have become, in time, either sects, denominations, or nullities. From at least the era of Channing onward, liberals had hoped to speak their minds without being forced to face, answer, or organize to combat an opposition. And repeatedly they had in fact been allowed to "preach abundant heresies" (as Theodore Parker boasted) until such time as opponents and erstwhile friends became aware that a serious movement was afoot.

This process is quite visible in the responses to the early statements of the New Theology. From 1877 to about 1883, scholarly and journalistic commentaries were predominantly favorable. After that, between 1883 and 1891, they became markedly more guarded, and the incidence of hostility to liberalism increased.[63] The New

---

[62]Munger, *Freedom of Faith*, pp. 68-69.

[63]For the purposes of this survey, as for others later in the book, I chose roughly fifty journals and newspapers, as widely representative as possible of American religious opinion, that might have reviewed the theological works in

Theology did not, on the whole, become more radical in this later eight-year period; nor does it appear that the popular liberal impulse waned. What happened, it would seem, was that the New Theology, by the time of Munger's *Freedom of Faith* in 1883 and partly because of it, had become recognizably a movement. Others besides Briggs became, during the 1880s, conscious of battle lines and in some measure willing to form ranks behind them.

Newman Smyth's early books were well received not only among the Congregationalists and Unitarians, but in the *Princeton Review* and among the Methodists and Lutherans. The reviewer for the *Lutheran Quarterly* articulated what was undoubtedly the strongest reason why many conservatives could set aside doctrinal objections and feel overwhelming gratitude for Smyth. The latter's interpretation of Schleiermacher had provided, in a time of severe threats from materialism, "a vindication of man's higher spiritual nature." When Smyth's *Old Faiths in New Light* appeared (1879), even Francis Patton was willing to concede that its arguments, while not acceptable for the theological classroom, were permissible as apologetics.[64]

The copious and mainly laudatory response to Briggs's *Biblical Study* in 1882 is somewhat more surprising. The *Presbyterian Review* (of which Patton and Briggs were coeditors) criticized the book for going too far; and the *Unitarian Review* found him too conservative; but nothing suggested the storms that were to come. The writer for the *Reformed Quarterly Review* (successor to the *Mercersburg Review*) thought the information in *Biblical Study* was "just such as every intelligent person needs who would understand the discussions which now agitate the religious world as to Sacred Scriptures." The Evangelical Lutherans found the book to be evidence for "one of the cheering facts of our time," namely for the intense and growing interest in the study of the

---

question. In the period 1877-1891 I sought reviews of all the writings of Smyth, Briggs, Munger, Allen, and the *Andover Review* editors. The conclusions in this section are drawn from the study of sixty of these reviews and articles, located in twenty-four periodicals. Table A in the Appendix indicates the locations of these reviews.

[64]*Lutheran Quarterly*, 7 (October 1877), 627-628. Smyth, to his own amusement, was as much patronized by Patton as by Briggs—Patton also being two years his junior. See Smyth's *Recollections*, pp. 100-103. Smyth remarks that *Old Faiths*

Bible. And a writer for the *Old Testament Student* predicted that the book, while it would "stir men up" and invite strong criticism, would, "a decade hence, be accepted by many of those who to-day so strongly condemn it."[65]

The responses to Allen's *Continuity of Christian Thought* and Munger's *Freedom of Faith* show such an alteration in tone that one is prompted to return to Gladden's gathering-storm imagery, and just at this point to picture woodland animals suddenly on the alert. From here on, reviewers increasingly object in principle to the New Theology, and express apprehensiveness about the future. In place of basically indulgent critics one begins to meet basically querulous ones.

Allen's work received a thorough going-over partly for reasons quite specifically related to his historical method. He had provocatively, even militantly, overargued the case for theological immanentism as the only proper formulation of the Christian tradition. He had, at the same time, done this with such candor and scholarly ability as to merit serious and lengthy attention. Two of the ablest critiques, interestingly enough, were penned not by conservatives but by Egbert Smyth of Andover and J. H. Allen of the Unitarians. But several journals that had accepted calmly the previous statements of New Theology saw in A. V. G. Allen's work the makings of a full-scale assault upon the theologies of transcendence they were committed to defend. A. A. Hodge in the *Presbyterian Review* launched that journal's steady denunciation of the New Theology by asserting, among other things, that history has made evident the superiority of the Augustinian-Calvinist mode of religious thought over more oriental styles of theism. "Western thought dominates the world," Hodge wrote, "and in this era of missionary activity, we are not likely to accept our theology from the Dormitories of the East. The old dreams will again be found out of place in this working world." The conserva-

---

received "deprecatory criticism" from defenders of verbal inspiration, but I was unable to find examples of such criticism in print.

[65]*Presbyterian Review*, 5 (January 1884), 154-157; *Unitarian Review*, 20 (November 1883), 479-480; *Reformed Quarterly Review*, 31 (January 1884), 149-150; *Lutheran Quarterly*, 14, (January 1884), 161-163; *Old Testament Student*, 3 (February 1884), 213-216.

tive Congregational journal *Bibliotheca Sacra,* which a year earlier had praised Briggs for "fearless honesty, infectious enthusiasm, and reverent piety," found Allen's work promotive of pantheism and "radically vicious."[66]

The responses to Munger's *Freedom of Faith,* and two years later to *Progressive Orthodoxy,* the Andover publication, were more clearly indicative of a changed climate. Although one sees few signs of panic or anger, some two-thirds of the reviews, at a minimum, would have to be classed as unfavorable. The most common objection was the one which, some forty years later, would link critics as divergent as the fundamentalist John Gresham Machen and the humanist Walter Lippmann: that the liberals were trying to fill the old wineskins of traditional terminology with the new wine of nineteenth-century science and humanism; and that this endeavor was bound to fail. John E. Todd's point-by-point response, in *Bibliotheca Sacra,* to Munger's introductory essay on the New Theology abounded in shocked phrases about what had "always been believed," and what was "held by the entire Christian church with but little dissent." Like the plea of Machen in the 1920s, the argument—too crudely framed by Todd—was that whatever other merits the New Theology might claim, it was certainly not Christianity. And Nicholas Gilman, in a valuable exposition of similar reservations as phrased by the theological left, used facetious synonyms like "advancing immobility" to highlight the apparent hedging and contradiction in such a phrase as "progressive orthodoxy." That the Andover men had "safely harnessed the 'wild filly Progress' and the sober nag Orthodoxy to one and the same carriage," Gilman wrote, and that they would be able to manage this remarkable team, "we greatly doubt."[67]

---

[66]*Andover Review,* 3 (March 1885), 286-291; *Unitarian Review,* 25 (February 1886), 157-172; *Presbyterian Review,* 6 (July 1885), 562-564; *Bibliotheca Sacra,* 41 (April 1884), 414-417; 42 (April 1885), 394-395. Allen was favorably reviewed in *Christian Register,* 64 (January 1, 1885); *Index,* 16 (May 14, 1885), 550; and *New Englander,* 44 (May 1885), 450. His thesis was questioned with greater or lesser severity in *Lutheran Quarterly, Reformed Quarterly Review,* and *Unitarian Review.*

[67]*Bibliotheca Sacra,* 43 (April 1886), 335-356; *Unitarian Review,* 25 (May 1886), 443-462. In response to Munger, the *Independent* and the *American Church*

When Briggs, in the years around 1890, assailed Presbyterian and other creedalists as apostates to traditions they had thought they were guarding, the responses to his writings provided commentary on what one might call the denominational sources of critical perceptions. Nearly all non-Presbyterian reviewers found Briggs admirable and utterly convincing in demonstrating that his own denomination had drifted from its moorings. But the *Methodist Review* assured him that "the Methodist Episcopal Church is not drifting, but holds to its theology with a tenacity that the conviction of its truth inspires." The Baptist reviewer thought Briggs had made his case for revision or abandonment of the Westminster Confession, but found his exegesis weak on the question of baptism by immersion. The *Lutheran Church Review* advised Presbyterians to "throw overboard Dorner as well as Calvin, and come to the study of the Augsburg Confession." And George Harris at Andover, in an otherwise admiring notice, found Briggs too conservative on the question which to such a large extent had defined Andover liberalism, the question of future probation.[68]

The New Theology as a scattering of biblical scholars and somewhat daring apologists had been one thing. The New Theology as a movement, with a movement's way of linking welcome and unwelcome ideas, with its potential for ideological acceleration and institutional subversion, was something quite different; and from the mid-eighties onward liberalism would have to contend with substantial external opposition.

Review offered few reservations. The *Congregationalist*, the *New Englander*, the *Lutheran Quarterly*, and A. A. Hodge of the *Presbyterian Review* all gave predominantly unfavorable reviews. The latter two, interestingly, praised Munger's sermons, but disapproved whenever the assumptions of the New Theology were stated, in so many words, as a theological program. The *Congregationalist*, in a separate article in the issue of June 7, 1883, gave succinct answers to six major contentions of the New Theology. In doing so it sharply contradicted its own reviewer's insistence that the younger men were preaching nothing really new.

Other reviews, mainly negative ones, of *Progressive Orthodoxy* are in *Unity*, *Presbyterian Review*, *New Englander*, *Bibliotheca Sacra*, *Baptist Quarterly Review*, *Lutheran Quarterly*, and *American Church Quarterly Review*.

[68]*Methodist Review*, 72 (January 1890), 147-149; *Baptist Quarterly Review*, 12 (January 1890), 123-128; *Lutheran Church Review*, 9 (January 1890), 82; *Andover Review*, 12 (November 1889), 552-555. Briggs continued, however, to

In this somewhat mechanical sense, the New Theology had to pay the price of its successes in spreading and institutionalizing liberal ideas. On the ideological plane, too, every success in vindicating the notion of divine immanence, every advance in broadening the base of revelation, raised new difficulties or intensified older ones.

Most striking was the reemergence of perennial anxieties about the finality or uniqueness of Christianity. For many of those moved by the new liberalism, the "freedom of faith" that it proposed was sufficiently exhilarating and empowering in itself; one need not worry about exclusive claims for any one religion. But for the New Theology as a whole this could not suffice. So far as most liberals were concerned, the rationale for religion must be embellished with a rationale—constructed, to be sure, on new foundations— for the special, supreme validity of the Christian faith.

---

draw admiring notices. One gains the feeling that for many thoughtful critics, his obstreperousness was more acceptable than the milder compromises of Andover. See *Old and New Testament Student, Bibliotheca Sacra, Reformed Quarterly Review*, and *Open Court*.

But Why Christianity?
Liberal Extension and
Apologetics in the 1890s

The question of the salvation of the heathen is
simply one aspect of the fundamental religious
question of our time: the claim of Christianity
to be the one perfect and final religion for mankind.

EGBERT SMYTH, 1885

Professor Lewis Stearns of the Congregational
seminary in Bangor, Maine, told an English
audience in 1891 that, so far as American religious thinkers were concerned, "the great philosophical and apologetical questions" of the recent past had been
virtually settled, and the time for serious theological construction
had arrived. The period since the Civil War, in Stearns's view, in
a small way had constituted an epoch. It had been a period when,
of necessity, theologians had discussed religion more than theology, had turned their thoughts "from the niceties of the Calvinistic system to the defence of the foundations of religion itself."
That had meant dealing with the theory of evolution, answering
agnostic and pantheistic philosophies with a revised theism, and
making religious experience more prominent in the scheme of
Christian evidences. All of this, he said, had now been accomplished to the extent that one could predict a heightening of
affirmative interest in theology and theological construction,
though not, certainly, a return to pre-Civil War Calvinism.[1]

Stearns, who had just turned down a call to Union Theological

---

[1]Lewis F. Stearns, "The Present Direction of Theological Thought in the
Congregational Churches of the United States," reprinted in Stearns, *Present-
Day Theology*, pp. 533-535.

Seminary because of the unsettled conditions there, and who undoubtedly knew in early 1891 that Charles A. Briggs would be tried for heresy, was not predicting an end to controversy. What he correctly foresaw was a period in which liberals would feel sufficiently secure that they would concentrate on consolidation, popularizing, systematizing, and the various social applications of the liberal ideas. More profoundly, Stearns's prediction of a turn from religious and philosophical issues to "theological" ones referred to a very fundamental shift on the apologetic side of liberal religious discussion: from a preoccupation with the vindicating of religion, and of man's religious nature, to an anxious concern about proving the uniqueness of Christianity itself. If, as liberals had been proclaiming, human culture is infused and alive with God's spirit, how does one make a case for the preeminence—to say nothing of finality—of the Christian revelation?

The Mauricean answer, and that of the New Theologians, began with the assertion that God is Lord of the world and that man's sin consists in thinking otherwise. Such an answer rested on faith that an Incarnation had occurred, ratifying both God's rule and his immanent nature. But again, given the erosion of literal acceptance of scripture, what was the status of this ratification? Why is it needed? Does it change the truths otherwise ratified and assured? Or are preeminence and finality insisted upon for sentimental and even political reasons having to do with the self-preservation of Christianity as an institution?

Liberals, both in Europe and in America, offered their theoretical answers to these further perplexities mainly in the context of the so-called "Ritschlian theology," a system of thought that strove to ground the argument for Christianity on forms of religious experience that could be considered both singular and adequately witnessed. But in America especially, the practical arena for debate about the essence and finality of Christianity was the foreign missionary movement. Such revisionists of missionary ideology as George Angier Gordon gave themselves less to profound restatements of the essence of Christianity than to ringing assertions that the nonessentials, the parochially cultural accretions to Christianity, must somehow be stripped away.

With respect to the development of modernist thought, both the Ritschlian theological answers and the more programmatic contributions of spokesmen like Gordon revealed that liberal Christians did indeed want to have it both ways; that they wished both to affirm a God-infused natural and cultural order and to maintain the specificity of a Christian revelation.

The Spread of Liberalism

The New Theology made impressive gains in the 1890s. Because of the many shadings of advocacy, adherence, and allowance, estimates of the number or percentage of Protestant congregations affected might well be misleading. In very general terms it can be suggested that by the end of the decade liberalism, while still probably in a numerical minority, had attained a voice equal to those of the older and newer conservatisms that opposed it; and that its dynamism or momentum as a movement by that time was at least as great as that of any opposing faction. The evidence for such an assessment lies in the history of the denominations—with factors of size, influence, and geographic distribution kept in view—and perhaps even more in the story of a liberal popularization and systematizing that went on outside or across the denominations.

The chief older forms of liberal organization—Unitarianism, Universalism, and the Society of Friends—all remained relatively small, though interestingly enough they reached a peak of numerical strength in the years around 1900.[2] The decline that each experienced after the turn of the century undoubtedly reflects, among other things, the increased opportunities for liberal expression within the main Protestant bodies. Among the seven major "families" in 1900, such opportunities were most readily found in the two smallest—that is, in the Congregational and the Episcopal churches.[3] But the movement had also made

---

[2]The largest of these three bodies, Quakerism, claimed about 115,000 members in 1900. Edwin Scott Gaustad, *Historical Atlas of Religion in America* (New York, Harper and Row, 1962), pp. 96, 131.

[3]Ibid., pp. 52-53. For an overview of the movement within American Episcopalianism, see Brown, "Christocentric Liberalism."

serious inroads by 1900 in the two denominations that were far and away the largest—the Methodist and Baptist.

Methodism, with its roots in Arminianism and experiential religion, moved with relatively little strain or controversy into broad alliance with the liberal forces.[4] By 1920 nearly all the major theologians of the Methodist Episcopal church (the Northern Methodist body) would be identified with liberalism. Back at the turn of the century that could not yet be said. Yet conservative efforts around 1900 to gain heresy convictions against the philosopher Borden Parker Bowne and the biblical scholar Hinckley Mitchell failed almost ludicrously, while Southern Methodism showed a degree of openness to the new science that easily ranked it with Episcopalianism as the most liberal of major southern bodies.[5]

After the Methodists, the two groups most deeply affected were the Baptists and the Disciples. These bodies, which were disparate in size (four-and-a-half million Baptists as against one million Disciples), were alike in certain other respects. Both were congregational in polity and both—partly for that reason— had experienced sharp divisions between a liberal faction that was largely northern and urban and a biblically conservative wing that enjoyed its greatest strength in southern or in rural areas. The northern branches of both bodies produced especially outstanding leaders of liberalism and more than their share of theological radicals. In both of these church bodies, moreover, the liberal and radical leadership became centered in Chicago

---

[4]Moncure Conway, a radical Unitarian leader of the generation of O. B. Froth-ingham, initiated his ministerial career as a Methodist, but did so, according to Loyd Easton, mainly under the influence of Emerson's essays, which "offered many points of agreement with the Methodist emphasis on the personal character of spiritual life and general indifference to dogma. 'I cannot remember,' Conway observed, 'ever hearing a Methodist sermon about the Trinity.' " Easton, *Hegel's First American Followers*, p. 126.

[5]Bucke, ed., *American Methodism*, II, 605; III, 263; II, 597-598. See also Chiles, *Transition in Methodism*, pp. 49-75 et passim. The lone conservative among Methodist theologians ca. 1920, according to W. J. McCutcheon, was Professor John A. Faulkner of Drew. Bucke, ed., *American Methodism*, III, 263. The comparative statement regarding southern religious bodies records the present writer's impression; but it is supported, certainly with respect to the contrast with the Southern Baptists, in Farish, *Circuit Rider Dismounts*, pp. 293-304.

where Baptists dominated the University of Chicago and its Divinity School, and where the *Christian Oracle* (later named *Christian Century*) capped a long controversy among Disciples journals by providing what eventually would become the prime journalistic medium for liberal and modernist ideas.[6]

The Presbyterian and Lutheran bodies, each of which at just under two million members ranked in the middle of the mainline denominations, stood forth as the most resistant to change. Powerful confessional traditions and—especially in the Presbyterian case—denominational structures made it relatively more possible in these churches to discipline or extrude dissenting elements when the predominating opinion in the denomination favored doing so. The Presbyterian pattern in the 1890s and for a generation thereafter involved a constant, unsuccessful pressure for creedal revision, together with an unequaled number of heresy trials, expulsions, induced resignations, and such institutional alienations as the break over the Briggs issue between Union Seminary and the General Assembly. The various Lutheran bodies, meanwhile, were able to resist more quietly—but on the whole more completely—because, for linguistic and other reasons, theological issues as phrased in American discussions remained fairly remote. The historian of eastern Lutheranism in this period finds a progression in that segment of the Lutheran churches "from simple resistance to genuine accommodation"; but no branch of Lutheranism, eastern or midwestern, at this time produced any notable advocates of the theological liberalism that was infecting all the other large denominations.[7]

The spread of liberal ideas in the 1890s was also a function of conscious, basically nondenominational efforts toward popularization. The trial of Charles Briggs at the beginning of the

---

[6]Newman, *Baptist Churches*, pp. 514-522; Garrison and DeGroot, *Disciples of Christ*, pp. 430-434. For the preceding controversies among the Disciples journals, see Corey, *Fifty Years*.

[7]Loetscher, *Broadening Church*, pp. 39-89; Wentz, *History of Lutheranism*, pp. 238-247; Deitz, "Eastern Lutheranism," p. 283. J. H. W. Stuckenberg, a Lutheran minister and sociologist, took a prominent part in the Social Gospel movement; but both Wentz (p. 330) and Deitz (p. 216) indicate that he did so at the expense of his influence within the Lutheran church.

decade, which has been called "a landmark in the popularization of the Higher Criticism,"[8] achieved that status more by indirection than by anyone's conscious intention; and popular preachers like Phillips Brooks (who lived until 1893) were practitioners of liberal religion more than crusaders for it. But a number of the liberal writings of the nineties were specifically designed, and were destined, to reach and persuade a wide popular readership. The most eminent and successful of the intentional popularizers during the decade were Washington Gladden and Lyman Abbott.

Gladden, who since 1883 had been minister of the First Congregational Church in Columbus, Ohio, published *Who Wrote the Bible? A Book for the People* in 1891; and added another volume with the same subtitle but a more provocative title—*How Much is Left of the Old Doctrines?*—at the end of the decade. In between, besides a number of contributions to the developing Social Gospel movement, Gladden sought to interpret what he called the *Ruling Ideas of the Present Age* (1895), and to show the credibility, given scientific modes of interpretation, of *Seven Puzzling Bible Books* (1897).

The champion popularizer, however, was not Gladden but Lyman Abbott, Whereas Gladden had virtually left journalism for the parish ministry, Abbott in the nineties was moving in the opposite direction. He had succeeded Henry Ward Beecher both as editor of the *Christian Union* and as minister of Plymouth Church. But Beecher's performance as an orator proved a much harder act to follow than his work as an editor; and by the end of the 1890s Abbott, partly for that reason and partly for reasons of health, decided to set aside one of his two hats and devote himself to journalism.[9]

The enormous success of the *Christian Union* under Abbott's direction also figured in this decision. The paper's circulation, which had stood at 15,000 when Abbott became associated with it in the mid-seventies, numbered 30,000 in 1893 and 100,000 by

---

[8]Brown, *Abbott*, p. 151.
[9]Brown, *Abbott*, pp. 70, 113-127.

the end of the decade. The name by then had been changed to *Outlook* in recognition of a marked broadening of the paper's interests since Beecher's day.[10]

But Abbott's role as popularizer involved much more than the *Outlook*. He published a half-dozen books in the nineties, all of which displayed what Ira Brown calls his "remarkable talent for bridging the gap between the aristocracy of the mind and the thought of the masses," and most of which involved the harnessing of evolutionary with higher-critical ideas—for example, by means of arguments for the developmental character of the Bible and of Christianity. Although such books enjoyed merely respectable sales of between five and ten thousand copies each, Abbott's lecturing on the university and general circuits put him in regular and direct touch with several hundred thousand more persons at any given time.[11]

Along with popularization in this decade went systematization. This process, though mainly directed by and to religious professionals, contributed just as much in the long run to the spread of liberalism. The outstanding systematizers were William Newton Clarke of the Hamilton (later Colgate) Theological Seminary in Hamilton, New York, and William Adams Brown of Union Seminary in New York City. Clarke was Baptist, Brown Presbyterian. Both men found themselves, as teachers of theology in liberalized institutions, unable to use any of the available textbooks and therefore forced to evolve "outlines" that grew gradually into published compendia of the liberal Protestant faith.[12]

Clarke was an unspectacular, slightly crippled, quietly impressive academic who influenced American religious thought both directly and through such students as Harry Emerson Fosdick (who inherited his realism and his mildly acerbic style). Clarke's *Outline of Christian Theology* discussed in its opening

---

[10]Ibid., pp. 69, 77-78, 168.

[11]Ibid., p. 238. Abbott's volumes of the 1890s were *The Evolution of Christianity* (1892), *Life of Christ* (1895), *Christianity and Social Problems* (1896), *The Theology of an Evolutionist* (1897), *The Life and Letters of Paul the Apostle* (1898), and *The Life That Really Is* (1899).

[12]Clarke, *An Outline of Christian Theology* (1898). Brown's *Christian Theology in Outline* was not published until 1906.

William Newton Clarke

pages what it meant to build a theological system on liberal premises. It meant beginning not with allegedly irreducible facts of scripture, as Charles Hodge and others had done, but with what the school of Schleiermacher, both in Europe and in America, had usually called "the religious sentiment." "Religion is natural to man," Clarke declared on his first page, and "being natural to man, religion is universal among men."

Then, in the familiar pattern, came assertions that religion or religious feeling is the source of particular faiths and forms, and that the religions of the world differ not as the false differs from the true, but rather as a more complete grasp of truth differs from a less complete one. "All the great religions contain some truth concerning religion." The formal structures of the various religions are therefore derivative, epiphenomenal. Because "the intellectual unfolding of a great experience like religion is a necessity of the mind," theology becomes a necessity; but any given theology must be at best a partial representation of the truth.[13]

Clark later delineated with exceptional clarity the differences he discerned between orthodox and liberal conceptions of theology. Preceding methods and his own method differed, Clarke thought, in their respective assumptions about divine inspiration and the status of biblical proofs. For the new theology as for the old, the Bible must be the chief source. But the older theology had assumed, Clarke said, that if the Bible is to be regarded as a source it must first be vindicated as divinely inspired. The new generation had outlived the necessity for such theories. "We are now able to take the Bible as it is, and listen to its testimony, without first proving that it must be listened to." The new theology held a more interior and spiritual idea of the presence and agency of God. "If God is in a book he will be found: we do not have to justify our sense of his presence there by building up a theory to show how he got there. God shines by his own light." How the book was written, Clarke said, "is a matter of indiffer-

---

[13]Clarke, *Outline*, pp. 1-4. For the views of Hodge, the orthodox Presbyterian champion, on the use of scriptural "facts" as the basis for theology, see his *Systematic Theology*, I, 9-16.

ence to me: what it contains is the point." The time had come, he said, to stop allowing mere theories of inspiration to tell people what they are supposed to find in the Bible.[14]

Clarke, in thus disavowing theories of inspiration, appeared a bit disingenuous. One can question whether he had really rejected all theorizing on the point or simply had adopted a theory contravening that of plenary inspiration. His way of rejecting the proof-text method in theology suggested the latter. The "ancient and familiar" mode of operation in theology, Clarke said, had entailed the belief that if the Bible could be quoted for a doctrine, that doctrine must be true; no other proof had been considered necessary. The theologian had been expected to bolster a doctrinal statement with all the texts that bore upon it, and in fact to construct a proposition that would encompass the teaching of virtually all of them.

As for his own contrasting method, Clarke quoted a critic's comment on his work: "that although the pages were freely marked with Scripture references—'spattered,' I think he said— the work was not really an expression of the results of exegesis." The critic had been "wrong in the deeper sense," Clarke said, but superficially right. It was true that he had not, in his theological works, simply reported what the Bible said upon the Christian doctrines. His technique (which probably he should have been willing to call a theory of inspiration) allowed for "intermediate processes" between exegesis and theology. A person's theology, instead of being dictated by the Bible, "should be inspired in him by the Bible—or, more truly, inspired in him through the Bible by the Spirit." The Bible, while unique—"most full of God, most helpful to man"—is not itself the ultimate authority: "the authority of the Scriptures is the authority of the truth that they convey."[15]

---

[14]Clarke, *Sixty Years*, pp. 195-200. Clarke's view of the formation of the canon followed logically from this view of inspiration: "It was not done by direct command or authority from God, nor was it done by any formal agreement of men, or by churchly decree . . . Revelation first produced its own divine life in men, and then through that life produced, collected, and organized its records and other literary memorials." *Outline*, pp. 22-23.

[15]*Sixty Years*, pp. 200-203; *Outline*, p. 42.

Clarke's 500-page theological outline lacked discussion of the church and the ministry; and that omission, together with a paucity of "historical material," caused William Adams Brown, despite his veneration of Clarke, to issue his own systematic theology several years later.[16] But in general Clarke adhered to time-honored canons of coverage and organization, with sections on the doctrines of God, man, sin, Christ, the Holy Spirit, and "things to come" or eschatology. In treating these matters he showed a refreshing tendency to seek straightforward phrases like "things to come," or "the work of Christ" to replace more technical usages, but otherwise the distinguishing mark of the work was its pervasive assumption that the Holy Spirit working in humanity, working in individuals and in human culture, is the arbiter of truth in theology.

Between the popular writings of Abbott and Gladden at one extreme and the systematizing of Clarke and Brown at the other stood a rich literature of theological and social liberalism that conformed somewhat to both descriptions. John Bascom, Lewis Stearns, David Beach, and George Gordon published synoptic accounts of the New Theology, to which Henry Churchill King added his *Reconstruction in Theology* in 1901.[17] The new social emphasis became an established part of the literature with George Herron's *The Larger Christ,* and with contributions by Shailer Mathews, by the Unitarian Francis Peabody of Harvard, and by William DeWitt Hyde, longtime president of Bowdoin College. Gladden, who had pioneered in this field with *Applied Christianity* in 1886, added a number of further Social Gospel writings in the 1890s. Newman Smyth and Borden Parker Bowne (the latter a professor of philosophy at Boston University and the chief American exponent of "personalistic" liberalism), produced systematic studies in Christian ethics that were at least adaptable to the support of the Social Gospel. George Harris's

---

[16]Brown discusses the relation between his work and Clarke's in *A Teacher and His Times,* p. 109.

[17]Bascom, *New Theology;* Stearns, *Present-Day Theology;* Beach, *Newer Religious Thinking;* Gordon, *Christ of To-day;* King, *Reconstruction in Theology.* See also J. Vyrnwy Morgan and others, *Theology at the Dawn of the Twentieth Century.*

social conservatism, however, as expounded in *Moral Evolution* and *Inequality and Progress*, gave aid and comfort to those who wished to stay on good relations both with evolutionary conceptions in religion and with the status quo in society.[18]

Ritschlianism and the Uniqueness of Christianity

A further tendency of the 1890s, along with the spread and systematizing of liberal ways of thought, was a broadening of the intellectual base; and this in turn proved to be very much a matter of establishing a firmer liberal-Christian apologetic.

As accounts of the movement have always noted, a new form of German influence began to be apparent, if not yet dominant, in this decade. A Germanizing trend is certainly evident if one includes persons like Walter Rauschenbusch and George A. Coe who, though already active teachers and writers, had not yet produced the work for which they would be best known. Even under a stricter definition of prominence, however, more than half of the most important younger contributors to liberal thought in this decade had received part of their training in Germany.[19]

Among the large number of German theologians, philosophers, linguists, biblical scholars, and historians with whom the American liberals studied, three names stand out with particular prominence: the philosopher Rudolf Hermann Lotze (1817-1881) and the theologian Albrecht Ritschl (1822-1889), both of Göttingen; and the church historian Adolf von Harnack (1851-1930) of Berlin.

Though each of these men enjoyed an independent reputation, Lotze and Harnack can legitimately be seen as among the brightest lights in a constellation dominated by Ritschl. Lotze was Ritschl's older colleague and a prime contributor to his thought;

---

[18]Herron, *Larger Christ*; Mathews, *Social Teaching of Jesus*; Peabody, *Jesus Christ and the Social Question*; Hyde, *Outlines of Social Theology*; Gladden, *Applied Christianity*; *Tools and the Man*; *Social Facts and Forces*; Smyth, *Christian Ethics*; Bowne, *Principles of Ethics*; Harris, *Moral Evolution; Inequality and Progress*.

[19]Borden Parker Bowne had studied in Göttingen, Halle, and Paris; William Adams Brown, George A. Coe, Henry Churchill King, and Shailer Mathews at Berlin; Walter Rauschenbusch at Kiel, Berlin, and Marburg; Arthur C. McGiffert

Harnack was his student and the most influential explicator of his central meaning.

It seemed at the time, and still seems in retrospect, that Ritschlianism was fundamentally an effort to regroup the scattered Christian forces around a new and revitalized statement of the uniqueness of Christianity.[20] "The century of Schleiermacher" had vindicated the reality of religion; the Ritschlians concentrated on vindicating the finality of a particular historic faith. The appeal to the human "religious sentiment," as they saw it, had been sufficiently—perhaps even too fully—elaborated, and it was time to go on to the next question: "But why Christianity?"

No one claimed that the followers of Schleiermacher had ignored this question.[21] But the feeling by the time of Ritschl was that the predominating Hegelian or speculative approach to an answer could never satisfy. The Hegelians, like Schleiermacher, had begun with a definition of religion and then sought to approve Christianity as the most fully developed and otherwise most satisfactory form of the impulse thus defined. But the Hegelian formulation, Ritschlians thought, was especially vulnerable because under its directives Schleiermacher's "religious feeling" had ceased to be feeling—even, many would say, had ceased to be religious—and had become sheer intellection.

The German influence that began to operate among American liberals in the 1890s, therefore, was philosophically part of a broad course-correction in the pervading Hegelianism of the time.[22] Some were ready by the end of the nineties to call the correction

---

at Paris, Berlin, Marburg, and Rome; Lewis Stearns at Berlin and Leipzig. George Herron at the end of the 1890s traveled and studied, partly for health and apparently in a more desultory way, in England, Germany, Italy, Switzerland, and Austria.

[20]This is the theme running through William Adams Brown's extensive treatment of Ritschl and the Ritschlian School in Brown's *Essence of Christianity*. See pp. 227-228, 267, and 223-319 passim.

[21]Nor, certainly, that Schleiermacher himself had ignored it; his *Glaubenslehre* and much of his later work aimed to root his philosophy of religion in the Christian revelation and to show the latter's indispensability.

[22]See William Wallace, *Lectures and Essays on Natural Theology and Ethics* (Oxford, Clarendon Press, 1898), pp. 481-510.

a revolt;[23] yet like most such revisions, this one retained and strengthened central elements of the movement against which it reacted. Idealism as a philosophical principle was not fundamentally renounced; the Hegelian avidity for distinguishing between ideas and their historic deposits was not lost; and the Hegelian sense of the importance of historical development was probably intensified. The Ritschlian generation is perhaps best understood, in fact, as seeking to retain the benefits of these characteristic elements in the heritage of the speculative philosophy and *still* to find a way to strengthen the case for Christian finality.

Somehow, without either renouncing idealism or returning to older assertions of supernatural facts immune from scientific investigation, one needed to show that Christianity takes its start from its own unique factuality. In trying to cope with this assignment, which was a far from easy one, the Ritschlians called back both to Schleiermacher and to Immanuel Kant for help. The result was an idealism that took seriously the claims of late-nineteenth-century scientism and belief in progress, but that refused, as Schleiermacher and Kant had refused, to make religion primarily an intellectual matter.

It is at just this point that the thought of Hermann Lotze became important to Ritschl, and important to the wider effort of theological restatement Ritschl was trying to synthesize. The value of Lotze's contributions to philosophy and to several other fields of investigation in no way depended upon Ritschlian appropriation; one of his twentieth-century interpreters in fact accords Lotze a significant early place in the epochal redirection of philosophy from its historic preoccupation with explaining the universe to its latter-day concern for the analysis and clarification of concepts.[24] But it was Lotze who provided Ritschl with the needed philosophical justification for assigning reality—and

---

[23]Brown, *Essence of Christianity*, pp. 223-225.

[24]Cecil Alec Mace, "Rudolph Hermann Lotze," *Encyclopaedia Britannica*, XIV, 329-330. But Mace also underlines the point that Lotze moved less far from Hegel than he liked to think, that he was very much a first-stage figure in this transition.

hence scientific credibility—to the data of individual religious experience. Neither Platonic idealism nor the Kantian correction thereof had solved the classic problem of what Kant had called the "thing-in-itself"—the reality behind any phenomenon—and its relation to the correlative object of sense experience. But Ritschl thought Lotze had solved that problem, had found a way to assert the reality of the physical world directly experienced without thereby denying or diminishing the reality of the ultimate Idea, of God. He interpreted his friend as saying that the human mind in its knowledge of phenomena does attain knowledge of ultimate reality, which it knows as "cause," as "end," and as "law."[25]

The language of ends and causes in Lotze was extremely significant and helps further to identify the part he played in the development of liberal theological thought. In a liberalism that would continue at least into the 1920s to be dominated by philosophical idealism, the concept of purpose was destined to gain an increasingly large place. In the face of repeated admonitions from science and from empirical philosophy that the universe is far more fragmented and changeable than idealists had customarily asserted, the almost standard adjustment of idealism and idealistic theology would be to reinterpret the unitive principle as purpose, as dynamic and in process, not finished or static. Lotze, while he rejected traditional teleological arguments for God's existence, nonetheless saw all of nature, and man as part of nature, as constitutive elements in one great and necessary ethical reality —a final good that "must be." This kind of teleological idealism (Lotze's own phrase)[26] was to be fundamental, and one might well say indispensable, to the survival into the twentieth century of the philosophical systems that underlay classic theological liberalism.

---

[25]Lotze, Ritschl said, held that in phenomena "we cognize the thing as the cause of its qualities operating upon us, as the end which these serve as means, as the law of their constant changes." Ritschl, *Christian Doctrine of Justification*, pp. 19-20.

[26]Wallace, *Lectures*, p. 505. For Lotze's concept of cosmic unity see his *Microcosmus*, I, 443-464. For his rejection of more standard teleologic proofs, ibid., II, 666-671.

Better known, or at least better remembered today, than Lotze's emphasis on teleology was his insistence that reality must be defined in personal terms. The personalistic version of idealism sponsored by Lotze in Germany and by Borden Parker Bowne, Henry Churchill King, and others in the United States, was again an attempted mediation between Hegelian intellectualism on one side and scientific positivism on the other. Its enormous appeal would be hard to understand if one were to ignore the dilemma— more precisely the crisis of faith—presented by that apparent set of options. It seemed that would-be believers were being offered the intolerable choice between a God who might or might not emerge from the chemist's beaker and a God who, as opponents of liberalism were later fond of saying, resembled a large oblong blur. In this situation, the answer of the personalists—an eminently traditional answer, but one now supported, supposedly, by the overwhelming data of human religious experience—was that God is "at least personal" and that human beings both know God and share the reality of God by virtue of their own personhood.[27]

Personalism offered strong support for the emerging Social Gospel, both because the God and goal of the personalist was defined in ethical terms and because the "world of persons" Lotze and Bowne talked about was a seamless web of ethical relationships in which each person was diminished or enlarged by the actions of anyone else. This social line of application was pursued by Ritschl, and much more by American Ritschlians like Brown.[28]

More immediately pertinent to the present discussion, however, than the reformist uses of personalism is the manner in

---

[27]Ibid., II, 659-688. Lotze's relation to the subsequent development of personalism in Europe and America is discussed in Knudsen, *Philosophy of Personalism*, pp. 61-67 et passim. See also Valentine, *Philosophy of Lotze*.

[28]Ritschl's emphasis on the Kingdom of God helped directly to structure the American Social Gospel, but the Americans so inspired found it necessary to engage in a good deal of extrapolation: "As presented in the classrooms of Germany," Brown writes, "the ethical program of Ritschl remained somewhat vague . . . But this did not trouble us . . . We went back to our own country in a mood of exaltation." William Adams Brown, in Roberts and Van Dusen, eds, *Liberal Theology*, pp. 261-262.

which this philosophy served to provide the theologians with a new, more empirical and secure set of starting points for Christian apologetics. Here the message of Lotze's revised idealism, as understood by the Ritschlians, was that the irreducible data of Christianity, the data supporting its claim to uniqueness, are matters of living moral experience. The special claims of Christianity rest neither upon uniquely inspired words and miracles, as traditional supernaturalism had supposed, nor upon the pristine spiritual ideas of the speculative philosophy of religion, but rather upon the actual experiences, recorded or recordable, of Christian individuals and communities in moral and ethical action. William Adams Brown, the most lucid and thorough (though also critical) American Ritschlian, stated succinctly the way in which this theology, reverting to the basic Kantian distinction, was attempting to renounce the intellectual certification of religious truth in favor of moral certification. "What the theoretical reason cannot afford," Brown wrote, "the conscience and the religious experience provide. In Christianity we do actually experience a power which delivers us from our weakness, our ignorance and our sin, and transfers us into the glorious freedom of the children of God."[29]

The Ritschlians therefore, much like Dorner and his followers in preceding decades, were avid about winning for the spiritual and ethical facts of Christian experience a status equivalent to that accorded the facts involved in scientific judgments. Value judgments, as Ritschl called them, were not to be confused with theoretical ones, but they were not to be subordinated to them either. The two epistemological modes were separate but quite definitely equal. Thus Brown could insist that the experience of God's redemptive power is "as positive a fact as any of those which enter into the catalogue of the positivist philosopher." Ritschlians were willing to claim, in fact, that more evidence is available for the reality of God as savior than can be adduced for many of the conclusions of physics or biology.[30]

---

[29]Brown, *Essence of Christianity*, p. 256.
[30]Ibid., 256-257.

Despite such claims, the specter of subjectivism haunted the Ritschlians almost as much as it had haunted the tradition of Schleiermacher which they were reviving in an allegedly less subjectivist form. And like those same predecessors, the Ritschlians sought to drive away this specter by demonstrating, scientifically and historically, how widely the subjective experience in question had been shared. Just as the romantics had sought prodigiously to document a widespread human agreement in religious and moral ideas, the Ritschlian generation, using more sophisticated scientific and historical instruments, dwelt at length upon the verifiable evidences of specifically Christian experience. Like idealists in any obtrusively scientific age, the Ritschlians saw no choice but to stride boldly along the path of inferential reasoning. Through the documenting of Christian experience, individual and collective, the singularity of Christ and of Christianity could, they thought, be established beyond a reasonable doubt.[31]

The attempt to define on such a basis "the essence of Christianity" became the most conspicuous common endeavor of those who called themselves Ritschlians. The students and disciples of Ritschl seemingly moved in such different directions that the very existence of anything resembling a school became a phenomenon to be explained. William Adams Brown listed the names and impressive bibliographies of the seventeen leading Ritschlians in Germany; and he gave an account of their divergences—from Julius Kaftan on the right to Ernst Troeltsch on the left—that amounted to a short course on the major disputes of the time.[32]

---

[31]A major difficulty in all this, for liberal theologians who were still convinced of the reality and efficacy of the human religious sentiment, was that only those who had experienced Christianity could logically be expected to acknowledge fully its claims to truth. Brown's response on this point may lead one to question how far the Ritschlians really had moved on their road to certainty: "No apologetic, it is true, can take the place of the Christian experience . . . But to one who shares this experience, it is possible to defend its legitimacy by such considerations as we have indicated [that is, actual evidence of saved persons and changed lives]. And even to him who has it not, the position of the Christian may be made to commend itself as one not unworthy of an educated man." *Essence of Christianity*, pp. 257-258.

[32]Ibid., pp. 264-275.

But then Brown sought to provide an explanation for the Ritsch-lians' sense of common identity. Their common bond, he said, was not precisely a personal loyalty to Ritschl, who had been "unmagnetic in person, obscure and unattractive in style." Nor was it the unity and symmetry of Ritschl's system, though surely the great theologian had attempted systematization. What made them Ritschlians was a common indebtedness to their teacher for posing or sharpening the central religious problem of their age—that of the uniqueness and finality of Christianity—and for restating a fundamental answer to which they could agree despite their individual variations: that the uniqueness of Christianity, as Brown put it, "is to be found in the person of its founder."[33]

Beyond this elemental structuring of a common effort, Ritschl's legacy had been the "multitude of new viewpoints" and provocative suggestions which he had left for his students and epigoni to follow out.[34] Ritschl, in other words, had been taskmaster to a generation even more than its mentor. It would not be unfair or unduly psychologizing to say that the influence of this very uncharismatic leader rested on the fact that he had brought fully into the open the central anxiety that had tortured nearly a century of romantic theology—the anxiety lest Christianity, having been identified as one expression of human religiosity, should be reduced to a status of mere equality with other expressions.

The centrality of this concern helps explain not only the massive influence of Ritschl but the even wider or more popular celebrity of his pupil Adolf von Harnack. Harnack had taught at Giessen and Marburg in the 1880s before moving to Berlin. American liberals studied with him at all three places; and since they continued to do so until his retirement in 1921, Harnack affected

---

[33]Ibid., pp. 266-267. For Brown's own major divergence, which had to do with Ritschl's reliance on an insufficiently defined historic Christ, see pp. 277-280. H. George Anderson provides interesting commentary on the nature of Ritschl's influence in "Challenge and Change within German Protestant Theological Education during the Nineteenth Century," *Church History*, 39 (March 1970), 48 and 36-48 passim.

[34]*Essence of Christianity*, p. 267.

many more of the Americans directly than had either Lotze (who died in 1881) or Ritschl (d. 1889). Harnack also, like Lotze but unlike Ritschl, made disciples by the excellence and clarity of his teaching, the breadth of his interests, the awesome erudition of his scholarship, and the warmth of his personality.

Brown, a committed champion of both Ritschl and Harnack, was probably typical in drawing a sharp personal contrast between them. To Ritschl, Brown said, all that mattered were ideas. But Harnack, supremely the historian, saw flesh-and-blood persons fighting for their places in a resistant world; and he sought to understand what they felt as well as what they did. Where Ritschl dealt with an anatomist's model, Harnack dealt with the living man. And just as important, Harnack in a special sense *was* a living man. Brown depicted the great scholar, at a time when his personal bibliography was growing toward 1,600 items, as having been terrified about the prospect of lecturing in English at Union Seminary. Later Harnack accepted a job as director of the Royal Library in Berlin because "I have *done* so little in my life."[35]

Harnack's lectures of 1899-1900 on "Das Wesen des Christentums" (almost immediately published in English as *What is Christianity?*) not only stated and extrapolated the results of his own lifelong studies in early Christianity; they came as close as any single statement could come to epitomizing the answers Ritschlians had evolved for the riddle of Christian distinctiveness.[36]

In one sense Harnack minimized questions of distinctiveness, or at least of the finality of Christianity. He claimed to eschew apologetics, professing a simple lack of interest in any other religion but Christianity: "Is it not after all with the Christian

[35]Brown, *Teacher and His Times*, pp. 83-92. For analogous tributes to Lotze's humanity and humility, see McConnell, *Bowne*, p. 37; Wallace, *Lectures*, 487-496; Leonhard Stählin, *Kant, Lotze, and Ritschl: A Critical Examination*, trans. D. W. Simon (Edinburgh, T. and T. Clark, 1889), p. 117.

[36]Brown, *Essence of Christianity*, p. 280. For the enormous influence of this book and a concurrence fifty years later in Brown's estimate of its importance, see Rudolf Bultmann's introduction to the paperback edition of Harnack, *What is Christianity?* vii-xviii.

religion alone that we have to do? Other religions no longer stir the depths of our hearts." But as Brown remarked, Harnack's disavowal of apologetic purpose was about as convincing as Ritschl's avowal of disdain for metaphysics (or, we may add, Clarke's dismissal of theories of inspiration). In each case the theologian in question had rejected a bad form of the method, not the method itself. There was more apologetic purpose, as Brown suggested, in a single volume of Harnackian history than in many volumes of Bridgewater Treatises.[37] So Harnack's modest statement of intent must perhaps be discounted. His emphasis upon a quintessential Christianity, rising superior to changing cultural embodiments and persisting through all of them, certainly provided ready material for those who did wish to style themselves Christian apologists.

In Harnack's view, Christianity means "one thing and one thing only: Eternal life in the midst of time, by the strength and under the eyes of God." But he also stressed, as strengths and proofs of this message, its adaptability and universality; and the very identification of such qualities involved claims of originality and of special access to truth. The "adaptability" of Christianity meant, explicitly, an ability to embody *eternal* truth in changing categories. And to ascribe universality to Christianity was to say that it is the perfect expression of that which all humanity is seeking.[38]

Jesus, according to Harnack, had taught the essential message in three different forms, one relating to the Kingdom of God, a second to the fatherhood of God and the infinite value of the human soul, and a third relating to righteousness and the commandment of love. Harnack's rendering of each of these elements of the Gospel entailed claims of novelty and singularity. Though Jesus made use of all the prevailing conceptions of the Kingdom, Harnack wrote, his culminating and most powerful idea was that

---

[37]*Essence of Christianity*, p. 285. Eight treatises, financed by the estate of the eighth Earl of Bridgewater and arguing the natural proofs for the validity of Christianity, had appeared in 1833-1836.

[38]Harnack, *What is Christianity?* (1901 edition), pp. 8, 13-14, 17. See also pp. 47-48, and Brown, *Essence of Christianity*, pp. 281-282.

of a "power that works inwardly," a Kingdom that comes individually and spiritually; on that point Jesus had synthesized traditional conceptions "in a new way and from a deeper knowledge." Jesus' teaching regarding the fatherhood of God entailed a degree of divine caring for humanity that raised the estimate of human worth and dignity beyond anything previously expressed. "A man may know it or not," Harnack said, "but a real reverence for humanity follows from the practical recognition of God as the Father of us all." And finally, Jesus' message in its ethical form transcended ritual elements, or any preoccupation with outward behavior, to emphasize the fundamental disposition of the heart and to show, as never before, the inseparability between the service of humanity and the love of God.[39]

Mission Theology—the Search for an Exportable Christianity

In the United States, while the Ritschlian theology was reported and widely discussed in the 1890s, and while younger men like Brown were already arguing for its conclusions, no Ritschlian school could be easily identified before 1900.[40] Most of the American interest in the problem of Christian uniqueness, during the 1890s at least, ran parallel to the thought of German contemporaries rather than drawing directly upon it.

Among the American liberals, questions about the essence and finality of Christianity arose in the context of a continuing but broadened discussion of the rationale for foreign missions. The mission enterprise, more than any other activity of the churches, demanded that the question of uniqueness be faced, and that it be given an answer that would convince outsiders. Brown was warning as well as extolling when he concluded his *Essence of Christianity* with the assertion that "in the world's high debate concerning Christianity, the missionary is the true apologist."[41]

To win approval and a working influence for Christianity at

---

[39] Ibid., pp. 51, 56-60, 70-74.

[40] See Smith, "Quarter Century of Theological Thinking," 579. Albert T. Swing of Oberlin, who perhaps did most along with Brown to promote an American Ritschlianism, identifies much of the descriptive literature of the 1890s in the bibliography of his *Theology of Albrecht Ritschl*, pp. xiii-xiv.

[41]*Essence of Christianity*, p. 319.

home was exacting enough. But at home the preacher or apologist could at least count on a general feeling among his audience that Christianity, whatever else it might claim, represented a civilization superior to those of other parts of the world. The missionary could count on no such prepared acquiescence, and the people most involved in missions were quite likely to feel uncomfortable with a Christian apologetic that fudged the question of Christianity's relation to the other religions and cultures of mankind. Discussions of missions in the 1890s, therefore, as the older debate over eternal punishment and future probation ran its course, turned rather naturally toward the more positive work of defining just what it is that Christianity has to offer the world, and on what terms the offer should be made.

The more discerning of the combatants in the earlier dispute had seen from the beginning that future probation was not the real issue. "The question of the salvation of the heathen," Egbert Smyth had written in *Progressive Orthodoxy* (1885), "is simply one aspect of the fundamental religious question of our time: the claim of Christianity to be the one perfect and final religion for mankind."[42] This is not to say that the disputants had disagreed about the perfection and finality of Christianity. They had agreed Christianity is final; the question of the moment had been whether or not this claim could be convincing without an accompanying conviction about the bitter fate of those unreached by the Gospel.

As the liberals of the nineties, along with many of their opponents, sought to move this discussion to broader and more positive ground, they articulated a program—or at least a coherent and connected set of attitudes—that was prophetic of twentieth-century changes in mission theology throughout the mainline Protestant denominations. The program for which they contended entailed the search for a quintessential Christianity suitable for export; the conversion of the idea of Christian finality into an almost purely ethical conception; a professed devotion to the ideal of establishing native churches free of Western control; a questioning of the right of Western Christendom to lecture the

---

[42]Smyth and others, eds., *Progressive Orthodoxy*, p. 178.

rest of the world; and a steady assertion that it was the old theology, not the new, that threatened to "cut the nerve of missions."[43]

Several of these objectives, especially those that involved direct criticism of American and Western cultures, were to be stated more explicitly after the rise of the new imperialism at the turn of the century. But the attempt to identify an exportable Christianity had gained expression by the mid-nineties, most notably in a pivotal address on "The Gospel for Humanity" that George A. Gordon delivered before the 1895 Annual Meeting of the American Board of Commissioners for Foreign Missions.

The very invitation to Gordon had been a symbolic act proclaiming the end of the future probation dispute and the unambiguous triumph of the liberals. For more than a decade conservatives, having failed to keep men like Gordon out of pulpits at home, had worked desperately to keep them from going abroad. The board's executive secretary, Dr. Alden, had consistently refused to approve candidates who would not affirm the doctrine of eternal punishment, and until 1893 the ABCFM in its annual meetings had voted to support Alden. By the latter year, however, the climate had changed, and the board, under a covering reassertion of belief in eternal punishment, reversed its actual policy by placing decisions about theological fitness in the hands of sponsoring congregations.[44]

The subsequent invitation to Gordon constituted a rather clear recognition of the need for a new agenda. Any of a number of men could have spoken for the triumphant New Theology, but Gordon in a special way represented the theologically sophisticated, somewhat amused impatience of a new generation with the controversies that had preoccupied their elders.

The first and nearly the only immigrant among the leaders of the New Theology, Gordon was the son of a Scottish overseer and

---

[43]To call this a liberal configuration is not to say that all its tenets were scorned by the opponents and predecessors of the liberals. Some of the main features in the liberal program—such as its doubts about American and Western culture— found ready if differently based agreement in conservative theology.

[44]The Meeting of 1893 also signaled the change of heart by approving a candidate whom Alden had rejected. Tucker, *My Generation*, pp. 152-158.

George Angier Gordon with daughter Ruth in 1897

surveyor. He had arrived in the United States in 1871 at age eighteen and eventually had made his way into the ministry by way of Bangor Theological Seminary. Reversing the usual procedure, he had then entered Harvard College, joining the class of 1881 in their senior year and being graduated with them *magna cum laude*.[45] Under the indirect influence of F. D. Maurice and the direct tutelage at Harvard of William James and George Herbert Palmer, Gordon emerged as a brilliant preacher and theologian, wholly aligned with the liberal movement but also—through James, Palmer, and others—well attuned to the changes of thought and preoccupation to which others were being introduced through study in Germany. Harvard was Gordon's Göttingen;

---

[45]Gordon, *My Education*, pp. 131-149, 191-212.

and though he remained, fittingly enough, staunchly British in his solutions—an incarnational theologian in the mold of Maurice and Robertson—still he had been moved as his German-trained contemporaries had been to a new urgency about finding the essence and peculiarity of the Christian message.

Gordon's quick wits, rugged attractiveness, and slightly exotic personal history had made him, from the first, a likely person to run interference for others equally weary of old obstructions but less able to surmount them. He also had come along at just that point in the future probation dispute when a dry Scots sense of humor was needed and appreciated. Before an installing council at Greenwich, Connecticut, in 1881 he had responded to the inevitable question about eternal punishment by stating that he did indeed believe in "the everlasting punishment of the finally impenitent." But

when questioned if I believed in the final impenitence of any individual person, I replied that on that question I was wholly without knowledge; that the only adequate authority on such a matter was the omniscient God, and that so far as I was aware, He had not made known His judgment. I was installed.

As for the yearly debates over this same issue in the ABCFM, Gordon's reactions oscillated between amusement and revulsion. Recalling later the session at Springfield in 1887, he remarked that "to me the whole business was so preposterous, such a matter of miserable detail, that I could not be serious over the great meeting." The absorption of his fellow delegates, however, was complete. As the debate raged, ex-Governor Washburn of Massachusetts fell dead from excitement, whereupon "a pause was made, a hymn sung, the dead man was carried out, and in five minutes all thought of what had happened was wiped out of the mind of the assembly." Toward the end of the eight-hour meeting ("with a recess of an hour for refreshments, which were needed"), Dr. Parker of Hartford finally succeeded in relieving the atmosphere by telling of a citizen in the street outside who had complained that the churchmen, having deprived ordinary people of most of their pleasures, now were seeking to impose "prohibition after death." The anecdote seems to have provoked a major catharsis among the delegates. Their merriment at length subsided, but then kept recurring in uncontrollable and contagious waves. From those moments on, or so Gordon felt, eternal punishment ceased to be a real issue: "The work had been done, not by logic, but by laughter, inspired by Him, I cannot doubt, of whom it is written, 'He that sitteth in the heavens shall laugh.'"[46]

Since Gordon also remarked in dead seriousness, in a sermon given national circulation by the *Christian Union*, that the theology of the ABCFM traditionalists had been "a libel upon Christian ethics and a stupendous insult to the church of Christ,"[47] his rise to the role of spokesman in the 1890s implied a pressing responsibility to propound something better, to set forth the affirmative theology of missions for which his protests and the protests of others had cleared the way.

In attempting to do this, Gordon took his start from the New Theology's principle of universality. This is God's world, not partly God's and partly the devil's. Christ lived and died for all humanity, not for a part of the human race.[48] Christ is in the world and in humanity; it is inconceivable that all will not somehow (if only in a second chance after death) have the opportunity to acknowledge Christ's Lordship.

But at this point Gordon led the way from the concerns of the 1880s to those of the following two decades, from a universalistic refutation of Calvinism's alleged elitism toward a new attempt to define essential Christianity. His ABCFM sermon of 1895 began with Paul's avowal to the people of Corinth that he had "determined not to know anything among you save Jesus Christ and Him crucified." To the revivalist or fundamentalist this text might well imply biblical literalism, no-nonsense decisions for Christ, and even anti-intellectualism; but for Gordon it meant something quite different, namely that the missionary must try to "preach Christ" rather than preach doctrines about Christ or impose the

---

[46]Ibid., pp. 214-215, 329-330.

[47]Gordon, "Missionary Motive," pp. 17-19.

[48]Gordon and his fellow liberals were frequently charged with being universalists. "I am not a Universalist," Gordon insisted. "The Universalist affirms the salvation of all men. I make no such affirmation." Ibid., p. 18. The liberals assumed that many would hear the Word but reject it.

gospel of a particular sect. David Swing had pictured Christians in alien settings as necessarily suppressing the dividing dogmas they have learned at home. Gordon, concurring, assured the ABCFM that "we are not under obligation to export our entire body of belief." The fundamental Christian message, one that must be shown as much as taught, is "the pure idea of self-sacrifice embodied with transcendent fidelity in the career of Jesus Christ." Beyond that, there is no particular call, he suggested, "for our church polity, our special theology, or the traditions of our Christian life. These are not wanted; if sent, they would prove unsuitable." The exportation of these trappings as "the Gospel" is not only impolitic; it is inaccurate. We should prize our ideas of the gospel, Gordon allowed, "but we must never make the mistake of supposing that our ideas are the gospel."[49]

This conviction about the cultural relativity of Christian doctrines worked in tandem with a professedly high estimate of non-Christian religions and cultures. Gordon, himself an admiring student of classical culture, made a good deal of St. Paul's expressed willingness to accept nearly the entire framework of Hellenistic thought and civilization. Paul had "swept within the compass of his vision the rich results of Greek and Roman civilizations; he saw what these people had attained, and he concluded that it was not worth his while to carry to them, even in nobler form, teaching that they already possessed." Not only was their "poetry and art and philosophy and history and oratory" of surpassing excellence; their systems of ethics sincerely sought the highest moral truth, "in many cases successfully finding it." And Gordon was ready to draw a rough parallel between ancient Greek culture and contemporary non-Christian cultures. "God," he contended, "has not left any of these peoples without witness of Himself."[50]

The implications for missions were plain enough. "No people having in them a spark of original genius," Gordon said, would tolerate the imposition of someone else's theology. And the for-

---

[49]David Swing's Sermons, p. 43; Gordon, Gospel for Humanity, pp. 5, 9, 7.
[50]Gordon, Gospel for Humanity, pp. 5, 14.

eigner's resistance is not merely prideful; the fact is that any attempted transfer of cultural forms is unfeasible. "Contrasted previous civilizations and the total diverse character of inheritance and environment will forever make impossible the domination of one division of the race by the rigidly formulated mind of another." A civilization in its immature state may accept that kind of tutelage; barbarian Europe was happiest, after all, while in bondage to Plato and Aristotle. But growth to maturity entails intellectual variation, and "the nations that are good for anything, and to whom Providence has assigned any considerable task in the advancement and enrichment of the kingdom of God . . . simply must go their own way; to arrest them or force them into another way would issue in a measureless sacrifice of power. The nations are to be left to the control of the Holy Spirit."[51]

Gordon's resulting plea for cutting umbilical cords between mission agencies and native Christian churches was not a new one. Rufus Anderson, secretary of the American Board in the earlier part of the nineteenth century, had advocated "self-government, self-support, and self-propagation" as the three watchwords for native churches. But Anderson's advice had been largely forgotten since the 1850s.[52] Premillennialism had been gaining strength; and while premillennialism in theory supports a conception of missionary work as a short-term business, its practical effect had been to keep the Western missionary at his post: when the millennium failed to arrive, the missionary stayed on. Against such a tendency, Gordon and other liberals now pitted the conception—a postmillennial one—of the missionary as a planter, as one who sets the receiving society on the long road to salvation and then gets out.[53]

From a later liberal perspective Gordon's attitude toward non-Christian religions, despite such concessions, remained con-

---

[51]Ibid., pp. 17, 14.

[52]R. Pierce Beaver, ed., *To Advance the Gospel: Selections from the Writings of Rufus Anderson* (Grand Rapids, William B. Eerdmans, 1967), pp. 16, 38. Anderson's advocacy of native churches had not entailed liberality toward ethnic religions. Beaver writes that Anderson "had no respect for Oriental, Pacific, and African cultures and religions." Ibid., pp. 35-36.

[53]Gordon, *Gospel for Humanity*, pp. 14, 9.

descending, while some of his reasons for urging collaboration with other cultures appear self-serving or even downright ominous. The Hindu "race," Gordon said, "have a marvelous faculty and fertility of spiritual imagination," but their thought seemed to him like a great fog bank rolling ashore under a blazing summer sun: "It is a wonder of beauty, but after all it is thin and cheap and unwholesome." Christianity can collaborate with such a system of thought and society because Christianity will be able (assuming that it comes as the pure unencumbered message of Christ) to conquer and assimilate any such inferior system. Gordon's tactic, in other words, was to warn the missionary, on the one hand, that he must be humble, tolerant, and restrained; and to assure him, on the other hand, that he could afford to be all those things because of the "absolute incomparableness" of Christianity. A comprehensive generosity is possible, Gordon asserted, because in the last analysis "there can be no possible competition between the idea of the cross and anything that these natives have to offer."[54]

To castigate Gordon extensively for these limits to his intercultural sympathies could be somewhat unfair. It is altogether easy to exaggerate the contrasts between his attitudes and later ones by mistaking later accessions of tact for improvements in fellow feeling. It must be remembered, moreover, that Gordon in 1895 was addressing a body whose neural system, if not destroyed as conservatives thought, was undergoing a major rearrangement. It is scarcely surprising that the speaker, well aware of his mediating and healing role, tried to bolster the confidence of the missionaries and their supporters as they contemplated their new world of cultural diversity. He was not the first, and surely would not be the last, to sweeten the study of comparative religion with a somewhat paradoxical claim to Christian incomparability.

Vital to the entire argument—substance, tactics, and all—was the notion of a stripped-down Christianity suitable for export. To Christians looking outward Gordon urged sharply increased cultural sympathies; to the same Christians looking to their own

---

[54]Ibid., pp. 12-13.

faith he advised a radical shedding of both doctrinal and cultural impedimenta. Modern Christians, he thought, like St. Paul, would find that diffidence about the transient "forms" of Christianity would free them to proclaim that which is lasting and of supreme value. Christianity proclaims "the eternal sacrifice in the heart of God mediated by the personal sacrifice of Christ."[55] That essential message, and not any theory about eternal punishment, was what had fueled the missionary movement in the past. That and not the threat of perdition was the theological "nerve of missions" that must not be cut.

There were numerous difficulties in the Gordon prescription, and many of them would still be disturbing liberal apologetics several decades later, despite a good deal of hard work and theological refinement in the interim. The principal problems had to do with the empirical grounding—or lack of it—for the claim of Christian absoluteness, and secondly with the extreme difficulty of actually achieving a nondoctrinal and deculturized Christian message.

Gordon, in his own solutions to such questions, remained closer to the British liberalism of the 1880s than to the newer Germanic infusions of the 1890s. It is evident that he had been touched by the Jamesean critique of idealism and by the personalists' determination to see the fundamental religious experience as an encounter between persons rather than the grasping of an abstract idea. But even so he still spoke in the mode that the Ritschlians were deciding was too speculative. His basic definition of Christianity, for example, alluded to the "pure idea" of sacrifice "embodied" in the career of Jesus. And his cosmology was Platonism as reworded by the personalists:

Our outward world is but a soap-bubble . . . and its collapse leaves man face to face with the Personal Spirit behind the pageant that we call nature. Berkeley is right; our sensuous experience is nothing if it be not the speech of the Infinite Spirit to the finite, the continuous communion of the Eternal with those made in His image. And so of history.

No conceptions or symbols, he added, can convey the reality of

---

[55]Ibid., p. 5.

God or of God's sacrificial love. "Only life can yield life; only personality can reveal personality"; and therefore "only the perfect personal Christ can utter to mankind the being of the perfect personal God."[56]

If this, from the point of view of Gordon's more Germanized colleagues, left the status of Christianity among world religions too vague, his striving for a purified statement of Christian truth also faced classic difficulties that were to remain especially persistent ones for mission theology in the twentieth century. Appeals to the "simple religion of Jesus," after all, whether instigated by liberals or conservatives, by critics of form or despisers of philosophy, in the past had presaged many of the great frustrations as well as great reforms of Christian history. One person's essential, reconciling Christian message had too regularly been another's dividing dogma. And thus, periodically, the church had needed a Channing or a James Marsh to insist that it is futile for theology to try to get along without metaphysics, or had needed a Charles Hodge to question whether there can be such a thing as a non-doctrinal Christianity.[57] Neither Gordon nor several generations of twentieth-century missionary theorists and practitioners would solve the agelong problem of separating the advocacy of Christianity from the implicit urging of particular cultural forms.

The dilemma and its relation to themes running through the larger rationale for imperialism, was illustrated in Gordon's allusions to the possibly redemptive uses of Western and American civilization. Not surprisingly, he dealt with such questions much as Emerson and Maurice had dealt with them. Of missions interpreted as the spread of Christian civilization he had little enough to say, but what he did say rested on the Mauricean base. He argued, that is, that the culture is redeeming only to the degree that it has first been converted and redeemed by Christ. In itself it is nothing; it is a soap-bubble. If we wish, therefore, "to see Christian civilization carried over the earth, we must go to the root of the matter. We must trace the truth and grace of that civilization to

<hr />

[56]Ibid., pp. 6-8.
[57]Hodge, *Systematic Theology*, I, 2-3.

its source." Gordon did not question the superior truth and grace of Christian civilization—"the confidence of reason, the moral idealism, the incomparable character, the varied, astonishing achievement in every line of lofty interest . . . the quenchless optimism"—but he insisted that all these glories must be traced back to that ultimate common source which makes all cultures one in their present innermost meaning and makes them all equal in their future prospects. The leveler of all religions and cultures, the great equalizing fact, is "their origin in the overshadowing and ineffable thought of God."[58]

As a matter of theory this presented no difficulties that further theories could not rectify. But the everyday world, which had forced transcendentalists on occasion to lay aside abstract neutrality and state a preference between past and present cultures, forced late-nineteenth-century liberalism to bring into the open its assumptions about the actual differences in quality—or, if you like, in degree of blessedness—between Western and non-Western cultures. And it was the missionary's special everyday world that focused and forced this issue most sharply, because it was there that the conjunction between a liberal, incarnational theology and a continued insistence on the finality of Christianity presented a clear demand for evidence of the ethical superiority of Christianity.

It was all very well to say, with Gordon's genuine conviction and humility, that the successful Western culture, like Emerson's "times," was but a masquerade of the eternities; the fact remained that the argument for Christian finality now depended heavily, whether or not it had done so under preliberal auspices, upon judgments of the ethical worth of Christian persons and societies. This meant that, however hard and nobly one might strive to distill the Christian essence from the cultural embodiment, there was no escaping the minimal demand that the sending culture show itself to be ethically superior. Even if the missionary should insist that the fruits of the spirit display themselves mainly in individual lives, still his or her effort as a missionary could be

---

[58]*Gospel for Humanity*, p. 8.

undercut by almost any palpable evidence of moral unsoundness in the so-called Christian societies.

Had liberals felt able to modify substantially the claim of Christian finality and the accompanying rhetoric of universal spiritual conquest, then much of the pressure to inject cultural claims would also have evaporated. But Christianity, unlike most other world religions, had held with some consistency since the time of Paul the Apostle that the claim to religious truth implies an obligation to convert all mankind to the truth. Liberals by and large had no intention of reneging on that formula. The claim to Christian absoluteness had been ethicized but not abandoned.

So long as liberals could feel at least Gordon's degree of confidence in "the incomparable character" of Western civilization and its "varied, astonishing achievement," their rationale could be made to hold together. It not only did seem to hold, well into the twentieth century; it also spread until in the 1930s it had become in effect the official foreign policy of American mainline Protestantism.

Among the theologians themselves, however, a more querulous tone would be apparent well before that time.

A Prophetic Minority:
Liberal Perceptions of
Cultural Crisis, 1900-1914

> The cry of "Crisis! crisis!" has become a weariness
> . . . yet in the widest survey of history Western civili-
> zation is now at a decisive point in its development.
>
> WALTER RAUSCHENBUSCH, 1907

The turn of a century is one of those events that offers the historian such great conceptual and literary convenience that he or she may be tempted to construct "watersheds" where none existed. Yet the *fin de siècle* experience can be a telling and even traumatic one for a people, or for particular groups of people within a culture. It is quite possible, therefore, that liberal theologians in the United States were affected in some degree by the sheer fact of passage from the nineteenth into the twentieth century, or by revulsion against the self-congratulatory publicity surrounding that event. Such contemporaneous occurrences as the Boxer Rebellion and the divisive, rather sudden American ventures into overseas imperialism administered more specific shocks to older dreams of concord. Whatever the external sources, a sharpened note of "crisis" appears in the liberal literature after 1900.[1]

---

[1]Except in certain Social Gospel writings such as Herron's *Larger Christ* or Josiah Strong's *Our Country*, I find almost no use of a crisis terminology or concept in the liberal literature before 1900. Between 1900 and 1910 such terminology is common but still not the dominant mode. From 1910 to 1915 the major writers (for example, King, Rauschenbusch, Lyman, Mathews, Tucker, G. B. Smith, G. B. Foster) tend generally to cast their work in these terms. In other words, unlike the group of "cataclysmists" treated by Frederic C. Jaher, these men grew steadily more apprehensive after the late 1890s. Jaher, *Doubters and Dissenters*:

This would have some significance even if it represented a modish change of rhetoric among theological writers. But it seems to have been more than that. The theme discovered an audience. Authors like Walter Rauschenbusch who had thought they would at best gain a hearing from other theologians, instead found themselves men of the hour. *Christianity and the Social Crisis*, Rauschenbusch said later, "was a dangerous book and I entered upon my task with fear and trembling . . . To my great astonishment, everybody was kind to it." Had there been no change in clerical and popular mood after the 1890s, the relatively unknown Rauschenbusch might have remained so—in fact might have been accorded the dismissal from his seminary post which his biographer, Dores R. Sharpe, says he expected. Instead, Rauschenbusch gained overnight such public acclaim that he was virtually beyond the reach of enemies, though never left alone by them. "Seldom," Sharpe suggests in a statement that may be tautological, "had a great book ever appeared at so precisely the right moment."[2] Notions of social and international crisis, by no means new, did appear to have gained a new resonance.

In another important sense, however, the increase in crisis thinking depended very little upon external stimuli of any sort, because it was simply a function of the liberal movement's further coming-of-age. "Applied" liberalism, for example in the literature of the early Social Gospel, had always made some use of the terminology of crisis; and applied liberalism was now becoming far more visible. The liberal ideology after 1900, having largely come to terms with itself and with its public, was being elaborated in more and more areas of Christian concern.

Some combination of external influence and internal dynamic, in any case, produced writings on international relations, on education, on social reform, and on Christian unification that gave the liberalism of 1900 to 1915 an increasingly apocalyptic tone.

Cataclysmic Thought in America, 1885-1918 (New York, Free Press of Glencoe, 1964), pp. 25-29, 60-74. Paul R. Meyer has shown that Josiah Strong himself grew far more pessimistic. Meyer, "Fear of Cultural Decline." For the appearance of similar querulous notes in English religion around 1900, see Elliott-Binns, *English Thought*, pp. 357ff.

[2]Sharpe, *Rauschenbusch*, pp. 231-233.

Conclusions remained optimistic, and the call for theological modernization became, if anything, more strident. But liberals also seemed genuinely apprehensive that if Christians did not act, if churches failed to act, frightful things could happen to this civilization that had nurtured such hopes, even though nothing frightful could happen to the ultimate scheme of God.

Missions: Pause and Reassessment

Edward Caldwell Moore of Providence, later of the Harvard Divinity School, in October of 1900 faced the unenviable task of preaching the Annual Sermon to an American Board still stunned by the tragedy of the Boxer Rebellion. All board personnel, Western and Chinese, had been lost at the Shansi station, and literally indeterminate numbers were dead or missing elsewhere. Some of the returned survivors sat in Moore's audience. Nearly everyone there had undergone some form of personal loss. Twice in the three-day meeting, the delegates sang:

Let every kindred, every tribe, on this terrestrial ball,
To thee all majesty ascribe . . .

but Moore's sense of his audience as conveyed in the Annual Sermon makes it difficult to imagine that anyone sang these confident words without a feeling either of their irony or else of sheer defiance.

Moore had known from early June onward that he must eschew the usual message of inspiration or financial pleading, and he avoided equally the more common clichés of comfort to the bereaved. Instead he preached from the passage in First Kings in which the angel of the Lord tells the weary, heartsick Elijah to "arise and eat, for the journey is too great for thee." In expounding this text Moore was recommending not a giving-up but a letting-go, a relaxing of the anxiousness and idealism of modern Elijahs who had asked too much of themselves and expected too much from the enterprise to which they were committed.

Elijah, Moore said, is the very picture of the man "whose zeal for the good is wearing him out before his time." Having been overconfident of himself, the prophet responded to adversity by almost despairing of God. In the same way, "the giant of the humane and Christly spirit of the age seems to me sometimes to lie prone today, waiting the touch of the angel. Precisely because of the responsibilities which we have assumed, of the work we plan to do, of the journey for the blessing of our fellows that we mean to take —the more do we need to hear God's voice saying to us, 'but the journey is too great for thee.'"[3]

It seems clear that Moore wished to advise the whole missionary army, not just the troubled people sitting before him in October 1900, to revise the expectations formed in a romantic age of world-conquering enthusiasm. But whether he did or not, other sym-pathetic counselors believed a new realism of that kind was precisely what was needed. William Newton Clarke, in a volume that also appeared in 1900 and that presumably had been composed well before the outbreak of the troubles in China, had delineated a severe "crisis in missions," and done so very much in Moore's terms.[4]

Many other theological writers, including George Gordon, were finding the close of the nineteenth century an excellent occasion for celebrating the achievements of Western civilization. Most missionary conferences of the time seemed to be dominated not by a mood of discouragement or even of caution but by an ebullient hope for "the evangelization of the world in this gen-eration."[5] Clarke, however, made short work of all current notions that the dawn of the new century heralded a great age of human brotherhood. Humanity had in fact, Clarke feared, entered upon an age of passion, unrest, racial antagonism, and

---

[3]*Annual Report of the American Board of Commissioners for Foreign Missions* (Boston, ABCFM, 1900), pp. iii-xii; Moore, *The Vision of God*, pp. 5-6. Paul C. Nagel found an analogous sense of exhaustion in nationalist ideology coming to a crisis in the late 1890s. *This Sacred Trust: American Nationality, 1798-1898* (New York, Oxford University Press, 1971). See also Sidney E. Mead, "American History as a Tragic Drama," *Journal of Religion*, 52 (October 1972), 358-360; and Winthrop S. Hudson, "Protestant Clergy Debate the Nation's Voca-tion, 1898-1899," *Church History*, 42 (March 1973), 110-118.

[4]Clarke, *Christian Missions*, pp. 170-195. It is entirely possible that Moore had seen and been influenced by Clarke's work, although I have found no hard evidence on that point.

[5]See Gordon's *New Epoch for Faith*. John R. Mott's *The Evangelization of the World in this Generation* appeared in 1900 (New York, Student Volunteer Movement for Foreign Missions).

national ambition. And he was none too sure which mood was dominant in the missionary movement itself. That movement, instead of overflowing with enthusiasm for a new age, seemed to Clarke to be beset by underfunding and criticism and uncertainty. "Something has happened," he mused, "to chill the ardor."[6]

What had happened? The "sense of pause," in Clarke's view, signified an inevitable relapse from the fine careless raptures of early missionary self-confidence. The expectations of quick and relatively easy triumph had been romantic and unintelligent. Clarke remarked incredulously that the nineteenth-century missionary enthusiasts had "really expected that vast masses of organized humanity would slide easily and without resistance into the kingdom of God, so that a nation would be born in a day, and born into satisfactory Christian life." Rhetorical talk about "planting shining crosses on every hilltop," he said, had almost been taken seriously. A warm enthusiasm had been relied upon "not only to do its own indispensable work, but to do a great deal of work besides." Such a period of romantic feeling had had to come, but it also must pass away. The missionary movement would need to live in the real world or not live at all. "The rush is over," he warned, "and the steady pull begins."[7]

Clarke thought the Westerner's new knowledge of the world in the later nineteenth century had brought the first daylight into a Western world-consciousness previously enveloped in "the darkness of ignorance colored only by a glamour of strangeness." But this was intensifying the crisis as much as relieving it, Clarke suggested, because modern knowledge, commerce, and communications were at the same time depriving the heathen of their salutary ignorance of Western civilization. "The defects of Christendom," he wrote, had "freely and unsparingly advertised themselves in foreign parts. The governments of the so-called Christian nations have appeared exactly as they were"; and while the impressions thus created had sometimes been favorable to the reputation of Christianity, too often they had offered only "a most

---

[6]Clarke, *Christian Missions*, pp. 192-194, 171.
[7]Ibid., pp. 171-174 and 182-183.

unhelpful commentary on the character of the religion that missionaries were seeking to commend." Worst of all, said Clarke, was "the hypocrisy with which nations allege Christian motives in justification of their land-grabbing, oppression, and unrighteous wars."[8]

Despite their very strong aspersions against traditional practices and illusions, neither Clarke nor most other liberals proposed to abandon the missionary movement. Clarke's *Study of Christian Missions* argued that the enterprise, if it was to recover, needed a quickened and on the whole a simpler faith. It needed more realism, more scientific knowledge, and far more patience. Above all, the idea of spreading the faith by either war or commerce showed "incredible effrontery" and should be foresworn. Yet the obligation of Christians to preach the uniqueness, finality, necessity of Christianity for all people was not to be questioned. The unprejudiced reader (if one could be found) might consider Clarke's opening chapter in which the finality of Christianity is asserted relatively unconvincing and somehow "unconvinced." But clearly the author had no conscious reservations about desiring and predicting world conquest for Christianity, which, he wrote, "deserves possession of the world. It has the right to offer itself boldly to all men, and to displace all other religions, for no other religion offers what it brings. It is the best that the world contains."[9]

The kind of doubts that Clarke expressed within this context were cropping up particularly among those liberals who were most sympathetic to the Social Gospel. Though such spokesmen displayed many shadings of opinion about the defects and the destiny of Western Christian culture, few voiced the national and racial self-assurance so often quoted from the writings of Josiah Strong. And those who did use the language of an ideal Anglo-Saxon supremacy, or right to spiritual conquest, were quite likely

---

[8]Ibid., pp. 174, 178-179. For a later, somewhat overdrawn indictment, in much the same terms, of the ignorance and naiveté lying behind the nineteenth-century missionary movement and the interest in comparative religion, see Ahlstrom, *American Protestant Encounter.*

[9]Clarke, *Christian Missions*, pp. 243, 19.

to be the same persons who employed especially strong language about moral flaws in the existing home culture.[10] Conservative evangelicals, who were also acutely conscious of domestic evils, complained principally about such things as drinking, material- ism, and vice and their international projections. Liberals agreed, but were inclined to add observations about structural flaws in American society. And because of their theological relativism liberals were more ready to use terms like "presumptuousness" and "effrontery" to characterize the missionary pretensions of an unsaved society.[11]

The liberal, in his dual role as spiritual expansionist and social critic, relied very much upon distinctions between ideals and actualities, between Western civilization as a process or destiny and that civilization in its present state of imperfection. Hence a common formula that ran somewhat as follows: "Christ and Chris- tian ideals must and will conquer the world. The West, and especially America, historically has embodied those ideals most fully. But the evils in our own society provoke severe doubts about the future. To the extent that these evils are allowed to continue, Western and Christian credibility will suffer. Yet we must persist in missions, both because Christianity is true and because it would be disastrous to allow Western commercialism and power to run over the world untempered by Christian influences."

Almost without exception liberals would have acquiesced in the statements in that formula. Some were reluctant to develop its negative aspect, the critique of American society: Gordon, who literally had found an earthly salvation through the educational and other opportunities of the New World, never could bring himself seriously to cloud the picture of a Kingdom coming in

---

[10]Strong himself, probably because so much attention had been focused on the Anglo-Saxonism of one section of *Our Country*, has recently received more sympathetic treatment. See especially Muller, "Josiah Strong," pp. 487-503.

[11]One finds counterexamples, however, of very great assurance about the credentials of American or Anglo-Saxon Christendom. See the ABCFM Sermons by Nehemiah Boynton (*The Commission of a Recovered Life*, Boston, ABCFM, 1897) and Washington Gladden (*The Nation and the Kingdom*, Boston, ABCFM, 1909).

and through America. But others such as Rauschenbusch and King combined a mighty nationalism and Westernism with excoriations of Western society that clearly implied doubts about its missionary pretensions.

Rauschenbusch's well-known opposition to World War I has led some admirers to assume that he could never at heart have been a militant nationalist or expansionist. Rauschenbusch in fact thought the Spanish-American War "one of the mountain ranges in the geography of times," and was willing to sit on the speakers' platform at the Republican Convention of 1900—a bit embarrassed, his biographer thinks, by the domestic program of the party but not questioning the rightness and necessity of American expansionism. Yet Rauschenbusch surely was anything but complacent about American society and about the effects of injustice at home upon the missionary enterprise. "The social wrongs which we permit," he wrote in 1907, "contradict our gospel abroad and debilitate our missionary enthusiasm at home." The non-Christian peoples see "our poverty and our vice, our wealth and our heartlessness, and they like their own forms of misery rather better."[12]

Henry Churchill King exhibited the same pattern still more sharply. Unlike Rauschenbusch, whose physical mobility was hampered by deafness, King traveled extensively and observed the morally ambiguous expressions of Western civilization directly in their foreign settings. King is also a particularly clear example of the kind of liberal who took Western expansion as a given and went on to ask how it could be tempered and civilized.

Economic and religious expansion were not the same thing, King asserted—and he thanked God they were not—but inevitably they interacted. While the interaction had been advantageous to economic expansionism, it had usually worked to the disadvantage of religion. And the whole process had been less than fortunate for the peoples of the non-Western world. With table-pounding italics King reminded his readers that "Western

---

[12]Sharpe, *Rauschenbusch*, pp. 358, 150-151; Rauschenbusch, *Christianity and the Social Crisis*, pp. 317-318.

civilization was *introduced* into the Orient . . . *for commercial reasons*, and in almost all cases practically by force." He thanked the current Japanese prime minister for having said that America had gently awakened Japan out of a dream life; but King, declining the compliment, went on to deplore Western "exploitation of the less advanced peoples" and Western use of a "method of force . . . at obvious variance with the underlying principles of the civilization so introduced."[13]

When he later, in spite of all this, referred to the spread of Western civilization as somehow good as well as inevitable, King testified to the power of a fervent cosmic idealism to dissolve contradictions. The West, he suggested, is not great nor noble nor indispensable; yet the West is the chosen instrument of ideals— of underlying principles—that have all those qualities. The East will need to westernize in any case; for without Western science, technology, and education, the nations of the East cannot compete in the world and will not survive. But they have a still better reason to westernize; and that is that the underlying principles of our civilization are necessary and eternally right—for them and everyone else—even if we ourselves are failing miserably to live up to them. "The Orient," King wrote, "must take on generally, and in its inner spirit, the great fundamental moral and religious convictions and ideals of Western civilization, if it is steadily to reap its fruits." The conditional clause in this statement might be taken as signaling that King's advice was purely pragmatic, but he made it clear that the principles he was talking about would be right even if American and Western civilization should cease entirely to embody them.[14]

The heart of the matter, as King's subtitle emphasized, was "reverence for personality." The West would be privileged to lead the world only insofar as it reformed its current practices and became a thorough champion of this humanistic piety. King's passionate denunciation of imperialism, though it managed to leave his optimism about such a consummation intact, left it in a

---

[13]King, *Moral and Religious Challenge*, pp. 344, 348.
[14]Ibid., pp. 348-360, 361.

most precarious balance. At best, Western civilization would have to "pay, sooner or later, the full penalty for its deeds of oppression." But the triumph of a great idea—that was something else. That was not in doubt. Whether or not it was to be given to America, "or to the English-speaking peoples as a whole, or to the still broader Teutonic races, or to some other people or groups of peoples" to lead the way toward the civilization of the future, "reverence for personality" was destined to continue as the guiding principle of all human progress. If American and Western peoples chose not to ride this wave of the future, then they, as surely as anyone else, would be overwhelmed by it.[15]

Here—in spades—was Gordon's determination to deculturize the pure message of Christ for the purpose of exporting it. The difficulties had more to do with the feasibility than with the desirability of the operation. Those difficulties were underlined— though not intentionally—by King's own argument that the nations of the East must not try to adopt Western technical civilization without Western religious principles. There was great danger, King remarked, that the Eastern nations would "fail to realize how unified a thing, after all, Western civilization is; and how impossible, therefore, it becomes permanently to reap its fruits and reject its roots."[16] The warning was itself redolent of cultural preconceptions that would later be sharply questioned, but that fact merely adds another persuasive turn to the proposition that what the liberals were calling for—the abstraction of Christianity from Western culture—might be impossibly difficult.[17]

The liberals' answer to such objections, besides the sheer obligation to preach an ethically supreme religion and the necessity of taming a dangerous imperialism, was a pragmatic answer:

---

[15]Ibid., pp. 371, 384; see also pp. 363-372.

[16]Ibid., p. 365.

[17]A recent, quite brilliant and discriminating, reconsideration of missions by Arthur Schlesinger, Jr., argues in effect that there was no way for Christianity, however deculturized, to avoid cultural aggression, and that of a most insidious kind. Schlesinger, "The Missionary Enterprise and Theories of Imperialism," in John K. Fairbank, ed., *The Missionary Enterprise in China and America* (Cambridge, Mass., Harvard University Press, 1974), pp. 336-373.

that the new theology in actual fact converted more souls to Christianity than the old. The stripped-down Christian idealism, like the bumblebee with its inadequate wing span, could not fly but did fly. The Andover men in the 1880s had argued enthusiastically that ridding the gospel of a bad eschatology would insure "a progress in its extension beyond anything as yet realized"; and liberal writers over the next forty years reported regularly that liberalism, far from cutting the nerve of missions, had made possible the unparalleled missionary expansion of that period.[18]

No amount of historical quantification will yield fully satisfying judgments about the validity of that claim. The distinguishing attitudes of the liberal theology did spread widely among the missionaries and mission boards of the mainline Protestant denominations after the turn of the century and were transmitted through such undenominational agencies as the Student Volunteer Movement and the YMCA. But from the conservative point of view (which will be examined in the next and succeeding chapters of this book), expansion under such auspices offered no refutation at all of the standard charge that liberalism had cut the nerve of missions. By 1920, the hard-line objection to liberalism in the mission field would be not "Is it effective?" but "Is it Christianity?" Fundamentalist and conservative tracts by then would become lengthy—frequently almost interminable—testimonies to the expansion of an evangelistic, educational, and medical enterprise that the writers considered disastrous.[19]

Crisis in Christian Nurture

Liberal prescriptions for Christian education, like those for

---

[18]*Progressive Orthodoxy*, p. 189; Clarke, *Christian Missions*, pp. 40-49; Macintosh, "New Christianity and World-Conversion." The *Missionary Review of the World* recorded an increase in American missionary personnel from 2,500 in 1886 to 10,000 in 1914. "Native communicants" attached to American missions increased from 300,000 to 1,500,000 (rounded figures). *Missionary Review of the World*, 9 (November–December 1886), 552-553; ibid., 29 (March 1916), fold-out charts.

[19]See, for example, Horsch, *Modernist View of Missions*; Thomas, "Modernism in China"; Machen, *Modernism and the Board of Foreign Missions*. For a brief discussion of later developments in this controversy, consult Hutchison, "Modernism and Missions," pp. 126-131.

missions, began with assumptions and observations that in some ways were utterly traditional. George A. Coe of Northwestern University, the leading liberal theorist in this area,[20] was to gain a reputation as a controversialist in personal style, as a passionate fighter for pacifism and social justice, and as an all-round radical. His early study (1904) of *Education in Religion and Morals,* however, described the emergency of the times somewhat as conservative evangelicals or spokesmen for the Salvation Army might have described it. At a time of social upheaval, Coe wrote, when the massing of the people in cities was "exposing children as never before to the forces of evil," religious education, inconveniently, had entered a period of hiatus. This had occurred because both the old certainties and the methods of imparting them had suffered discrediting; and nothing had yet taken their place. Though the growth of popular government had increased the need for high character in the people, no new modes of character training had replaced the old dogmatic religious instruction that had so properly been expelled from the curricula of the public schools. At the same time, family training had weakened; and though the Sunday school movement might appear to have entered a "bloom period," its real ineffectuality showed in decreased accessions to the churches and in a continued, perhaps heightened, ignorance of the Bible.

Society, Coe thought, was not lacking in resources with which to meet the crisis. It could call on the experience of the public schools and Sunday schools, together with the knowledge and inspiration gained in a century of innovative thought in psychology, educational philosophy, and religious studies. The great problem of the moment was to bring needs and resources into closer contact.[21]

Up to this point the author and the more individualistic

---

[20]Smith, *Faith and Nurture,* pp. 26-27; Seward Hiltner, "Pastoral Theology and Psychology," in Nash, ed., *Protestant Thought,* p. 186. See also Smith's chapter, "Christian Education," in the Nash volume; and his "Coe: Revaluer of Values," pp. 46-57.

[21]Coe, *Religion and Morals,* pp. 5-6.

revivalists shared much common ground. But Coe already had passed both personally and professionally beyond individualist solutions. The old-time religion, in his view, was too much a cause of the social crisis to serve well as a response to it. As the son of a Methodist minister, Coe had been trained to expect that his own conversion would come in dramatic fashion and, like a remarkable number of others who became liberals, had felt chagrin and uncertainty when this did not happen.[22] That experience, together with exposure to personalist philosophy and advanced biblical scholarship at Boston University and the University of Berlin, had led him not only to reject the common evangelicalism but also to set aside theology, professionally, in favor of philosophy and then in favor of the psychology of religion. The first work that brought him wide notice refracted much of this personal history. In 1899 he published a pioneering study—much praised by contemporaries and competitors such as Edwin Starbuck—of the characterological differences between those who undergo sharply defined conversion experiences and those who do not.[23]

In 1909 Coe moved from Northwestern University, where he had been professor of philosophy, to accept a post as professor of practical theology at Union Theological Seminary in New York. There, because of his own movement toward the theological left, but also undoubtedly because of radical views on capitalism and war, he came increasingly into conflict with his fellow liberals; and in 1922, in the wake of Union's failure to promote a colleague, Coe accepted a position at Teachers College, Columbia University. In the 1920s and after, although he intensified his

[22]The context of this experience, for Coe as for other liberals, had been a home atmosphere that was conservative but apparently not rigid or repressive. "Though I recall no instance of parental pressure to make me conform, and though my childhood and youth were more than ordinarily free from sense of restraint, nevertheless I was a young conformist." Coe, "My Own Little Theatre," in Ferm, ed., *Religion in Transition*, p. 92. For further suggestions about parental guidance and conversion experience among those who became liberals, see Hutchison, "Cultural Strain," 398-411.

[23]Bremer, "Coe," pp. 64-71. Coe's "A Study in the Dynamics of Personal Religion" appeared in the *Psychological Review*, 1899.

insistence upon making Christian education "more Christian," it was the socially revolutionary elements that he had come to emphasize in the message of Jesus.[24]

Coe was to be remembered by at least one Union alumnus as "the real 'modernist' of my day in the Seminary." He seemed so, and the religious education movement seemed a particularly vivid expression of the modernist impulse, because of the religious educationists' intense enthusiiam for a contemporary movement—progressive education—that others saw as specifically secular or secularizing. For Coe himself, of course, this partially misstated the problem. There was such a thing as a devout Zeitgeist; hence the new education and religious education were arising, not within a hostile environment of secular educational thought, but within a culture suffused with religious and ethical aims. He argued that social adjustment, which John Dewey had called the driving aim of progressive education, surely was an ethical conception. And progressive educational theories in general, he said, while they contrasted sharply with medieval, didactic modes of religious training, posed no threat to an emancipated Protestantism for which salvation involved the cultivation of inborn tendencies.[25]

To put the matter more affirmatively, Coe was saying that the partners to this heaven-made marriage brought highly compatible gifts. Liberal theology contributed a receptivity to the so-called secular culture, which meant an openness in the curriculum of Christian education to insights from the arts and sciences. It brought an emphasis upon growth and continuity in the religious life, in place of the sharp discontinuity commonly assumed between man's lost and his regenerate condition. It brought a view of children as the children of God rather than of

---

[24]Coffin, *Half Century*, pp. 87-90, 105-106, 185; Bremer, "Coe," pp. 201-203, 236ff. The colleague, Hugh Hartshorne, later taught and conducted research in the psychology of religion at Southern California, at Teachers College, and at Yale. Shelton Smith, unlike Coffin, thinks the Hartshorne incident more important than the longer-standing clashes of personality and ideology. (Smith to author, July 28, 1972). See also Swift, "[Coe] at Union Theological Seminary," p. 95.

[25]Coffin, *Half Century*, pp. 89-90; Smith, *Faith and Nurture*, p. 27; Coe, *Religion and Morals*, pp. 17-19, 70-74.

wrath, a stress upon religious experience as more fundamental than the creeds or other necessary objectifications of that experience, and a conception of divine authority as working "within the individual as an impulse, not without him as compulsion." Liberalism prescribed, finally and perhaps most obviously, utilization of the principles of modern biblical criticism in decisions as to what is to be taught about the background and message of the Christian religion.[26]

From progressive education and from the functional psychology that underlay it came an insistence upon the interrelatedness of doing and knowing, and a concomitant tendency to reject any sharp separation between physical being on one hand and mental or spiritual existence on the other. Progressive education articulated the need for a child-centered rather than creed-centered religious curriculum, and suggested a rationale for religious education as contributing to an exalted form of social adjustment. A large number of other progressive ideas were really, as Coe saw them, Christian teachings that had been reinterpreted with such originality that one could now speak of them as "contributions of modern education to religion." The principle of universal education, for example, was based upon a conception of human worth that Jesus had "emphasized as no other teacher has done." The same was true of the principle of development from within, of the notion of educating the whole child, of the preference for concreteness over abstraction, and of much else associated with the advanced movement in education.[27]

At one point Coe reverted to revivalist terminology in declaring that society, when it had appropriated these waiting educational and religious resources, would "get a new heart." Very probably the rest of that favorite evangelical text—"for why will ye die?" —echoed in his mind also. But such resemblances to revivalist formulas were superficial, because what Coe was proposing was

---

[26]The quotation about religious authority is from *Religion and Morals*, p. 78. That and the other themes mentioned in this paragraph appear throughout the book, but see especially the summaries on pp. 195-197 and 387-388. See also Smith, *Faith and Nurture*, pp. 1-32.

[27]Coe, *Religion and Morals*, pp. 85, 87, and 82-96 passim.

a massive institutionalization of the Bushnellian theories of Christian nurture. The church at large, and not just a Sunday-morning department thereof called religious education, would turn its attention radically toward youth, would begin finally to think of regeneration as occurring early in the cycle of life. Religion under the influence of revivalism, Coe thought, had persisted in trying to salvage mature persons instead of addressing itself, as it now must, to persons in formation.[28]

Coe outlined in the minutest detail his prescriptions for the family, the Sunday school, the public schools and colleges, and all other institutions engaged in the nurture of the young. Though his books are saved from pedestrianism by a style that expresses an interesting and forceful personality, Coe's students sometimes complained that he seemed more concerned about the detailed physical setting for learning than about what was to be learned. A former student recalled that "we ridiculed the instructions he gave us about the exact height of the chairs for a kindergarten child, or how much light should enter the windows of a classroom, as if religious education were wholly dependent on its setting."[29]

Certainly it is true that Coe's writings, in this early period at least, were intended as handbooks as well as theoretical discussions. The aim of *Education in Religion and Morals*, he said, was to end the isolation of "our philosophy of life" from "practical methods of training for life," and to exhibit principles and forces "in their highest concreteness." Coe therefore set out guidelines and described materials or techniques with a kind of specificity that does suggest enormous reliance upon mechanical arrangements.[30]

Some of his proposals, in addition, seemed anticlimactic, as though he had brought his readers by a new route to an old and

---

[28]Ibid., 389-406.

[29]Quoted in Coffin, *Half Century*, p. 89.

[30]Coe, *Religion and Morals*, pp. 6-7. Smith defends Coe at this point by emphasizing that he intended "method" to remain child-centered, and objected whenever it became "material-centered." Smith to author, July 28, 1972.

obvious destination. Coe advocated, for example, a simplification of living to allow time for "family companionship"; the devising of "home occupations" and projects to which all members would contribute; and the reestablishment of family devotions. Yet the revitalization of sometimes venerable practices by means of a modern rationale was a significant part of Coe's contribution.[31]

In 1912, Charles Scribner's Sons published, with an introductory essay by Coe, the Sunday school curriculum that had been developed at Center Church in New Haven during the pastorate of Newman Smyth. It provides excellent illustrations of the methods that Coe and the Religious Education Association (founded by Dewey and Coe) had been advocating. In this curriculum the course of serious instruction began, in good Bushnellian fashion, with the Cradle Roll (ages one, two, and three years); the idea being "to associate the child from birth with the Sunday School as a part of the Church." The program directed to children aged six through eight focused the child's attention on the loving qualities of God and on the human, serving activities of Jesus. The lessons prepared for the next age group illustrated the effort to appeal to children by way of their natural interests, more specifically by a heavy, five-year-long preoccupation with the heroes of the Bible and of the history of Christianity. Teen-aged children were introduced to historical and critical methods of understanding the Bible and were involved in active social service. By age seventeen they were also exposed to comparative religion and the principles of psychology.[32]

Such plans, as those who opposed them readily agreed, did bring the resources of religion and modern education into harmony and did forge them into some kind of response to the social crisis. But the question was, what kind of response? Opponents contended, here as in the case of the Social Gospel and the liberal theology of missions, that solutions might be appealing and apparently effective, yet still constitute a further falling-away

---

[31]Coe, *Religion and Morals*, pp. 282-285, 304-306.

[32]Coe, *Good Teaching*, pp. 10-16. For further specification of contents and approach, see pp. 20-32 of the same pamphlet.

from Christianity. Coe offered, in response, a defense of the continued necessity of Christianity, together with a religious critique of any wholly secularized progressive education.

Few passages in all the liberal literature convey so strong a sense of the mutuality of religion and the secular. In Coe's plans for religious education, Munger's depiction of religion as the completion of culture was given a working, speaking embodiment. Coe's strong tendency to identify the origins and aims of modern religion with those of modern education precluded any sharp separation of Christian from secular elements, and he could therefore not argue that Christian education is "different." He could, however, claim that it is "more." Christianity, he argued, provides an enrichment and completion without which educational theory in its most enlightened form will turn out to be regressive.

Building upon the conceptions of wholeness that were central to advanced educational theory, Coe suggested that if education lacks a religious dimension it fails in its stated aspiration to deal with "the whole personality of the child, the whole content of civilization, and the whole ideal of human life." Education, he said, according to modern theory is not an aggregation of discrete bits of knowledge, but rather is a unified process. The correlative psychological theory holds that the child itself is a unit and not a bundle of faculties, while the supporting ethical position supplies the ideal of a completely unified self as the goal of the educational process. Modern education therefore seeks, on behalf of the child, to bring "into his fragmentary interests a principle of organization; into his life as a whole a purpose and a meaning." But all such aspirations toward wholeness must fail, Coe contended, if education lacks a religious dimension. The child's "whole personality," after all, includes a religious impulse or sentiment; and the world in which the child seeks self-realization includes not just physical objects and human persons but God and an unseen world. The question whether particular religious traditions have correctly identified the nature of the unseen world cannot be finally answered, but also is not decisive. "Whether or not religious faith is well founded," Coe insisted, the desire of the self for adjustment to this larger world, for "unity with the ultimate ground of our being," is something education cannot ignore. Therefore religion, "instead of being a department of education, is an implicit motive thereof. It is the end that presides over the beginning and gives unity to all stages of the process."[33]

Coe was not hesitant to suggest answers, from this point of view, to some of the specific complaints already lodged against progressive education. John Dewey had acknowledged in *The Child and the Curriculum* (1902) that "it is a danger of the 'new education' that it regards the child's present powers and interests as something finally significant in themselves." Coe concurred in that warning and suggested that the corrective would come precisely from a fuller recognition of the place of religion in a total education. Education, in being "brought close to the life that now is," had been tending to look backward (in an evolutionary sense) "to the laws and forces of the child's mind." That had been a necessary move; but education must also look to "the destiny that is to be achieved," must pay attention to goals. And this is what religious education is all about.

The correctives and completions offered for progressive education extended logically into the much controverted area of life adjustment or social adjustment. The higher the form of life, Coe argued, the wider its spheres of necessary adaptation. Creatures with eyes adapt to a wider world than those without them; beings with mind and memory, beings with conscience and social instinct, adapt to successively wider environments; and the human religious faculty demands that human beings work out an adaptation to the ultimate ground of being, to God. Those critics of progressive education who complained of "adjustment" as a mean or narrowly pragmatic objective were correct, Coe said, unless adjustment can be interpreted cosmically as well as socially. "Accepting the notion that education consists of acts performed by society for social ends . . . in religious education organized man provides for a progressive adaptation of the race to its divine environment."[34]

All of this argued rather powerfully for a dimension of religious

---

[33]Coe, *Religion and Morals*, pp. 96, 29-32.
[34]Ibid., pp. 13-14, 24-25.

questioning, and even of religious affirmation, in education. But again, why Christianity? What was Christian about a mere sensitivity to religious questions, or about the religious education that resulted therefrom? Coe's answers perhaps foreshadowed his subsequent move to greater theological radicalism. One argument, that the Christian rubrics are necessary because religious experience must be "named," plainly left the door ajar for a thoroughgoing relativism. But Coe did add more particularizing claims. He held that Christianity in its various fundamental expressions, including of course those at the base of modern educational theory, constitutes "a distinctive attitude and a distinctive utterance." Jesus was unique in teaching, for example, that children already possess the Kingdom of God, and that their experiences offer a demonstration of the ideal human society. More than that, Coe was still able to say, with the tradition that had formed him, that Christianity is necessary because Christ was and is the unique manifestation of God, the only means through which man can gain the union he seeks "with the one being who is higher than himself."[35]

The Social Crisis

The affinity between a vigorously "applied" form of liberalism and a preoccupation with cultural crisis was made more obvious by the contrast between liberals who championed a Social Gospel and those who did not. The rhetoric of crisis was far more common among the former group.

Few if any liberals actually campaigned against the Social Gospel or would have admitted hostility to it. Its goal, the Christianization of society, was one that only the most extreme premillennialists could oppose; and there were no premillennialists among the New Theologians. More important, the Social Gospel's distinctive attitudes about the ways of achieving this goal had sprung from, and remained at least congenial with, liberal views of the nature of religious experience. The new social Christianity proclaimed not simply that society must be saved

---

[35]Ibid., pp. 151-170, 44-47, 63-64. For one view, largely a negative one, of the effectiveness of the liberal "professionals" in the Sunday school movement, see Robert W. Lynn and Elliott Wright, *The Big Little School: Sunday Child of American Protestantism* (New York, Harper and Row, 1971), pp. 79-86.

but that this goal could be attained by collective or directly environmental modes of action, and in fact could not be reached if the church continued to fix its attention on saving sinners one by one. The strongest animus of the movement, therefore, lay against the individualistic, primarily revivalistic Protestantism that was also a major target of theological liberalism.[36]

Liberals who rejoiced in any discomfiture of revivalism were not, however, certain to be pleased by attacks on economic and other forms of individualism. The carry-over in many cases was simply not made. Where it was not, the result was usually a tacit form of dissent—a simple matter of not preaching, as the Social Gospel clearly implied one must preach, against the structural evils and defects in American society. Though Phillips Brooks in his early career denounced racial segregation and Johnsonian Reconstruction, he tried thereafter to keep politics out of the pulpit; and men like George Gordon seem consciously to have emulated Brooks in that respect.[37] A number of others, particularly among those who were scholars rather than preachers, appeared to lack interest in the movement. Among the thirty-three most prominent leaders of theological liberalism in the period from 1875 to 1915, about one third took no discernible part in the Social Gospel.[38]

---

[36]The term Social Gospel has sometimes been lifted out of its late-nineteenth-century context and made a generic equivalent of "religious social reform." Under such an expanded definition an enormous number of theological conservatives, as well as many more liberals, can be called proponents or prophets of the Social Gospel. I think, however, that any attempt to make the term so inclusive muddies the waters considerably. Orthodox Calvinists, revivalists, and other religious conservatives had always been prominent and instrumental in "social reform" crusades—from temperance, peace, and antislavery movements to city mission work and the general denunciation of social vices. It was something else again to argue, as the Social Gospelers did, that social salvation precedes individual salvation both temporally and in importance. Even to give social reform an equal, nonderivative status was a move quite distinct in theory from what evangelicals generally could support. It was this theoretical elevation of social salvation, therefore, that made the Social Gospel a distinctive movement.

[37]Albright, *Focus on Infinity*, pp. 110, 126. Allen, *Phillips Brooks*, p. 416; Gordon, *My Education*, pp. 299-301; Likens, "Awareness of Social Problems," pp. 4, 160, 328.

[38]Hutchison, "Cultural Strain," p. 411. Liberal leaders whom I would classify as lacking interest in the Social Gospel are Borden Parker Bowne, Charles A. Briggs, Phillips Brooks, Frank H. Foster, George Gordon, George Harris, A. C. Knudson, A. C. McGiffert, Theodore Munger, Egbert Smyth, and Lewis Stearns.

Among that majority of liberals who did participate in the social movement, positions ranged from a reformism still strongly tinged with individualist assumptions, to the advocacy of radical revisions in the political-economic system.[39] Walter Rauschenbusch, whose views of liberal Christianity and the cultural crisis are to be considered here, belongs in the leftward or more radical half of the spectrum, although the favorable reaction to his work of 1907 indicated that his pragmatic socialism was nearer to the center of reform thought than he or others had supposed.

On the whole, Rauschenbusch was a representative as well as leading figure, both theologically and socially, in the liberal movement. A second generation German-American who had returned to Germany for segments of secondary and postgraduate education, he was profoundly committed to the historical approach to Christianity and its doctrines, and was unusually explicit—even for a liberal—about the necessity for theology and the church to respond sympathetically to contemporary social and intellectual movements. He joined energetically in the attack upon "the old scheme of salvation," which he called "mechanical and remote." He stressed the socially innovative character of Christianity by asserting that, though Jesus had been neither a theologian nor an ecclesiastic nor a socialist, the founder of Christianity had belonged prospectively with the socialists and reformers, with "the men who are giving their heart and life to the propaganda of a new social system." And finally, Rauschenbusch represented, and greatly elaborated, the liberal emphasis upon an earthly Kingdom of God.[40]

Rauschenbusch, to be sure, impressed some contemporary and later observers as displaying greater historical and theological depth than his fellow liberals.[41] That is a reasonable appraisal.

---

[39]For Henry F. May's useful division of the pre-1895 Social Gospel into conservative, progressive, and radical wings, see his *Protestant Churches*, pp. 163-265.

[40]"The New Evangelism," in Hutchison, ed., *American Protestant Thought*, pp. 111-112; *Christianity and the Social Crisis*, pp. 92, 67. The emphasis upon the Kingdom runs through all of Rauschenbusch's writings, but was expounded most fully in his *Theology for the Social Gospel*.

[41]See Hudson, *Great Tradition*, pp. 226-242. Cf., however, Robert D. Cross's characterization of Rauschenbusch's understanding of the medieval church as "grotesque." Introduction to Torchbook edition of Rauschenbusch, *Christianity and the Social Crisis*, p. xiv.

Rauschenbusch seems frequently to have achieved a kind and level of discourse that transcended his own times; and to that extent he becomes hard to classify under the party labels of any particular time. But the differences between Rauschenbusch and his fellow liberals are matters more of richness and dimension than of ideological variation. A later neo-orthodox generation would seize appreciatively, for example, upon Rauschenbusch's acknowledgment that "there is no perfection for man in this life."[42] Yet that same acknowledgment had been essential to the arguments of the Andover men, and of Gordon, Newman Smyth, and others when they contended for the likelihood and necessity of a completion beyond the grave.

Rauschenbusch's position on such points was archetypal rather than atypical. Apart perhaps from his protest against American participation in World War I, he was never a "prophet without honor," but was widely heard and responded to. His message was one that his contemporaries were ready to hear and Rauschenbusch projected—both directly and in print—personal qualities that helped him gain a hearing. His writing combined passion and critical acuity with clarity of diction and a notable lightness of touch. His analogies and figures of speech were peculiarly effective. His spoken discourse, formal and informal, benefited from a notable kindliness and sense of humor, and probably even from Rauschenbusch's deafness and frail appearance.[43]

The crisis of which Rauschenbusch wrote in 1907 was an unprecedented social revolution that he claimed was now recognized "by universal consent" as the overshadowing problem of the times. His figurative introduction to the details of the crisis showed how ready some liberals were to deride the boastings of the recently deceased "glorious century." Rauschenbusch pictured the spirit of the nineteenth century descending to "the vaulted chamber of the Past, where the Spirits of the dead centuries sit on granite stones together." He had the newcomer respond to the queries of his predecessors by reporting almost casually that "I am the Spirit

---

[42]*Christianity and the Social Crisis*, p. 420.

[43]Sharpe, *Rauschenbusch*, pp. 66-67, 142-145. See also the tributes to Rauschenbusch and to his teaching in *Rochester Theological Seminary Bulletin*, November 1918, especially pp. 6-8, 72.

Walter Rauschenbusch

of the Wonderful Century. I gave man the mastery over nature
. . . I freed the thoughts of men . . . I broke the chains of
bigotry and despotism . . . I have touched the summit of
history." But his hearers make short work of him. "We all spoke
proudly," says the First Century, "when we came here in the
flush of our deeds." The First Century then asks whether the
mastery of nature has really made humanity free from want,
whether increased human wisdom is anything more than cunning,
whether people have learned to control their passions, or have
learned to dispense justice; and the Spirit of the Nineteenth Century acknowledges that the long-promised redemption did not
come in his time. "But it will come," the centuries assure each
other.[44]

"I am not a despiser of my age and its achievements," Rauschenbusch told his readers. But he then devoted some sixty-five pages
to the maladies of his society. Human beings, he contended, had
conquered nature but not themselves. Land had been monopolized.
Working conditions had deteriorated, and with them the physical
condition of working people. Inequality had grown, and the pre-
dominance of commercial over human values had brought corrup-
tion to the political system and moral decay throughout the
society. At the end of the chapter, after labeling the theory of inevitable human progress an "optimistic illusion" and laughable,
Rauschenbusch launched into a peroration comparing the current
situation of Christendom to that of Rome before its fall. Whether
modern Western civilization could avoid Rome's fate, he said,

will depend almost wholly upon the moral forces which the Christian nations can bring to the fighting line against wrong, and the fighting
energy of those moral forces will again depend on the degree to which
they are inspired by religious faith and enthusiasm. It is either a revival of
social religion or the deluge.[45]

When Rauschenbusch turned to the posing of solutions, his
great seriousness, professionally and personally, about historical
theology did not preclude his indulging in a most explicit

---

[44]Rauschenbusch, *Christianity and the Social Crisis*, pp. xii, 211-213.
[45]Ibid., pp. 220, 279, 286, and 213-286 passim.

modernism. He was, in fact, most modernist in method when most theological in the treatment of his major theme. *A Theology for the Social Gospel* (1917) opened with a warning that "if theology stops growing, or is unable to adjust itself to its modern environment . . . it will die." The greatest danger facing theology, he contended, "is not mutilation but senility." Many of the ideas once needed to hold the church together had lost any such unifying function. "Our reverence for them," he said, "is a kind of ancestor worship. To hold laboriously to a religious belief which does not hold us, is an attenuated form of asceticism; we chastise and starve our intellect to sanctify it by holy beliefs."[46]

Nearly all of Rauschenbusch's earlier work had sounded a similar call for theological change. In "The New Evangelism" (1904) he had asserted that humanity, like the individual, "must reconstruct its moral and religious synthesis whenever it passes from one era to another." He had noted, mildly enough, that "when all other departments of life and thought are silently changing, it is impossible for religion to remain unaffected"; but then he had made it clear that the response he was calling for entailed, specifically, adaptation to what is best in the spirit of the age:

The Gospel, to have power over an age, must be the highest expresssion of the moral and religious truths held by that age. If it lags behind and presents outgrown conceptions of life and duty, it is no longer in the full sense the Gospel . . . If the official wardens of the Gospel from selfish motives or from conservative veneration for old statements refuse to let the spirit of Christ flow into the larger vessels of thought and feeling which God himself has prepared for it, they are warned by finding men turn from their message as sapless and powerless.[47]

Rauschenbusch carried these statements of 1904, some of them verbatim, into his epochal volume three years later.[48] That volume constituted, among other things, an elaboration upon his long-standing insistence that individualism was the decisive fault of the Old Theology. Repeatedly he proclaimed that "individualis-

---

[46]*Theology for the Social Gospel*, pp. 1, 12-13.
[47]"The New Evangelism," in Hutchison, *American Protestant Thought*, p. 109.
[48]*Christianity and the Social Crisis*, p. 339.

tic Christianity," having given all its attention to personal salvation, stood discredited and disqualified among contenders for a prophetic influence in modern society. "Religious individualism," he wrote, "lacks the triumphant faith in the possible sovereignty of Jesus Christ in all human affairs . . . It lacks that vital interest in the total [sic] of human life which can create a united and harmonious and daring religious conception of the world." The prevalent evangelicalism, "while rich in men of piety and evangelistic fervor," had been "singularly poor in the prophetic gift." If Christianity was to hold an influential relation to society; if it was to stand—in the phrase later popular among critics of liberalism—"over against" the demonic forces making for social evil, then Christian theology must become social theology. This above all was the adaptation required by the present moment of history.[49]

Adaptation to the present was also, of course, construed as realignment with the original message of Christianity, and with what Rauschenbusch took to be the most powerful and valid tradition of Old Testament prophecy. But critics could argue that this move still, in effect, left modern culture in the position of prophesying to Christ, more than the reverse. Modern culture— or at least the dynamic, better spirit thereof—was being granted the right to decide what is most valid both in the prophetic tradition of the Old Testament and in the teaching of Jesus. One function of social Christianity, Rauschenbusch said, was to "take the veil from our eyes when we read the synoptic gospels." And social Christianity itself had reemerged because of the imperatives of a "vast historical movement" of the present day.[50]

Rauschenbusch rendered himself still more vulnerable to objections that he was making "modern culture" normative by contending that, whereas "culture" in the past had placed obstacles in the way of social Christianity, the culture of his own day was removing the obstacles—in fact had already removed them. The social message of Jesus, he said, with its primary concern for

[49]Ibid., pp. 338-340.
[50]Ibid., pp. 1-92, 340, 336.

justice and its appeal to the poor and downtrodden, had been deflected in the earliest years by "alien forces penetrating Christianity from without." Yet all these cultural obstacles had "strangely disappeared or weakened in modern life." As a result, in the opening years of the twentieth century the church was blessed with a providential convergence between two lines of development, one from within organized Christianity and one external to it: "At the same time when Christianity has . . . attained to its adolescence and moral maturity, there is a piercing call from the world about it, summoning all moral strength and religious heroism."[51]

This suggests the nature of Rauschenbusch's response to questions of proximate historical causation. The ultimate, consistent cause was God—standing, in James Russell Lowell's phrase, "within the shadow, keeping watch above his own." But at the level of historical action, the relations of Christ and culture were reciprocal. Throughout Rauschenbusch's treatment of such historical epochs as that of the Reformation runs his refusal to press the claims either of religious ideology on one hand, or of economic and social forces on the other:

> In all the greatest forward movements of humanity, religion has been one of the driving forces . . . But in turn the greatest forward movements in religion have always taken place under the call of a great historical situation. Religious movements of the first magnitude are seldom purely religious in their origin and character.[52]

If, as he believed, this interaction has produced a modern culture that is "better," less obstructive, than preceding ones, that gives some warrant for a hope of the eventual coming of the Kingdom. It does not guarantee, however, that the upward climb will be automatic, or even that continued upward movement is a certainty. Nor does it mean, simply because the balance of forces within the secular culture may now be tipped toward true Christianization, that institutionalized religion no longer has a prophetic role to play. The interaction must continue: "If Chris-

---

[51]Ibid., pp. 199, 198, 201, 210. Rauschenbusch details the disappearance of each obstacle on pp. 201-209.

[52]Ibid., pp. 209, 332.

tianity would add its moral force to the social and economic forces making for a nobler organization of society, it could render such help to the cause of justice and the people as would make this a proud page in the history of the Church."[53]

But what, exactly, is this Christian addendum? Is it an indispensable one? Rauschenbusch had a clearer or at least a more forceful and impressive answer to the first question than to the second. "All the teaching of Jesus and all his thinking centered about the hope of the kingdom of God." Social salvation is the heart and essence of Christianity. No matter how hard Rauschenbusch tried on occasion to concede an equivalent importance to individual salvation, the individual kept coming out second, and individual salvation proved always to be derivative in importance. "It is not a matter," he wrote, "of saving human atoms, but of saving the social organism. It is not a matter of getting individuals to heaven, but of transforming the life on earth into the harmony of heaven."[54]

That this distinctive Christian addendum is also an indispensable one for the life of humanity, Rauschenbusch seems never to have doubted. The current crisis could not be met, he argued, without a dedication to Christ's vision of the Kingdom: "The religious spirit is a factor of incalculable power . . . Unless the economic and intellectual factors are strongly reenforced by religious enthusiasm, the whole social movement may prove abortive, and the New Era may die before it comes to birth." Concomitantly, Rauschenbusch was thoroughly dedicated to ensuring, so far as he could, that preachers of the Social Gospel would not become simply spokesmen for secular reform or "the megaphone of a political party." Like John Dewey and most other leaders of great innovative movements, he issued warnings that some followers would ignore and that most critics would fail to credit him for. "One of the most serious charges that can be raised against preaching on social questions," Rauschenbusch wrote in 1907, "is that it is unreligious. It is the business of a

---

[53]Ibid., p. 336.
[54]Ibid., pp. 67, 65. For Rauschenbusch's effort to give personal religion its due, see, for example, pp. 22-32, 60-61.

preacher to connect all that he thinks and says with the mind and will of God.''[55]

Rauschenbusch, however, did not think of apologetics as his major task. In all of his major writings, the immediate and pressing aim was the reform of the church and of Christianity. Rauschenbusch addressed himself chiefly to an audience that already professed to believe in the world's absolute need for Christ; so that this point was not really, as it was with other liberals, up for discussion. In the views on missions mentioned at the beginning of this chapter, Rauschenbusch accepted enthusiastically the traditional missionary objective; his concern was the extent to which the enterprise could prosper if the home religion and the home society went unreformed.

In another sense, however, the entire Social Gospel was an apologetic. It did not "contain" an apologetic; it was one. The church must learn its own proper message, the Social Gospel contended, and start performing in accord with it, before it either attempts to instruct others in "the truth" or tries to defend its own claims to special inspiration. But having once accomplished this, having set its house in order, the Christian church will be persuasive as embodying the final religion.

Get the social message of Jesus through the head of the church, Rauschenbusch was saying, and the superiority of Christianity will be proven by what the church will do as an active force in the world. The result will make a formal theological apologetic easy to frame, but also superfluous.

"The Passing of the Protestant Age of History"

In March of 1908, Newman Smyth addressed himself to a crisis related to the others and in a sense overarching all of them—Protestantism's loss of control of "the forces of life." Human affairs, as Smyth contended in an idiom very specific to the social sciences of that time, are problems of forces. History is a dynamic process, the study of which, as much as that of physics or biology, is a study of energy. Religion or any other social enterprise is alive

---

[55]Ibid., pp. xxii, 362-364.

only insofar as it discerns and masters this dynamism, and a religion that fails here will be able to make no exclusivist claims. "Christianity must become the mastery of human life, or it is not the final religion."[56]

Smyth thought that Protestantism, in its earlier stages of protest and systematic construction, had remained sensitive to social forces and thus had maintained a sense of mastery in their midst. And he insisted that he had no wish to minimize the achievements even of the modern church. But everywhere he saw signs that the "Protestant era" was ending, that Protestantism as theretofore conceived was losing control or had already lost it. The religious bonds of family life were coming undone. Religious discourse was "withdrawing from the churches" to become privatized or else located in other institutions of intellectual and spiritual life. Concomitantly, the kind of specifically Christian discourse once known among ordinary people was being stifled by the failures of religious education and by a consequent ignorance about Christianity. But more fundamental and serious than all these constituents of crisis was that loss of Christian unity which the Pope had called "the synthesis of all heresies," and which a Protestant liberal hastened to rephrase as "the summation of the losses of Protestantism." Smyth claimed it was a matter of "general consent" that nothing is "more fatal to religious efficiency everywhere than the loss of the unity of the Church."[57]

Smyth, like his liberal colleagues, thought ample resources were at hand for resolving the crisis he had described. A new age was imminent if human beings could read the signs of God's will and respond to them. The implication here was not that the new age would be perfect, or even glorious. The great movements of the past had been providentially right and good for their times without directly bringing in the Kingdom, and one could not be sure that the "coming Catholicism" would differ in that respect. The choice was not between disaster and a foreseeable Kingdom

---

[56]Smyth, *Passing Protestantism*, pp. 13-14.
[57]Ibid., pp. 1-22. Smyth writes of a completed "Protestant era" on p. 8.

on Earth, but rather between disaster and the unobstructed continuation of the long, dialectical, upward movement of history.

Smyth's mood, on balance, remained optimistic even with respect to the immediate future. "If we point without hesitation to
the darkest clouds of the present hour," he wrote, "it is because
we see also across them the sweep and radiance of the bow of
promise." But he seemed not to fall into the logical error of those
who rely upon a dialectic to explain the past and then abandon
such explanations for anything beyond the immediate future.
Smyth's phrasing was revealing in this regard: he saw the numerous hopeful signs of the present converging in the promise not
of a perfect day, but of "another of the days of the Son of man."
History was to remain open.[58]

Smyth's critique of Protestant decline and his vision of Christianity's future were conceived on an unusually grand scale, but
there was nothing singular about his attitude toward Christian
disunity. Liberals regularly had supported the cooperative and
unifying tendencies within Protestantism, and, to a somewhat
lesser extent, the movements toward *rapprochement* with the
Roman Catholics. There were some apparent exceptions: Henry
Ward Beecher, when he became editor of the *Church Union* in
1870, changed its name to *Christian Union* because he thought
the notion of actual organic union of the churches "as absurd as
the union of families in philanstery [sic]."[59] And Theodore
Munger as late as 1904 warned against the tendency to condemn
all sectarian divisions; religious multiplicity, he argued, is an
inevitable adjunct of religious freedom. Munger thought that
"'our unhappy divisions,' as they are sometimes called, might be
more unhappy if they were absorbed in large unions."[60]

Yet even Beecher and Munger scarcely constitute exceptions.
Beecher's blast against organic union came, after all, at a moment
when he was assuming leadership of one of the two major ecumenical enterprises in religious journalism—a paper devoted specifically to "the promotion of a unity of feeling and a cooperation of

---

[58]Ibid., pp. 12, 36.
[59]Brown, *Abbott*, p. 67.
[60]Munger, *Essays for the Day*, p. 11.

effort of all Christian churches." Munger, similarly, opposed church union, not Christian union. His hesitations were those not only of a pluralist but of a committed congregationalist and doctrinal liberal; he feared that a church union would require a more exact and oppressive creedal agreement than any found in the "sects" constituting the union.[61]

The divisions within liberalism, on this matter, had not pitted sectarians against supporters of unity; they had involved various degrees and kinds of ecumenists. The most common liberal ecumenism was federationist, favoring continued denominational identity but opposing sectarianism, creedal rigidity, and duplication of effort. The liberal statesmen and politicians of the church unity movement—for example, William Adams Brown, Edward Scribner Ames, William DeWitt Hyde, William Jewett Tucker, and Shailer Mathews—were predominantly of this persuasion.[62] But an important minority, led by Newman Smyth and Charles A. Briggs, pled for more thoroughgoing church union.

Rigid lines were not always visible between federationists and proponents of organic union. It was possible to favor one or another combination of these principles and common to move from one to the other—usually from federative to more unitive thinking.[63] Yet for some the distinction was crucial. Mathews, a federationist from the early years of the twentieth century, felt that from the first the two approaches had involved differing social psychologies and had claimed the loyalties of quite different sets of people. The organic ideal, he said, "carried over from the Roman Empire and the Middle Ages the imperial idealism; the federation movement sprang from democratic experience like that of the United States. To one movement denominationalism is a

---

[61]Abbott, *Reminiscences*, p. 328; Munger, *Essays for the Day*, pp. 42 and 3-15 passim.

[62]Brown, *Teacher and His Times*, pp. 335-365; Ames, *Beyond Theology*, pp. 78-85; Burnett, *Hyde of Bowdoin*, pp. 234-247; William Jewett Tucker, "The Church of the Future," in Abbott and others, *New Puritanism*, pp. 217 and 215-236 passim; Mathews, *New Faith for Old*, pp. 153 and 152-170 passim.

[63]Newman Smyth was delighted to find his friend Munger warming to the organic ideal shortly before Munger's death in 1910. Bacon, *Munger*, p. 366. Smyth himself had been something of a convert. He had had relatively little to say about church union—organic or federative—before the middle of the decade.

matter of disloyalty to the Lord, to the other it is a datum to be recognized in all plans."[64]

"From my understanding of social process," Mathews explained, "my sympathies were and are" with the federationists. But others found federation inadequate and even dangerous. Newman Smyth deplored "the complaisance with which even broad-minded men in all the churches are contented to welcome lower and beggarly substitutes" for the ideal of a visible universal church:

They will follow some flickering expedients of fraternal conventions, or courtesies of limited exchange of ministerial functions, and friendly greetings on neutral platforms, and other such manifestations of mutual respect and occasional charity. Such approaches of religious bodies are indeed to be welcomed, as flags of truce may be between long hostile forces; but this is not the marching on as one triumphal host of Love for the overcoming of the world. The recovery of the ideal . . . is our Protestant need, if we are to have in this century a gospel for all men.[65]

Among proponents of organic union, Briggs unquestionably was the most formidable technician, minutely concerned with scriptural validation and with distinctions between essentials and nonessentials in the various creeds. Smyth, in contrast, dealt more directly with the evaluation of modern culture and with Christianity's obligation to assert a prophetic role within that culture.

Smyth's response to the alleged Protestant loss of cultural control was not to assert that Protestantism deserved to regain mastery. On the contrary, he said that Protestantism was finished; it had done its great work and must now make way for something better. The new church Smyth envisioned would embody far too much of historic Protestantism to suit either secularists or Catholic traditionalists; and to such persons his announcement of the end of the Protestant era may well have seemed too much of a flourish, perhaps even disingenuous. Yet the very willingness to relinquish the term Protestant indicated the seriousness of Smyth's conviction that a real break had occurred in history. Historic

---

[64]Mathews, *New Faith for Old*, p. 153. The most adequate analysis of the Federal Council of Churches—and thus of the working out of the federative ideal—is John Hutchison, *We Are Not Divided.*

[65]Mathews, *New Faith for Old*, p. 153; Smyth, *Passing Protestantism*, pp. 24-25.

Protestantism would help shape the future, but it could not itself provide the shape of the future.[66]

Even more surely, however, the "coming Catholicism"—despite Smyth's willingness to use that term—would be unlike the old. Among a number of features that made Smyth's vision a liberal rather than reactionary one, probably the most important was his enthusiastic acceptance of a "mediating modernism" as the key-stone in the structure of reunification. Much depended, in his calculations, upon the success of the Roman Catholic modernists, the men who with varying degrees of radicalism were reworking Catholic doctrine in the light of contemporary historical and scientific knowledge. Two Papal pronouncements in the year 1907, while vigorously condemning this multifaceted movement, had served to publicize and unify the persons admonished and to fix the term "modernism" upon their efforts.

Smyth, though he saw further perils in the way of Catholic modernism, nonetheless believed that this movement was a part of God's plan for the next stage of Christian development. Its eventual success was entirely probable; its more immediate prospering depended upon the election of a "modernized Pope," or at least of a Pope willing to call a General Council to consider the relation of the church to the contemporary world. Though reluctant to predict the timing of such a change, Smyth believed the pressures of "outside" opinion—the pressures of modernity itself—would force the Papacy to allow progressive adjustments. This part, too, of the contemporary crisis was soluble if Christians would use and develop the resources that God seemed plainly to have placed at their disposal.[67]

Catholic modernism, as Smyth saw it, could serve as mentor to Protestantism in two related respects: in its understanding of the historical development of doctrine and in its championing of the organicism that Protestant thinking had lacked. How could

[66]Ibid., pp. 2-3, 8, 10.

[67]Ibid., pp. 40-131, 175-209; John Ratté, *Three Modernists: Alfred Loisy, George Tyrrell, William L. Sullivan* (New York, Sheed and Ward, 1967), pp. 13-19. See also Bernard Reardon, ed., *Roman Catholic Modernism* (Stanford, Calif., Stanford University Press, 1970), pp. 16-52.

Newman Smyth

Christianity find its way back to unity, Smyth asked, through the bewilderment of its creeds? "These Modernists," he suggested, "are learning an answer for us all."

Protestantism may find itself more indebted than we know to those Roman Catholic thinkers and historians for the answer which they have been compelled to discover in order to save the loyalties of their own faith. It is given in their principle of the historical development of the dogmas of the Church.

Protestant scholars, including Smyth and his older brother, had also contributed steadily to the historical reconsideration of dogma. But the Catholic modernists were now integrating this historical approach with their own traditionally organic conception of the church. And the resulting model of ecumenicity would be far more valid and effectual than the mere undenominationalism so often practiced by liberal Protestants.

Apply without hesitation the first principles of organic evolution to the development of the Church and its dogmas, and you will have secured both the integrity and historical continuity of its life, and at the same time the progress and ever renewed adaptations of it to the knowledge and life of the world.[68]

As this implied, Smyth wished to take the creeds of the church, as well as the church itself, more seriously than American liberalism, at least, had been wont to take them. Placing the most positive construction upon creedal relativity, he found all the great creeds valid because they "witness to the true Christian life in the language of each age." Creeds should not be viewed as rubber bands that we stretch to the breaking point, but as "pearls and jewels of diverse colors which are strung together on the same unbroken thread." An ecumenical consensus, then, either among Protestants or among all Christians, would reflect "the orthodoxy not of a single creed, or of a finished formula, but the truth of all Christian creeds which the one Catholic Church rejoices to own."[69]

This sort of solicitude for the creeds had not—despite Bushnell

---

[68]Smyth, *Passing Protestantism*, pp. 169, 171-172. See also his "Wanted: Church Statesmanship," p. 282.

[69]Smyth, *Passing Protestantism*, pp. 169-172.

—been characteristic of the American liberals, but it could be made to harmonize with their more typical attitudes. Indeed, Smyth's kind of broad churchmanship served to keep the way clear for a strong and steady adaptationism. The possibilities in that formula were perhaps best exploited in the later career and thinking of Charles Briggs, who became an Episcopalian in 1898 and who thereafter became increasingly fierce both in support of specific doctrines such as the virgin birth and in support of a catholicity that would enable churchmen to hold differing fierce beliefs. Briggs, as George Park Fisher of Yale once remarked, loved church unity so much that he was "willing at any moment to fight for it."[70] He was able, to the befuddlement of more conventional minds, to berate another accused heretic, A. C. McGiffert of Union Seminary, for not upholding the virgin birth, and at the same time to declare almost complete solidarity with the modernist critique of doctrines. The only significant warfare in Christendom, in fact, as Briggs insisted in his usual military phraseology, pitted modernism against "medievalism," with "Progressive Protestants and Catholic Modernists . . . lined up in the same ranks" on the modernist side.[71]

If the more churchly ecumenists could be accused of simply preaching an older rationalistic adaptationism from more respectable headquarters, they were even more vulnerable to the charge that their professed love of creeds was a way of compromising all specificity of belief. Briggs remarked to Smyth that he would accept as many ordinations as there were churches to give them to him.[72] While he and most other champions of comprehensiveness did feel strongly about certain doctrines, the church they were envisioning could scarcely, it would seem, feel strongly about anything except the principle of comprehensiveness. To Munger's youthful question, "What shall I preach?" Smyth's

---

[70]Smyth, *Recollections*, p. 102.

[71]Coffin, *Half Century*, p. 40; Briggs, *Church Unity*, pp. 438 and 435-442 passim. Briggs had made this point about the broad division in the theological world—though without as yet using the term modernism—as early as 1889. See *Whither?* chap. 9, and especially p. 296. Briggs's incisive summary of the common tenets of Catholic and Protestant modernism appears in *Church Unity*, pp. 439-440.

[72]Smyth, *Recollections*, p. 102.

new church might have to answer: "Everything." Would the coming catholicism be so very different from a federation of churches when it came to standing for something theologically?

The champions of organic union thought such criticism simply reflected a superficial understanding of the church. Even if an actualized new catholicism should resemble a federation, which they doubted it would; even if, contrariwise, the proposed Federal Council of Churches should resemble a church, which they thought was too much to hope; still the difference in starting point was vital. The organic unionists believed that the One Church already exists, and that the problem was to make it visible. It followed that in the agonizingly difficult enterprise of overcoming Christian divisions, one must not handicap oneself by surrendering to assumptions of disunity that are superficially plausible but fundamentally false and wrongheaded.[73]

Whatever the merits and outcome of such arguments, it is fair to say that the organic or churchly stance involved, in Smyth's case as in that of the classic typology of church and sect, a high degree of accommodation to the general culture. It is also clear that Smyth, at this point in his varied career, remained sanguine about the movement of culture and contemporary events.

In *Passing Protestantism* he conveyed with earnestness and obvious conviction the sense of *kairos*, of the pregnant moment, that Paul Tillich would later explore more profoundly. There were negative elements in this view of the world, elements that were to be intensified by the coming of the war and by the later apparent failure of Smyth's efforts toward Congregational-Episcopal union. Though Smyth was a congenitally cheerful and contented man, the picture of the dignified octogenarian pleading

---

[73]Smyth, *Passing Protestantism*, pp. 138-139. The given oneness of the church became the ruling assumption of the movement for Christian reunion in the second quarter of the twentieth century. Peter Gordon Gowing's "Newman Smyth: New England Ecumenist," emphasizes Smyth's importance as a pioneer spokesman for such an assumption. See pp. 2-3, 233. The Smyth papers, in the Yale University Library, are concentrated in the long postretirement career. They show Smyth to have been not only an advocate of church union, but also a prodigious activist and political leader. As Raymond Calkins remarked, "he was a campaigner; he was a soldier." Gowing, "Newman Smyth," p. 79.

for speaking time in the church councils of the early twenties has much the same pathos as the better-known picture of Walter Rauschenbusch mourning the calamity of the war.[74]

But all that was to come. The tone of *Passing Protestantism,* meanwhile, like that of many other liberal works just after 1900, was neither despairing nor "Onward and Upward Forever." It was a tone that spoke of imminent crisis, of providentially ordered possibilities, and of hope that human beings acting freely might yet give Providence the necessary cooperation.

One reason for liberalism's ultimately upbeat response in each of these four areas of external crisis was the fact that the crises *were* external to liberalism and did not involve—at least not explicitly—the challenging or decay of its own premises. A real convergence between perceptions of outward social crises and of liberalism's possible incapacity for meeting them would come only with World War I.

But those later difficulties were foreshadowed in the problems social gospel theorists and liberal activists still seemed to experience in explaining why their social or educational or humanitarian programs required Christianity. This suggested, at the least, a certain fragility in the theological premises.

During the same period—that is, in the quarter-century before the outbreak of World War I—the questioning of liberalism as a religious ideology was indeed developing, both among an opposition consolidating itself as fundamentalism and among liberals who, turning inward, began to question their own most basic assertions with a view to revising them. For the latter, and increasingly for the former, the main question by 1914 would be not—or not merely—whether liberals were reading the Bible correctly, but rather whether they were correctly reading human history and the action of God within it.

---

[74]Ibid., p. 226.

The Emergence of a Critique: Liberalism Under Scrutiny, 1891-1913

To a serious thinker, Modern Liberalism
often seems too jocund for life as it really is.
WILLIAM WALLACE FENN, 1913

If any occurrence in the history of the modernist
impulse can be called entirely predictable, it is
the development of a full-fledged opposition. As
religious liberalism demonstrated strength and
effective institutional expression in the 1890s, conservatives
responded not only by continuing to write and preach in their
accustomed ways, but also by putting their heads and arguments
together for the purposes of direct rebuttal. As liberals, particularly after 1900, addressed various cultural crises from the
theological platform they had so recently established, their opponents of course felt obliged to explain why liberal thought
could not deal either with the new crises or with the older and
recurrent difficulties of human society.

It was also to be expected that as liberalism became established
and in some quarters even a rather old story, the reservations of
its own adherents would become more patterned and would be
more freely voiced. In the early years of the new century, though
such advocates as the men of Union Seminary either were still
embattled or were tending recent wounds, liberalism in some other
places had long since ceased to be on the defensive. The theological crises of Unitarian Harvard and Boston, for example,
barely echoed in the memory of the oldest inhabitant; and that

circumstance, together with avant-garde philosophical tendencies that were affecting both Harvard and Chicago, appears, in those quarters at least, to have tipped a balance in the direction of liberal self-scrutiny. Thus the consolidation of external opposition was paralleled by a deepening and also a readier explication of internal doubts.

Benchmark for Criticism: The Optative Mood in Liberalism

In order to put either of these critiques in perspective, it is necessary to take a closer look at the progressive optimism which still, despite a rising sense of crisis, was the dominant mood among liberals at the turn of the century. When the questioning of liberalism reached a culmination in the early 1930s, John Coleman Bennett remarked that the best short cut to an understanding of the then-current theological situation was "to realize that liberalism diverges from orthodoxy and neo-orthodoxy . . . in its doctrine of man, and that other differences follow from that."[1] The historian must be wary of allowing the preoccupations and urgencies of a later time (either the historian's own time or the 1930s) to shape perceptions of what mattered most to liberals of 1900. Yet it does seem that the critics of the thirties, when they trained their firepower upon optimistic views of human nature and destiny, were examining a genuinely central point in the liberal argument, even if they exaggerated, and even if they examined this issue too much in isolation from other interests.

On the more euphoric flank of the liberal movement stood a few supremely confident celebrants of progress, who, like the prophets of crisis discussed in the previous chapter, gained an appreciable public response and the concurrence of many popular preachers and religious writers. While none of these more optimistic spokesmen admitted to being soft on sin, and none thought progress was assured regardless of the follies human beings might commit, they planted themselves firmly on the sunnier side of the liberal street and refused to be moved either by social or by international upheaval. Lyman Abbott, though he dissociated himself

---

[1]Bennett, "After Liberalism," p. 1403.

from the more jejeune slogans about evil being good-in-the-making, interpreted human sin as an atavism, a reversion to animalism. Henry Churchill King, though a critic of chauvinism and moral complacency, came exceedingly close to a theory of inevitable progress based upon the power that accrues to virtuous action. To the question "whether we may reasonably expect the forces of righteousness finally to prevail" in international affairs, King's answer was that the righteous nation, assuming its virtue to be real and not just latent or rhetorical, cannot fail to be more efficient militarily. Thus, in a world in which war is almost inevitable, the triumph of right and justice is also nearly certain. Still others were able, as Abbott and King were not, to spice their optimism with generous doses of acquiescence in social inequality and a ruthless struggle for existence. Abbott could not accept the "survival of the fittest" as applied to human society; but George Harris, despite disclaimers about fatuous optimism ("I am not so foolish as to claim that the problem of suffering, waste, and cruelty is completely solved"), insisted in two books that "all the native impulses of humanity," including those that result in some people crushing others, "are essential to the making of a man and to the well-being of society."[2]

About midway between this exultant progressivism and the crisis thinking of Rauschenbusch or Smyth stood the reasoned, deeply theological optimism of which George Gordon was the most eloquent spokesman. No one among the liberals wrote more extensively on the theological implications of the idea of progress, and no one else developed so careful a rationale for optimism as an obligation of religious thought and preaching. While it is not possible to say just what balance of moral idealism and moral realism was normative for liberalism, Gordon's comprehensiveness, in the Coleridge-Maurice tradition, meant that he gave voice to attitudes toward culture that cover a fairly wide range within

---

[2]Abbott, *Theology of an Evolutionist*, pp. 45, 31-49, 6-7; King, *Moral and Religious Challenge*, pp. 228-234; Harris, *Moral Evolution*, p. 443; *Inequality and Progress*. For another and very early example of the extreme evolutionary optimism about which later critics made such sport, see Minot Judson Savage, *The Religion of Evolution* (Boston, Lockwood, Brooks, and Company, 1876).

the liberal spectrum. At the same time, since Gordon for about two decades was both the leading preacher of liberalism and one of its two or three most creative theologians, critics were justified in supposing that he spoke for a large part of the movement and its popular constituency.[3]

Gordon once epitomized his own cultural outlook as "optimism founded upon the Divine intention."[4] It was also, as he readily admitted, an optimism founded on seemingly conclusive personal experience. Besides being the sole European immigrant among prewar liberal leaders,[5] Gordon was one of the few who had grown up in relatively impoverished surroundings. His had been one of the unusual American success stories that hucksters for the system liked to suppose were usual. While Gordon neither shared that supposition nor ignored the dangers of construing an individual pilgrimage in universal terms, he did seem deeply to feel that his own progress from a Scottish croft to a pulpit in Copley Square must be a figure for the progress of the race.

The more others doubted the reality of progress, the more plaintively Gordon protested that the doubters simply could not know, as he could, how terrible man's past has been. "Is human progress a delusion?" he asked a few years after World War I, or is the prayer of Christians for the coming of God's Kingdom a "reasonable exercise of the human mind? Is there such a thing as the reign of God in the souls of men?"

As the calm affirmations of progress rolled out in the course of that sermon, so did the persistently Scottish metaphors of the life that the human race allegedly had left behind:

You have been in Holyrood Palace in Edinburgh, and you have visited the apartments of Royal Mary Stuart, and you are aware that you could not get a self-respecting mechanic in all of Scotland today to live under those conditions. You have seen the little cottage in which Robert

---

[3]Gordon's production of twelve books is not greatly above the average for liberal theologians; but there are at least one hundred more separate publications —mainly sermons and addresses—listed in the Harvard Library catalogue, and Gordon also published extensively in popular magazines.

[4]*Ultimate Conceptions*, p. 135.

[5]D. C. Macintosh and Shirley Jackson Case were Canadians. For further data, see Hutchison, "Cultural Strain," pp. 408-409.

Burns was born one hundred and sixty-six years ago this very day; there
is not a peasant in Scotland who would live in such a hovel today . . .
There is not a valley, a dark and dangerous road, a cliff-shadowed walk,
a glen or byway in Scotland that has not a history of brigandage,
savagery and pillage compared with which our hold-ups of today are
child's play. We are pessimists because we do not know.[6]

The pessimist was also a person who had failed to grasp the
moral obligation of optimism. Gordon, though apparently far
less afflicted by spiritual and psychological stress than his mentor
and friend William James, nonetheless had appropriated James's
conception of a Will-to-Believe that can remake circumstances and
that must therefore be maintained in spite of circumstances.[7] Thus
in Gordon's writings one is confronted with an acute sense of
human limitation—present as well as past—that would make it
questionable to say he minimized human sinfulness; yet also with
a vision of the continuities of progress that seems to rule out even
the conceptualizing of a crisis in current affairs.

Gordon delimited the principle of optimism by first of all
recognizing the close connections between personal experience
and moral outlook. "It seems ignoble," he wrote, "but it is nevertheless true, that personal fortune in this world has much to do
with the optimistic and pessimistic moods in which men view the
universe." To be sure, one could find exceptions. History records
the serenity of Epictetus the slave, the misery of the emperor Nero,
the trustfulness of Christ on the Cross, the fearfulness of Pilate.
But in general, he said, few men climb to such summits of intellectual disinterestedness and moral heroism that they are able to
regard the universe in the light of pure reason.[8]

Presumably this was a way of recognizing not only that one's
own optimism may be suspect but also that the despair of others
should be discounted. Yet Gordon could understand the objective
provocations to despair. He found in the dolour of James Thomson's "City of Dreadful Night"—a poem he much admired—

---

[6]Gordon, *New Epoch*, pp. 213-220; *Jesus and the Individual*, pp. 13, 18, 21-22.
[7]Cushing Strout, "The Pluralistic Identity of William James: A Psycho-
Historical Reading of 'The Varieties of Religious Experience,'" *American Quarterly*, 23 (May 1971), 135-152; Gordon, *Ultimate Conceptions*, p. 213.
[8]*New Epoch*, pp. 213-217.

"the only adequate voice for a large section of the experience of human beings in the nineteenth century." Thomson's alcoholism and personal tragedy undoubtedly had affected the poet's outlook; but Gordon thought it would be folly to understand that outlook, personal tragedy and all, "as other than sadly representative." The gap between human aspiration and individual or social reality was enormous, and despair about this gap could not sensibly be set down as idiosyncratic.[9]

Gordon's essay in *The New Epoch for Faith* on "the discipline of doubt" offered one of the most appreciative and least condescending treatments of nineteenth-century skepticism that was to appear among the religious writings of Gordon's generation. Ignoring easy targets in popular agnosticism or fanatical atheism, Gordon surveyed the scientifically based skepticism of Huxley; the magnificent literary expressions of doubt in Arnold and Tennyson; the philosophic streams flowing from Hume and Kant. These traditions were not of merely cautionary value, nor was submission to them just a discipline through which the very conscientious pass on the way to faith. On the contrary, skepticism in Gordon's view actually destroys what needs to be destroyed. It uncovers and cultivates the solid truth of things by removing "the loose rubbish heap of tradition, covered up by accumulations of superstition, false opinion, inadequate notions, superficial, distorted, and incredible interpretations."[10]

The anomalies and evils to which skepticism points cannot, moreover, be set down as atavisms. Man's so-called "animal nature," he argued, should not be loaded down with the essential blame for what has gone wrong with mankind. Equally culpable is the vaunted human reason that rationalizes the most brutish of human activities. "The idealizing faculty," Gordon wrote, "has been to a painful extent the organ of human selfishness." And the human will is the most derelict agency of all:

Until he has recognized . . . the force of sheer perversity, the reformer has not measured the strength of his enemy . . . The pious dreams that

---

[9]Ibid., p. 219.
[10]Ibid., pp. 200-203, 245, and 183-245 passim.

see no perverse will in the way of human progress are the worst kind of wild-cat currency.

All three of these causes of personal evil—animalism, ignorance, and perversity—gain new force, Gordon explained, as they come to be expressed through institutions: "The evil in men's hearts has gained immense influence through expression in custom, law, government. Inhumanity has fortified itself in the institutions of trade, society, politics, and religion."[11]

Given such extensive and ingrained faults in human nature and society one could not, Gordon said, "define the issue of earthly history. It had a beginning; some time it may have an end. What the history of man upon this planet will be when the record is complete, it is impossible even to guess." This was one important reason why he thought belief in a just God implied belief in a future life and even in a future probation. Christ asked men to be perfect. "Than that ideal there could be nothing more hopeless or absurd if for man there is no history beyond this world."[12]

Reinhold Niebuhr, prime theological spokesman for a generation that largely repudiated modernism, would warn in the 1940s that "history moves toward the realization of the Kingdom but yet the judgment of God is upon every new realization."[13] Gordon could have agreed to that formula, even with the word "judgment" in it. Yet the differences between what the two men were saying were far from negligible. In comparing such thinkers one finds sober truth in the old witticism about optimists who call bottles half full and pessimists who call them half empty. "No, but . . ." and "Yes, but . . ." may each preface a balanced estimate of the elements of glory and degradation in humanity, yet still express important differences of temperament and of historical and polemical context. While Niebuhr's principal word to his generation would be the necessity of a corrective moral

---

[11]Ibid., pp. 37-39, 41-42, 43.

[12]Gordon, *Ultimate Conceptions*, pp. 249, 250. See also his *Immortality and the New Theodicy*, pp. 83-86, 92-93; *New Epoch*, pp. 382-383; *Ultimate Conceptions*, p. 217.

[13]Niebuhr, *Nature and Destiny*, II, 286.

realism, Gordon's overriding message was the moral necessity of optimism. His negations and hesitancies served, in context, as preludes to larger affirmations; and Gordon's affirmations, unlike Niebuhr's, formed the ideological base for his popular reputation.

Gordon, after all concessions to realism, took his stand upon the assertion that the universe is ultimately favorable to man. Tension surely exists, he acknowledged, between man and the cosmos. "There is no procedure more insane than the attempt to reconcile man's world with the worlds beneath him." Humanity is not "the simple pulling out of another part of the cosmic telescope." But he could see no such hostility between natural and moral progress as that which Thomas Huxley had depicted in his famous Romanes Lecture of 1893. Affirmation and optimism were necessary attitudes because of the self-fulfilling potentialities of the will either to believe or to disbelieve. But they also were possible, credible attitudes—made so by what practical experience and cosmic theory, in collaboration, had proved in the course of the nineteenth century.[14]

Gordon was willing to assert that "upon the whole, history is the record of the defeat of inhumanity." But he rested the empirical case very heavily upon what he liked to call the "uncontradicted experience" of the nineteenth century. Like the earliest New Theologians, he argued that the nineteenth had been the century in which mankind had become not Christian, but truly ready for Christianity. Although Gordon never unambiguously predicted the extirpation of evil from human society, his *New Epoch for Faith*, a book much caught up in the enthusiasm of the opening century, came extremely close at some points to just such a prediction. "Thus much the new vista of history seems to make good," Gordon wrote "—that injustice and inhumanity

---

[14]Gordon, *Ultimate Conceptions*, p. 325; Thomas H. Huxley, *Evolution and Ethics and Other Essays* (New York, D. Appleton and Co., 1896), pp. 46-116. For the antihumanism of Augustine, Calvin, and Edwards, Gordon found "palliating circumstances" in their terror-filled surroundings. Today there could be "no valid excuse" for similar slanders upon God's justice. *Immortality and the New Theodicy*, pp. 73-75. See also *New Epoch*, pp. 358-361.

are not here to stay. The moral evil of society is among things temporal."[15]

Human existence is not purely temporal, in Gordon's view, and neither will human fulfillment be temporal, whether it is achieved in an afterlife or in an earthly coming of God's Kingdom. His humanism at its most sanguine worked within that understanding. But Gordon did, after all qualifications are counted, stand for conceptions of humanity and human culture as infused with divinity and moving toward a divine event called perfection.

External Criticism: Biblical Revelation vs. Cultural Revelation

Most of the outside response to liberalism in the years around 1900 dealt only lightly and indirectly with issues in the philosophy of history or with the liberals' relative optimism about human progress. Among the theologians and academics as well as in popular consciousness the immediate fight concerned the reliability of the biblical record and the immutability of the creeds built upon it. And yet, the more seriously the conservatives took their task—and their antagonists—the more clearly they saw that mere reassertions of the finality of biblical revelation would not suffice, that the counterclaims for a cultural revelation must be answered directly.

After 1890, as before, the responses to liberalism often fail to fall neatly into denominational or other patterns. One certainly finds in the religious press a general consciousness of opposing ideologies and parties; the writers know there is a liberal movement and know what it stands for. But among two dozen religious journals and approximately 100 different reviewers, only about half can be said to have followed a strict denominational or party line. Reviewers even for the journals of very conservative denominations appear often to have been left free to treat individual liberal works on their own merits.[16]

---

[15]*Ultimate Conceptions*, p. 185; *New Epoch*, pp. 384-386, 104, 361, and 357-373 passim. See also *Ultimate Conceptions*, pp. 188, 239, 322-327; and *Witness to Immortality*, p. 274.

[16]The generalizations made here are based upon a search for reviews of 21

Still, denominations do select editors, and editors choose reviewers. Strong group attitudes and recurrent themes of approval or criticism are therefore discernible in much of the periodical literature. At the consistently approving end of the spectrum stood the *Independent*; Lyman Abbott's *Outlook*; and the *Biblical World*, the most important American vehicle of the Higher Criticism. At the other end, alone and quite unapproached in either consistency or quality, stood the theological journal of Princeton Seminary, in which nothing was ever uncertain except a constantly changing name.[17]

Although most other periodicals were ranged between these two positions, one important set of journals falls entirely outside the spectrum. These were the journals of the Unitarians. The Unitarians were nearly as critical of the New Theology as Princeton was, but of course for reasons the opposite of Princeton's. The *New World*, successor to the *Unitarian*, tried to maintain an open and catholic stance, but the *Christian Register* reflected a self-conscious denominational attitude made up of approval, indulgence, and, not infrequently, condescension. In 1892 the *Register* greeted Newman Smyth's *Christian Ethics* as an encouraging sign that the orthodox were finally taking an interest in the ethical teachings of Christ, but at the same time regretted that Smyth had obscured the simplicity of Christianity by clinging to outmoded

---

outstanding liberal publications, from Stearns's *Present-Day Theology* in 1891 through Borden Bowne's *Personalism* in 1908. Frank Luther Mott estimates there were about 1,000 religious periodicals of all kinds at any one time in the years around 1900. I worked from a select list of about 40 publications representing the denominations and nondenominational religious life between 1890 and 1910, and found reviews of one or more of these liberal works in 24 of them. Eighteen of the publications carried two or more reviews, and therefore account for the largest part (126 out of 132) of the reviews located. The six journals containing the most reviews also, fortunately, provide an excellent spectrum of consistently voiced theological opinions. From most liberal to most conservative these journals are: *The Outlook* (11 reviews), *Biblical World* (8), *Hartford Seminary Record* (12), *Bibliotheca Sacra* (13), *American Journal of Theology* (in its preliberal phase) (12), and *Presbyterian Review* (11).

[17]The title before 1880 had been *Princeton Review*. From 1880 to 1889, both a *Princeton Review* and a *Presbyterian Review* were published. These combined in 1890 as *Presbyterian and Reformed Review*, and then continued from 1903 to 1929 as *Princeton Theological Review*. (The present-day successor is called, refreshingly, *Theology Today*.)

doctrinal assumptions. The *Register*'s reviewer thought George Harris' *Moral Evolution* (1896), while it was a fine book, harbored the ghost of Calvinist determinism. And Clarke's *Outline of Christian Theology* (1898), drew the barbed remark that "it is interesting to see how cheerfully positions are abandoned which but a little while ago were held as absolutely essential."[18]

At the middle of the spectrum, the most mixed responses were those of the Lutheran, Baptist, Methodist, and Reformed publications. Lutherans, probably because of a continuing relative isolation, remained detached and rather indulgent on most of the issues raised by the liberal writers, but at the same time became especially upset when a liberal pronouncement touched the quick of sectarian sensitivities. The *Lutheran Quarterly Review* applauded Rauschenbusch's *Christianity and the Social Crisis* except where Rauschenbusch contrasted Calvin and Luther, to the disadvantage of the latter, in social outlook. Newman Smyth's *Passing Protestantism* offended the *Lutheran Church Review* by its expressed regret that the "sudden lightning bolt of Luther's Reformation" had frustrated a more gradual and less divisive process of reform. And the *Quarterly Review* took Smyth to task for proposing that the Episcopal church, rather than the Lutheran, was likely to be the mediating force in the coming new catholicism.

Methodist reviewers, showing less sectarian defensiveness, voiced objections to liberalism whenever men like Abbott appeared to accommodate Christianity to Darwinian science, but little resistance when the issue was the Social Gospel. Baptists, without a reviewing vehicle after the demise of the *Baptist Quarterly Review* in 1890, reentered the discussion with a voice generally friendly to liberalism when the *Review and Expositor* was established in 1904.[19]

---

[18]Since all reviews have been identified in table B in the Appendix, footnote references to them will be given only in cases where the length of the review makes it desirable to specify the page from which a quotation was drawn.

[19]The *Review and Expositor*, published by the Southern Baptists, showed more indulgence toward liberal writers than the usual image of that denomination would lead one to expect. Though its reviewers condemned the work of George B. Foster, the radical Baptist theologian of Chicago, they placed Rauschenbusch's work of 1907 second only to the Bible as a manual of social reform.

The German Reformed Church, as represented by successor publications to the famous *Mercersburg Review*, responded more favorably to liberal writings than did any other in this group of evangelical bodies. Their unsigned review of *Jesus Christ and the Social Question*, by the Unitarian Francis Peabody, was one among many indications that the Mercersburg men had been moving to the left both socially and theologically. The review criticized Peabody for directing his gospel of regeneration too much to "poor and unfortunate sinners and not enough to the rich and prosperous sinners." And it faulted this Unitarian spokesman for insufficient immanentism, for locating Jesus' social teachings too much in the New Testament utterances and too little in the "present and ever-living spirit" of Christ.

Also divided in their reactions, but more analytic and substantially more negative or querulous, were a group of impressive scholarly journals consisting of the *Andover Review* in its final years, the Chicago *American Journal of Theology*, the powerful *Bibliotheca Sacra* published at Oberlin, and the *Hartford Seminary Record*. Though an enlarged tolerance for liberalism is detectable in this group after 1905—most noticeably in the *American Journal of Theology*—before 1905 they represented a fairly consistent uneasiness about the Christology, the commitment to evolution, the attitude toward miracles, and, so far as the *Andover Review* was concerned, the socialist tendencies in liberal thought.

The most consistent or consolidated answers to liberalism in these years appeared in *The Fundamentals*, the twelve volumes of essays published by the Testimony Publishing Company between 1910 and 1915; and in the theological journals of Princeton Seminary. While the second of these sources is far richer than one might expect, the first is less so. The essays in *The Fundamentals* were not generally rancorous or shrill, as so much popular fundamentalism came to be in the 1920s. But neither did they directly engage most of the principal issues the liberals were raising. *The Fundamentals* were designed as straightforward "testimonies to the truth," and that objective seems to have precluded their being detailed responses-in-kind to liberal writings, even though in the broadest sense the combatting of liberalism was what the fundamentalist enterprise was all about.[20]

Only a small proportion of the ninety articles in *The Fundamentals* attacked particular liberals or specific liberal doctrines with any degree of explicitness. Among those that did, the largest number assailed the Higher Criticism of the Bible. Others accused liberals of minimizing the virgin birth, the deity of Christ, the seriousness of sin, the justice of divine punishment, or the miraculous effect of Christ's atoning death. Still others directed their attacks more generally against modern philosophy, worldly learning, evolutionary and materialist thought, and liberal over-adjustment as allegedly shown, for example, in the secularizing of the Sabbath.[21]

Taking the few explicitly antimodernist essays of *The Fundamentals* together with the many that are implicitly so, one can venture to summarize what this sector of the opposition was saying. In response to Higher Criticism, the repetitive, somewhat frenzied, yet simple assurance offered by the fundamentalist writers was "Not Proven." Evolutionary thought and the "assured results" of modern science, though the attention devoted to these in *The Fundamentals* was minor compared with the attention given to biblical criticism, drew the same objection. "You need not be intimidated," the writers said in effect, "by all these 'assured results.' We too have doctorates. We have access to scholarship. And we can tell you that the scientific evidence is incomplete, contradictory, sometimes absurd, as well as impious." By the methods of the higher critics, one writer asserted, it would be possible to throw doubt on the historicity not only of Jesus Christ but also of Theodore Roosevelt.[22]

The Fundamentals, for all their relative gentility and partly because of it, remained at two removes from any grappling with

---

[20]*The Fundamentals: A Testimony to the Truth.* Contrasts in tone between the fundamentalism of the original pamphlets and the popular fundamentalism of the twenties are noted in Sandeen, *Roots of Fundamentalism*, pp. 188-207; and Carter, "Fundamentalist Defense," pp. 179-214.

[21]See *The Fundamentals*, I: article 1; II: 3, 4, and 5; III: 4; IV: 3; VI: 3 and 7; VII: 1; VIII: 2; IX: 3; X: 1 and 4; XI: 2; XII: 5.

[22]John L. Nuelson, "The Person and Work of Jesus Christ," in *The Fundamentals*, VI, 103-105.

the roots of modernism. If men like Gordon were to be taken seriously, if because of their success they were dangerous and had to be taken seriously, then conservatives would need to enter more explicitly into doctrinal discussion with liberalism and, beyond that, would need to develop a critique of the liberal philosophy of history. Whether *The Fundamentals* took even the first of these steps is questionable; the tendency of the doctrinal essays is to labor to prove simply that a given doctrine in fact is biblical. The second step, the questioning of the liberal philosophy of history, they did not attempt except in the most general, out-of-hand way.

Whether the lack of dialogue with liberalism reflected the intent of the sponsors or the uneven abilities of the writers—and most interpreters, I think, will conclude that it was both—it helped insure that *The Fundamentals* would be virtually ignored in those sectors of the theological community that might otherwise have been expected to respond. Despite the emphasis among writers for the series upon biblical criticism (the one issue on which they did meet the liberals on their own ground), liberal journals like the *Biblical World* seem to have paid no attention whatever.[23] More surprisingly, the reaction even of conservative journals to the massive and at least quasi-scholarly effort of *The Fundamentals* was a virtual silence. Wave upon wave of these free booklets went out—probably three million copies in all—over a five-year period; but only a half-dozen of the leading journals reviewed them, and these reviewed only one or two of the twelve volumes.

It would be possible to make too much of a stand-offishness that the fundamentalists themselves would have explained as mere *hauteur* on the part of the academic theological establishment. But it is also possible that the alliance between scholarly and popular versions of fundamentalism was less viable, even temporarily, than has been supposed.[24] The *Princeton Theological Review* seems quite definitely to have joined in the general

---

[23]Cf. Sandeen, *Roots of Fundamentalism*, p. 199.

[24]I believe Sandeen has overestimated the success and effectiveness of the *mariage de convenience* between Princeton and the Bible-Conference conserva-

indifference to *The Fundamentals*. William B. Greene of Princeton welcomed volume one, and Caspar Wistar Hodge mentioned the existence of volume three; but both reviews, the second of which was utterly noncommital, were perfunctory 150-word notices that contrasted blatantly with the extensive essays that Princeton lavished on nearly every liberal work.[25]

Despite new attention to the Princeton theology in recent scholarship,[26] the singular force, consistency, and importance of this conservative ideology have still, probably, received less than their due. As the preceding discussion suggests, the critique of liberal doctrine elsewhere, even in the most serious and intellectually impressive journals, was marked either by a highly selective approach (for example among Lutheran writers) to the issues raised by liberalism; or else by the varied uncertainties of old liberalisms grown conservative (*Bibliotheca Sacra* and *Andover Review*), old dogmatisms grown tolerant (Hartford), or strong theological positions that had become severely attenuated (Mercersburg). The inspired obstinacy of the Hodges, Pattons, and Warfields, and later of John Gresham Machen, shone in marked, self-conscious contrast with all such flickering lights.

Book reviews offer a limited picture of Princeton's reaction to liberalism, but it is a revealing one. The editors seem to have been able to call upon a stable of orthodox reviewers of very marked theological and literary abilities, chiefly from outside the seminary

---

tives. That relationship might well be investigated more thoroughly, particularly through further scrutiny of the personal papers of the Princeton theologians during the period of *The Fundamentals*.

[25]*Princeton Theological Review*, 9 (January 1911), 130-131; 10 (January 1912), 122. Benjamin Warfield, William and Charles Erdman, Robert E. Speer, and a few others identified with Princeton Seminary contributed to *The Fundamentals*. But on the whole Princetonians were notable for their absence. Speer and Charles Erdman, moreover, contributed two of the most nearly liberal articles to appear in the series. In Speer's essay on missions, several quotations were printed without attribution, though not without quotation marks. Since Speer in other instances did name his sources, one suspects it was the editors who removed the attributions. Speer, to their embarrassment, was quoting from William Newton Clarke. See Speer, "Foreign Missions or World-Wide Evangelism," *Fundamentals*, XII, 64-84; Erdman, "The Church and Socialism," ibid., 108-119.

[26]For able accounts, see Sandeen, *Roots of Fundamentalism*, pp. 114-131; and Ahlstrom, "Theology in America," pp. 260-266.

faculty; and their lengthy, courteous antiliberal essays poured out, through these years, as mighty waves of sound from the same well-planned orchestration. Their central theme was one that would reach a culmination and gain greater popular expression some years later in Machen's *Christianity and Liberalism*. The realistic, if sometimes disingenuous, message of Princeton was that while liberalism and modernism were attractive, perfectly respectable religious systems that good men might choose—some of one's best friends were liberals—they were also systems that should stop claiming the name and sanction of Christianity.

The reviews ranged in severity from a respectful citing of theological defects in Gordon, to Greene's opinion that the work of George Burman Foster was so radical and absurd that it constituted its own refutation. Yet the same, unvarying demand for a choice ran through all of these articles. It was not the revivalist's proferred choice between God and the devil; the Princeton writers were not so crude as to intimate that liberals conspired with the devil. It was, in their minds, a choice between Christianity and a well-intended, quite inadequate humanism. One must begin, they said, either by accepting a revelation, which to them meant scriptural revelation, or by consulting the "Christian consciousness of the age." The latter was what they insisted the liberals were invariably doing; and they thought the result, whatever else it might be, was not a Christian theology.

The Princeton writers never admitted to any lack of sensitivity to contemporary science or thought. They were willing, in fact, to acknowledge the necessity of a certain degree of theological adaptation. George S. Patton, who reviewed Harris' *Moral Evolution* in 1897, rejected the theological implications of Darwinism, yet claimed to support the right and necessity of seeking accommodations between Christianity and culture:

Let it be understood that we do not criticize Dr. Harris for his desire to reconcile Christianity with the dominant thought of the age. The human mind is so constituted that it is constrained to seek consistency; the harmonizing tendency is most logical and natural.

But Patton (who was Francis Patton's eldest son) had made a more sweeping concession at that point than the Princetonians of his father's generation could condone. Benjamin Warfield, Charles Hodge's most notable successor as a theological scholar, scorned adaptation as a weak-kneed and lethargic submission to the fads of the moment. Reviewing David Beach's *The Newer Religious Thinking*, Warfield complained that the chief characteristic of this new thinking was "its confounding temporary drifts of thought with progress in thought; its practical acceptance of the Carlylean doctrine that whatever is at any time dominant is right."[27]

That, said Warfield, was what the liberals' prized "comprehensiveness" really meant. It was a weariness of "thinking, distinguishing, defending." It reflected a listless desire to melt all types of thought into one "structureless, homogeneous mass." Here Warfield gave expression to an especially interesting and persistent dimension of the Princeton rhetoric of choice, namely the appeal to a kind of theological *machismo*, a virile contempt for all weak, spineless, compromising systems of quasi-belief. The contempt showed when Warfield used quotation marks to scoff at liberals like Beach as "thinkers" in self-evaluation only, and hurled at them the dreadful word "invertebrate." (In refraining from using a more colorful term such as, say, "jellyfish" he illustrated one important distinction between the Warfields and the Billy Sundays of American conservative religion.)[28]

Instead of fuming, as did so many writers for *The Fundamentals*, about the inconclusiveness of liberal scholarship, Princeton appeared to acknowledge scholarly inconclusiveness on both sides, but then to drive to a deeper level and demand a choice, as a matter of faith, between differing premises of scholarship. Thus, to Daniel Gregory, Newman Smyth's ethical system was "not the

---

[27]Patton, in *Presbyterian and Reformed Review*, 8 (July 1897), 540; Warfield, ibid., 5 (January 1894), 188.

[28]Ibid. Billy Sunday's contrasting mode of expression is illustrated in the following: "Lord save us from off-handed, flabby-cheeked, brittle-boned, weak-kneed, thin-skinned, pliable, plastic, spineless, effeminate, ossified three-karat Christianity." Quoted in McLoughlin, *Billy Sunday*, p. 175. While claims of superior intellectual virility were especially strong in the Princeton rhetoric, they were also to be found among liberals, as the account above (chapter 2) of David Swing illustrates, and as the rhetoric of Theodore Parker also makes plain. See Hutchison, *Transcendentalist Ministers*, p. 117.

Christian ethics needed for these times," because in the last analysis it appealed to these times for the foundation principles of ethics. Supposedly, "love" as embodied in Christ formed the groundwork of Smyth's ethics. "In reality, however," Gregory said, "the Christian consciousness of the present age, as interpreted by the author . . . is made the final arbiter of duty." Smyth's theory gave its adherents "an apparent claim to Biblical authority, while actually making another authority, Christian faith in its latest evolution, the supreme arbiter of ethical principles." Dorner in Germany, Briggs and Smyth and others in America, were seeking, Gregory said, to enthrone the scriptures and the religious feeling as coordinate and equal authorities, but they were failing because they were not really willing to let the Bible have even this much of a voice in any final adjudication. "When the Bible and Christian faith come into apparent conflict," such liberals merely "refuse to formulate a doctrine on that point." However plain the scriptural statement might be, the liberals will not recognize it "unless the Christian consciousness also teaches the same thing."

One cannot have it both ways, Gregory insisted. The student of morals, and also society at large, must make a fundamental decision:

Is morality to be judged by the plain revelation of Christ; or by the finished product of evolution? If by the latter, who is to decide between Spencer and Smyth and all the rest? Does it ultimately rest on Christ's authority in the Word; or on the changing, evolving, and often contradictory dicta of the so-called Christian consciousness? Are we at anchor, or at sea?[29]

For the liberals, of course, the simple presumption that Matthew, Mark, "and all the rest" provide a sufficient anchoring for ethics had been invalidated by modern biblical criticism. But one might share their doubts about biblicism and still, like some humanists in the 1920s,[30] find Princeton's demand for choice a source of relief in the weary land of theological equivocation. Gregory, providing

---

[29]Daniel S. Gregory, in *Presbyterian and Reformed Review*, 5 (April 1894), 350-353.
[30]See Lippmann, *Preface to Morals*, pp. 30-35.

a gloss upon Charles Hodges' notorious boast that no new idea had ever originated at Princeton, thundered that "Christ's ethical principles have never changed, and will never change. They will never be accommodated to human society or development; but must shape that society and development if it is not to end in decay and destruction. The Christian will continue to prefer Christ to Dorner and Smyth."[31]

Again and again the theme was repeated. The dreaded agnosticism of George B. Foster was taken as an object lesson in the perils of trying to make doctrine the product instead of the necessary condition of the Christian life. The more acceptable modernism of Shailer Mathews was called defective because Mathews tended to see real religion and doctrine as antithetical. Princeton, through George Patton, could clasp George Harris' Darwinian social theory to its bosom, but Harris' contention that evolutionary thought implied necessary changes in Christian doctrine would not do at all. The mere mention of such an interpretation provoked Patton to a forceful, if casuistic, corrective statement to the effect that while Christian doctrine had of course elevated man's moral consciousness, the reverse cannot be true. The idea that the dialogue continues, that an elevated human consciousness has some effect on formulations of the faith, needed, as Patton wrote with almost an audible clearing of the throat, "some elucidation."[32]

Patton would go as far as to acknowledge that the moral ideals derived from Christian belief have, in their turn, "modified and clarified" theology. Yet certain doctrines—those "concerning the Fatherhood of God, the person, character, and teaching of Christ, the kingdom of God, and immortality"—are in principle unchangeable and cannot be touched by a new moral consciousness of whatever derivation. Progress in theology can therefore mean no more than "that we may gradually enter into clearer understanding and truer interpretation of the teachings of the Scriptures." It cannot mean that doctrines are to be "modified, changed,

---

[31]*Presbyterian and Reformed Review*, 5 (April 1894), 353.
[32]Ibid., 8 (July 1897), 537.

revolutionized, so as to bring them into accord with the fancied demands of the ethical Zeitgeist."[33]

Patton rose to his peroration with a style and cadence highly reminiscent of his father's appeal to the invertebrates of the Chicago Presbytery two decades earlier:

> Let us be honest with ourselves. Let us face the question whether Christianity is a supernatural religion or not, whether it is from heaven or of men, whether it is the absolute religion or simply the purest form of religion that has yet appeared in the developmental history. If the former be true, then there is still need, as there always has been need, of a Christian apologetic. But if we believe the latter, let us give up the old terminology and the old method of defending the faith. And when we have given up the God-man Christ Jesus, and the miracles He wrought, and His resurrection from the dead, and His atonement for sin, then at least, if not before, let us pause and ask, as Strauss asked long ago, whether we are still Christians.[34]

The reviews coming out of Princeton, as the latter part of this utterance may suggest, supported their central contention with an entire litany of particular doctrinal objections to liberalism. A lengthy complaint by Thomas Nichols against Stearns's voluntarism was the work of a man who had not yet reconciled himself to a much earlier revision of Calvinism by Nathaniel Taylor and the so-called New Haven theology. The writer seemed a throwback even in a Princeton publication. But when Nichols also charged the liberals with minimizing sin, he assayed a kind of criticism that was to sound increasingly "modern" as allegedly civilized human societies in succeeding decades used their free will to make primitively evil choices. The Calvinist, said Nichols, is perfectly ready to match liberals text for text, either in the Bible or in the book of experience. If experience teaches the love of God, it also reveals "the love in the heart for all within itself that is alien to the character of God, and that lies at the root of evil choices." Such, he pointed out, is the testimony of the greatest saints, whose consciousness of sin always seemed to grow in proportion to their own apparent growth in likeness to Christ.[35]

---

[33]Ibid., p. 538.
[34]Ibid., p. 540.
[35]Ibid., 5 (October 1894), 738.

Along the same line, Daniel Gregory pointed out that Smyth had illustrated the fallacies in the liberal doctrine of God by making God's goodness rather than his righteousness the foundation of ethics. Correspondingly, Smyth had made happiness instead of righteousness the chief end of man. Nichols and Patton both expatiated upon liberal Christology, which according to Patton made Jesus the "son of God only in the sense in which we are all sons of God, except that He was in closer communion . . . and better understood the divine nature."[36]

James Good wrote appreciatively of Clarke's *Outline of Christian Theology* as "the clearest statement of the new theology that can be found in English." But among the consequences of liberalism that were clear to this reviewer were a fading into the evolutionary haze of any doctrine of creation; a renunciation of the doctrine of the two natures of Christ; a complete moralizing of the atonement; a subjectivizing of justification; and a virtual evacuation of meaning from the doctrine of election—which, he said, becomes the choosing of individuals to earthly service instead of their ordination to an eternal destiny.[37]

The proposals for Christian education coming from George A. Coe and Shailer Mathews looked to the Princeton writers like excellent examples of the chronic liberal failure to distinguish between Christianity and religion-in-general. Mathews' proposals for broadened seminary curricula made sense, William Greene said, only if one should decide that the Bible is not a supernatural revelation. And Henry C. Minton complained, with increasing exasperation, that Coe had removed creeds and catechisms from the Sunday school in favor of the Bible, and then had minimized the Bible in favor of "religion." "Just exactly what is it," Minton asked pleadingly, "that is to be studied in the Sunday-school?"

Indeed, we are warned to be very careful about having children memorize Scripture . . . We had supposed this time-honored and heaven-blessed custom innocent enough, but alas! it must go. While an unfriendly criticism would fain cut away our Bible, is a friendly pedagogy to warn

---

[36]Ibid., 8 (July 1897), 539.
[37]Ibid., 9 (April 1898), 354-356.

us not to have our children store their memories with what little Bible the critics are constrained to leave us?[38]

Queries from Within: The Undermining of Idealism and Humanism

The biblical literalism of *The Fundamentals* and of Princeton Seminary probably changed few minds among the liberals. It was destined, indeed, to be challenged and then defeated even at Princeton during the 1920s. Yet wherever the Princeton writers complained about the humanism and the alleged semantic vacillations of the liberal theology, or saw inadequacies in its outlook on human history, Princeton had entered into at least a partial dialogue with expressions of doubt arising within liberalism itself. By the second decade of the twentieth century, countercurrents inside the movement were quite apparent—not just in the various acknowledgments of precariousness and crisis, but in heightened discomfiture with idealistic philosophy and the traditional theism, and in a direct querying of the progressive attitude toward human history.

The American reaction against philosophical idealism, whether or not it found its major stimuli outside the classroom of the technical philosopher, certainly found cognate, highly supportive expressions in that broader ambience.[39] Reformers in one area of American thought after another were seeking to combat a formalism that at this particular stage of history had embodied itself, allegedly, in the cool, ordered Greek temples of a nonfunctional architecture and psychology, a literature and painting hamstrung by classical rules and the *Beaux-Arts*, and a remote Platonic idealism infecting various sectors of the academy. Louis Sullivan, the architectural reformer, urged the Young Turks in his profession to disdain the Gothic and other supposedly irrelevant styles as well as the classical revival. But the classical modes, par-

---

[38]Ibid., 6 (January 1895), 169-171; 3 (April 1892), 306-309.

[39]In the now considerable literature descriptive of the broad value-changes in American intellectual life at this time, Henry May's *The End of American Innocence* provides the most thorough analysis. For a brief and especially sensitive discussion of this historiography and of the dynamics of cultural reversal, see Paul F. Bourke, "The Social Critics and the End of American Innocence, 1907-1921," *Journal of American Studies*, 3 (July 1969), 57-61.

ticularly after the Columbian Exposition of 1893, had become the major target. "There is a certain grim, ghastly humor in it all," Sullivan remarked:

libraries that might be mistaken for banks, hospitals that might be taken for libraries, department stores that might be taken for hotels; a Doric column proposed as a memorial to the hardy American pioneer; the suggestion to transform the city of Washington into an American Rome, and to make of the Potomac an American Tiber. The suggestion in general that if anything in particular is to be done it shall be done in the most unnatural way.[40]

"Grim, ghastly humor" may seem a bit strong as a response to Doric columns. But it was at least ironic that the fresh, clean, "honest" expressions of earlier cultural rebirths had now apparently come to represent senescence.[41] Philosophical idealism was perhaps the most notorious illustration of this melancholy process. Idealism, once the philosophy of antiformalism, of Emerson's newborn bards of the Holy Ghost, now in its numerous academic variants had come to represent not only formalism but a kind of scholasticism that seemed utterly remote from the everyday concerns of real people. By the 1890s, therefore, the new Emersons preaching immediacy of experience were blaming a rigidified idealism for what they perceived as a dangerous separation between thought and life. "The world of concrete personal experiences," William James told students, "is multitudinous beyond imagination, tangled, muddy, painful and perplexed." Yet the world presented in most philosophy classrooms, James said, was

simple, clean, and noble. The contradictions of real life are absent from it. Its architecture is classic. Principles of reason trace its outlines, logical necessities cement its parts. Purity and dignity are what it most expresses. It is a kind of marble temple shining on a hill . . . It is far less an account of this actual world than a clear addition built upon it,

---

[40]Sullivan, "Natural Thinking: A Study in Democracy," a paper read before the Chicago Architectural Club, February 13, 1905, unpublished. Quoted in Hugh Morrison, *Louis Sullivan: Prophet of Modern Architecture* (New York, W. W. Norton and Co., 1935), p. 258.

[41]The productions of this new antiformalist generation would of course come in their turn to seem formal. Henry May quipped that the rebels of Sullivan's era wanted to repudiate all absolutes as a means of advancing "toward truth, freedom, and justice." *End of Innocence*, p. 141.

a classic sanctuary in which the rationalist fancy may take refuge from the intolerably confused and gothic character which mere facts present.

James always was careful to include other "rationalisms" among the systems he indicted. But it was the absolute idealism of James's Harvard colleague Josiah Royce, far more than the positivism of Auguste Comte or even of Herbert Spencer, that served as the American representative of rationalism—particularly if one was referring to the academic classroom. James considered Spencer's philosophical structure "skinny" and, compared to idealism, scarcely worth considering. The great object of his professional life, as he said, was not to score victories over positivism but to demolish his friend and antagonist Royce. "You are still the centre of my gaze," he told Royce in 1900. "I lead a parasitic life on you, for my highest flight of ambitious ideality is to become your conqueror, and go down into history as such."[42]

Whether or not James attained that objective—or truly meant to —the story of adaptive response to pragmatism among the philosophers of religion can be said to begin with Royce's own assertion in 1913 that his theory of ideas had led him to "a sort of absolute pragmatism."[43] But a more extensive convergence could be seen by that time in American personalism, which like its European counterpart had been from the first a correction almost as much as an advocacy of idealism. In 1898, at the very moment when Borden Parker Bowne of Boston University an- nounced a heightened insistence upon the idealist position, he also underlined the distinction between the mind's activities and the "substantial self"—an objective or "solid" entity—that he in-

---

[42]*Pragmatism: A New Name for Some Old Ways of Thinking: Popular Lectures on Philosophy* (New York, Longmans, Green and Co., 1907), pp. 21-22, 38-40; James to Royce, 1900, in F. O. Matthiessen, *The James Family: Including Selections from the Writings of Henry James, Senior, William, Henry, & Alice James* (New York, Alfred A. Knopf, 1947), p. 543.

[43]The theory alluded to saw an idea as a "plan of action." Royce, *Problem of Christianity*, pp. 122-123. Bruce Kuklick's recent study of Royce argues that the issues between pragmatism and idealism have been "muddied" by undue emphasis on the technical differences between James and Royce. James was a "pluralistic idealist," and Royce had flirted with pragmatism "as early as 1880." Kuklick, *Josiah Royce: An Intellectual Biography* (Indianapolis, The Bobbs-Merrill Company, 1972), p. 5.

sisted underlay those mental activities. And in *Personalism*, Bowne's manifesto of 1908, the rebukes to absolute idealism clearly were meant to be equal in force with the rejection of naturalism.

Naturalism and idealism were both implicated in what Bowne called "the failure of impersonalism." Impersonality in the realm of ideas, he insisted, is a "pure fiction":

All actual ideas are owned, or belong to some one, and mean nothing as floating free . . . The various categories of thought, apart from their formal character as modes of intellectual procedure, get any real significance only in the concrete and self-conscious life of the living mind.

Whether or not personalism succeeded in vindicating an ultimate reality that was ideal yet not pure idea, spiritual without being sheer unsubstantial spirit, it is clear that this is just what Bowne hoped to do. He refused to concede that his conception of an invisible, "unpicturable" ultimate reality rendered the objective order unreal. The consciousness "points to" phenomena; and to Bowne, as his biographer McConnell contends, this "outward pointing, by the human consciousness, was an indication of a true objective order which could not be disregarded."[44]

William James, who respected and liked Bowne but also was amused by his philosophical self-assurance,[45] complained that the Boston philosopher, with his doctrine of the substantial self, had crawled into a hole and pulled the hole in after him. Bowne retorted that James relied too much on picturesque figures of speech to get himself over dangerous spots in philosophy. He also, showing just the sort of self-assurance that James found annoying, complained—almost with a sigh—that the pragmatists were offering little that was new or exciting. Where they displayed

---

[44]Bowne, *Metaphysics*, pp. iii and 421-429; *Personalism*, pp. 253-254; McConnell, *Bowne*, pp. 102-103. McConnell's study of Bowne, which is an exceptionally able intellectual biography, was written at a time of heightened attacks upon idealism, and unquestionably goes farther than Bowne himself would have gone in stressing the realistic elements in personalism.

[45]James liked to say, only half jokingly, that he was a better Methodist than the "rationalistic" Bowne was. But he is also supposed to have turned, in the midst of his lectures, to volumes of Bowne's with the remark: "Now let's see what God Almighty has to say." Ralph Barton Perry, *The Thought and Character of William James* (Boston, Little, Brown, and Co., 1935), II, 329-332; McConnell, *Bowne*, pp. 76-77.

a lack of moral ideas, or seemed to make mechanical or material success the effective goal of living, he could not take them seriously. Where they avoided such materialist pitfalls, on the other hand, he could not see that their outlook and his own were very different. When Bowne called himself a "transcendental empiricist" in epistemology, and when McConnell credited him with a "higher pragmatism" in philosophical method, the adjectives covered a good many sins so far as the pragmatists were concerned—and covered them quite inadequately. But Bowne's phraseology in protesting against absolute idealism shows that his points of contact with the pragmatist movement were more than incidental:

Concepts without immediate experience are only empty forms, and become real only as some actual experience furnishes them with real contents . . . We conceive some things, but we not only conceive, we also live ourselves. This living indeed cannot be realized without the conception, but the conception is formal and empty without the living . . . In this fact the antithesis of thought and being finds recognition and reconciliation; but the fact itself must be lived, it cannot be discursively construed. Thought and act are one in this matter, and neither can be construed without the other.[46]

Most of the liberal philosophers of religion shared Bowne's reservations about pragmatism. Few found it a position to which they wished permanently or definitively to attach themselves. This was not, usually, because they found pragmatism committed to mean or materialistic ends. What they were more likely to comment upon was pragmatism's apparent lack of commitment to definite ends of any kind. While some of them found this open-endedness unsatisfactory and a little frightening, others accepted and exploited the opportunity it presented. In such cases, the liberal momentarily or transitionally enthusiastic about pragmatism went on to supply the commitments in metaphysics that the pragmatic method had quite purposely left open. He decided, as pragmatism said he should, what worked in the realm of the

---

[46]Ibid., p. 151; Bowne, *Personalism*, pp. 258-259. James himself felt, after the publication of *Personalism*, that except for Bowne's insistence upon a "substantial self" their points of view were fundamentally alike. McConnell, *Bowne*, p. 77.

largest ideas and action, and he then identified himself not by the term pragmatist but by the theism or personal idealism or realism to which the method had led him.[47]

All of which is to guard against any impression that the most broadly important philosophical movement of this time had negligible effect among the liberal theologians. To illustrate more concretely the nature of the effect it did have, one turns to those for whom pragmatism was a firmly occupied way station in the journey from idealism to realism—those who embraced the pragmatic method to the extent of making what they thought was a clean break from philosophical idealism. The most prominent and illuminating of the liberals who appropriated the benefits of pragmatism in this fashion was Eugene Lyman—later of Union Seminary in New York—who during these earlier years was teaching theology and philosophy in the Congregational seminary at Bangor, Maine.

Lyman, a leading liberal practitioner of the philosophy of religion and one of the great classroom teachers associated with the liberal movement, in 1910 identified four great "highways of thought" that were available to the religious philosopher: supernaturalism; absolute idealism; the neo-Kantianism promoted by the followers of Ritschl; and pragmatism. He thought that the standpoint of the older supernaturalism, picturing religious truth "as let down from heaven like the New Jerusalem," had been sufficiently criticized, and he was inclined to let it off with a few passing rebukes. That of absolute idealism, however, was still rampant and fairly confident. Idealism, Lyman suggested, was living on the prestige acquired in its nineteenth-century triumphs over materialism, much as the Republican party—"in spite of grave delinquencies"—sometimes maintained its ascendancy on the strength of ancient triumphs over slavery.[48]

The great contribution of idealism, Lyman thought, had been its

---

[47]Anna Louise Strong, the journalist and onetime student of Edward Scribner Ames at Chicago, made the same point conversely in an article of 1908: "The religion of a pragmatist is the result of many conditions, one and only one of which is his pragmatism." Quoted in Rucker, *Chicago Pragmatists*, pp. 107-108.

[48]Lyman, *Theology and Human Problems*, pp. 9, 5, 16.

support for the idea of divine immanence. But in proportion as idealism had become more "absolute," it had negated this very contribution by making God timeless and thereby removing him once again to a remote distance from the moving scene of human history. While the biblical deity was a God "of activity, of infinite purposes and of redeeming power," the timeless Absolute of the idealists reminded Lyman of a "huge spherical aquarium" enclosing the world—"encompassing within itself motion and life, but as a whole rigid, glassy, and motionless." He suggested (multiplying architectural metaphors, as this generation liked to do) that the idealists' intellectualism resulted in elegant, irrelevant philosophies, much as the reliance upon church legends in the siting of cathedrals produced magnificent structures remote from the avenues of daily life. The fact that absolute idealism makes space and objects in space dependent upon consciousness bothered Lyman very little; but he thought that an adequate doctrine of the immanence of God must take time much more seriously.[49]

Lyman saw greater merit in the neo-Kantian efforts of the Ritschlians. Kant had limited knowledge to make room for faith; and the Ritschlian return to Kant had had the great merit of reasserting the place of faith as one of the cardinal principles of philosophy. Kantianism, Lyman wrote, "furnishes the entering wedge for that larger recognition of religious experience for which we are seeking." Yet the attendant sharp separation between scientific and religious spheres of knowledge neutralized the effectiveness of the approach. Reason, Lyman complained, in the Kant-Ritschl scheme becomes "a kind of Austro-Hungarian empire without even a Franz-Joseph to preserve outward unity."[50]

By way of these critiques Lyman arrived at the judgment that pragmatism, though it by no means had all the answers for religious thought, provided the "highway"—a highway still, he cautioned, under construction—along which that thought should move. Lyman, almost as much as Bowne, would demand a higher pragmatism. Pragmatism reunited thought and action by making

---

[49]Ibid., pp. 9-24.
[50]Ibid., pp. 38, 29, 26, 37.

experience the precedent of thought and workability the test of truth. But if the new method was to be at all serviceable to theology, its test of workability must speak of success and failure in the largest cosmic terms and over the whole course of human evolution. The experience that is precedent to knowledge must mean not just the experience of the five senses but that of our whole nature. And a higher pragmatism would take seriously the function of moral belief in bringing about new objective events.[51]

In an earlier article Lyman had considered and rejected one other highway of thought that was coming to be much traveled: that of empiricism "as science has developed it." The empiricism to which Lyman objected sought "the explanation of a thing, the truth about a thing . . . in an enumeration of the component parts into which that thing could be resolved." Such a method, he argued, had always been inadequate in its attempts to explain religion because it could only deal with the static and the ahistorical, whereas religious phenomena have their meaning as part of a dynamic or dialectical process.[52]

Other liberals, however, were more ready by this time to talk the language of empiricism even "as science has developed it." D. C. Macintosh of Yale, who in 1910 had agreed with Lyman about the superannuation of idealism and the theological potential of pragmatism,[53] several years later announced—most ponderously—his formulation of a "critical realistic monism" that unfortunately sounded more remote and scholastic than the systems he was repudiating.[54] By the World War years, however, his thought seemed to have come untangled, and he was writing more felici-

---

[51]Ibid., pp. 41-58.

[52]Lyman, "The Influence of Pragmatism upon the Status of Theology," in Tufts and others, ed., *Studies in Philosophy*, pp. 224-225.

[53]Macintosh, "Can Pragmatism Furnish a Philosophical Basis for Theology?" pp. 125-135.

[54]"What we are here to defend might perhaps be called epistemological monism and *critical* realism (critical realistic epistemological monism), as opposed to the epistemological monism and dogmatic realism (realistic absolute epistemological monism) of the typical neo-realist . . . Other appropriate but simpler designations for this position are critical realistic monism, critical epistemological monism, and critical monism in epistemology." Macintosh, *Problem of Knowledge*, pp. 310-311.

tously on the requirements for a truly empirical theology. The introductory chapter for his *Theology as an Empirical Science* offered a stunning critique of each of the philosophical highways Lyman had considered, and of several others. Macintosh then took his stand for a scientific empiricism that would demand objective information, not just about religious states of mind, nor about the person of Christ as revealed in the historical record, but about the ultimate religious datum called God.

All the theologies that took religious experience as their starting point were improvements, so far as Macintosh was concerned, upon idealism and similarly deductive systems. The mystical, the eclectic, and the Ritschlian subtypes were successive advances in the direction of a truly empirical method; and the attempt of Ernst Troeltsch to rectify the narrowness of Ritschl's concentration on the historic Person of Christ constituted a further advance. As for pragmatism, Macintosh took the interesting position that if theology should fail to become fully scientific, then pragmatic theology in its current relatively undefined state would probably be the best one could hope for.[55]

Macintosh, however, felt confident that theology could become fully empirical. Pragmatic theology could reach this consummation on the two conditions that it form its propositions out of scientifically verified materials and that the criterion of "working" be defined as a demand for reasonable scientific verification. Macintosh's proposals for effecting these advances constituted a research design and plan of campaign for a generation of empirical theology. In the shorter run, what Macintosh illustrated was the decisiveness with which an advance party of religious liberals had departed, before the war, from the philosophical idealism that had informed the early stages of their movement.[56]

What this departure implied for the understanding of God, human nature, and the uses of religious language is best seen if one turns to two other striking personalities in the liberal com-

[55]Macintosh, *Theology as an Empirical Science*, pp. 1-46.
[56]Ibid., pp. 23-24. For an illuminating discussion of the theological empiricism of this and other periods, see Daniel Day Williams, "Tradition and Experience in American Theology," in Smith and Jamison, *The Shaping of American Religion*, pp. 443-495.

munity of the prewar period, George Burman Foster and William Wallace Fenn. Both men were heavily influenced by pragmatic and functional approaches to religious thought. Foster, who had been Macintosh's teacher at Chicago, remained closer to the older philosophical certitudes of liberalism than Macintosh did, but he strayed farther from the theistic certitudes. Fenn, dean of the Harvard Divinity School and close friend of Foster, began rather systematically around 1910 to ask the loaded questions about liberal optimism that were to be asked with steadily rising effect from that time until the advent of the neo-orthodox movement in the 1930s.

Foster—tall, craggy, and intense in appearance, unkempt in intellectual and literary style—raised deeper, more passionately felt questions about the liberal outlook than any of his contemporaries. He and Macintosh perhaps, if any comparison is possible, exercised roughly equal influence upon later revisions of liberalism; but a sharp contrast in style suggests how different was the nature of the influence in each case: Macintosh's penchant for meticulous outlining of his material contrasted, in Foster, with a mode of presentation so headlong that Foster himself, probably, could not have made an outline of it. Passionately honest, generous to new thinking as it appeared and approved itself, uninhibited by any sense that substantive reversals should occur in orderly fashion and toward prepared positions, Foster gave vent to his doubts as they assailed him, and did so without the careful press-agentry of self-justification that most doubters employ. The difficulty of his prose protected him. Had he been as clear as, say, H. L. Mencken (with whom he had affinities), Foster would have been both a better-known and a more vilified figure in our intellectual history. As it was, he exerted his influence through the students, of all kinds and subjects, who sat under him at Chicago and who caught the man's message from the passion and kindliness of his personality as well as from his statement of propositions.[57]

Foster said that "persons save persons," just as "fire, and not

---

[57]Foster's relation to theism is discussed, and a guide to materials on Foster provided, in Arnold, "Death of God," pp. 331-353. For a portrait and several descriptions of the man, his teaching, and his intellectual style, see Fenn, untitled memorial article.

George Burman Foster

some theory about the nature of flame," kindles fire.[58] That aphorism encapsulated a great deal about the nature of his own radicalism. His opus of 1906, *The Finality of the Christian Religion*, stood no farther to the left than personalistic idealism in philosophy and Ritschlianism in theology. Its central theme, the finality of Christianity as a system of ideals, ranged it nearly as much against naturalism as against what Foster called authority-religion. What was radical about Foster, really, was none of these positions but rather the driving, probing, somewhat heedless intellectual habits that kept him from tidying up the rooms of thought as he swept through them. His conclusions, in the *Finality* at least, were not wild or uncompromising; but Foster as often as not let traditional beliefs and slogans lie where they fell, instead of refitting them for use within the newer context. Thus Foster's critics were often objecting, as the Chicago *Tribune* did in 1906, to negations that had long been standard in liberalism but that usually had been more diplomatically phrased. The *Tribune* headline complained that Foster "Assails Canon of Bible . . . Declares Miracles Incredible and Says Proof of Resurrection Is Lacking."[59] Liberal uncertainties became radical ones in Foster's hands because his writing and his person conveyed the message that, though he by no means doubted everything, he would continue to call the shots as he saw them. There was an unsettling impression that he would continue to probe, that more was coming.

The direction of Foster's probings became apparent in the questions he raised in 1906 about theism. The discrediting of authority-religion, he said then, had made obsolete the traditional ways of referring to the deity. God was not dead, but "a God outside the cosmos is dead." God dies to live, just as the older concept of man dies to live. A radically transcendent conception gives way to a radically immanent one.[60]

At this point, however, God for Foster was still very real. The contrast between a transcendent and an immanent God had

---

[58]*Finality*, p. 187.
[59]Quoted in Arnold, "Death of God," p. 333.
[60]*Finality*, p. 177.

always seemed enormous to conservatives; and to a conservative Foster's position was already sheer pantheism. But so far as Foster himself was concerned, even a radical immanentism was still theism. The contrast between immanence and transcendence might in fact turn out to be "a mere matter of words," because, he said, the new cosmos with its immanent God had been invested with "all the ethical and rational values . . . all the ontological attributes . . . all the physical energies, which were predicated of the transcendent God of the old world-scheme."[61]

"All the ontological attributes"—in the last decade of Foster's life that assertion acquired a question mark. He planned and apparently drafted a volume of constructive theology to follow and balance the more analytic *Finality*, but he told colleagues that new currents of philosophical thought were forcing him to revise what he had written.[62] The unsettling nature of this philosophical change may account for the nonappearance of the sequel volume; we have no other ready explanation. The new current was pragmatism—but pragmatism in its broadest sense, as a movement that articulated the Darwinian undermining of absolutes. Foster by 1908 had been strongly affected by a functional interpretation of religion as one of the instruments the human organism uses in adapting to its environment.[63] In Foster's thinking, such a functional interpretation led, just as his earlier critics would have predicted, to doubts as to whether God is an objective reality or simply a magnificent ideational convenience.

Through the last decade of his life, as he oscillated between subjectivist conclusions and his conviction of the reality of God, Foster foreshadowed and helped instigate several of the more

---

[61]Ibid.

[62]Tufts, "Foster," p. 182.

[63]Foster's *Function of Religion* had its origin in lectures at Berkeley in 1908. For excerpts from the latter, see Hutchison, ed., *American Protestant Thought*, pp. 136-146. The most useful treatment of the brand of pragmatism that surrounded and affected Foster is Darnell Rucker's *Chicago Pragmatists*. Rucker makes the pertinent distinctions between Jamesean and Chicago formulations (p. 5), sketches Foster's relation to the Chicago movement (p. 130), and treats extensively the functional psychology of Edward Scribner Ames, whose radicalism contributed nearly as heavily as Foster's to the critique of liberal religion (pp. 107-115).

prominent religious positions of the 1920s: theistic realism, non-
theistic humanism, and what Joseph Wood Krutch and Walter
Lippmann were to identify memorably as the sense of loss associated with both these positions.[64] In July of 1912 he told Macintosh that "I have passed through the slough of epistemological
subjectivity, and see more clearly and hold more firmly the objective and social reality of religion . . . A real God, a real man,
a real world—our need of these is too imperious to give them
up." But by 1918, the year of his death, he was again convinced
"that we are witnessing the passing of theistic supernaturalism."
Mankind was outgrowing theism, he thought, "in a gentle and
steady way," but it was outgrowing it: and the result for Foster
was anything but the exhiliration of a new freedom. He had lost
a son in the war, and two children before that. The resulting
personal need for assurance had not settled the facts that would
provide assurance, and Foster's career as a thinker ended with
questions rather than with answers—despairing or otherwise. "By
and by," he wrote, "when your children have died and your life
is almost gone, and you seem to have done almost nothing, is
there anything that can give you heart and hope? Or is it the condition of nobility in man that the All should be against him? If
there were a foregone assurance of victory, what kind of man would
that give?"[65]

Macintosh—he of the ready outlines of human knowledge—
patronized his old friend and teacher by remarking that though one
"must admire, revere, and perhaps pity the man," it was difficult
to absolve him entirely from blame for the religious and intellectual difficulties he encountered.

He was possessed with such a curiosity as to the quicksands of modern
scepticism and unbelief that he must needs step into them, and such
courage, amounting almost to bravado, that he must tramp around there
. . . until at last, apparently, it was too late. And all the while, not far
away—or so at least it is claimed by some—there stood the perfectly sound
and solid rock of religious realism.

---

[64]Krutch, *Modern Temper*; Lippmann, *Preface to Morals*, pp. 3-151.
[65]Macintosh, *Religious Knowledge*, pp. 106 and 118; Foster, review of *The
New Orthodoxy*, by Edward Scribner Ames, *Christian Century*, 35 (October 24,
1918), 17-18.

But William Wallace Fenn had offered a rather different interpretation of Foster's personal struggle which Macintosh, since he
said he agreed with it, may not quite have grasped. "He died,"
Fenn wrote, "with pilgrim staff in hand and nobody can tell
what would have been the final resting-place of his thought, if,
indeed, it had ever found one." Macintosh and Fenn were describing the same pilgrim, but one of them left him in the Slough
of Despond, while the other left him climbing the Hill Difficulty.[66]

Foster and Fenn had first known each other during the latter's
Chicago pastorate of the 1890s. They had spent extended periods
of time together.[67] Whether because of Foster's influence or
otherwise, Fenn had acquired some of the same tentativeness,
and a great deal of the same dissatisfaction with the liberal habit
of calling new notions in religion by the old names. Unwilling
to risk being locked into his own past ideas, he wrote relatively
little for publication, even though in learning and intellectual
acuity he exceeded some liberals who wrote twenty books apiece.
Though he understood Foster's habit of expressing boldly and
in print "opinions concerning which he had not made up his
mind," Fenn himself could not quite do that.[68]

In spite of this diffidence, Fenn was outspoken in his interpretations of the current religious situation. He seems to have
responded readily when called upon, as he was in 1913, to expound
publicly his estimate of religious liberalism. In that year he wrote
an article for the *American Journal of Theology* that took for
granted the breakdown of philosophical idealism, advocated the
revision of liberal theism, and warned, more directly than any
critique had done previously, that liberal humanism was becoming
dangerously out of touch with the realities of the human situation.

The type of religious thinking "now often called Modernism but
formerly called Modern Liberalism" could be defined negatively,
Fenn thought, by its free attitude toward tradition, and affirmatively by its insistence upon unity—"unity of the mind in itself

[66]Macintosh, *Religious Knowledge*, pp. 119, 115.
[67]Fenn, untitled memorial article, pp. 178-179.
[68]Macintosh, *Religious Knowledge*, p. 115. See also Dan Huntington Fenn,
"William Wallace Fenn," pp. 25-26.

and with the whole being of man." Theologically, the fundamental expression of liberalism lay in its principle of divine immanence; and Fenn outlined, approvingly, the consequences of immanentism for particular Christian doctrines. As these doctrinal restatements demonstrated, Fenn was not ready to retreat. Liberalism represented a "distinct advance in Christian thinking."[69]

But there were objections nonetheless, and these, he wrote, were principally of two kinds. One kind, coming from outside the movement, chided the dependence of liberalism upon the historical Jesus. Albert Schweitzer's documenting of the apocalyptic world view and assumptions of Jesus had allegedly trapped liberalism "in a salient where the only alternatives are unconditional surrender or complete annihilation." The Jesus discovered by historical research, according to this criticism, had turned out to be "quite incompetent to fill the place which Liberalism has accorded him."[70]

Fenn professed to feel no great difficulty in battling his way out of the salient. His Unitarian blood rising, he asserted that "the Liberal has no inclination to return to traditional Christianity, still less to the church which anathematized his departure and now arrogantly commands or patronizingly invites his submission." If forced to choose between the clear results of scholarship and the Jesus figure relied upon in early stages of the liberal movement, he was sure liberals would accept the former. Those who made such a choice, moreover, might well "feel all the nearer to the Jesus whose apocalyptic hopes were vain but whose love of God and man was not thereby diminished." Religious certainty might be lessened, but the liberal, Fenn said, had always been more concerned about reaching the truth than about the comforts of absolute certainty. "He would far rather have the Jewish apocalyptic Messiah with all his limitations than

---

[69]"Modern Liberalism," pp. 509-513.

[70]Ibid., 513-514. This view of the dilemma of liberalism had been put forward by James Denney in *Jesus and the Gospel* (New York, A. C. Armstrong and Son, 1909). See also K. C. Anderson, "The Collapse of Liberal Christianity," *Hibbert Journal*, 8 (January 1910), 301-320.

the ecclesiastical Christ with delusive promises of certainty and finality, never to be expected of a growing mind in a growing world."[71]

The concept of a growing world, of a world in process, was crucial to Fenn's thought. It provided the foundation for his response to the other, much tougher kind of criticism directed against liberalism, the criticism of its view of evil. The hardest question about liberalism, Fenn suggested, was "whether it can bear the weight of the tragedies of human existence." Its greatest vulnerability lay in its tendency to minimize the depth and seriousness of sin.

It may be conceded that traditional theology made too much of sin, but surely that was better than to make light of it . . . If a Jesus rebukes the doctrine of original sin, a Judas similarly condemns that of original righteousness. To a serious thinker, Modern Liberalism often seems too jocund for life as it actually is . . . We would not have Modern Liberalism return to a belief in the devil—that is too easy a solution of the problem—but it must deal more justly with the crushing tragedies of life, with evil and with sin, if it is to command the respect of candid and thoughtful men. The saviors of the world always have been and always will be men of sorrows and acquainted with grief.

Fenn spoke of liberalism's "amiable faith in inherent goodness" as one source of the trouble. But probably little could be done about that, he said, unless liberals revised their "favorite concept" of unity by infusing it with more dynamic elements. The idea of unity, and indeed theism itself, was salvageable only on the condition that monistic idealism be discarded. A static and mechanistic conception must yield to "unity interpreted in terms of purpose." Pragmatists and pluralists had justly complained about a logical unity that permits no contradictions or inconsistencies, and about a mechanical unity that knows only necessity. "But unity conceived as purpose not only admits of contradictions and possibilities but would even seem to require them," since without these things purpose has no sphere of operation.[72]

---

[71]Fenn, "Modern Liberalism," 514-515.

[72]Ibid., pp. 516-517. James Luther Adams called attention to this and other pre-Niebuhr critiques of liberalism in "The Changing Reputation of Human Nature." Adams in a more recent article locates one possible inspiration for Fenn's critique of idealism in a 1910 address of Ernst Troeltsch. Adams, "Fenn as Critic," p. 17.

The technical difference between this sort of purposive theism and the idealisms which had called themselves dynamic or teleological does not seem immense, as Fenn would probably have acknowledged. The more unusual element in Fenn's argument was his candid questioning of the view of human nature that generally had come in the same package with the older theism. Fenn renounced a rhetorical starting point that had been taken for granted. Liberal reservations about human nature and progress—and these had been many[73]—had usually begun, in effect: "Though we all know liberalism is basically right about inherent goodness . . . ." Fenn's may have been the first prominent voice raised to say, "Perhaps we do not know this. Perhaps liberalism is not basically right on that point."

He was to be followed in this kind of critique, and in a most striking way, by his successor as dean of Harvard Divinity School, Willard Sperry. That fact raises the possibility, mentioned at the beginning of this chapter, that Unitarian Harvard, long habituated to religious liberalism yet no longer chargeable in the old way for its alleged errors, felt a high degree of detachment and hence of readiness to criticize.

Whatever the explanation, Fenn felt able not only to raise the rather demeaning possibility of liberal naiveté, but also to express impatience with the time-honored practice of fitting traditional terminology to sharply revised doctrines. In a sermon of about 1910, Fenn echoed George Patton's injunction of 1897 on that point. If we discard the substance of basic doctrines, Patton had suggested, and retain only their names, "let us pause and ask . . . whether we are still Christians."[74] Fenn now warned his fellow liberals that if they failed to deal adequately with the reality of sin and the need of salvation, it would be time "to consider seriously the question whether we are Christians in any proper sense." In the past, he added, Christians had "suffered because of devotion to the name; now the name is in danger of losing all distinctive meaning because of the devotion of those who would retain it at all hazards." To distinguish between things

---

[73]Hutchison, "'End of Innocence,'" pp. 129-132.

[74]George S. Patton, review of Harris, *Moral Evolution*, in *Presbyterian and Reformed Review*, 8 (July 1897), 540.

that differ, Fenn asserted, is the second great duty of the theologian. "The first is to fit his thought to the fact and his word to the thought."[75]

The complaint about liberal language, which came almost as an afterword in this sermon, seems to have grown more positive in Fenn's mind by the time he wrote "Modern Liberalism" in 1913. By then he had decided that liberalism should stop trying "to adapt old phrases and usages to fit the religious life of today." The urgent need of the moment was, instead, "to aid that religious life in creating its own forms of expression." Fenn said that he sympathized with the urge to retain venerated forms of expression. "To give up the verbal form seems like renouncing the reality which originally fashioned it." But Protestantism, he said, has always insisted upon translations into the vernacular, "and it must now face the necessity of translating the sacred page of the soul into contemporary speech at whatever hazard or cost." It was painfully evident, Fenn wrote, that current liberal Protestantism was not willing to do this.

Indeed, readers of current theological literature must often wish that every writer were obliged to furnish a glossary in order that his teaching might be fully intelligible . . . Until theological writers are willing to cast aside their patched and baggy terminology—the race set before us is not a sack-race—they can hardly expect a sympathetic hearing from thoughtful men. And in addition, looseness and vagueness of utterance inevitably react upon thought. A smear of words and a smouch of ideas are reciprocally related. The supreme need of Modern Liberalism, so far as wide appreciation goes, is for definite, precise thinking and direct, plain speaking.

It was true, Fenn said, that when one is dealing with mysteries, "with objects too vast for exact definition," words can only be "thrown out" in the direction of the mystery being explored. But "they should at least be thrown with an eye single to the object, and with accuracy of aim . . . That the mystery is incomprehensible is no excuse for unintelligible statements concerning it— patient silence were better."[76]

---

[75]Fenn, "Meaning of the Christian Religion," pp. 8-9.
[76]"Modern Liberalism," pp. 518-519.

That Fenn's 1913 critique of liberalism now seems a culminating document is partly an accident of chronology. Less than a year after its publication, an unexpected war gave a fairly sharp twist to the kaleidoscope through which worldviews and theologies were perceived. But the essay also, in a brief and modest way, provided a summation because its author managed to synthesize so many elements of the external and internal criticism that had been voiced up to that time. Not only did he repeat and integrate parallel kinds of reservation about static idealism and static theism; he also provided integration between the complaints of outsiders and those voiced by liberals themselves.

Toward the Princetonian insistence on tough minded either-or thinking Fenn felt little enough sympathy. That emphasis was not to be adopted widely among critics of liberalism until naturalism on the left flank and neo-orthodoxy on the right voiced it after 1925. But even in such areas Fenn suggested some common ground between external and internal critics: like the Princetonians, he complained that liberalism was trying too hard to pour the new wine into the old wineskins, and was thus falling into an imprecision or even sleaziness of religious terminology.

Finally, in its uncommonly direct questioning of liberal attitudes toward human nature and history, Fenn's work marked an agreement with outside critics that was the more startling for its sharply differing context. Conservatives, standing atop the barricades of exclusive biblical revelation, had proclaimed that no sure revelation can come through cultural development. An apparent upward movement in human culture, they said, means little or nothing; sin is still real and desperate, the human outcome very uncertain. Liberal self-criticism was beginning to reach the same conclusion, not through denials of cultural revelation but by way of changed observations as to what the development of human culture actually reveals.

The Great War and
the Logic of Modernism

The true successors to the Calvinist with his agonized
conscience and his initial dogma of original sin are to
be found to-day among the biologists, the
psychologists, the novelists and the dramatists.
WILLARD SPERRY, 1921

The outbreak of world war in 1914 played a con-
firmatory more than an originating role in the
development of liberal self-questioning. Munger's model of the cognitive process—"I gain
knowledge slowly . . . I gain the meaning of knowledge instantly"—was sadly illustrated as the leisurely introspection of the
prewar period gave place to sharp, graphic recognition of inadequacies in the church and the liberal world view. Preceding
analyses of crisis in the culture and the liberal faith now looked
like prophecies of the current debacle. They had been such only
in the sense that any prophecy is really an insight into what is
already happening, based on unusual power to read signs of the
times that others are unable or unwilling to read. Yet, just as the
war confirmed long-resident international tensions, the agonized
responses to it represented prewar apprehensions in realized
form.

The effect of the war as a concretizing event, and more specifically as a compelling datum for modernists claiming special
sensitivity to cultural development, nonetheless ought not to be
minimized. Reinhold Niebuhr later, in one of his typical
quadrilateral epigrams, expressed the impact of the experience
even upon one who continued for some time afterward to consider
himself a liberal: "When the war started I was a young man trying

to be an optimist without falling into sentimentality. When it ended and the full tragedy of its fratricides had been revealed, I had become a realist trying to save myself from cynicism."[1] Fenn, very much in a minority, had called in 1913 for a new, more diffident startling point for liberal discourse. With the outbreak of war, that starting point became widely accepted. After June 1914 the conventional wisdom, what "everyone knew," was that severe doubts had been raised about the liberal outloook and about the very viability of Christianity.[2]

"The Failure of the Christian Churches"

While for some the rhetorical shift from optimism to realism would be merely that—rhetorical and temporary—for many others it was more solidly based. In either case, the response of liberals and of liberal theology to World War I was immediate, very vocal, and deeply troubled. William Adams Brown told a London audience in late 1914 that "we had underestimated the forces which resist progress. We had supposed that the great prize for which we had been contending was to be quickly won; that war on a grand scale belonged to the past, and that our more enlightened age, in spite of of its underlying selfishness and cruelty, could somehow slip easily into the Kingdom of God. We have had a rude awakening." George Gordon, apostle of reasoned optimism, agreed. Sympathizing with "the deepening sense of the brutal forces in man," he remarked in 1915 that

during the last three light-hearted decades, we have been smoking the opium pipe of evolution, telling the world how far it has risen, chiefly by its own force, from the depths in which it began, describing the speed by which it has mounted under our sage and dreamy eyes, and prophesying of its complete ascension in the near and sweet bye and bye. Recent events have broken the opium pipe and dispelled the delusion.[3]

---

[1] Niebuhr, "What the War Did," p. 1161.

[2] The impression that liberals and the clergy generally were little affected by the experience of the war seems to rest upon the observation that American religion in the twenties did not adopt a pessimistic theology, and also upon a preceding assumption—never a well-documented one—that most liberals and other religious leaders had accepted the necessity of war with complacency or enthusiasm. See Ahlstrom, "Continental Influence," p. 260.

[3] Brown, *Is Christianity Practicable?* p. 57. Gordon, *Infinite Mystery*, p. 260.

What the consequences might be for the church and for theology no one pretended to know at this early date. L. P. Jacks of Oxford, editor of the *Hibbert Journal*, advised his Anglo-American readership not to expect clarification of the meaning of the war "till long after the issue is determined." Still, as an editor observing the flow (or, currently, the ebb) of theological manuscripts, Jacks confirmed the general impression that the crisis had produced theological paralysis. Paraphrasing William James, he suggested that the Western world was on "theological holiday."[4] "Almost on the very day" of the war's outbreak, the torrent of theological and philosophical articles had been reduced, then had become and remained a mere trickle. New writers had appeared, on new subjects, but the old writers and topics had virtually disappeared. Jacks seemed not to assume the theologians were too busy; he thought they were stunned, appalled, silenced. They were on enforced holiday.[5]

Superficially, one could account for the paralysis by the temporary immobilization of German scholarship, particularly so far as it had operated as an influence upon the English-speaking world. "The age of German footnotes," as Jacks wrote, was on the wane because the rest of the world, since the sinking of the *Lusitania* and the acquiescence of German scholars therein, had begun to wonder about the Germans as moral mentors. At a deeper level, religious thinkers had become querulous not about particular scholars but about the methods of reasoning these scholars had so admirably and influentially represented. Jacks cited, and deplored, current assertions by German academicians that ordinary standards of morality are inapplicable to the state; and that war discharges the belligerents from all obligations to the moral law.

We feel there is a twist in the culture of these great minds. We see that what the British mean by immorality is rapidly converted by German logic into morality; and this has caused suspicion to fall on the whole

---

[4]James in a famous characterization of philosophical idealism had said that such forms of monism offered philosophers a "moral holiday" for which he personally had to find some alternative justification. William James, *Pragmatism: A New Name for Some Old Ways of Thinking* (New York, Longmans, Green and and Co., 1907), pp. 74-79.

[5]Jacks, "Theological Holiday," pp. 1-5.

method of reasoning which achieves these surprising transformations. Morality, we are now saying to one another, will stand a good deal of argument and is all the better for being argued up to a certain point; but the German example seems to show that, after this point is reached, further argument only serves to render the conscience more and more confused; so that if you argue a moral question long enough, you are certain to reach an immoral conclusion.[6]

But Jacks also thought, quite apart from the Germans and their logic, that the war had thrown entire structures of thought into confusion. Theology, along with most of the social philosophy of the Western world, had been, before the war, "unconsciously but obviously accommodated to permanently peaceful conditions." American liberals agreed. As Eugene Lyman remarked shortly after American entry in 1917, "publishers cannot issue the same books, magazines cannot print the same articles, lecturers cannot give the same courses, as before the war . . . There is an intellectual *status quo ante* to which it is impossible now peacefully to return."[7]

If liberal theologians were unable to deal conclusively, on short notice, with the questions of human guilt raised by the war, they were quite ready, especially after a number of years' training in the Social Gospel, to indict what they called "the failure of the Christian churches." Led by William Adams Brown and Washington Gladden, they now rang all the changes on a traditional argument of liberal social ethics—that though Christianity is perfectly valid and practicable, it has in fact never been tried.

Gladden, taking that line, distinguished between "vital Christianity" on one hand and the actually operative assumptions of the church and of "Christian civilization" on the other. Vital Christianity, he claimed, "has not wholly failed, though its work has been greatly crippled by its divisions and the perversions of its message which have been produced by ecclesiasticism." Organized Christianity, however, had been "a signal and dismal failure."[8]

---

[6]Ibid., p. 6; Jacks, "England's Experience," p. 438.

[7]Ibid., p. 441; Lyman, *New Age*, pp. 2-3. For further expressions of the sense of disjunction from preceding modes of thought see Coffin, *Social Rebuilding*, pp. 2-5; Tucker, *New Reservation*, p. 138.

[8]Gladden, *Great War*, p. 29.

Gladden's indictment, issued at the very beginning of the European fighting, came as near to truly apocalyptic vision as a liberal was likely to venture. He saw the war as a last horrible convulsion, utterly without redeeming features except that it would finally convince mankind of the worthlessness of force, of arming, of alliances, and of all the machinations of "the lords of privilege." The war, he predicted, would be short, would make a wreck of the world, and would eventually prove to have been the birth-agony of a new and glorious world order.[9] Brown's vision of the future was less vivid; but the rebuke to organized religion was scarcely less harsh. Brown charged that the churches had failed "to exercise any controlling influence upon the national policy of the so-called Christian nations." In a day when the church, with its great ecumenical conferences and international outreach, might have been expected to intervene effectively against war, virtually nothing had been done. "Not only were the churches powerless to prevent the war, but they made no serious attempt to do so." Now, with the nations lined up in battle, "the Christians within each are found heart and soul in support of their respective governments, not only in the physical struggle in which they are engaged, but . . . in their interpretation of the moral issues at stake." Christians as individuals doubtless had shown unselfishness and nobility, but Christian society and the church had "shown no consciousness of independent responsibility." To be sure, neither the academy nor the professions nor the various agencies of international idealism—including the peace movement—had done better. "But of all these failures, signal and discouraging as they are, none is more surprising, and none more disheartening, than that of the Christian church."[10]

The prewar peace movement came in for a kind of derogation that prefigured later, more wholesale critiques of religious and secular liberalism. William Jewett Tucker in 1915 criticized

---

[9]Ibid., pp. 8-11, 22. By the time he preached the fourth sermon in this series, Gladden was admitting he had been oversanguine about the speed with which rational, horrified mankind would end the fighting and convict the perpetrators. But he by no means relinquished the idea of a great world conversion as the war's end result. Ibid., pp. 33, 39-40, 58.

[10]Brown, *Is Christianity Practicable?* pp. 3-7.

pacifists for imagining that peace itself, rather than righteousness or justice, could be made the primary consideration in human affairs. He thought it evident that "peace has no moral significance except as it is an exponent of justice . . . The so-called concert of Europe has seldom prevented war except at the cost of freedom and justice." The broader peace movement, if free from some errors of the doctrinaire pacifists, had suffered from an equally grave delusion that peacemaking is an easy matter. John Chamberlain later identified the "technique of liberal failure" as a disposition to quit when the going gets rough, but Tucker placed the fault at an earlier stage. The liberals of the peace movement, he said, had never understood "the tremendous seriousness of their business." Neither they nor the nations they represented had had any conception of what would be required of them.

When the nations are willing to make sacrifices for peace in any degree commensurate with those which are made for war, we shall have peace . . . But this means at least the readjustment of many "existing rights," concessions in respect to trade and commerce, the restraint of racial pride,—in a word, it means sacrifice. Disarmament would be futile if the occasions and incentives of war were to remain in force.[11]

Shailer Mathews, who had been much more of a peace activist than Tucker had been, later confirmed Tucker's view of what had been wrong. Except for brief flurries of interest, he said, churchmen before 1914 had lent little support to the peace movement because "we were incredibly optimistic, which is another way of saying we were incredibly blind." His own participation, Mathews recalled, had been "in a rather dilettante spirit" up to the time of Andrew Carnegie's founding of the Church Peace Union in the winter of 1914. Even then, he said, when Carnegie read a paper on the evils of war "I recall thinking that his apprehensions were unfounded."[12]

---

[11]Tucker, "The Ethical Challenge of the War," reprinted in his *New Reservation of Time*, pp. 119-145. See especially pp. 140-142. John Chamberlain, *Farewell to Reform: The Rise, Life, and Decay of the Progressive Mind in America* (New York, Liveright, Inc., 1932), pp. 304-305.

[12]Mathews, *New Faith for Old*, pp. 195-196. George Coe wrote in 1916 that before the war "men had spoken of divine love and of human brotherhood; but

American Participation and the Roots
of Theological Reassessment

It was this common conviction of ecclesiastical and liberal failure that contributed most directly to subsequent reassessment of liberal assumptions. But arguments, on both sides, about American involvement in the war also contributed to later revisionary thinking. Those who favored preparedness or, later, joined avidly in the American war effort, produced the beginnings of a critique of liberal political sentimentality that neo-orthodoxy would resume. Those, on the other hand, who opposed preparedness and who, after American entry, maintained a running criticism of chauvinism and intolerance, formulated a brief against national pride and economic exploitiveness that also was important to later denigrations of the liberal bourgeois culture. And quite a large group managed convincingly to combine these sometimes-polarized forms of realism. William Adams Brown was the most prominent exemplar of a position that, after American entry, relentlessly linked a realistic conviction about the war's necessity with a determination to combat the persecution, hate-mongering, and national self-righteousness that infected American wartime thinking.

Liberal leaders, like other churchmen, tended to oppose preparedness;[13] but those few who supported it were men of great influence. The notorious and vitriolic Newell Dwight Hillis, of

---

men had not counted the cost of brotherhood . . . Brotherhood was a sentiment, a hope, an ethical fragrance." Coe, "Contemporary Ideals," p. 387. The involvement of clergy, and surprisingly minor involvement of social-gospel clergy, in the prewar peace movement is discussed in Marchand, *American Peace Movement*, pp. 323-380. Charles Chatfield offers a discriminating picture of the prewar international arbitration pacifism and its disintegration in "World War I and the Liberal Pacifist in the United States," *American Historical Review*, 75 (December 1970), 1920-1937.

[13]Mathews, *New Faith for Old*, p. 197. Ray Abrams, though the severest scholarly critic of the clergy's actions in relation to American entry and participation, offers a number of statistics that confirm the reality of clerical opposition in the earlier preparedness controversy. Petitions by several dozen clergymen in favor of preparedness were swiftly answered by counterpetitions bearing hundreds of names. A preparedness organization polled 1,000 clergymen and got a predominantly militant response, but only from the 165 who bothered to reply. Abrams, *Preachers Present Arms*, pp. 36-44.

Plymouth Church in Brooklyn, probably (whatever his effect upon popular audiences) aroused more thinking persons to the dangers of bigotry than to the dangers of Germanism. But the milder Lyman Abbott reached his hundreds of thousands through the *Outlook*; the Britisher George Gordon preached Americanism (though not intervention) to his fellow immigrants; and several venerable college presidents or ex-presidents—Tucker, Harris, Hyde—reached wide audiences with implicit or outright support for preparedness.[14]

Tucker's articles for the *Atlantic Monthly* in 1915 and 1916 stated most adequately the argument for a new, armed realism in the peace movement. The retired Dartmouth president offered no illusions about the motives of democratic states, or about the dangers involved in arming them. "The Ethical Challenge of the War," published in June 1915, in fact blamed the Anglo-Saxons for originating those doctrines of racialism and *Realpolitik* on which the Central Powers were now operating, and Tucker denied that a democratic polity is proof against the diabolic uses of patriotism. Ten months later, however, he was arguing that "the crux of the peace problem" was an understandable public suspicion that the peace movement was an expression of selfishness, of an unwillingness to make sacrifices on behalf of justice. "Peace, in itself essentially good, may lose moral character from the failure to identify itself with a righteous cause in the time of its extremity." He foresaw a possibility that American neutrality would come to mean abandonment of suffering democracies and "a peace established in militarism and guaranteed by militarism."[15]

The position involved a conditional approval for the policy of neutrality, so long as neutrality contributed to a righteous settlement; and Tucker accorded that approval. But it also implied support for preparedness, which according to Tucker gained a new breadth of meaning: "It means self-defense in all contingencies,

---

[14]Hillis' barnstorming for the Allies, both before and after American entry, provided the most solid material for Granville Hicks's attack in *American Mercury*, "The Parsons and the War." Ira Brown, *Lyman Abbott*, pp. 214-216; Gordon, *Appeal of the Nation*; Tucker, *New Reservation*, pp. 154-155; Harris, *Century's Change in Religion*, pp. 265-267; Burnett, *Hyde of Bowdoin*, p. 255.

[15]Tucker, "Ethical Challenge," pp. 122, 144-145, 148-149, 150-155.

but it means in certain contingencies the wider defense of liberty."[16]

Support for the contemporary peace movement in the face of such denigrations emerged from many liberal quarters, notably in articles against preparedness by John Wright Buckham, George A. Coe, and Shirley Jackson Case. Brown, Mathews, and King also campaigned actively against preparedness, and Gladden bitterly denounced American departures from neutrality. But the most blistering and comprehensive refutation of the Tucker position came in a notable sermon delivered by Henry Sloane Coffin, pastor of the Madison Avenue Presbyterian Church, as the ticker tape and confetti settled on the streets of New York after Preparedness Day, 1916.[17]

The thirty-nine-year-old Coffin told his hearers that the great march "so far as it was a demonstration for military preparedness . . . was a march into yesterday." It had also been a march away from Christianity. Christ to be sure had counseled the overcoming of evil, and Paul the putting-on of armor; but evil was to be overcome with good, and the armor was supposed to be the moral armor of godliness. Thus the only national preparedness that can be Christian is a preparation "of the nation's soul"; and for the purposes of such a rite, the speeches and demonstrations of the preceding day had been highly inappropriate. Americans should be engaging in acts of repentance for all participation, past and current, in the follies of militarism and imperialism and nationalistic pride.

What did it mean to arm oneself "with the mind of Christ"? The mind of Christ, Coffin said, is first of all emptied of self. That would dictate that the United States must covet nothing

---

[16]Ibid., pp. 154-155.

[17]Buckham, "Good-Will"; "Principles of Pacifism"; Case, "Religion and War"; Coe, "Contemporary Ideals," pp. 385-387; Brown, *Is Christianity Practicable?* p. 116; Mathews, *New Faith for Old*, pp. 197-198; King, *Fundamental Questions*, pp. 217-221, 232-233; Dorn, *Gladden*, pp. 416-430; Coffin, *Preparedness*. Gordon identified a division along generational lines when he said that "some of the ablest and best of my younger brethren in the ministry differ from me" on the pacifist question. *Appeal of the Nation*, p. 40. For a discussion of King's somewhat uncertain later stand on the preparedness issue see Love, *King*, pp. 192-206.

for itself in its international dealings, least of all on any excuse relating to "national honor."

Much has been said of "national honor," and almost everything that has been said reveals a pagan conception of honor . . . A nation's honor is impugned only when its own bad manners or quick temper or pride or vengefulness [or] self-seeking prevent it from being useful. We lose our honor when we lose our courtesy, our temper, or our conscience. So our honor remains entirely in our own hands; no one else can hurt it in the least.

Similarly, the nation's "rights" are not a Christian concern. "The value of having rights," Coffin suggested, "is mainly to be able not to insist upon them." Nor could the United States claim substantive physical or economic imperilment, since "the gravest danger to our peace at present lies not in the attack of some foreign power jealous of our wealth, but in our imperialistic commercialism eager to preempt for its selfish advantage the markets of the world."[18]

Under various covering rationales, some Americans wished to "rescue" one or another small nation or "clean up" Mexico. New York City needs cleaning up, Coffin remarked, but we would not want some patronizing world power to come in and attempt it. As for rescue operations, "it is one thing to go to the rescue of a bullied little nation pleading for your help; another to foist yourself upon a little nation that does not want your help."

The talk of benefits to be derived from military training was also, Coffin argued, largely incompatible with the mind of Christ. "Military discipline is unchristian in that it teaches unquestioning obedience," whereas "Christianity demands that no man do anything of which his own conscientious judgment is not persuaded." What is worse, military discipline, "however one may try to forget it, has just one end—to train effective butchers of men; it is training to kill, and everything in it is subordinate to its dominating purpose." If American young men need disci-

---

[18]Coffin, *Preparedness*, pp. 2-6. A later generation of readers will recognize the distinct family resemblance between Coffin's objections to World War I and those of his nephew, William Sloane Coffin of Yale University, to Southeast Asian wars of the 1960s and after.

pline, Coffin suggested, let us find some other way to inculcate it.

Coffin managed to find in his one short quotation from St. Paul ("Arm ye yourselves also with the same mind") rebukes to nearly every conceivable feature of militant nationalism. He stressed the dangers of American power ("Our big country is not little Switzerland; our very size and wealth make us dangerous"); the qualitative equivalence between British and German violence ("The cruelly stupid executions of misguided Irish rebels . . . only breed hatred"); and the evil contagiousness of an arms race ("Already the preparedness campaign in this country has had sinister results in Japan, where we need most to allay the ill-will engendered by our execrable manners").[19]

At one point, in the course of a summary statement of his argument, Coffin managed even to express support for those escaping military service:

On behalf of the thousands who have sought our shores to escape the compulsory military service of Europe, on behalf of those enslaved nations whose wealth has gone year after year to support this military establishment which has brought them not peace, but the most hideous war in history, let us as American patriots and as loyal believers in Jesus Christ resist to the utmost this attempt to deamericanize our beloved America and dechristianize our Christianity.[20]

When America entered the war in April of 1917, nearly all the leaders of religious liberalism went along with that decision in one degree or another. A great many were silent, and few have been shown, in even the most ex parte denunciations of clerical participation, to have lent themselves to the intolerance and hyper-Americanism that threw such a grotesque light upon American war aims.[21] It is true that men like Rauschenbusch, Lyman, and Coe who balked at American participation tended to accept

---

[19]Ibid., pp. 6-9, 11-12.

[20]Ibid., pp. 11-12.

[21]Of the 156 clergymen who had achieved a reputation for leadership of religious liberalism in the mainline denominations before World War I, 95 lived at least through the year 1917. Although this collection of men is undoubtedly more hawkish than it would be if it included the young men of Coffin's generation, very few are mentioned in studies of clerical participation as having made inflammatory statements. Professor Darrel Bigham, in a letter to the *American*

the superior moral position of the Allies in a war that from their point of view need never have occurred. Rauschenbusch himself, in May of 1918, wrote that Germany had become "the chief exponent of the philosophy of expansion and of the anti-democratic idea," and that "a victory for the central powers would doubtless fasten this philosophy of imperialism and militarism on the world." "I should regard this," he added, "as a terrible calamity."[22] This degree of loyalty to the United States, and of willingness to state a moral preference for the Allied cause, was, admittedly, virtually universal among the main-line liberals, and even extended into the leadership of the "peace churches."[23] Unless one wished to imply guilt by association, however, there would be no reason to place such evidences of loyalty to the nation in the same category as expressions of vindictiveness and hate against the enemy.

A most significant and portentous distinction, in fact, within the pattern of loyalism was the distinction between those who conceived their principal business in relation to the war as whipping up moral enthusiasm and those who felt, especially after

---

Historical Review, questioned my estimate that 50 percent of the liberal leaders should be classified as "reluctant" about the war. Yet Bigham's own dissertation quotes only two of these 95—Mathews and Abbott—as expressing intolerant sentiments. He mentions twelve others, including three who he agrees were opponents of the war, at one point or another in his chapters on World War I. Darrel E. Bigham, letter to the Editor, *American Historical Review*, 76 (December 1971), 1631-1632; "American Christian Thinkers and the Function of War, 1861-1920," Ph.D. dissertation, University of Kansas, 1970, chaps. 7 and 8 passim. See Hutchison, "Cultural Strain," p. 411. Granville Hicks and Ray Abrams cite, between them, 12 of these 95 prominent liberals as "presenting arms," generally by means of militant statements insisting upon the morality of the Allied cause and the immorality of the German. Twelve others (again including virtual opponents like Rauschenbusch) are mentioned by one or both of these two authors as in some way going along with the war. Hicks, "Parsons and the War"; Abrams, *Preachers Present Arms*, passim. There were of course liberal militants whom these authors have not happened to mention, but all the evidence suggests that the greater number—probably far more than half—should be called "reluctant"; and that these men remained critical, in many cases openly so, after American entry.

[22]Sharpe, *Rauschenbusch*, pp. 386-387.

[23]W. A. Brown, *Teacher and His Times*, p. 228. Cf. J. A. Thompson, "American Progressive Publicists and the First World War, 1914-1917," *Journal of American History*, 58 (September 1971), 364-383.

the onset of widespread intolerance, that their principal job, and that of the churches, was to exercise a moderating influence.[24] In the first group were Abbott, Mathews, Henry Churchill King, and Harry Emerson Fosdick. Each of these men warned against extremism, but each devoted himself principally to justifying, in Abbott's phrase, "the twentieth-century crusade." For Abbott the world of 1918 could be divided rather neatly into sufferers (Belgium), repentant sinners (America, Britain), and sinners (Germany). The sinners of course must be defeated and punished. Fosdick later, deeply repentant, recalled that he had "learned to bring down the house with out-and-out militaristic appeals."[25]

Other equally prominent liberals took the opposite tack. Gladden, who had been one of the doughtiest fighters for neutrality, reluctantly accepted the breaking of diplomatic relations in February 1917 and later became a convert to American participation. But he continued even then to seek publication (unsuccessfully) for an antiwar manuscript entitled "Killing Wrong-Doers as a Cure for Wrong-Doing." Newman Smyth, contending publicly for a negotiated settlement, betrayed serious reservations about American war aims. And A. C. McGiffert, newly elected president of Union Theological Seminary, in late 1917 deplored the extent to which religion had become "simply the creature of the various warring nations"; he attacked the "arrogance and censoriousness of judgment" that impede reconciliation, and the tendency to attribute "irreligion and hypocrisy to all one's enemies."[26]

The atmosphere of Union Seminary, in spite of the trustees'

---

[24]In general the division ran along the lines formed in the preparedness debate. Clergymen are sometimes pictured as having undergone a sharp reversal of position in 1917 from pacifism to militancy. A few, like Mathews and Fosdick, had been involved in the peace movement and then became militant. But other alleged examples of the phenomenon are less than convincing. Gladden, a thoroughgoing peace advocate before the war, turns out to have been considerably less than a superpatriot after April 1917. (Dorn, *Gladden*, pp. 429-432). Henry Churchill King, on the other hand, while he never became strident or bigoted, might be said to have experienced "reversal"; see his *The Way to Life*. George Herron would serve as the strongest prototype of reversal, except that Herron had left the ministry in 1901.

[25]Abbott, *Twentieth Century Crusade*, pp. vi-xii; Fosdick, *Living of These Days*, p. 122.

[26]Dorn, *Gladden*, pp. 429-432; Gowing, "Smyth," p. 74; McGiffert, *Seminary*

dismissal of one faculty member, Thomas C. Hall, for an outright pro-German stance, appears to have fostered a distinctly critical attitude toward the war. George A. Coe had hinted at his own persecution in 1916, and seems to have remained silent while the war lasted.[27] But Coffin, Lyman, McGiffert, and Brown all were able to be forthright in protesting the excesses of the war hysteria and in calling for national repentance. Coffin, affiliated with Union as well as with the Madison Avenue Church, continued in his Beecher Lectures of 1918 to deplore arms races, economic exploitation, and "the entire system of preserving international equilibrium by mutual fear." Lyman, though willing to say, in his Union inaugural address of 1918, that "the Great War has become for most of us a mighty struggle for the preservation of democracy," continued to condemn the war. His language in *The Experience of God in Modern Life* (1918) was not remotely similar to that of the militants; or rather, it was similarly strong language applied to an opposite purpose. He wrote of the war as "palpably irrational and . . . colossally hideous . . . wholesale waste and debauchery." "In what sense," he asked, "can moral progress be claimed for a civilization which can issue in such a debacle as is now taking place, in which the human race is slaughtering or deforming its toilers by the million?"[28]

William Adams Brown had gone on record in 1916 as deprecating the manipulation of public opinion through propaganda, and had held sinister economic and power interests responsible for that manipulation. Hatred and distrust are not natural feelings among men, Brown said. One has got to be carefully taught:

It is . . . the result of a process of education, in part deliberate, in part

---

and the War, p. 12. One of Gladden's last articles, rejected by *The Congregationalist* as overly controversial, attacked superpatriotism; another, printed posthumously, suggested that those who asked God to damn the Kaiser had learned their prayers from the Kaiser. Dorn, *Gladden*, p. 432.

[27]Coffin, *Half-Century of Union*, pp. 186-187; Coe, "Contemporary Ideals," p. 387.

[28]Coffin, *Social Rebuilding*, pp. 2-5; Lyman, "Religion of Democracy," p. 44; *Experience of God*, p. 104. Coffin, like McGiffert and others, was also convinced of Germany's special culpability, and in particular that Germany had committed outrages against humanity in Belgium and on the high seas. See Coffin, *Social Rebuilding*, p. 3.

unconscious, through which men have been taught to associate all good with their own country and to look upon the countries to which at the time they happen to be opposed in policy, as dangerous and unprincipled rivals whom it is the highest duty of the patriot to oppose and if need be to crush.

Brown was also an early exponent of a "merchants of death" explanation of the war's causes. Though he thought some militants could be credited with good motives, there were others "to whom war or at least the fear of war means personal profit and enhanced prestige; manufacturers to whom it brings increased dividends, capitalists to whom it opens new markets, journalists who see in it the material of a new sensation." "It is these men," Brown insisted, "and the influences which they set in motion which constitute the real danger against which we need to be on our guard."[29]

Brown, though he called his autobiography *A Teacher and His Times*, was best known for his international ecumenical statesmanship and for forthright, even if patricianly, ventures in social activism. He was a natural choice to be secretary of the Wartime Commission of the Churches, to which post he was appointed in the summer of 1917. With that appointment, both the representativeness and the obduracy of Brown's critical view of the war and the warmakers were put to the test. The main purpose of the Wartime Commission, certainly from the government's point of view, was mobilization of the churches for the war effort and for spiritual services to the troops; but its mission was also, so far as its leaders were concerned, to see that the church's pretensions as a reconciling force be made real. The agency was placed under considerable pressure to stress the first objective and not the second.[30]

The meetings from which the Wartime Commission grew, though instigated by the Federal Council of Churches, were purposely augmented to include religious groups not represented on the council. The resulting body, which Brown called "the most representative body of American Christians which up to that time

---

[29]Brown, *Is Christianity Practicable?* pp. 125-127.
[30]Piper, "Federal Council," pp. 201-298 et passim.

had ever assembled," adopted unanimously a lengthy statement of war aims that Brown had composed. The statement promised the nation "support and allegiance in unstinted measure," but also asserted that loyalty to God, "whose loving purpose embraces every man and every nation," rises above and beyond loyalty to the nation and its ideals. Along with admonitions about the inspiriting of the people, the worthiness of the ideals being defended in the war, and the need for concern about the spiritual welfare of American troops, the manifesto included a number of commitments to the cause of reconciliation. Christians were urged, for example,

To purge our own hearts clean of arrogance and selfishness . . .
To unite in the fellowship of service multitudes who love their enemies and are ready to join with them in rebuilding the waste places as soon as peace shall come . . .
To be vigilant against every attempt to arouse the spirit of vengeance and unjust suspicion toward those of foreign birth or sympathies;
To protect the rights of conscience against every attempt to invade them.[31]

Brown later acknowledged that in actual practice the churches had fallen considerably short of such ideals, and that individual Christians in some cases definitely repudiated them.[32] Whether Brown and his colleagues in the clerical leadership backed down, whether they ceased to exercise a moderating leadership, is a different question.

The inducements to do so, in the form of direct attacks upon the patriotism of the commission, of the religious newspapers, and of the clergy generally were very intense. As John Piper demonstrates, the leaders of the Federal Council were, with some justification, more often accused of pacifist than of militarist sympathies. In February of 1918, the Reverend Joseph H. Odell, of Troy, New York, published an article in the *Atlantic Monthly* excoriating the American clergy for insufficient zeal against the

---

[31]Brown, *Teacher and His Times*, pp. 227-230.
[32]Ibid., p. 228. See also John A. Hutchison's assertion, which I should think is substantially correct, that officials of the Federal Council and the Wartime Commission did not actually denounce American policies in prosecution of the war. Hutchison, *We Are Not Divided*, p. 182.

Kaiser and against German theology. At the end of the same month, Robert E. Speer, who as chairman of the Wartime Commission was Brown's immediate superior and close colleague, was attacked severely in the letter columns of the New York *Times* for having devoted a speech before YMCA workers chiefly to criticisms of American society. And in August of 1918, A. C. Dieffenbach, the very militant editor of the major Unitarian periodical, issued an even more comprehensive attack than Odell's. "We have listened to speech after speech by so-called religious leaders," Dieffenbach complained in exasperation, "as we have read thousands of editorials and articles in the church papers, and only once in a hundred times does either speaker or writer go to the centre and soul of the business and utter a ringing challenge to win the war for God and Christ and mankind."[33]

From militant churchmen such criticisms of course elicited new assertions of militance. From those who had been fighting intolerance, however, they drew unhesitating protestations both of loyalty to the country and of determination to go on opposing the superpatriots. Speer showed no timidity whatever about repeating in the *Times* the very criticisms of American chauvinism that had brought him under fire in the first place. He in fact added deeper criticisms:

My conception of loyalty at this time does not require of the loyal man that he should believe in the impeccability of our national past or in the ethical perfection of our present national life . . . Whoever takes any other view and requires of the man who would be loyal that he must deny facts or tolerate in America what he is warring against elsewhere comes perilously near to the "insidious disloyalty" of [which] one of your correspondents speaks . . . To tolerate or to conceal behind our armies the policies, the prejudices or the passions which are before them is disloyalty. To try to make our own hearts pure and our own hands clean . . . is loyalty, and it is the only kind of loyalty that will stand the strain that is before us.[34]

---

[33]Piper, "Federal Council," p. 110; Odell, "Peter Sat by the Fire"; New York *Times* (February 23, 25, 26, 27, 1918); Dieffenbach, "Failure of the Religious Press," p. 727.

[34]New York *Times* (February 26, 1918), p. 8. The most complete account of the Speer controversy, and of Speer's direction of the Wartime Commission, is in Piper, "Robert E. Speer."

Brown later asserted that during his association with Speer on the commission "there was not, so far as I know, a single major issue on which we differed." Certainly there seems to have been no disagreement at all about the fight against intolerance. Writing in May of 1918 on "The Place of Repentance in a Nation at War," Brown contended that "we must guard against those who would persuade us that, in this time of storm and stress and instant need, we have no time for self-examination and penitence."[35]

In August, when Dieffenbach's indictment of clerical luke-warmness appeared, the *Congregationalist*, like Speer, Brown, and the Federal Council, reaffirmed its intention to combat the spirit of hatred. The paper, said its editors, would continue,

while doing all it can to help win the war speedily and conclusively, to keep alive . . . the vision of a kingdom founded not on force alone but on righteousness and love . . . to incite the nation to win the war worthily, to arouse the mighty forces of prayer and to direct their exercise, to repress the spirit of indiscriminate and implacable hatred.[36]

Odell, Dieffenbach, and other militants may have underestimated the incidence of warmaking zeal among the clergy. But they were entirely right in discerning that a critical loyalism, and a very qualified enthusiasm for the war, were more prevalent among the clergy—whether conservative or liberal—than extreme zealotry in the cause.[37]

Patterns of Theological Response

Against this background of a predominating critical loyalism, liberals developed a number of different attitudes concerning the sufficiency of their theology or its need of revision. One prominent

---

[35]*Teacher and His Times*, p. 231; *North American Student*, 6 (May 1918), 366.

[36]*The Congregationalist and Advance*, 103 (August 15, 1918), 183.

[37]Sydney E. Ahlstrom asserts that Abrams' *Preachers Present Arms* has been accused but never successfully convicted of exaggerating the militance of the clergy; he predicts that it will not be so convicted. (Ahlstrom, *Religious History*, p. 884.) My own findings, together with John Piper's work on the Federal Council (which Ahlstrom had not seen, or at least does not cite or refute) convince me that Abrams' critics have been, if anything, too easy on him. A thorough reworking is needed.

line of argument, represented especially by Gladden and Brown, held that the war showed the need not for a new Christian theology but for new attempts to apply the one already professed. A second position, defended by Lyman and Fenn, was that the war had confirmed and vivified a need for theological change that ought to have been evident long before. And a third stance, taken just after the war by Fosdick and by Willard Sperry, concentrated upon the implications of the entire war experience, including its aftermath at Versailles, for the liberal doctrines of human nature and human progress.

Gladden's biographer rightly refers to the Social Gospel leader's "amazing optimism" during these years when his world appeared to be crumbling.[38] In the spirit of that optimism, he insisted that the liberal world view required no basic alteration. For Gladden, the great problems were institutional—not a need for new ideals but a need for the church and similar institutions to come abreast of their ideals. The churches, he thought, would become regenerate as a result of the war and would berate themselves for their "horrible, deadly failure"; but if such repentance were to mean either going back to the old theology or attempting to go "beyond Christianity," the results could be tragic. "Let us not listen any longer," he proposed, "to those who prate to us about going back to the religion of some old day." But the churches, far from being called upon to go beyond Christianity, must try "to overtake it if they can."[39]

Fenn and Lyman agreed with Gladden that the war had changed nothing essential, but followed a somewhat different reasoning. The need for rather fundamental changes in theological structure had existed before the war, they contended, and had even to some extent been acted upon. The current crisis, according to Lyman, had simply accelerated a shift from preoccupation with physical nature to preoccupation with humanity. In the earlier days of liberalism, theology had dealt mainly with natural law, with the nature of cosmic forces, with biological evolution. Even

---

[38]Dorn, *Gladden*, p. 431.

[39]Gladden, *Great War*, pp. 30-32. For Brown's similar view, see *Is Christianity Practicable?* pp. 49-54.

when liberals had discussed history, psychology, and sociology, their point of view had been shaped by the physical sciences; and theology had been occupied with adjusting itself to the assured results of science. But the war was underlining the need to discuss more humanistic issues of "autocracy versus democracy, nationalism versus internationalism, militarism versus disarmament." And in the approach to such problems the whole question of human improvability had been thrown open. Divine immanence could no longer simply be taken for granted; one must ask what immanence means in a civilization capable of so much evil. Human potential for good could not be flatly assumed, but must be reexplored.[40]

Both Lyman and Fenn, despite the latter's recognition of flaws in the liberal doctrine of man, showed more concern to redefine theism than to reconsider liberal definitions of human nature. The jarring disjunctions between the older conceptions of God and the newer observations of humanity and the world were to be resolved largely by redefining God.

This redefinition followed the lines laid down a few years earlier as these two men, along with many others, had passed through the pragmatic revolt. For Lyman, "the God of the new age" must be a God of creative personality—one who, instead of simply defining human goals once for all, works with human beings to achieve them. "Men at this tragic moment of history," Lyman wrote, "need a God who is accessible, who can enter into the most intimate relations with them."

If he is immanent in nature and history—and doubtless that way of conceiving him will still be needed—it must be . . . as the organizing genius of a vast workshop who is transforming raw material into a structure the lines of which are only beginning to appear, but which shall yet prove to be strong and beautiful and abiding. [Men] will need that God whose very nature is creative personality.[41]

Fenn in 1918 preferred the terminology of "purpose," just as he had in his prewar critique of idealistic theism. The progress of mankind, in the new schema, was to be seen as "a living adventure, not a dead sure thing." God, accordingly, must be thought of "in

---

[40]Lyman, *God of the New Age*, pp. 4-10.
[41]Ibid., pp. 11-15.

William Wallace Fenn in 1909

terms of becoming rather than of being." Without acceding explicitly to H. G. Wells's notion of a finite God, Fenn approached within hailing distance of that conception when he said that theologians in the prewar period had already come to hold "that God Himself was making the best of things and of men, and to believe that it was up to man to join issue with God in the glorious enterprise. Things were not best as they were: God and man must labor together to make the best of them."[42]

Lyman's observations about what was happening in the relations between religion and evolutionary theory were significant and prescient. One of the meanings he discerned in the shift of concern from nature to humanity was that the old supernaturalist objections to Darwinism would be giving way to objections framed by moral realists. The new tension would be between "the actual facts of evolution and the idea that the cosmos is realizing a moral purpose."[43] Lyman thus foresaw to a considerable extent the later movement from a fundamentalist to a neo-orthodox set of objections to evolutionary liberalism.

Neither Lyman nor Fenn, however, was willing, when it came to considering human nature, to define man as radically sinful. The key attribute of man, they thought, was not his sinfulness but his freedom. They had, in their own conception, extricated humanity, as well as God, from its former rigidly determined place within a system of absolute idealism; and the human person thus liberated did not seem to them primarily a miserable sinner dependent upon grace. Man was, instead, a potential co-worker with God, one whose terrible sinning was a way of retarding God's unfolding purpose.

By such a method, by making both man and God free co-workers within a grossly unfinished evolutionary process, Lyman avoided going "outside of human evolution" for evidence of God. Human beings are indeed sinful, and in fact, as both Lyman and Fenn insisted, must take responsibility for such tragedies as the war. The explanation of evil, however, is reached not by emphasizing the

---

[42]Fenn, "War and the Thought of God," in Hutchison, ed., *American Protestant Thought*, pp. 152-153.

[43]Lyman, *Experience of God*, p. 103.

moral distance between humanity and God, but by stressing human responsibility in a way that incidentally decreases that distance. "The new thought of God," said Fenn, "will be one in which the assertion of human freedom will be definitely and emphatically made. There is the gist of the whole matter." In the new-style conflict over evolution, such thinkers would seek to maintain the credibility of the evolutionary concept by, fundamentally, dampening all earlier illusions about the great distance humanity had come, or about the extent to which God had thus far been able to effectuate his abiding purposes.[44]

Fenn's avoidance of theodicies based upon humanity's radical sinfulness and distance from God was a very conscious avoidance. Like many others, he feared an overreaction that would undo all the salutary work of the liberal movement. "Granted that the facts of evil have been forced into the forefront of our thinking," he wrote, "and that upon them our minds are now focused, yet for that very reason the danger is that we shall now consider these as disproportionately as we have been wont to consider the opposite class of facts." The war had brought out unsuspected nobility as well as unsuspected baseness in the human makeup. "The valleys run deeper, the peaks rise higher than we had suspected." The faith in an orderly universe therefore remained intact—"not a single natural law has suspended operation"—even though unity and order must now be seen as concomitants of purpose rather than of mechanism.[45] Like Gladden, Fenn was leery, despite his critical attitude toward liberalism, of anything that appeared to be a real return to Calvinist conceptions of sin and transcendence.

Among several British writers who addressed themselves to Americans on the meaning of the war for theology, one in particular shared the apprehensions of Gladden and Fenn that all the gains of the past could be lost. Alfred E. Garvie, of New College, London, feared "a relapse from the conception of the Holy Father to that of the Righteous Ruler." In reality, "a world stricken as it

---

[44]Ibid., p. 92; Lyman, *God of the New Age*, pp. 44-45; Fenn, "Thought of God," pp. 153-154, 157.
[45]Ibid., p. 155.

is today needs not so much the terror of the Lord as his tenderness"; and Garvie warned that political reaction and intolerance could not be stemmed, nor brotherhood and internationalism promoted, if religious thinkers returned to a despotic conception of God.[46] Other British writers, however, such as L. P. Jacks and William Inge, seemed to be moving toward a reassertion of traditional Christian convictions about original sin and about the estrangement of human beings from God.

Inge, dean of St. Paul's in London, earned his sobriquet of "gloomy dean" in these years not because he suddenly became pessimistic but because his pessimism began to be heeded. His gloominess related only to the world and the flesh; with respect to a higher world of transcendent values, and the Christian's ability to live in that higher world, Inge was an optimist. Thus he could take the serene position that "for the Christian, nothing absolutely vital is at stake in any secular conflict"—the Great War definitely included. But he also thought the war would make it impossible any longer to assume or preach an Emersonian explanation of evil. The idea that "justice is done universally, here and now, if we could only see it," had been possible only to "the successful literary man of the nineteenth century, living in perfect security and considerable comfort," and knowing "little of the darker mysteries of human suffering." "Could Emerson have borne to turn his graceful epigrams," Inge asked, "if he had lived in Belgium in 1914, or in Armenia in 1915"?[47]

L. P. Jacks, attempting to predict more directly what the war would mean for theology, proposed that everything would depend upon the impression of human nature that people absorbed during the current theological hiatus. If the heroism and nobility of men at war seemed most impressive, that would mean a boost for "the theology of moral excellence." But Jacks plainly thought this unlikely. If all the newspapers, statesmen, professors, and other users of language in Europe "were to speak the truth consistently for a week on end," the war would cease automatically;

---

[46]Garvie, "Danger of Reaction," pp. 325-338.

[47]Inge, "Justice of God," pp. 446, 457, 442-443. For criticism of Inge by a more hopeful Platonist, see Buckham, "Dean Inge."

but since that was not likely to happen, the reputation of human nature would probably continue to suffer. As a result, "the theology which interprets religion as the pursuit of moral excellence will remain below the horizon for some time to come." In its place, Jacks expected the ascendancy of the kind of "theology of salvation" which always asserts itself "when all goes ill and the devil seems master of the world." Men would "fling themselves, as they have often done in darker times, on the grace and mercy of God."[48]

On the American side, Charles G. Shaw in 1916 took up the question of revisions in the liberal estimate of human nature and progress. Shaw, a graduate of Drew Theological Seminary (Methodist) who had become professor of ethics at New York University, acknowledged the rights and accomplishments of the rationalistic, emancipatory liberalism of Voltaire, Renan, and A. D. White; but he insisted there is another valid liberal tradition—on the whole a more pessimistic one—that provides a more full-bodied response to humanity's real situation in the cosmos. Rationalistic liberalism, as it "writhed its way through the seventeenth and eighteenth centuries," had attended too exclusively to the emancipation of the human intellect. Shaw now asked whether the cognitive process were the only function of consciousness that stood in need of freedom or had the capacity to enjoy it.[49]

Over against the tradition of rationalistic liberalism Shaw set the ideas of Goethe, Ibsen, Nietzsche, and especially Dostoyevski. These thinkers, instead of contending for a mere "liberty of the thinking process," had spoken for "the full freedom of the soul in its human unity." Their conception of freedom, which Shaw traced farther back to Jeremiah and to St. Paul,[50] involved liberation from the kind of parochialism and present-mindedness that had often prevented rationalism from valuing any ideas except those of its own age. It also implied an untrammeled insistence upon the ideal; and it was by this route, especially, that Shaw arrived at a

---

[48] Jacks, "Theological Holiday," pp. 12-14.
[49] Shaw, "Two Types of Liberalism," pp. 360-363.
[50] He also linked Homer, Dante, Milton, Blake, Baudelaire, and Wagner to this tradition. Ibid., pp. 361, 368.

conjunction among the three ideas of freedom, humanism, and relative pessimism. "It is the harsh contrast between the Ideal and the Actual," he wrote, "that begets the pessimistic mood." The national need of Americans, and of American religion, he concluded, was for "an intensive, humanistic liberalism, even when this is sure to entertain us under the auspices of pessimism."[51]

Although Shaw's attempt to retain the *cachet* of the term "liberal" for his realistic humanism seemed just a bit forced, his article helped initiate a phase of self-criticism that in some ways was modernistic liberalism's finest hour. Shaw and a succession of others, in their willingness to turn to the literary and scientific culture for insights into the darkening human condition, were adhering to the logic of the modernist position. If some liberals thought it was only the orthodox who were supposed to open themselves to correction from those secular quarters, men like Shaw did not agree. Where the theological establishment—liberal or otherwise—seemed not to be providing adequate responses, the modernist, they assumed, should be the first and freest to turn elsewhere. The modernist should also be the one best equipped to make new secular insights available within the going religious ideology.

The most forceful and prominent critiques of the liberal idea of progress in the years immediately following the war were unequivocal in stating the necessity for religious liberalism to turn to the novelists, the dramatists, the philosophers, and certain of the scientists for help in reinterpreting their own religious tradition. Willard Sperry, Fenn's successor as dean of Harvard Divinity School, said in 1921 that the most effective exponent of Christianity at that moment was not the preacher but "the free lance." And the distinctive contribution of the free-lance theologian lay in his understanding of human sin.

In the backlash of the war Western intellectual life, according to Sperry, was rejecting "Romanticism and its bastard child Sentimentalism." The magnificent nineteenth-century romantic movement having done its work and gone to seed—in a descent

---

[51] Ibid., pp. 368, 371.

from Cowper and Wordsworth to Oscar Wilde and Aubrey Beards-
ley—"the wholesome prophetic spirit of mankind" was once again
reasserting itself. But the reassertion was coming from outside the
churches. The most notable current fact of religious life, Sperry
thought, was the turning of the unchurched mind to the message
of Jesus. People were turning to the gospel of Galilee "because
the gospel of Manchester has proved such a shoddy substitute";
and these new informal adherents seemed to understand, better
than the preachers and theologians, what Christianity is all
about.[52]

The preaching ministry of Jesus, Sperry pointed out, "opened
with an unqualified command to repent." And in successive centuries the Christian life invariably began "as an effort to roll
away the burden of sin and guilt from the bowed shoulders of the
human conscience." But the culture of modernity, both elite and
popular, had forgotten about sin and repentance, and liberal
religion was not doing anything to jog its memory. "There is no
point," said Sperry, "at which modern liberal Protestantism
stands in sharper contrast to historic Christianity as a whole than
in its indifference to this initial mood of Christian experience."
The church's too-ready acquiescence in modern man's satisfied
view of himself was a betrayal of its own heritage and a major
reason for "the apparent impotence of the Christian religion in
modern society."[53]

Sperry was not recommending a return either to preliberal
dogmas of original sin or to an earlier individualistic moralism.
To say once again that "in Adam's fall we sinned all" would be
to say nothing useful to modern man; and similarly, Christianity
would discredit itself if it returned to a petty conception of sin
as "the sort of transgression which is confessed by the sower of
wild oats at a Salvation Army mourners' bench." Dancing, drinking, cheating, and sleeping in church, however deplorable these
peccadilloes may be, did not add up to the "sin" for which St.
Paul or Luther had suffered an agonized conscience. For the Calvinist, also, the moral problem had not been "to keep his petty

---

[52]Sperry, *Disciplines of Liberty*, pp. 4-6.
[53]Ibid., pp. 59-61.

cash account with God balanced week by week. What haunted his soul was the knowledge that there was a mortgage on the whole business."[54]

The appointed spokesmen of the churches, despite ample provocations, had not in Sperry's opinion met the occasion of the war with a credible statement of the human need for repentance. No official voice in all of Christendom, during or since the war, had "begun to rise to the moral level that Lincoln reached in the Second Inaugural." Instead, "the true successors to the Calvinist with his agonized conscience and his initial dogma of original sin are to be found to-day among the biologists, the psychologists, the novelists and the dramatists." Scientists like Huxley, literary persons like George Bernard Shaw, admittedly were moral diagnosticians rather than moral penitents. But they were offering at least the rudiments of a modern doctrine of original sin, a conception under which man is "not so much a sinner in nature, as a sinner through society." Their writings spoke from the depths of the agonized human conscience to which Calvinism formerly had given the most eloquent expression. Although this conscience "now speaks a new dialect, its central consciousness is qualitatively unchanged."[55]

Harry Emerson Fosdick, the most widely-known religious liberal of the 1920s, concurred in Sperry's warnings—only in stronger language. When Fosdick in 1928 told readers of the *Christian Century* "What the War Did to My Mind," he wrote mostly about what that event had done to his militarism: the young seminarian who had chided his teacher William Newton Clarke for his strictures against the Spanish-American War had become in the twenties the chastened preacher vowing not "to bless war again, or support it, or expect from it any valuable thing."[56] But Fosdick also, throughout the decade, spiced his liberal apologetics with warnings about "The Dangers of Modernism" and "The Perils of Progress."[57] And while the war could

---

[54]Ibid., pp. 64-66.
[55]Ibid., pp. 79, 67, 70, 67.
[56]*Christian Century*, 45 (January 5, 1928), 10-11.
[57]The first of these two chapter titles appears in Fosdick's *Adventurous*

not provide the entire explanation for these reservations, clearly it had played its part in generating them. There was no need, Fosdick said in 1922, for either the theologians or the psychologists to "conjure up a sense of sin. All we need to do is to open our eyes to facts." The current "desperate endeavors to save this rocking civilization from the consequences of the blow just delivered it by men's iniquities" were sufficient to indicate "that this is no fool-proof universe automatically progressive, but that moral evil is still the central problem of mankind."[58]

Fosdick's *Christianity and Progress,* offered originally as the Cole Lectures at Vanderbilt University in 1922, was not a rejection of the progressive faith. The speaker thought the idea of progress, upstart though it was in the world's long intellectual history, had come to stay; and he reiterated the familiar applications of that idea to the interpretation of the scriptures and to the ideology of Christian social reform.[59] Fosdick's intent was not to discredit progressivism but to save it from its friends. His effort to reinterpret Christianity's relation to the doctrine of progress, he said, was a defensive measure "to save the Gospel from being unintelligently mauled and mishandled" by progressive doctrine. Fosdick was as offended as Clarke had been by visions of the easy triumph of Christianity and idealism. Noting that a recent writer had suggested that "over the crest of the hill the Promised Land stretches away to the far horizons smiling in eternal sunshine," he retorted the

the picture is nonsense. All the progress this world will know waits upon the conquest of sin. Strange as it may sound to the ears of this modern age, long tickled by the amiable idiocies of evolution popularly misinterpreted, this generation's deepest need is not these dithyrambic songs about inevitable progress, but a fresh sense of personal and social sin.[60]

Among the major perils of a fatuous progressivism, Fosdick said,

---

Religion, pp. 258-274; the second in his *Christianity and Progress,* pp. 167-206. Fosdick was so persistently concerned about this matter that in his homiletics classes at Union he regularly assigned the writing of a sermon on "The Perils of Liberalism." See Horton, *Realistic Theology,* p. 4.

[58]*Christianity and Progress,* pp. 177-178.
[59]Ibid., pp. 41-48, 87-165.
[60]Ibid., pp. 48, 175.

was its tendency to take the backbone out of social radicalism. Because they imagined progress to be easily attainable, reformers relied upon palliatives instead of opting for radical solutions. In the matter of preventing wars, for example, disarmament conferences would not 'suffice; people must be induced actually to put loyalty to Christ above loyalty to the nation. Whenever Germans refused to place morality above the state, or Japanese gave blind obedience to the Mikado, we had been ready enough, Fosdick said, to condemn them. "When, however, a man says in plain English: I am an American but I am a Christian first . . . and, if ever national action makes these two things conflict, I must choose God and not America—to the ears of many that plain statement has a tang of newness and danger."[61]

The heart of the problem—which affected all human social relationships, not just national loyalties—was the discrepancy between the unselfishness of individual persons and the ruthless selfishness of these same persons as members of their various collectivities:

We are unselfish so far as our group is concerned; we make it a point of honor to support our economic class; it is part of our code of duty to be loyal there. But while we are thus unselfish with reference to the group, the group itself is not unselfish; the group itself is fighting a bitter and selfish conflict, avaricious and often cruel.[62]

Ultimately there was no way out of this situation except through the activities of persons whose loyalties transcended those of their particular groups. But Christianity would never generate such sacrifice so long as people operated under the illusion that progress comes without sacrifice. And Fosdick, like Charles Shaw and Sperry, was convinced that the preachers badly needed the help of secular thinkers in ridding themselves of their illusions. After centuries of thundering against sin, the preachers in recent years had become "very reticent about it." But literary people had not been reticent—there had been no great novel or play that was not "centrally concerned with the problem of human evil." The

---

[61]Ibid., pp. 179-181.
[62]Ibid., pp. 183-184.

scientists, meanwhile, far from predicting with Tennyson that every grim ravine will become a garden, were warning that the earth, once uninhabitable, may become so again.[63]

Religious liberalism had not simply taken the war in stride. The experience of war had strengthened the process of self-criticism already under way before 1914; had vivified for many the fears about liberal inadequacy and sentimentality; and had directed a glaring spotlight on humanistic issues that had received relatively less attention in prewar controversies. The questioning of liberalism had not taken hold as strongly or noticeably in 1920 as it would seem to after 1930. But even that difference should not be exaggerated. Church people of the twenties can be accused of continuing obliviously with their lawn socials, while "overhead the banner of Normalcy fluttered listlessly."[64] But there is little evidence that the rank and file in church or clergy adjourned the theological lawn social in the thirties, despite the palpable inducements of depression and Hitlerism.

Within the liberal ideology, the modernist idea seems in retrospect to have suffered profound disintegration at the very moment of its most forthright application. The logic of modernism had always demanded that theological revision take account of the observable movement of history and of ideas arising from the so-called secular culture. Liberals like Fenn, Sperry, and Fosdick, in their absorption of the war experience, followed this logic faithfully; and the result was an increasing sense that the progressivist component of modernism, its reverently hopeful interpretation of the immanence of God in culture, had become deeply problematic.

---

[63]Ibid., pp. 177, 32-37.
[64]Ahlstrom, "Continental Influence," p. 260.

The Odd Couple: Fundamentalism and Humanism in the Twenties

We shall do well to listen to Dr. Machen.
WALTER LIPPMANN, 1929

The most powerful challenges to religious liberalism in the two decades after 1920—fundamentalism, secular humanism, and neo-orthodoxy—were in most respects mutually exclusive or at least discontinuous movements. The people who called themselves fundamentalists, for example, abhorred any notion of kinship with the neo-orthodoxy and theological realism that entered the lists against liberalism after 1930. Secular humanists, pessimistic naturalists, and others who joined in the same general attack were equally anxious, on those few occasions when anyone confused them with their co-belligerents, to make clear how much they differed from either fundamentalists or the neo-orthodox. And so it went. Even within movements like fundamentalism that the public tended to view stereotypically, differences could be large and deeply or bitterly felt. Princeton conservatives felt sufficiently disturbed by what most people were calling fundamentalism in the twenties that they would gladly have repudiated the very term, had it not been too late in the day to do so.

The fact that, despite disagreements and historic antagonisms of a most essential kind, some small degree of intellectual collaboration was effected in the 1920s between fundamentalists and secular humanists suggests how pervasively the flaws in the liberal posture were being felt. The particular flaw these two sets of critics found themselves agreeing upon was not the liberal overestimate of human nature—the point on which neo-orthodoxy would later fix attention. Fundamentalists did generally disapprove of liberal anthropology; and many secular humanists in the 1920s were moving, despite that designation, in the direction of a brave despair about human nature. But in this period the real ground for agreement lay in an old Princetonian refrain: the alleged necessity of a clean choice between Christian orthodoxy and no Christianity at all. Liberals, in response, averred not only that the modernist method had historically been the one by which Christian doctrines had been formed but also that for most of those who adhered to modernist ways of thought, the actual choice had been between liberal Christianity or none at all.

"It is not Christianity": Fundamentalist Reactions to Liberal Success

The intense and growing fundamentalist demand for choice, for an end to comprehensiveness and equivocation, operated at various levels of stridency. Popular and political fundamentalism tended to pose the issue as one between biblical literalism and atheism, while conservative scholars were likely to denounce the alternatives to literalism merely as "not Christian." In either form, this heightened exclusivism constituted a response to the same phenomenon; namely, to liberal success. As liberals, or those who were tolerant of them, came to power in mission boards, social service agencies, and educational institutions, fundamentalist rhetoric took a line that, while not inconsistent with earlier conservative positions, was distinctive enough to give a special coloration to the controversies of the 1920s. The theme that united different kinds of fundamentalists involved a concession—"Yes, liberalism is succeeding"; and a disclaimer—"No, it is not Christianity."

Again, as in the 1880s, missions provided the entering wedge for new controversy. Harry Emerson Fosdick might have become the chief heretic of the era in any event, but it was fundamentalist activities in the mission fields that in fact provoked his famous protest of 1922—"Shall the Fundamentalists Win?" And these provocative activities had themselves been responses to a liberal takeover of missions that allegedly had got completely out of hand.

From the earliest days of the New Theology until at least the period of *The Fundamentals,* the central conservative argument, *pace* George Gordon and William Newton Clarke, had been that liberalism would surely "cut the nerve of missions." Conservatives had meant by this not just that the message preached would be insipid and untrue—though they were sure it would be—but that the heathen would not accept it. Mission organizations, it was said, would fail; missionaries would have to come home.

Cyrus Hamlin, founder of Robert College in Istanbul, in 1886 had offered a modest, half-serious proposal to those who wished to carry the new, less urgent message of salvation into the mission field. They should, he said, form their own board and secure a field all to themselves, preferably in the heart of Africa. The organization could be called The Dissenters' Board of Missions for the Congo, and "those who should prefer it to the American Board could send in their contributions accordingly." Such a plan would enable enthusiastic young men to go into Africa and "tell the heathen how happy have been their ancestors in knowing nothing of Christ, for their trial has been in far more favorable circumstances." If, in response to such a message, "Ethiopia shall soon stretch out her hands unto God" and conversions abound everywhere, then, Hamlin said, the liberals would have proved their point.[1]

But Hamlin and conservatives of his generation had been confident that nothing of that kind would happen. The Reverend Charles Bowen, in volume nine of *The Fundamentals,* insisted that the doctrine of the Atonement—in its strict substitutionary form—not only does not offend prospective converts; it is the only thing that wins them. Bowen, like George Gordon, wished to preach solely "Jesus Christ and him crucified," but to Bowen this meant preaching about a God who, in the form of the Christ, dies for the sake of men and in legal expiation of their guilt. Nothing

---

[1]Hamlin, "New Departure," p. 769.

less, he said, impresses the heathen as superior to their own religions.[2]

By the early 1920s, however, the conservatives, thoroughly alarmed by liberal successes and by postwar projections of eclectic "church unions" throughout the world, were arguing almost the reverse of what Bowen had contended; and Hamlin's idea for a Dissenters' Board of Missions had ceased to amuse. *The Ministers' Monthly*, founded in 1922 as a counterweight to the "controlled press" of the liberal religious establishment, contended that "the fearful situation in most of our foreign mission fields" had come about precisely because liberalism was so much more attractive and so much more easily absorbed by "an ignorant, idol-worshipping heathen" than orthodox Christianity could be. The flood tide of liberalism had engulfed the missionary movement as it had the seminaries, the religious press, and "the ecclesiastical machinery in nearly all of the leading denominations." This had happened because liberals had "outwitted and outgeneraled the orthodox forces at nearly every turn of the road." Liberal missionaries were gaining entrée, moreover, because foreign peoples and governments had come to associate a socially oriented Christianity with cultural and economic progress. "Missionary activities," the *Monthly*'s editors fumed, "have become popular with statesmen, economists, chambers of commerce, and who and what not!" A serious misunderstanding had arisen about the real purpose of missionary activities because the liberals "with their theories of social Christianity, ethical culture, intellectual development and general civic advancement have drawn the eyes of men from off the Christ of God."[3]

Conservatives returning or writing from specific mission fields documented the situation in lurid detail. One of the earliest and most influential documents was the 1921 report of W. H. Griffith Thomas, an Episcopal clergyman, on "Modernism in China." Thomas' lectures in China during the preceding year had made

---

[2]Charles A. Bowen, "A Message from Missions to the Modern Ministry," *Fundamentals*, IX, 96-102.

[3]"Flood Tide of Liberalism," pp. 3ff. An earlier installment, surveying the situation in the theological schools, had appeared in the September number.

him a figure, somewhat against his will, in the controversy over the founding of a new organization called the Bible Union of China. The Union's purpose was to see that only believers in "the whole Bible" would thenceforth be sent into the mission field in China or, by implication, anywhere else. Clearly, Thomas approved such an objective. He quoted a British observer who complained that in Canton, which he said offered a typical urban instance, none of the foreign missionaries was engaged in evangelistic work. Such efforts were being left to native Christians, while Westerners with "loose views about the authority and inspiration of the Bible" busied themselves with educational and other institutional work. What this meant, of course, was that the Higher Criticism and allied heresies were subverting the faith that the real evangelists were trying to teach. Thomas was appalled and apparently convinced, also, by the report of Pastors Lo and Hutchinson, who told the East China Educational Association that "we have not found a single student body in our schools [that is] not deeply affected by ideas which, whether in the realm of politics, economics, sociology or religion, can hardly be called orthodox . . . Within the schools conducted by the Christian Church you will find as much radical thought, and thought as dangerous in its implications, as is to be found anywhere in this seething land."[4]

Thomas' account of the depradations of modernism in China continued for another twenty-five pages. This massively documentary approach was one that came to be standard in the 1920s and early 1930s in the literature of fundamentalist opposition to modernism. While conservatives could not concede the spiritual effectiveness of liberalism,[5] they did now concede its practical success in winning at least nominal adherents to Christianity. That the views enjoying these successes were not really Christian views was commonly taken for granted or was demonstrated by simple reference to scripture.

Against such a background, the great contribution in the

---

[4]Thomas, "Modernism in China," pp. 630-647.
[5]See ibid., pp. 668-669.

1920s of the Princeton scholar J. Gresham Machen lay in his willingness and ability to argue out—rather than just assume or proof-text—the premise that modernistic liberalism was not Christianity. Machen on the whole agreed with the Chicago modernist Shailer Mathews, who contended that fundamentalism and liberalism represented contrasting social minds and contrasting attitudes toward culture. But Machen thought real religious differences were also involved; and he excluded decisively all possibility of the sort of accommodation between the parties that liberals like Fosdick and Mathews considered workable and essential.

Machen maintained, most carefully and studiously, an attitude of personal charity toward those who held liberal views. "We are particularly anxious not to be misunderstood," he wrote at the beginning of *Christianity and Liberalism* (1923); "'Un-Christian' . . . is sometimes taken as a term of opprobrium. We do not mean it at all as such." Socrates and Goethe were not Christians, Machen explained, and yet they towered over the common run of men. If those who are least in the Kingdom are greater than such non-Christians, this is by virtue of "an undeserved privilege," not because of any inherent superiority. The fact remained that the Christian-liberal confrontation represented a clash between different religions:

What the liberal theologian has retained after abandoning to the enemy one Christian doctrine after another is not Christianity at all, but a religion which is so entirely different from Christianity as to belong in a distinct category.[6]

It was to underline this view—as well as, no doubt, to forestall facile identification between his ideas and those of relatively unwashed conservatives—that Machen so far as feasible avoided the term "fundamentalist."[7] To use such a term would imply that there are Christian subcategories of which liberalism might be one. And that was not the case, in Machen's view; whatever is not fundamental is not Christianity at all.

---

[6]Machen, *Christianity and Liberalsim*, pp. 8, 6-7.
[7]Machen, "Christianity in Conflict," in Ferm, ed., *Contemporary American Theology*, I, 270.

J. Gresham Machen

It was quite possible to interpret this stance as disingenuous. To suppose that it can ever be "not opprobrious" to call other professing Christians un-Christian struck some critics as either naive or unctuously dishonest. Dean Sperry complained about the peculiar "mixture of theological patronage and theological vitriol" in such positions.[8] But it is also credible, if one thinks of Machen in the context of the long Princeton tradition, that he was indeed able to separate his convictions about the moral worth of persons and his passion for the purity of doctrine. The maintenance of such high and impersonal standards for inclusion in the Christian body could leave the more room for genuine, if still penultimate, appreciation of moral virtues in those who could not meet the doctrinal test. It was the paradox of the poet Lovelace—"I could not love thee, dear, so much/Loved I not honor more"—applied within the warfare of orthodox Christianity.[9]

Though charity to nonbelievers was an aspiration and where achieved provided a kind of safety valve, still the central obligation was that of identifying the real Christians. What then were the essential doctrines? What must one believe? According to Machen, the believer must first of all accept the primacy of doctrine itself. Machen took direct exception to Fosdick's oft-repeated dynamic conception of Christianity as a matter of "abiding truths in changing categories." Liberals, he said, make doctrine the historical product of Christian experience, but this reverses the true situation. Christian experience is impossible without doctrine.[10] Both truth and categories "abide"; neither changes. If it could be decisively shown that Jesus himself did not propound doctrine, we would still have to attach the name "Christian" to the system of doctrine promulgated after his death. ("It is very doubtful whether a name which through nineteen

---

[8]Sperry, "Theological Vitriol," *Literary Review*, 3 (July 14, 1923), 828.

[9]Richard Lovelace, "To Lucasta, Going to the Warres" (1649). There is no reason to doubt Machen's sincerity in such startling passages as the following: "Many ties—ties of blood, of citizenship, of ethical aims, of humanitarian endeavor—unite us to those who have abandoned the gospel. We trust that those ties may never be weakened." Machen, *Christianity and Liberalism*, p. 52.

[10]Ibid., pp. 19, and 17-53 passim. For an even more direct refutation of the Fosdick position, see Machen, "Christianity in Conflict," pp. 266-267.

centuries has been so firmly attached to one religion ought now suddenly to be applied to another.") But Jesus did preach a doctrine: that of his own Messiahship. Jesus made the "stupendous" claim that "he was to be the chief actor in a world catastrophe and was to sit in judgment upon the whole earth." And this is the fundamental of fundamentals, according to Machen. To qualify as a Christian, one must believe in the coming and work and resurrection of Christ, and believe in all of these as supernatural events.[11]

What made liberalism "another religion" was, above all, its disbelief in the supernatural Christ-events. Other liberal disqualifications followed from that one: liberalism erred in trying to believe in a God who is immanent, who can be known through individual experience, and who is Father to all humankind rather than just to the redeemed. Liberalism negated historic Christianity by minimizing human estrangement from God. It denied the unique authority of the scriptures. It viewed Christ as an example rather than as a supernatural person and the Savior of mankind. Liberalism, Machen claimed, made man rather than God the author of salvation. And finally, liberalism erroneously conjured up a "brotherhood of man" having divine or religious status, whereas Christianity speaks only of a "brotherhood of the Christian Church"—to which, however, all people are invited.[12]

The attitudes toward modern culture running through Machen's side of these Christian/liberal antinomies were reasonably clear, and Machen had no hesitation about expressing them candidly. While he could not assent to the liberal characterization of dogmatic Christianity as unsympathetic to the "forces that are making to-morrow,"[13] Machen showed a basic disinclination to trust—or, of course, to find primary religious insights—in the development of modern culture. *Christianity and Liberalism* offered, very much in the terms of nineteenth-century laissez-faire

---

[11]*Christianity and Liberalism*, pp. 30-37.

[12]Ibid., pp. 54-180.

[13]Mathews, *Faith of Modernism*, p. 17. Machen protested against "obscurantism"; thought modernity might be "regretted" but not ignored or avoided; and suggested that biblical literalists are really more scientific than their opponents. *Christianity and Liberalism*, pp. 9, 12, 2-3, 7-8.

individualism, repeated rebukes to the mechanization and vul-
garization of modern life. Ranging over the broader world of
culture, it painted a dark picture of science, education, and the
arts. Machen complained that "no great poet is now living" to
celebrate the admitted physical improvement in human living.
"Gone too are the great painters and the great musicians and the
great sculptors."[14]

Machen's autobiographical article of 1932 placed all such reservations in a context of real nostalgia for the days and ways of his
Baltimore boyhood, and for an Old Princeton which by then had
been virtually abolished through a reorganization of the seminary.
And while for Mathews or George Gordon a catalogue of social
evils always led to new statements that God is in the world and will
prevail, for Machen they led to a direct repudiation of the modernist premise. "In view of the lamentable defects of modern life,"
Machen wrote, "a type of religion certainly should not be com-
mended simply because it is modern, or condemned simply because
it is old. On the contrary, the condition of mankind is such that
one may well ask what it is that made the men of past generations
so great and the men of the present generation so small."[15]

Machen explained his personal choice of a traditionalist approach to religion by means of a metaphor learned from his
mentor and friend Francis Patton. Patton had told of a man who,
obliged to cross the ocean, had been presented with a choice between two ships. One was in despicable condition; the other was
firmly built, with a competent captain and a high rating at
Lloyd's. The man in the story, concerned that he could not be
absolutely certain about this second ship, was foolish enough to
choose the first one. The person suffering nagging doubts about
literal Christianity, Patton said, is in a similar position. He
should not be foolish. He should choose the safer ship.[16]

Much of the response to *Christianity and Liberalism* was entirely predictable. Machen's book—except for certain regrettably
un-Lutheran pages—had "gladdened the hearts" of two different

---

[14]Ibid., pp. 9-15.
[15]"Christianity in Conflict," pp. 249, 264; *Christianity and Liberalism*, p. 15.
[16]"Christianity in Conflict," pp. 262-263.

reviewers for the Lutheran *Theological Monthly*; and the *Bibliotheca Sacra*, without such reservations, was "embracing every occasion" to recommend it. From the other side, the *Methodist Review* introduced Machen to its readers as "one of the ablest of the diminishing number of reactionary theologians." The *Crozer Quarterly* criticized the Princeton theologian for picking a fight and for attempting to resurrect discredited biblical theories. Gerald Birney Smith, reviewing for Chicago's *Journal of Religion*, expressed resentment about Machen's "absurd" belief that liberals were "dishonest men, craftily scheming to gain a position in the church," and chided the author for providing only a caricature of liberal belief to set over against his own views.[17]

Other responses were more surprising, and seemed to presage new public alignments. W. O. Carver, editor of the *Review and Expositor* and one of a staunch group of moderates at the Southern Baptist seminary in Louisville, took strong exception to Machen's book. As an evangelical and a "profound believer in doctrine," Carver could not wholly disapprove of one whom he called "the great champion of scholarly orthodoxy." But plainly he found his own annoyance with Machen hard to control. The author, Carver complained, had overgeneralized and thus misapprehended "the opposition against which he is contending." While it was true enough that much liberalism is really a "different religion" from Christianity, "legalistic, externally dogmatic interpretations" are also remote from what Christ taught; and Carver left no doubt that Machen had succumbed to legalism: "His interpretation of Christianity is far too external and too dependent on formal logic." Machen's biblical rationalism was "as dangerous to spiritual religion" as an unbiblical rationalism.

---

[17]*Theological Monthly*, 3 (June 1923), 189; ibid., 4 (April 1924), 126-128; *Bibliotheca Sacra*, 81 (January 1924), 89-90; *Methodist Review*, 106 (September 1923), 819-820; *Crozer Quarterly*, 1 (July 1924), 359-360; *Journal of Religion*, 3 (September 1923), 541-544. For other laudatory comments, see *American Church Monthly*, 13 (August 1923), 480-484; *Lutheran Quarterly*, 54 (October 1924), 501-502; and *Biblical Review* 8 (October 1923), 626-630. Further adverse criticisms are in *Anglican Theological Review*, 6 (March 1924), 350-351; *Congregationalist*, 108 (September 13, 1923), 336; and Dean Sperry's "Theological Vitriol," cited above.

Carver accused Machen of "special pleading, defective reasoning . . . a distressing pessimism" (particularly about the decline of nearly everything in modern civilization), and an inept and insulting strategy. The "passion for exclusion," which Carver and others were encountering and battling also in the Southern Baptist Convention, had led Machen to formulate everything in the spirit and phraseology of warfare, and to spend his time trying to show the un-Christian character of liberalism instead of concentrating on its fallacies as a professedly scientific system. Above all, Carver took issue with the entire Princetonian effort, of which Machen's work was the culmination, to denigrate the work and progress of the spirit of God within human culture:

In the volume before us one finds himself repeatedly inquiring where is the author's faith in the Holy Spirit and where his recognition of the Spirit's functions and work. Much emphasis is laid on the Spirit in the revelation and inspiration of the word in the original giving of the Bible. Some stress is given to the work of the Spirit in the Regeneration and Sanctification of the believer, interpreted in characteristically traditional fashion and with emphasis on the doctrine rather than on the experience. Beyond that, so far as this book goes he might reply if one asked him of the Holy Spirit, "I had not so much as heard that there is a Holy Spirit."

Evangelicals, Carver acknowledged, ought to agree with Machen that there can be no children of God apart from the redemption in Christ, "but let us not lose sight of [Christ's] undertaking to get the will of God done on earth." Machen's treatment of contemporary efforts to make Christianity include the social life of mankind had to be called "pathetic." Carver advised those who rightly make much of doctrine to heed "the 'doctrine' of the Holy Spirit"; and to bear in mind that Christ "will not fail or be discouraged till He hath set righteousness in the earth."[18]

---

[18]W. O. Carver, review of Machen's *Christianity and Liberalism*, in *Review and Expositor*, 21 (July 1924), 344-349. For accounts of Carver's career, see the articles written in honor of his eighty-sixth birthday, in *Review and Expositor*, 51 (April 1954). The significant work of the group of Southern Baptist moderates to which Carver belonged is recounted in Eighmy, *Churches in Cultural Captivity*, pp. 57-157. See also Wayne Flynt, "Dissent in Zion: Alabama Baptists and Social Issues, 1900-1914," *Journal of Southern History*, 35 (November 1969), 523-542.

For every conservative evangelical who failed to follow Machen's leadership, however, there were several religious radicals, humanists, and "realists" who found much to commend in his kind of fundamentalism, with its insistent demand for clean and unequivocal choices.[19] The leftward side of the spectrum of religious thought, in fact, was becoming almost as unfriendly to liberalism as the fundamentalist right. "I found myself . . . raked by fire from two directions," Fosdick remembered later, "and which was fiercer I do not know." A. C. Dieffenbach, the Unitarian editor who had been so infuriated by clerical recalcitrance in the war effort, launched almost a comparable attack upon the beleaguered champion of modernism. "If our sympathy goes over completely to Dr. Fosdick for his spirit," Dieffenbach wrote, "our intelligence goes over quite as completely to Dr. McCartney [who had initiated the charges in the Fosdick case] for his impregnable defense of the orthodox Presbyterian faith." Later the same critic added that "I have the profoundest respect for a man who is consistently a Roman Catholic, or for a man who is consistently a fundamentalist, but I have no respect for the attitude of Dr. Fosdick." In the view probably of the great majority of those liberals who, like Dieffenbach, had gone "beyond Christianity," Machen's analysis was right, and most welcome. "An evangelical Christian is not a liberal," Dieffenbach insisted, "in the accepted use of both words. They are mutually exclusive terms."[20]

Nearly as scathing about liberalism's alleged evasions, though less sympathetic to Machen's dichotomizing, were the "realist" philosophers of religion, those who were attempting to further and if possible complete the discrediting of philosophical idealism. In the later 1920s the ascendant figure in that campaign was Henry Nelson Wieman, who in 1927 was appointed professor

---

[19]Machen's conviction in the 1930s as a schismatic, which he and others contended was really a conviction for heresy, again brought forth this diverse kind of support. See Stonehouse, *Machen*, pp. 482-492. For an especially striking example, see H. L. Mencken's warm tribute to "Doctor Fundamentalis" in the Baltimore *Evening Sun* for January 18, 1937.

[20]Fosdick, *Living of These Days*, p. 166 (for both the Fosdick and the Dieffenbach quotations).

of the philosophy of religion in the Divinity School at Chicago. Wieman's *Wrestle of Religion with Truth*, published that same year, argued that in spite of the preceding efforts of the empiricists, religion was still urgently in need of "refining its method and establishing its presuppositions."[21]

The method called for would be not merely scientific, because scientific method, while indispensable, "is not self-sufficient." Empiricism as applied to ultimate questions involved, for Wieman, "the experimental method of religion, not of science." He deplored, along with more ancient dogmatisms, a doctrinaire adherence to science as the new guarantor of the human mind against error. Still, an open, experimental approach to the "facts" of religious experience was the great desideratum; and the illusions of the older liberalism, even more than those of conservative religion, stood in the way of such an approach. Wieman averred that insofar as he was engaging in any fight at all, it was "not against either modernism or fundamentalism as such, but . . . against all religion of illusion wherever it may be found." Liberal idealism, however, was for him the most immediate and formidable enemy.[22]

Throughout both of his major books of the twenties, the gravamen of Wieman's charge lay against the kind of religion that locates religious authority in the realm of abstract ideals, and that moreover tries to make God and the world into the pleasant, reassuring objects that humans would like them to be. In vigorous language replete with almost contemptuous similes, Wieman assailed "the religion of illusion, this religion of sugar and spice and all things nice." Such fatuity "may serve to draw people into the church as the ice-cream counter draws them into the drug store. But they will not stay to get the truth any more than the consumer of a 'Lovers' Delight' will stay to buy castor oil." A more substantial and, in the end, satisfying faith

insists that facts are more important than any cherished mistaken beliefs, no matter how unpleasant the facts and how delightful the beliefs. It

---

[21]Wieman, *Wrestle*, p. v.
[22]Wieman, *Religious Experience*, p. 236; *Wrestle*, pp. 17, 3.

insists that this is not a nice world and God is not a nice God. God is too awful and terrible, too destructive to our foolish little plans, to be nice.[23]

The problem about ideals, Wieman thought, either as ideals are understood formally by the philosophers or as they function in popular religion and life, is that we are satisfied with them, when in actuality we should be regarding them with the greatest suspicion and should be constantly revising them. The office and function of religion should be "the reconstruction of ideals rather than the enhancement and enforcement of established and recognized ideals." Wieman's synthesizing of the revisionary purposes of the older liberalism with the spirit of a tough new realism was most evident as he asserted that our ideals, which have in them "all the error, all the impracticality, all the perversity and confusion that human beings . . . can put into them," can be reconstructed and improved only by the free action upon them of the data of religious experience.[24]

Wieman's not-nice God, meanwhile, retained an immanence— indeed a greatly intensified immanence—in the world and in cultural processes, but as the totality of the concrete facts of the universe, not as a spirit or construct animating the human mind. God is real, said Wieman, in the way that a stone wall or a toothache is real. God is something that it is equally perilous to ignore or to idealize. This insistently objective kind of immanentism constituted perhaps as strong a rebuke to liberal idealism as could be mounted without moving in quite a different direction and repudiating immanentism itself—as the neo-orthodox were soon to do.[25]

Other varieties of literary and philosophic co-belligerency with fundamentalism appeared at the end of the twenties in the writings of literary critics Joseph Wood Krutch and John Crowe Ransom,

---

[23]Ibid., pp. 2-3.

[24]*Religious Experience*, pp. 267-268.

[25]*Wrestle*, p. 2. Wieman followed Alfred North Whitehead in retaining the concept, and even language, of immanence. See *Wrestle*, p. 186. The stress upon cosmic disharmonies, however, made Wieman's kind of immanentism hard to defend. By the later 1930s he was conceding much more to the arguments for "the otherness of God." See Wieman, "Blind Spots Removed," p. 118.

the Amherst philosopher Clarence Ayres, and Walter Lippmann, the journalist and political philosopher. Krutch, whose denial in *The Modern Temper* of man's harmony with the natural order may have done more than any other pronouncement of the time to cut the taproots of religious liberalism, could not advise a return to religious orthodoxy, nor could he sanction fundamentalism. "Skepticism has entered too deeply into our souls," he wrote, "ever to be replaced by faith" in Christian or humanist or Communist fantasies about man's reconciliation with the cosmos. Ayres, on the other hand, revealed a grudging preference for fundamentalism, with its "established church and . . . consecrated dogma" over what he called the enlightened unbelief of the modernists. And Ransom's "unorthodox defense of orthodoxy" ended by demanding a return to the creeds. Having reestablished the whole body of Christian supernaturalism at two strokes by declaring Christianity to be mythical and then declaring adherence to myths to be an absolute psychic necessity, Ransom offered militant advice to the modern man: "With whatever religious institution [he] may be connected, let him try to turn it back towards orthodoxy . . . Let him restore to God the thunder."[26]

Walter Lippmann, though similarly impressed with the ordinary person's need for myths, advocated continued strivings toward a scientific humanism rather than a return to orthodoxy or even to theism. Lippmann's *Preface to Morals* in 1929 expressed so much nostalgic appreciation for traditional religion, and so much respect for Machen's kind of fundamentalism, that one could doubt whether the author had ceased entirely to be a theist. George Gordon in fact accused Lippmann of being, despite his protests to the contrary, "a truly liberal and devout Christian." Were it not for his elitism, Gordon said, Lippmann would make an excellent deacon![27] But Lippmann made no case for theism as the religion of the present or future. Humanity was going to

---

[26]Krutch, *Modern Temper*, p. 167; Ayres, *Science*, pp. 183-185; Ransom, *God Without Thunder*, pp. 81, 327-328.

[27]George A. Gordon, "A Review of Mr. Lippmann's *A Preface to Morals*," *Congregationalist*, 114 (November 14, 1929), 637.

have to go it alone, drawing upon inner resources that were, to be sure, earnests and counterparts of larger cosmic realities, but without relying upon support from the kind of personal being connoted by the term God. According to Lippmann, the religion of the future, the faith that would rescue humankind from its current confusion and loss of mooring, would be a humanism based not precisely on science itself but on the kind of disinterestedness best displayed in the modern world in the scientific search for truth.

Of all the secular or religiously radical counterparts of the fundamentalist critique in the 1920s, Lippmann's gave the most direct and effective support to the demand for a clean choice between orthodoxy and humanism. He agreed with Machen and Dieffenbach that there could be no middle ground. "The historic churches . . . have founded faith on clear statements about matters of fact, historic events, or physical manifestations. They have never been content with a symbolism which the believer knew was merely symbolic." And the churches had been right, he said, to eschew self-consciously symbolic interpretations—not because such a method is invalid in itself, but because the common man cannot handle it. The orthodox believer "may be mistaken as to the facts in which he believes. But he is not mistaken in thinking that you cannot, for the mass of men, have a faith of which the only foundation is their need and desire to believe." Machen's argument, according to Lippmann, was "the best popular argument produced by either side" in the fundamentalist controversy; though Machen's view of reality was wrong, his definition of Christianity was consistent with the way in which the church had always, in historic fact and by necessity, distorted reality for the benefit of the unsophisticated.[28]

According to such a scenario, Christianity—ancient, hoary, heavy with the honors of its epochal achievements—was to be sent to a deserved rest, and not allowed with smooth talk to insinuate its way into a modern world. Face-lifting and attempted rejuvenation would be unconvincing if not pitiable. Fosdick's idea of immor-

---

[28]Lippmann, *Preface to Morals*, pp. 31-34.

tality, which spoke with relative vagueness of "the persistence of personality through death," might arise from a long tradition of Platonism, might be true and even be compatible with scripture; but the whole history of religion, Lippmann said, should warn us against assuming "that a statement of the purest truth is in itself capable of affecting the lives of any considerable number of people." The ordinary person (whom Lippmann throughout this passage also called "the worldling") simply finds the Fosdick version of immortality, along with the deliteralizing of other biblical doctrines, too impersonal and nonmaterial. The worldling's heart "is set on the enjoyment of worldly goods," and he cannot make any sense of a revised idea of heaven in which the enjoyment of these things is not perpetuated. More comprehensively, what the ordinary person demands in a religion, and fails to find in liberalism, is certainty. Certainty, the conviction that one's religion and morality are based on absolute authority that cannot be doubted—this above all, said Lippmann, is "what modernism leaves out."[29]

"What immeasurable folly!"
The Liberal Retort to Fundamentalism

Harry Emerson Fosdick sounded one keynote for the defense of liberalism when he protested in "Shall the Fundamentalists Win?" (1922) against the growing spirit of exclusivity among conservative Christians. That discourse, which led to Fosdick's own separation from the Presbyterian congregation that he had been serving in New York City, pled for mutual forbearance between the contending parties in an already "split and riven" Protestantism. The advice was intended for liberals as well as conservatives; young persons "intolerant about old opinions" could, as much as intolerant fundamentalists, harm the Christian church and their own cause. But clearly Fosdick thought the troublemakers of the moment were neither overzealous young liberals nor traditional kinds of conservative (who "can often give lessons to liberals in true liberality of spirit"). The greatest danger

---

[29]Ibid., pp. 42, 45-46, 44, 48, and 37-50 passim.

lay in a fundamentalism that insisted on defining professing Christians out of Christianity. "Just now," Fosdick said, "the Fundamentalists are giving us one of the worst exhibitions of intolerance that the churches of this country have ever seen." In the midst of a world situation that "smells to heaven," in the presence of "colossal problems, which must be solved in Christ's name and for Christ's sake, the Fundamentalists propose to drive out from the Christian churches all the consecrated souls who do not agree with their theory of inspiration. What immeasurable folly!"[30]

The folly of exclusivism and undue dichotomizing remained an important theme throughout all the liberal rebuttals of the twenties. But this was supplemented by two other forms of rebuttal that responded more fully to the charges that by now were commonly brought against liberalism. The first and central response was that modernistic liberalism not only is Christian but also is actually closer than its rivals to the genius of Christianity. The second was that unless Christianity can present people with a liberal option, it cannot function in the modern world and probably cannot survive there.

Shailer Mathews of the University of Chicago was the most prominent spokesman during the twenties—rivaled only by Fosdick—for both of these arguments. Fosdick's outspoken eloquence, and his involvement in a notorious public controversy, made him known to an especially wide circle of Americans. But Mathews, as dean of the divinity school that had become a sort of modernist headquarters, stood forth as the leading statesman, politician, historian, and systematic spokesman for the movement. In numerous households and church or college communities, Mathews was highly honored for striving to preserve Christianity as a possible faith in the contemporary world; in probably more households and pulpits, particularly throughout the Midwest, his name stood for the destruction of the faith.

James Luther Adams, the Unitarian theologian and ethicist,

---

[30]Harry Emerson Fosdick, "Shall the Fundamentalists Win?" in Hutchison, ed., *American Protestant Thought*, pp. 170, 179, 172, 181.

Shailer Mathews

recalls the shock of his first exposure, during a Mathews visit to the University of Minnesota, to the man who in Adams' Baptist and Plymouth Brethren circles had been known as the devil incarnate. Here instead was a kindly, bespectacled gentleman— looking, in physique, like the former baseball catcher that he was[31]—who spoke irenically and forcefully for liberalism and social Christianity, and who really thought young people should consider working for the church. "I think that if I had been exposed to Mathews earlier," Adams has said, "I would have remained a Baptist." This kind of persuasiveness—or, if you like, plausibility—made Mathews' volume of 1924, *The Faith of Modernism*, the most important liberal work of the 1920s and made his very phraseology common coin among adherents and opponents of modernism. One eulogist at the time of Mathews' death remarked that the dean's ways of expressing himself had often seemed—a bit like Shakespeare's —"disappointingly full of familiar quotations."[32]

The Faith of Modernism, while it was not presented as an answer specifically to Machen or to fundamentalism, appeared about a year after Machen's *Christianity and Liberalism* and offered an extended response to the question of legitimacy that that book had raised. Mathews argued that the essence of Christianity lay in a set of convictions and a governing method; and that both of these were most adequately represented in the twentieth century by modernist Christianity. The basic Christian convictions were humanity's need for salvation from sin and death; the love, fatherliness, and forgiving nature of God the creator; Christ as "the revelation in human experience of God effecting salvation"; good will as essential to the nature of God and as the foun-

---

[31]Mathews' only similarity, perhaps, to Billy Sunday lay in this area. While a baseball star at Colby College, he caught in one professional game and was offered a contract. "I have more than a suspicion," his son wrote later, "that he takes more pride in his prowess on this occasion than in all his later contributions." Professor Robert E. Mathews, in Krumbine, ed., *Process of Religion*, p. 5.

[32]James Luther Adams, interview with the author, October 8, 1966; unsigned editorial tribute to Mathews, *Christian Century*, 58 (November 5, 1941), 1362-1363. For Mathews' thought and development to 1924, see Wurster, "Shailer Mathews." Wurster emphasizes Mathews' role as an evangelist for modernism.

dation for human betterment; the persistence of individual human lives after death; and the centrality of the Bible as the record of God's revelation and as a guide for the religious life.[33] The "governing method" of Christianity had been associated throughout the ages with a spirit of cultural awareness of which the twentieth-century modernist was simply the most recent heir.

Modernists, Mathews explained, "ask and propose to exercise the same liberty in the choice of patterns in their day as Clement of Alexandria and the members of the Council of Nicea exercised in theirs." Modernism could best be defined, therefore, as a determination to use "scientific, historical, social method in understanding and applying evangelical Christianity to the needs of living persons." The idea that such a process accords normative status to science or secular culture instead of to the teaching of Christ was a serious misunderstanding, Mathews insisted, since the real starting point is "the inherited orthodoxy . . . Modernists as a class are evangelical Christians. That is, they accept Jesus Christ as the revelation of a Savior God." Loyalty to Jesus, he declared, is at the heart of the Christian movement; "the Modernist knows no other center for his faith."[34]

Since Christianity has always adapted its forms and language to particular cultural situations, the modernists in any given age have simply been those who were most candid and most creative in doing this. The forward movement of Christianity throughout its history has been guided by those who have discerned and responded to the social mind of a given era.

Mathews' conception of the social mind reproduced in more hardheaded, twentieth-century form both the enthusiasms and the qualifications of his predecessors' commitments to a "devout Zeitgeist" or to the spirit of the age. Sometimes he spoke as though there were only one social mind—the one that pressed for such ends as human solidarity and social amelioration. But at other times he seemed to speak in the plural. He characterized the modernist-fundamentalist conflict, for example, as a clash between

---

[33]Mathews, *Faith of Modernism*, pp. 76-81.
[34]Ibid., pp. 46-47, 138, 34-35, 146.

"two social minds" divided by "different degrees of sympathy with the social and cultural forces of the day."[35] As this phraseology suggests, however, the coexistence of various social minds at a given time did not involve their equality. They were equal neither in vitality nor in effectiveness; and in that sense the modern social mind could be discussed in the singular. The social mind represented by fundamentalism belonged to another age, not to this one.

Like its more romantic predecessors, Mathews' idea of a religiously vital social mind contained heavy concessions to the failures and the lack of fulfillment in contemporary human society; and these concessions led back to an insistence that humanity at its best cannot solve its problems without the help of God and the example of Christ. Though hopeful signs abounded, an easy optimism was not even to be considered. The threat of injury inherent in social change, Mathews warned, "is as loud as its promise of happiness. We have not yet learned how to use . . . our new knowledge, our new ideals, our new freedom. The dangers of progress are as real as the dangers of reaction."[36]

Mathews included in the opening chapter of his *Faith of Modernism* a distressing catalogue of continuing human ills. He decried "the survival of the psychology of war." He complained of the persistence both of inequality between social classes and of a selfish hedonism among the members of the more favored classes: "Nations with millions of their people starving abound in those who are feasting." Economic development, he said, has worked to intensify the hatreds involved in the class struggle; and hatred in turn has bred desperation and cynicism.

What were mankind's resources for fulfilling the aspirations of the social mind and for correcting the evils that stand in the way of these aspirations? Some might put their trust in democracy, but Mathews agreed with such critics as Lippmann and H. L. Mencken that the picture was less than clear. He recognized the current doubts as to whether democracy would "grade up or grade

---

[35]Ibid., pp. 16, 18.
[36]Ibid., p. 4.

down human life" and voiced apprehension about the Hobson's Choice according to which a democracy must either rely on dubious resources of good will and expert knowledge or alternatively give way to terror. He even paraphrased Mencken's frequent allegation that (in Mathews' words) "the worst enemies of democracy are democrats themselves."[37]

Despite his immense respect for science, moreover, Mathews like Wieman resisted any notion that science was a new religion. He rejected the facile hope that "as men come to see the facts of nature they will also come to wisdom." "When," he asked, "has knowledge meant virtue? . . . Knowledge is certainly not always identical with good will, however much good will must be directed by knowledge."

If democracy and science in their current state could not save mankind, perhaps human beings nonetheless were good enough, especially with all their new powers, to redirect democracy and science to desirable ends. "The answer is tragic," Mathews replied. "Humanity is not good enough."[38]

How then could one presume to offer liberal solutions? To answer that, a later observer must attempt to re-enter the world of thought in which the generation of Fosdick and Mathews had now lived half a lifetime or more. It was a world in which, so far as their own painful experience could tell them, orthodox answers were unutterably worse than liberal ones. Liberalism in a real sense was the only game in town.

In Fosdick's later writings, especially, this was a recurrent theme. In his autobiography and elsewhere he sought to recreate for a younger generation—for those who could afford to take the gains of the liberal movement for granted—some sense of the urgency with which his own generation had laid hold of a freer interpretation of Christianity. It had been a choice not between liberalism and orthodoxy, but (in a kind of ironic reversal of Machen) between liberalism and no Christianity at all. "Of

---

[37]Ibid., pp. 5, 7. Mencken's *Notes on Democracy* (New York, Alfred A. Knopf, 1926) would conclude—as Mathews did not—that the only sincere democrat is an aristocrat.

[38]Ibid., pp. 4-9.

course," Fosdick admitted in 1956, this ideology "left out dimensions in Christian faith which would need to be rediscovered!" But the point that latter-day critics failed to grasp, he said, was liberalism's "absolute necessity to multitudes of us who could not have been Christians at all unless we could thus have escaped the bondage of the then reigning orthodoxy."[39]

This was Mathews's response also. True, human society is full of evil; and human powers are dubious. But what has orthodox Christianity offered? In a passage reminiscent of Theodore Parker almost a century earlier, he ticked off the failures of conservative religion:

The world needs new control of nature and society and is told that the Bible is verbally inerrant. It needs a means of composing class strife, and is told to believe in the substitutionary atonement. It needs a spirit of love and justice and is told that love without orthodoxy will not save from hell . . . It needs faith in the divine presence in human affairs and is told it must accept the virgin birth of Jesus Christ.

If society suffers because of such dusty answers, Mathews asserted, the church in offering them decrees its own death. If Christianity, "while the swarming millions are desperately struggling to establish justice and fraternity," answers with "a system of doctrines authoritatively fixed in patterns of other times," Christianity will be abandoned. To the argument for the legitimacy of liberalism, then, one was bound to add the argument for its necessity—both to human society and to the survival of the faith.[40]

Mathews went on to a harsher indictment of conservatism. The religion of creedal subscription, he said, had always tended toward amorality. "Neither the Apostles', the Nicene, the Chalcedonian, nor the Athanasian" creed makes any reference to morality beyond the mere statement of the belief in the forgiveness of sin. "So far as each is concerned, the teaching of Jesus contained in the Sermon on the Mount might as well never have existed." Mathews hastened to acknowledge that this was less true of the great Protestant confessions, and that any flat allegation of

[39]Fosdick, *Living of These Days*, p. 66.
[40]Mathews, *Faith of Modernism*, pp. 10, 83.

the church's indifference to morality would be grossly unfair. But he insisted that the great moral reformers, conservative ones included, have usually operated in spite of creeds and dogmaticians, seldom with their support.[41]

Mathews repeatedly expressed understanding of the personal and political pressures that produce the dogmatist. "Confessions," he explained, "make easy tests. It was natural that conviction of the finality of such tests should become permanent in groups which originated in theological controversy and which were either prosecuted, or persecuted, or both." But the fact remained that the dogmatic mind, for all its reputation of nay-saying moralism, "has never been as severe with sinners as it has been with heretics." In that sense, anyone who seeks truly to come to grips with the moral problems of his own day must share the modernist temper. While Mathews did not complicate his already broad definitions by using the term "modernist" for conservative moralists like Dwight Moody, the great evangelist, he did allude to the "practical religion" preached and inspired by Moody as indicating recognition, even among conservative evangelicals, of "the insufficiency of dogmatic Christianity."[42]

Liberals and, indeed, religious commentators generally in the twenties paid much less attention to the fellow travelers of Machenite conservatism—to the promoters of various styles of humanism—than they paid to Machen himself.[43] They did, how-

---

[41]Ibid., pp. 25-27.

[42]Ibid., pp. 26-27.

[43]Even the *Humanist Manifesto* produced by John Dewey and others in the early thirties stirred little response from the liberal Christians whom it implicitly criticized. Only the *Christian Century* seems to have been at all interested in this genre. See Reinhold Niebuhr's review of Krutch in volume 46 (May 1, 1929), 586-587; Lloyd Douglas on Ransom, 47 (December 3, 1930), 1490-1491; and the unsigned editorial article attacking the *Humanist Manifesto* in 50 (June 7, 1933), 743-745.

Wieman's work was widely reviewed, but it provoked rejoinders only on relatively technical questions. See, especially, George A. Coe in *Religious Education*, 23 (January 1928), 167-170; an exchange between Wieman and Coe, ibid. (April 1928), 395-399; Julius Seelye Bixler in *Journal of Religion*, 8 (April 1928), 288-291; and "M.B.S." in *American Church Monthly*, 23 (April 1928), 172-173. W. O. Carver again showed the breadth of his sympathies by approving much of Wieman's enterprise; see *Review and Expositor*, 25 (January 1928), 86-87.

ever, comment extensively on Walter Lippmann's *Preface to Morals,* a book that was both thoughtful enough to be taken seriously and enough of a popular success that liberals had to make a public response.[44]

Those liberals who had themselves been critical of the liberal movement were, naturally enough, the ones least offended by Lippmann's treatment. Dean Sperry concurred in deploring the "trivial illusions" that modern religion sets in the place of "majestic faiths," and also sympathized with Lippmann's vision of a humanistic future (though partly because, like Gordon, Sperry was sure Lippmann was really more than a humanist). Reinhold Niebuhr, who had been highly appreciative of Krutch's *Modern Temper,* found Lippmann's volume "a relief and a joy" by contrast with the kind of humanism that championed a spurious freedom and a naive scientism. But Harry Emerson Fosdick, perhaps because Lippmann had made Fosdick the type-figure for all the unsatisfactory compromises of liberalism, spent most of a long article ringing the changes on Lippmann's essentially fundamentalist definition of Christianity. And Geroge Gordon, in the last piece of writing that he completed before his death in October 1929, similarly berated Lippmann for judging liberalism by entirely unrealistic standards of "certainty."[45]

Fosdick neatly summarized the objections of both men when he made sport of Lippmann's complaints about the unpicturability (and thus the uselessness to ordinary folks) of the liberal conceptions of God and heaven and hell. Let us admit for the sake of argument, Fosdick said, that the poor unlettered common man

---

[44]*A Preface to Morals* ran through five printings in its first year, and was a Book-of-the-Month Club selection. The phrasing of the frequent allusions to it over the next several years indicates that this was a book that "everyone" knew —or at least knew about.

[45]Willard Sperry, "From Pure Religion to High Religion," *Yale Review,* 19 (Autumn 1929), 161-163; Reinhold Niebuhr in *World Tomorrow,* 12 (July 1929), 313-314; Fosdick, in New York *Evening Post* (April 27, 1929), sec. M, p. 11; Gordon, "A Review of Mr. Lippmann's *A Preface to Morals,*" *Congregationalist,* 114 (November 14, 1929), 636-638. The extent to which Lippmann's book provoked a serious and creative discussion among religious liberals is reflected in the fact that the first article in a significant cooperative volume of 1931 was an extended critique, very much along Gordon-Fosdick lines, of *Preface to Morals.* Arthur K. Rogers, "Is Religion Important?" in Macintosh, ed., *Religious Realism,* pp. 3-32.

about whom Lippmann was so anxious could deal more easily with pictures than with abstract spiritual truths. But Lippmann's religion of the future was to be based on "disinterestedness." "May I suggest," Fosdick asked, "that sometime he try to secure an enterprising artist who will paint a picture of 'disinterestedness?'" Lippmann, knowing too little about the history of Christian thought, had been beguiled, Fosdick thought, into underestimating the sophistication of ordinary Christian believers, and then into the illogic of supposing that the common man had suddenly become sophisticated enough to be satisfied with the abstract ideals of humanism.[46]

Clearly Lippmann's assumptions in this area required careful unpacking. And three in particular were scrutinized in the Gordon and Fosdick reviews: (1) the assumption that the religion of the past had depended upon absolute intellectual certainties; (2) the idea that acceptability to the allegedly ignorant is somehow a standard for the validity of a religious position; and (3) the belief that, in any case, biblical and creedal literalism has been the Christian way and deserves exclusive use of the Christian name.

Lippmann's bewailing of the modern "loss of certainty," Gordon wrote, was "everywhere overdone. There has never been," he claimed, "in the followers of the ancient faith any such unclouded certainty as Mr. Lippmann alleges." If the author would read Christian biographies of all eras he would see that the certitude he held in such high esteem was "but a picture of his imagination." St. Paul, in no obscure or unpopular passage, had said that "we see through a glass, darkly." Admittedly there had always been dogmatists, but the only kind of certainty claimed by a great many Christians throughout history had been a qualified certainty, "held as faith and never as a system of demonstrated belief."[47]

In his solicitude about the capacities of the "intellectually simple," Gordon wrote, Lippmann was "sadly and superciliously out of date." One of Lippmann's key terms, along with disinterestedness, was "maturity." Even if it were true that

---

[46]Fosdick, *Post* review.
[47]Gordon, "Review of *Preface*," pp. 636-637.

Harry Emerson Fosdick, 1928

ordinary believers in the past had been too simple to grasp spiritual ideas, surely this would not be a problem under the conditions of coming religious maturity that Lippmann himself had projected. That the grounds of Christian faith cannot be pictured, Gordon said, "means nothing to an educated mind." The only question for such minds will be which kind of non-literalistic conceptions best accord with the actual religious experience of individual persons.[48]

But Lippmann's real problem, according to Fosdick, was that he had been completely taken in by a fundamentalist definition of Christianity. He could not grasp what modernists were saying because he was "temperamentally a fundamentalist" himself. "The only theistic religion he can understand at all is of the most naive and medieval sort." When Lippmann thought of God as physically walking in the Garden of Eden, Fosdick said, or as a transcendant king in the sky of a pre-Copernican universe, "he easily grasps that."

But when he comes within reaching distance of the idea of the immanent God, dwelling in the universe and revealing himself especially in the spiritual life of man, he is completely lost. The result is that he is not at home with any intelligent religion since the Deism of the eighteenth century went to pieces.

Fosdick thought that Lippmann, like the fundamentalists, really yearned for "the absolute certainty of an infallible system." Unable actually to accept the certainty offered by fundamentalism or Catholicism, Lippmann had hopes of finding it in the gospel of disinterestedness, which he dogmatically asserted to be "the only answer which completely suits the premises of the situation." But others, Fosdick said, share neither Lippmann's illusions about the attainability of absolute certainty, nor his apprehensions about society's getting on without it. Lippmann in his underrating of the popular intelligence was attributing "to everybody else his own religious disabilities."[49]

Gordon's obituary and his review of Lippmann appeared in

[48]Ibid., p. 637.
[49]Fosdick, *Post* review.

the same issue of the *Congregationalist*. In retrospect, the symbolism suggested by that coincidence extends broadly enough to be worth remarking upon. A part of the liberal impetus was itself "passing away"—the euphemism is here direct and fitting—at about the time of Gordon's death. And the part that was passing was the one Gordon had epitomized. With the onset of the depression, Hitlerism, and neo-orthodox questionings, liberals themselves came to be less and less confident about asserting, as Gordon had, that "upon the whole, history is the record of the defeat of inhumanity."[50]

Liberalism continued, through the thirties and after, to show remarkable resilience, both as a word and as a cluster of theological and biblical preferences forged in the great nineteenth-century battles. Liberals, under severe provocation, proved unwilling to renounce the idea of adaptation, and even less willing to modify significantly their more fundamental stress upon the immanence of God. But cultural immanentism and with it the assumption of human progress would come, within a few years after Gordon's death, under deep and widely-agreed suspicion. And the term modernism, which had depended for its richness and affirmative content upon confidence about God's immanence in cultural development, within that short time would nearly fall into disuse.

---

[50]Gordon, *Ultimate Conceptions*, p. 185.

Epilogue:
The Decline of Cultural Faith

> There is very little in our present social order
> that naturally suggests the Providence of God.
> WALTER MARSHALL HORTON, 1934

By the early 1930s it was evident that a new, more
potent configuration of antimodernist thought
had come into being—one in which secular
humanism had receded to the background and in
which fundamentalism was not an active or acknowledged contributor. To many of the theologians and preachers closest to
this movement, the change in theology seemed as cataclysmic as
the concurrent changes in economic life. It seemed, Halford
Luccock of Yale wrote later, as though "the elevator loaded with
humanity, due to shoot upwards to some sixty-fifth story of a
skyscraper of man's own construction," had jammed and dropped.
"In that drop," he quipped, "it was not only General Motors
and A. T. and T. and other similar hopes of salvation that were
deflated, but faiths as well."[1] There was a sense, among those
most affected, not only of sharp discontinuity with the immediate
American past and its ideologies, but of a reappropriation of
forms of Protestant Christianity that antedated all the modern
theologies—liberalism, fundamentalism, and also humanism.
Because of that sense of discontinuity and restoration, the term
"neo-orthodoxy" (rather than, say, "realism") was the one that at
length became the standard name for the movement.

---

[1]Luccock, "No Apologies," p. 972.

Liberals unaffected or little impressed by neo-orthodoxy of course lacked this sense of discontinuity with the attitudes of the immediate past. Yet in one vital area their way of speaking did change: by the end of the thirties they had almost ceased to use the term "modernism" except in historical reference.

In part, that term went out of fashion because like "fundamentalism" it had been loaded down with extreme and often unfair connotations during the more unsavory confrontations of the 1920s. But the change in rhetoric also signified that the modernist convictions, beset by internal questioning, external attack, and the pressure of events, had lost their coherence and credibility during the two decades after 1920.

The Neo-Orthodox Onslaught

The first stirrings of the new realism in the late twenties seem much like those of the New Theology in the late 1870s—like a gentle "going in the tops of the trees."[2] They were even more reminiscent, however, of the beginnings of transcendentalism a generation earlier. God once again seemed to be speaking German, and the moment's excitement and task lay in translation and transmission. In 1926, Professor Gustav Krüger of Giessen lectured at Union Seminary on "The Theology of Crisis," which he said had not previously been explicated in English. With sympathy, though not with complete approval, Krüger explained German crisis theology as a new pietism for which the great enemy was the Enlightenment—"the root of all evil"—instead of the Lutheran or Calvinist scholasticism to which pietism had objected in the past. The Enlightenment had made man the measure of all things, and religion "a mere function of the human soul, hence something belonging to this world and purely subjective." Against Enlightenment Christianity, said Krüger, the crisis theologians were setting what they conceived was the biblical and Protestant tradition: "faith in something given, objective, real—faith in the Word, the Word of God, who is above everything human and created; the Word that speaks to us out of the sacred

---

[2]See the opening of chapter 3, above.

documents of Christianity." They wished, furthermore, to speak not of "God *and* man," but of "God, *not* man"; to speak of a God "before whom man, his culture, and his values are as nothing."[3]

Krüger described the seminal influence of Friedrich Gogarten, for whom religion was not the soul of culture, as the Enlightenment allegedly had taught, but rather "the *crisis*, that is, the doom, of culture." He analyzed, at much greater length, the influence of Karl Barth, for whom "the reality of religion is man's horror of himself." Barth's dialectical method and fondness for paradox Krüger found maddening. "Dialectics are very difficult to deal with," he wrote, because "the arguments you were about to bring forward, your adversary always has disposed of in advance. And should you succeed in getting him into a corner, he will adroitly withdraw into the fortress of his paradoxes." But Krüger had no doubt of Barth's enormous importance; and he urged that the Swiss theologian's *Wort Gottes und die Theologie* be translated.[4]

Over the next several years, that book of Barth's sermons was translated (by Douglas Horton, in 1928), and a number of American scholars published brief critiques and interpretations of Barth, of the more moderate Emil Brunner, and of others associated with the German reaction against theological liberalism. While few of these American interpreters were entirely committed to Barth— some, like Reinhold Neibuhr, mixing appreciation with extremely sharp criticism—their observations converged at the same point at which the neo-orthodox movement itself would steadily find coherence: namely, in a common conviction that liberalism had failed and that something better—something more "realistic" and more "biblical"—must be found.[5]

The larger-scale works that established a kind of corpus of early neo-orthodox thought appeared mainly from 1931 through

---

[3]Krüger, "Theology of Crisis," pp. 233 and 227-258 passim.
[4]Ibid., pp. 233-239.
[5]Barth, *Word of God*; Jenkins, "Paradox Theology"; Horton, "God Lets Loose Karl Barth"; Niebuhr, "Barth: Apostle of the Absolute"; Pauck, "Barth's Religious Criticism of Religion"; Offermann, "Theology of Barth"; Homrighausen, "Counter-Revolt." For the disagreement between, respectively, Barth's sympathetic critics and his strongest defenders, see Niebuhr, "Let Liberal Churches Stop Fooling Themselves!" and Homrighausen, "Barthianism."

1934. In those years, Wilhelm Pauck and Walter Lowrie—the second much more enthusiastically than the first—offered further interpretations of "Barthianism." H. Richard Niebuhr, Walter Marshall Horton, and others collaborated in a symposium on religious realism that seemed to testify to the continuities, at least as much as to the reversals, in American development; and Horton in 1934 followed with a volume of his own on the same subject. The Neibuhr brothers specialized in a type of theological re-thinking that rested on broad political and cultural analysis of the crisis in Western civilization—Richard principally by way of a translation and introduction of Paul Tillich's *Religious Situation*, Reinhold through three important books written between 1932 and 1935. And finally, Edwin Lewis and George Richards each attempted fairly thorough systematic reconstructions in works produced in 1934.[6]

The spectrum of opinion within this body of literature ran from Lowrie's nearly wholesale endorsement of Barth to a position, represented especially by Walter Marshall Horton, that could be called neoliberalism as easily as neo-orthodoxy. Yet the catalogue of the faults of liberalism was a matter of broad agreement all across the spectrum.

The oldest and simplest conservative pleas for a return to biblical literalism and an individualistic moralism did not reappear in neo-orthodoxy. Yet the new realists contended that the word of scripture, even if it must now be understood as mediated by the poetry of human languages, represents a higher authority than individual or social experience. This was the meaning of Richards' proposal that "the gospel of God" lay beyond both fundamentalism and modernism. These two forms of Christian expression, though bitterly opposed to each other, according to Richards

---

[6]Pauck, *Karl Barth: Prophet of a New Christianity?* Lowrie, *Our Concern with the Theology of Crisis*; Macintosh, ed., *Religious Realism*; Horton, *Realistic Theology*; Tillich, *The Religious Situation*, trans. H. Richard Niebuhr; Reinhold Niebuhr, *Moral Man and Immoral Society*; *Reflections on the End of an Era*; *An Interpretation of Christian Ethics*; Lewis, *A Christian Manifesto*; Richards, *Beyond Fundamentalism and Modernism: The Gospel of God*. A further notable work in this period was H. Richard Niebuhr, Pauck, and Miller, *The Church Against the World*.

had committed an identical error: both had mistaken the language or the experience of mere men for the true gospel of God. "Both fundamentalism and modernism," he wrote, "are the outcome of adjustment. The fundamentalism of today is the modernism of yesterday crystallized and set." Modernism would always be needed, he said, to save the gospel from hardening into dogmas and institutions, "but modernism must be held in check by living contact with the word of God in Christ as set forth in the Bible." But would this not involve a return to some kind of biblical literalism? Richards thought not: "The word must be maintained not as a letter, but as spirit and life in the hearts of believers."[7]

A second weapon, drawn with less hesitation or modification from established arsenals, was an objection to the liberal stress upon divine-human continuities. The dichotomizing tendencies articulated especially by Princeton fundamentalism in the preceding decades now gained new life and richness. Walter Lowrie, a convert to Episcopalianism but a Princetonian in background and training,[8] provided the archetypal illustration. Echoing Machen, and in fact announcing a triumph of which Machen himself was quite unsure, Lowrie rejoiced that in the high places of German and American liberal religion, it had now been conceded "that Liberalism . . . is *not* Christianity." That concession, he said, had put an end to "a vast deal of hypocrisy." Perhaps people would now, all along the line, face the choices truly before them.

In the hands of Lowrie, translator and interpreter of Kierkegaard, the rhetoric of choice became less a go-getter's preference for manly incisiveness and more (as in much popular revivalism) an acknowledgment of anguish and despair:

The Either-Or, when it involves the great alternative, God or the world, eternity or time, life or death, creates the "Moment" . . . Such a

---

[7]Richards, *Beyond Fundamentalism and Modernism*, title page and pp. 205-206.

[8]Lowrie, after graduation from Princeton Seminary in 1893, had studied and worked in Germany and Italy, and for a time had considered himself a theological liberal. Voskuil, "Liberalism to Neo-Orthodoxy," pp. 103-108. The best presentation of the philosophical context of neo-orthodoxy and its successor movements is Walter Kaufmann, "The Reception of Existentialism in the United States," *Midway*, 9 (Summer 1968), 97-126.

Moment calls for a decision which is sharp and instant and complete
. . . This decision is the relief of "Anguish" (one of Kierkegaard's key
words), and yet it remains founded upon anguish. It is an act of faith,
and yet of a faith which continues to be founded upon doubt—yes, even
upon despair, "a comforted despair."[9]

Even those who were anxious to distinguish their own attitudes
on many points of theology from those of Barth or of Lowrie could
join the latter in promoting this revised form of Either-Or
thinking. Richard Niebuhr and two co-authors declared in a volume of 1935 that they wished only "to add our contributions to
. . . the task of the Christian community in defining and taking
its position against the world."[10] Such a declaration undercut
the most basic assumptions of liberal thinking about culture;
yet the idea by that time had ceased to shock, and indeed had
become an expected way of speaking in many seminary classrooms
and refectories.

Another theme carried over from much earlier eras of opposition
to liberalism was an aversion to all types of immanentism. "The
doctrine of divine immanence," Lowrie wrote, "*begins* as theism,
but only too readily it merges into pantheism." He agreed with
Barth in opposing a theology that sees the world "as the lumi-
nous revelation of God, rather than as the cloak which *hides* the
Godhead." Theology, as Barth had said, must reinstate the distance between the supernatural and the natural. God is not
revealed "in the heart of man, in human nature . . . in the
amazing world of life below man, nor in the realm of inanimate
nature." And above all, God is not, as the nineteenth century had
been dazzled into believing, revealed in the upward movement of
civilization, even where such upward movement is conceded to be
real.[11]

Here Lowrie and his more moderate colleagues were able to use
much the same language. Richards spoke for all of them in
asserting that the Christian God is not a god "who has gradually
come to self-consciousness in the mind of man, who consists of

---

[9]Lowrie, *Our Concern*, pp. 54, 101.
[10]H. R. Niebuhr and others, *Church Against World*, p. 13.
[11]Lowrie, *Our Concern*, pp. 114, 122, 146-147, 33-34.

the accumulated experiences of tribes and nations, who is an aggregate of the highest values that men have reached from the cave-dweller to Pericles." Scientific knowledge, historical development, and economic reform are "terrestrial by-paths that lead to the plains but not to the heights."[12]

While the foregoing reactions to liberal biblical attitudes and liberal ideas of nature and God linked neo-orthodoxy to critiques voiced early in the century, several others elaborated the special complaints of the 1920s. Pursuing the line of attack that associated liberalism with the terrible loss of certainty modern man had experienced, Lowrie drew up a hedging, vacillating "liberal creed" that was almost certainly an intentional caricature of one that Shailer Mathews had proposed in the closing pages of *The Faith of Modernism*.[13] Lowrie gallantly included himself among one-time subscribers to a fictitious creed that began as follows:

(1) Of all the religions of mankind, Christianity, we are sure, is the highest; (2) for we regard it as the climax of a long evolutionary process, (3) in which the people of Israel, because they were a race especially gifted for religion, played a conspicuous part, while above this high level of human attainment towered (4) the Founder of our religion, (5) a religious genius so unique that men may well hesitate to deny that (6) in some sense he was divine.[14]

Others like Wilhelm Pauck and Walter Marshall Horton, while less ready to ridicule liberal statements, agreed in deploring what Pauck called "this tentativeness of our beliefs." Horton, in the symposium of 1931 on religious realism, echoed Lippmann's concern about "bewildered novices" who were looking for certainty and getting no help from liberals. Horton's volume of 1934 then elaborated the realist response to the problem of certitude:

The word "realism" suggests to me, above all, a resolute determination to face all the facts of life candidly, beginning preferably with the most stubborn, perplexing and disheartening ones, so that any lingering romantic illusions may be dispelled at the start; and then, *through* these stubborn facts and not *in spite* of them, to pierce as deep as one may into the solid structure of objective reality, until one finds whatever

---

[12]Richards, *Beyond Modernism*, pp. 149, 22.
[13]See Mathews, *Faith of Modernism*, pp. 180-181.
[14]Lowrie, *Our Concern*, p. 29.

ground of courage, hope, and faith is *actually* there, independent of human preferences and desires.[15]

Biblical faith; the necessity of choice; transcendence; certitude; openness to "the most disheartening facts"—these emphases together very nearly define the neo-orthodox revision. But one element must be added. It is an element almost as important to neo-orthodoxy as the one character Hamlet is to the play. This is the neo-orthodox emphasis on human sinfulness. Of all the "disheartening facts," sin was the one that neo-orthodoxy would most insist upon, and with an intensity not prefigured in any opposition to liberalism since the time of the earliest break between Calvinists and Unitarians. As John Bennett wrote in 1933, the point at issue between liberals and their detractors was the interpretation of human nature; other differences, he said, "follow from that."[16] The "newest" element in neo-orthodoxy, distinguishing it from preceding movements of outright opposition if not from the long-standing internal critique of liberalism, consisted in a despairing anthropology based to a large and often an acknowledged extent upon contemporary observations of human failure.

This opposition to liberal ideas about human nature, deservedly the best known of all neo-orthodox arguments, appeared particularly in the work of the Niebuhrs. Richard Niebuhr's broad and perceptive analysis of "Religious Realism and the Twentieth Century"—a high point in the Macintosh symposium of 1931—took it for granted that the optimism and "the anthropocratic and anthropocentric spirit of the nineteenth century" were now on the defensive; and Niebuhr made no pretense of denying the cultural sources of the new outlook. Theological realism was rooted, he said, "in experiences no less significant than those which gave rise to anthropocentrism and idealism." It expressed, for example, "the point of view of a time which has learned that failure is no less symptomatic of reality than triumph, decline no less significant . . . than progress." The same theologian's preface to

---

[15]Pauck, *Barth*, p. 6; Horton, "Authority Without Infallibility," in Macintosh, *Religious Realism*, pp. 277-304; *Realistic Theology*, p. 38.

[16]Bennett, "After Liberalism," p. 1403.

Reinhold Niebuhr

The Religious Situation a year later stressed Tillich's abandonment of "the liberal myth of unending progress."[17]

Disillusionment about human nature and the idea of progress,
meanwhile, predominated in nearly everything Reinhold Niebuhr
was writing. *Moral Man and Immoral Society* assailed and revised the hopeful preconceptions liberals allegedly harbored
about the possibilities of disinterested action by groups or classes.
From there the attack widened, so that in *Reflections on the End
of an Era* Niebuhr could assert that "the real basis for all the errors
of liberalism is its erroneous estimate of human nature." And in
An Interpretation of Christian Ethics he chided the "curious
error" of E. Stanley Jones in thinking that the human mind was
becoming "more and more latently Christian."[18]

Niebuhr's patronizing of a Christian missionary statesman for a
cautious faith that Christ is really at work in human nature reflected the kind of overargument for which he was constantly
taken to task. Yet both Niebuhrs showed an unusual ability to
transcend the polemics of their own preoccupying times, and an
awareness that the new realism could easily commit the very sins
of overadaptation to the times that they thought liberalism had
committed.

Neo-orthodoxy as expressed in extreme form by a Lowrie, or in
relatively careless form by many preachers and students, seemed
often to be claiming a special immunity from entanglement in the
relativities of its own historical situation. Lowrie, for example,
denied that the premises of Barthian theology had been shaped
"by discouragement, by the failure of all efforts to argue from the
world to God." Crisis theology, he asserted grandly, "radically ex-
cludes *a priori* all such effort by its assertion of the infinite qualitative difference between time and eternity." But the Niebuhrs
generally avoided any such claim. Reinhold, in the final para-
graphs of *Moral Man and Immoral Society*, allowed that the

---

[17]H. Richard Niebuhr, "Religious Realism and the Twentieth Century," in
Macintosh, *Religious Realism*, pp. 416-417; translator's preface to Tillich,
Religious Situation, p. xv. For able discussions, strengthened by use of unpublished materials, of H. Richard Niebuhr's stance "between Barth and Schleiermacher," consult Fowler, *To See the Kingdom*, pp. 34-95, 201-203.

[18]Reinhold Niebuhr, *Reflections*, p. 48; *Ethics*, pp. 180-181.

practicability of the liberals' love ethic "depends upon time and circumstance." Richard, in the "Religious Realism" article, laid emphasis on the contrasts between German and American formulations, and did so precisely for the purpose of keeping theologians on both sides aware that their concepts were necessarily limited as patternings of eternal truth. Richard Niebuhr thought that if the Barthians and the American realists would each, in effect, keep accusing the other of subjection to cultural influence, both would be right, and both might avoid the ironic error of representing "only the experience and the spirit of the twentieth century." Neo-orthodoxy in the thirties produced more electrifying warnings than this one, but none, perhaps, that was more prescient, or more splendidly faithful to neo-orthodoxy's own presuppositions about the finiteness of all human expression.[19]

Liberal Response: The End of the Modernist Era

Immediate reactions among those who had been identified with liberalism suggested panic, or at least a sense that the liberal movement had ended. John C. Bennett asked in his influential article of 1933 what was to come after liberalism. Walter Horton a year later referred to the defeat and rout of the liberal forces. And Fosdick at the end of 1935, though still not prepared to disown the term modernism, issued another of his ringing declarations that "we must go beyond modernism!"[20]

It is noteworthy, however, that these key figures, all of whom had been affected by neo-orthodoxy and—with the partial exception of Fosdick—were actively seeking to interpret its meaning sympathetically to the liberal community, hedged their own statements about the demise of liberalism. Bennett closed the door on the liberal epoch, then immediately opened it a bit by stressing "the elements of liberalism which we must not lose in the present stampede." And Horton, instead of just noting the panic among

---

[19]Lowrie, *Our Concern*, p. 124; Reinhold Niebuhr, *Moral Man*, pp. 275-277; H. Richard Niebuhr, "Religious Realism," pp. 424-428.

[20]Bennett, "After Liberalism"; Horton, *Realistic Theology*, p. 2; Fosdick, "Beyond Modernism," p. 1552.

his fellow liberals, implied strongly that they were overreacting. Some of them, he said, had become so nervous as to "flee when no man pursueth," and to berate themselves "ten times as destructively" as they were berated by their assailants.[21]

It is clear, especially if one looks just beyond the earliest alarmist reactions, that the liberal movement had not been routed or driven underground. That it had been transformed in spirit, however, was evident well before the end of the thirties. The change was attributable in large part to the decline of modernism, the virtual withdrawal of all remaining reliance upon what had once been celebrated as "the spirit of the age."

One indication of the Americans' limited response to crisis thinking, and of the persistence of liberalism, was the predominating attitude toward Karl Barth and his theology. Even among those who considered themselves ex-liberals and realists, the general reaction to Barth, while respectful and even awed, was massively unaccepting. Reinhold Niebuhr in the late twenties had rejoiced that "we finally have direct contact with this man Barth"; but he had also deplored the "sorry victory" achieved by Barth's kind of absolutism, and had remarked that "ultimately there is no more peace in dogmatism than in magic." Wilhelm Pauck's book-length study of Barth a few years later had ended with the troubled conclusion that the great Swiss theologian was at least "not *the* prophet of a new Christianity," and that "we must wait for another."[22]

Liberals of course expanded the negative side of these initial appraisals. Liberal reactions in the early thirties ranged not-so-widely from those who thought Barth incoherent but important to those who found him incoherent and of little consequence. The *Methodist Review* complained that *The Word of God and the Word of Man* was informed more by hysteria than by history; the

---

[21]Bennett, "After Liberalism," p. 1403; Horton, *Realistic Theology*, p. 2.

[22]Reinhold Niebuhr, "Barth—Apostle of the Absolute"; Pauck, *Barth*, p. 220. For a highly illuminating introduction to the discussion of Barth's theology in Europe, see H. Martin Rumscheidt, *Revelation and Theology: An Analysis of the Barth-Harnack Correspondence of 1923* (Cambridge, Eng., Cambridge University Press, 1972).

Anglican Theological Review judged it out of touch with modern thought and "antiquated" in theology.[23] By 1939, when thirty-five religious leaders contributed to the *Christian Century* series called "How My Mind Has Changed," the term "Barthianism" had largely displaced phrases like "Theology of Crisis" as the code word, even among the neo-orthodox, for an unacceptable transcendent-ism, anti-intellectualism, and ignoring of social responsibility.

John Bennett, in this 1939 series, confided that he was now "more repelled than helped by the Barthian form of traditionalism"; while E. S. Brightman of Boston University wrote that wherever European Christianity seemed to be flouting empiricism, it had become simply "unintelligible . . . a speaking with tongues." Ernest Fremont Tittle, noted Methodist preacher in Evanston, Illinois, went so far as to indict the current "utter disparagement of man" as playing into the hands of fascism and militarism, and as "nicely calculated to develop . . . a sanctimonious and sterile piety." Russell Henry Stafford defined Barthians as "men who use all the apparatus of learning in a grim endeavor to defeat learning in principle and destroy reason root and branch."[24]

Continuing attempts by the Niebuhrs and the American realists to "reinstate the distance" between themselves and Barth did not prevent their being accused of many of the alleged Barthian errors. The broadest and probably, in the long run, the most telling accusation was that neo-orthodoxy was the product of undue subservience, not merely to "culture" but to a very transient cultural mood. Shirley Jackson Case of Chicago, while he thought Reinhold Niebuhr too earnest to be called a cynic, said nonetheless that Niebuhr had "looked upon certain evils in the social order so intently that desperation has gripped his soul." To Case's colleague, Edward Scribner Ames, even Horton's

---

[23]Reviews of Barth and of the neo-orthodox literature are identified in table C.

[24]Bennett, "A Changed Liberal," p. 179; Brightman, "From Rationalism to Empiricism," p. 277; Tittle, "A God-Centered Ministry," p. 797; Stafford, "Change Without Crisis," p. 849. See Robert M. Miller, *How Shall They Hear Without a Preacher: The Life of Ernest Fremont Tittle* (Chapel Hill, University of North Carolina Press, 1971).

realism appeared "a backwash from the tragedy of the war and a 'failure of nerve' in times of depression." By the end of the decade, an additional, terrible element entered the argument as liberals warned, with Tittle, that the overreaction against religious liberalism could help render the West defenseless against its Hitlers. Crisis theology, with Barth an exile from Germany, clearly could not be called a willing adjunct of Hitlerism. But John C. Schroeder of Yale let slip an allegation that the whole campaign against liberalism was a "Barthian *Putsch,*" while his colleague Robert L. Calhoun deplored attempts to adjourn that search for rationality "against which the cults of blood and soil are in revolt." Calhoun saw "no way in which theology can get on safely without history, philosophy, and common sense."[25]

Other staples of liberal or neoliberal response in the 1930s—all connected with those just named—were complaints about the pessimism of neo-orthodoxy, about its tendency to caricature the liberal tradition, and about its alleged failure to move beyond destructive criticism to the articulation of clear lines of action.

Even evangelical critics found it hard to see how social effectiveness comported with so much apparent pessimism. J. B. Weatherspoon of the Southern Baptists argued emphatically that while one might believe with Niebuhr in human depravity, "we must believe also in the power of redemption and regeneration." More distinctly liberal writers of course agreed. Theodore Hume quoted, and appeared to understand, Niebuhr's characteristic statement that "the religious ideal in its purest form has nothing to do with the problem of social justice." It was a position, Hume insisted, that brought Niebuhr perilously close to a fundamentalist rationale for social inaction.[26]

Charles Clayton Morrison, reviewing *Reflections on the End of an Era,* lauded the author's "good wholesome pessimism" and denied that it necessarily paralyzed social action; but he scolded

---

[25]For the Case and Ames reviews (in the *Journal of Religion* and *Christendom,* respectively) see the Appendix, table C. Schroeder, "A Deeper Social Gospel," p. 923; Calhoun, "A Liberal Bandaged but Unbowed," pp. 703-704.

[26]See Appendix, table C, entries for Reinhold Niebuhr's *Moral Man and Immoral Society.*

Niebuhr for indulging in caricature. Niebuhr's method, he said, was to construct social strategies that plainly were childish absurdities, and then to call these strategies liberal. Neibuhr had asserted, for example, that it was foolish to invite the oligarchs to live by the law of justice; but who, Morrison asked, had ever invited them to do so? Certainly not liberalism, which "proceeds on the democratic principle of dispossessing the privileged holders of power whether they are willing or not. This is the essence of the social gospel which is the essence of liberalism."[27] And which liberals, precisely, had given themselves (in Niebuhr's words) "to the simple faith that both the ideals and the needs of individuals can be fully realized in an ideal society?" Morrison did not think Niebuhr could find support for such a position in any liberal writer. Such aspersions were therefore "wholly gratuitous."[28]

A final, very prevalent query from the liberal side was whether the new realists had anything to offer besides negative criticism of their predecessors. E. E. Aubrey of Chicago found it frustrating that realists like Richards had thus far failed "to offer a clear alternative for coping with problems which modernism had honestly tried to meet." And at least three writers—Aubrey, Morrison, and Winfred Garrison—reacted in the same way to the Niebuhr-Pauck-Miller volume of 1935. The church, Morrison

---

[27]To those who are familiar with such famous attempts at persuasion as Gladden's "Is It Peace or War?" (1886), Morrison's protest at this point will seem too strong. What he presumably had in mind, however, was the nearly unanimous disposition among social gospelers, particularly after the turn of the century, to support coercive legislation when persuasion would not work. There can be little doubt that the oligarchs themselves thought they were being dispossessed by antitrust laws and regulatory legislation.

[28]For another attack on the new realists for their overgeneralizing about liberalism, see Ames's review, in *Christendom*, of Horton's *Realistic Theology*. One would expect that Lowrie must have been objected to on this score. I was, however, able to find surprisingly few reviews of Lowrie's work; liberals in particular seem to have ignored it. Reinhold Niebuhr was repeatedly criticized for his overgeneralizing technique, and his desultory attempts at documentation in *An Interpretation of Christian Ethics* may well have been intended as responses to such criticism. In a characteristic reply on this point a number of years later he admitted that "when Professor [Daniel Day] Williams names names I am embarrassed." "Reply to Interpretation and Criticism," in Kegley and Bretall, eds., *Reinhold Niebuhr*, p. 441.

observed, was to be freed from servile entanglement with the world. But the proponents of this laudable objective did not really say how such a difficult operation was to be accomplished, and did not "constructively define the kind of church which will emerge if their call to independence is heeded." Morrison went on to acknowledge that a short book could not do everything. But Garrison, reviewing the same book for the *Christian Century*, was less kindly: the authors, he said, demanded "a return to God and Christ without offering any fresh suggestion as to how one may either find God or be found by him . . . They sound a trumpet call to nothing in particular."[29]

Few of these liberal critics denied the powerful impact of neo-orthodox revisionism, both upon themselves and upon American theology and thought. Morrison, editor of the *Christian Century*, set about organizing the journalistic "testimony meeting" of 1939 in the conviction that the series would confirm "a radical and significant change in the thinking of Christian scholarship and leadership."[30] Yet it is evident, even if one assumes that Morrison fell somewhat short in his effort to recruit representative leaders of religious thought,[31] that the voice of liberalism remained strong in the American churches at large, and particularly in the traditional centers of liberal power. Of the thirty-five contributors to the series (thirty-four invitees plus Morrison himself), more than twenty still thought of themselves fundamentally—and in many

---

[29]Aubrey's review of Richards appeared in *Journal of Religion*. Aubrey, Morrison, and Garrison reviewed the Niebuhr-Pauck-Miller volume in, respectively, *Religious Education, Christian Century Pulpit,* and *Christian Century.*

[30]Morrison, "How Their Minds Have Changed," p. 1194.

[31]Morrison's original invitation had been sweetened with the announcement that the editors were attempting to enlist twenty of "the most interesting minds in the modern church." He said later that he had also wished the contributors to be "truly representative of the church in general, or of some part of the church, or of some school of thought in the church." And the editors, at least, felt that on both counts their judgments had been "fully confirmed by the outcome." But for whatever reason—because of refusals, perhaps, from fundamentalists, Catholics, and others—the contributors seem to have represented a cross-section not of American religion but mainly of that large liberal-to-evangelical stream within which most discussion of neo-orthodoxy was taking place. The group included only one fundamentalist (Clarence McCartney), one Anglo-Catholic (George Craig Stewart), and one Jew (Morris Lazaron).

cases vociferously—as liberals, while barely a half-dozen came out squarely for even the American forms of crisis theology.[32] The "bouleversement" of the 1930s, like a good many others in the history of American thought, had occurred—up to this point at least—very much as a modification within a persisting liberalism.

Among that majority in the 1939 symposium who did still call themselves liberals, several broad patterns of response to neo-orthodoxy had become discernible. The most adamantine response was that of men like Ames of Chicago; Bishop McConnell of the Methodist Church; and Russell Henry Stafford, Gordon's successor at Old South—all of whom averred that the challenge of crisis theology had merely strengthened their resolve as liberals. Ames, a bit maliciously, acknowledged that he had formerly erred in his estimate of human progress, and cited as evidence the continuing capacity of human beings to believe incredible theologies.[33] At the opposite edge of the liberal grouping were those who, like Horton, Luccock, and the Southern Baptist leader Edwin McNeill Poteat, considered themselves to have been led, in Horton's words, "to the verge of orthodoxy."[34] Somewhere between these two positions stood the largest subgroup among those who professed continued attachment to liberalism. This middle stance, reiterated in one article after another throughout the year 1939, involved (1) an assumption—not necessarily judgmental in nature—that neo-orthodoxy was equally or more responsive than liberalism had been to an immediate cultural situation; (2) a refusal to give much ground in the argument between immanent and transcendent conceptions of the nature and action of God; and (3) an acknowledgment that liberalism had theretofore counted too much on human

---

[32]Karl Barth (elected an honorary American, apparently, for the purpose of this series), Reinhold Niebuhr, Elmer Homrighausen, Edwin Lewis, John Mackay, and Frederick D. Kershner of Butler University are the six who were plainly willing to be identified with neo-orthodoxy. In another group of five contributors who do not quite announce an alignment, only one—James Luther Adams—might conceivably be listed as, at this time, neo-orthodox. For most of the remaining twenty-four, Robert Calhoun's title—"A Liberal Bandaged but Unbowed"— would have served rather well.

[33]Ames, "Liberalism Confirmed," p. 380.

[34]Horton, "Between Liberalism," p. 637; Luccock, "No Apologies," pp. 971-974; Poteat, "Greater Loyalties," pp. 244-247.

progress, together with a marked retreat from progressive phrasings of the idea of divine immanence.

By this time, the standing observation about the cultural sources of neo-orthodox theology was usually offered evenhandedly. It came as an observation about cultural influence upon all theology, and was directed against neo-orthodoxy only insofar as the neo-orthodox might suppose they were immune from this kind of limitation. Luccock remarked that although neither liberalism nor neo-orthodoxy could be explained fully by the methods of the economic determinists, it did seem that "in times of prosperity Christians tend to become Greek in their theology; in times of adversity they again become Hebrew." Currently, he thought, the movement from Greece to Judea had assumed the proportions of a Great Trek.[35]

Walter Marshall Horton discussed the same allegedly inevitable process in greater depth and with more attention to implications for the future of theology. Horton counted his own rediscovery of Augustine as one event that had changed his thinking during this ten-year period, and averred that Augustinian thought went far toward expressing "the truth that God is bringing home to mankind in times like these." But, as that phrasing suggests, Horton could see that the wheel would turn, that the need for a doctrine of immanence would recur. "When that happens, please God, the call will not be for an Augustine or a Barth, but for an Origen, a Thomas Aquinas, a Schleiermacher." Christians would need again to assert

the *self-imparting, world-pervading* character of the God who became incarnate in Christ and continues the process in and through the church. If in ages of peaceful construction it would have been well to warn our Schleiermachers of judgment to come, lest they grow too complacent, it is equally necessary in this time of crisis to warn our Barths of redemption to come, lest they grow too desperate.[36]

Bishop McConnell, however, added a further reproof that did in effect fall more heavily upon the neo-orthodox. McConnell, an

---

[35]Luccock, "No Apologies," p. 972.
[36]Horton, "Between Liberalism," p. 638.

Walter Marshall Horton

old and leading social gospeler, saw the current theological discussions as unduly preoccupied not only with the problems of a
particular time, but also with those of a relatively small segment
of humanity. He argued that the whole agonized discussion of
wars and economic depressions, and of a presumed decline of
Western civilization, showed an amazing self-centeredness and
provincialism. What did the people of the West, after all, know
about suffering? And how important—indeed how real—was the
decline of the West in any encompassing view of history?

> Taking the world over, the problem and the fact have always been about
> what they are now . . . There has not been for the majority of men any-
> thing even resembling a chance at human existence. In these dreadful
> respects the Western world has in ten years come to be just a little like the
> conditions in which the masses of mankind have always lived.

Were Christians in Germany and England and America crying
out about the pain of the world "because it is the common lot, or
because at last we are hit by it"? Despite all the moaning about
bread lines, McConnell pointed out, even the masses in America
were "in luxury compared with the millions of India and China."
If McConnell had known, at this time, about Halford Luccock's
fanciful depiction of the human elevator that crashed when the
stock market failed, he would presumably have asked who, precisely,
had ever been on that elevator in the first place. Again a convinced
liberal was turning the neo-orthodox weaponry on the neo-orthodox themselves: the theologies of crisis, ironically, illustrated
human inability to transcend narrow self-concern.[37]

Dean Sperry engaged in a similar analysis, but added a note that
had been characteristic of his attitude since the early 1920s, and
that brought him into closer sympathy with what the Niebuhrians
were saying. Like Horton with his rediscovery of Augustine,
Sperry tended to see permanent validity in the strains of Christian
thinking now being resurrected, even if this reawakening was a
historical accident, and even if the awakeners were provincially
bound to their time and place. Sperry might have made some
personal capital out of the fact that he himself, well before Niebuhr

---

[37]McConnell, "From Lausanne," p. 511.

had been heard of, had expatiated upon the consciousness of sin and suffering as "the initial mood of Christian experience."[38] Instead, he found himself rejoicing "with a certain fearful joy" that he was living in a time when such a rediscovery was being widely made.[39]

Sperry thus showed himself more willing than many of his liberal colleagues to credit the neo-orthodox correction with elements of permanent validity. On one central point, however, he did think neo-orthodoxy was both faddish and wrong. For all his concessions, Sperry would not renounce the liberals' stress upon divine immanence. "I am not prepared . . . to identify the case for religion solely with the revelation in Christ."[40] This kind of statement—embodying a firm refusal to narrow the scope of revelation—constituted another nearly unanimous theme on the liberal side. Its converse, the immanence and accessibility of God, was far and away the most persistent note of liberal reaffirmation.

McConnell's way of putting it was perhaps a bit perverse: The world being a poor place for God to be found, he said, "we look off to the transcendent. If, however, God were not in some fashion immanent we could never know him as transcendent." Albert Palmer, president of Chicago Theological Seminary (Congregational), spoke for more of the liberals when he insisted that "no conception . . . seems satisfactory to me which does not accept the whole universe as its primary data about God." "We do not do honor to God," John Bennett added, "by insisting upon . . . the 'parsimony' of his revealing or redemptive activity, assuming that God cannot be known apart from one channel of revelation."[41]

Here, above all, liberalism was taking its stand. The estimate of human nature had declined; but God's condescension to humanity, God's willingness to remain accessible and companion-

---

[38]Sperry, *Disciplines of Liberty*, p. 59.
[39]Sperry, "How My Mind Has Changed," p. 83.
[40]Ibid., p. 84.
[41]McConnell, "From Lausanne," p. 511; Palmer, "Spiritual Pilgrimage," p. 731; Bennett, "A Changed Liberal," p. 179.

able to human beings whatever their true state might be, was seen as directly proportional to human degradation. Liberals remained unwilling to make more of discontinuity and alienation than of continuity between the divine and the human—unwilling in anything like the Barthian sense to "reinstate the distance" between man and God.

What then had changed? Simply the estimate of human nature? And was the change, even in this area, perhaps a matter of degree rather than of qualitative difference? The shift seems to have been more decisive than such questions would suggest. One form of argumentation, the argument from human progress, had virtually disappeared. Despite the complaints that crisis theology had overreacted to current events, liberals themselves had reacted by ceasing to cite human progress as a datum for explaining the nature of God.[42] Despite the continued emphasis on the breadth and variety of God's modes of revelation, the idea that God reveals himself in and through the process of cultural development had been seriously modified—enough so that the old terminology of "modernism" seemed no longer appropriate. Modernism's confidence in the advance of the earthly Kingdom had become unavailable as an assumption in ordinary discourse.

While the large-scale assaults of the twenties and thirties, and particularly the neo-orthodox critique, had identified grievous flaws in the liberal outlook and method, they had also helped to place the necessity and contributions of the liberal movement in a new light. Though often deficient—whether uniquely so or not— in prophetic independence and moral realism, classical liberalism had championed some modes both of independence and of realism

---

[42]Bennett's carefully balanced statement rose, at its most optimistic point, to little more than Niebuhr's degree of faith in human progress: "I do believe that it is possible on this earth to have a structure of society within which men can live together in an interdependent world without destroying each other, within which individuals and groups can rise to high levels and within which they can live without intolerable compromise." Bennett, "A Changed Liberal," p. 180. See also, for a persisting hope of social improvement, McConnell, "From Lausanne"; Kern, "Hope Sees a Star," pp. 412-414; and Beaven, "Generation Ahead," pp. 820-822.

that were not necessarily scorned even in the neo-orthodox reaction. Liberalism at its best had asked the church and its people to say what they really believed, and then to make moral action consonant with belief. It had asked Christian theology to accept realistically the entanglement of religion in culture, and to make the best of that circumstance. "Proclamation" was not to be a substitute for ethical performance; nor was the church to assume too easily that it had actually achieved a critical or prophetic detachment from the larger society. Candor on such a point had been greatly encouraged and facilitated by progressive faith, and more easily achieved in that ambience. But whatever the initial incentives, liberalism under the modernist impetus had declared openly that the church is and must be in the world.

Neo-orthodox realism was never entirely uncongenial with this position. The neo-orthodox, to be sure, deplored and resisted Christianity's cultural entanglement; but they did not—except in moments of forgetfulness or arrogance—deny its inevitability.

Restatements and Prospects

By the 1960s, the prevailing attitudes among the heirs of liberalism and neo-orthodoxy once again bespoke acceptance and often celebration of continuities between the sacred and the secular. The most widely known assertion was that of Harvey Cox in 1965: "secularization rolls on, and if we are to understand and communicate with our present age we must learn to love it in its unremitting secularity." Two years later, the Presbyterian General Assembly, which despite changes since the time of Francis Patton had not become a hotbed of radical theology, approved a new confessional statement that conveyed far more equanimity about cultural adaptation than had been common during the neo-orthodox interlude. "In every age," this statement acknowledged, "the church has expressed its witness in words and deeds as the need of the time required"; the scriptures, though "given under the guidance of the Holy Spirit, are nevertheless the words of men, conditioned by the language, thought forms, and literary fashions of the places and times at which they were written. They reflect views of life, history, and the cosmos which were then current." The same Confession averred that "the Christian religion, as distinct from God's revelation of himself, has been shaped throughout its history by the cultural forms of its environment."[43]

This renewed cordiality toward culture and secularity remained, however, a sober acceptance. Langdon Gilkey of the University of Chicago saw theology and the church engaged in a renewed movement toward the world and a "sharp reversal of all that characterized the neo-orthodox period"; but he admitted that neo-orthodox doubts about human progress had not been reversed. Liberalism had assumed "that our culture is not only creative of value, but . . . increasingly creative in a visible progress to a better state of things." That assumption was the one that remained unusable: "We now feel our entire culture to be precarious, possibly mortal, and certainly relative to the onrush of historical forces. It might not last, it might be replaced."[44]

Looking to the future, one should allow for the possibility of new births of cultural enthusiasm, for new humanisms and accessions of this-worldly confidence imbibed, perhaps, from people whose histories and memories bear little resemblance to those of Western Christendom. For the time being, however, the acceptance of Christianity's cultural involvement persists without the comforts of the progressivist elation that first nurtured it—largely without the nineteenth-century liberal's "generous hopes of the world's destiny." So long as that remains true, the retrospective attitude toward the strain of this-worldly confidence in modernism will doubtless retain an air of nostalgia even when it manages to avoid condescension. The other two modernist ideas—adaptationism and the sense of divine immanence that supported it—remain with us not as historical curiosities but as the main elements of a controversial, still-vital heritage from the decades of modernist enthusiasm.

---

[43] Harvey Cox, *The Secular City: Secularization and Urbanization in Theological Perspective* (New York, The Macmillan Co., 1965), p. 4; United Presbyterian Church in the United States of America, *Constitution: Part I, Book of Confessions*, 2d ed. (Philadelphia, United Presbyterian Church, 1970), secs. 9.02, 9.29, 9.41.

[44] Gilkey, *Naming the Whirlwind*, pp. 107, 343-344.

Appendix

A. Reviews of selected liberal works in representative journals and newspapers, 1877-1891

	Smyth, *Religious Feeling* (1877)	Smyth, *Old Faiths* (1879)	Smyth, *Orthodox Theology* (1881)	Briggs, *Biblical Study* (1882)
American Church Review				
Andover Review				1, 1/84 101-103
Baptist Quarterly Review				
Bibliotheca Sacra				41, 4/84 414-417
Christian Register	56, 10/20/77			
Congregationalist		31, 12/10/79		35, 11/1/83
Hartford Seminary Record				
Independent	29, 10/11/77			35, 10/25/83
Index				
Lutheran Church Review				3, 1/84 73
Lutheran Quarterly	7, 10/77, 627-628	10, 7/80 461-464		14, 1/84 161-163
Methodist Quarterly Review	60, 4/78 365-366			66, 1/84 184
Nation				
New Englander	37, 1/78 72-79			
New York Times			11/21/81	
Old Testament Student [a]				3, 2/84 213-216
Open Court				
Presbyterian Quarterly and Princeton Review [b]	6, 10/77 759-760			5, 1/84 154-157
Reformed Quarterly Review				31, 1/84 149-150
Unitarian Review				20, 11/83 479-480
Unity				

[a] *Hebrew Student* (1882-1883), *Old Testament Student* (1883-1889), *Old and New Testament Student* (1889-1893), *Biblical World* (1893-1920).

Munger, *Freedom of Faith* (1883)	Allen, *Continuity of Christian Thought* (1884)	*Progressive Orthodoxy* (1885)	Briggs, *Whither?* (1889)	Briggs, *Holy Scripture* (1891)	Gladden, *Who Wrote the Bible?* (1891)
42, 10/83 508-510		48, 9/86 306-311			
	3, 3/85 286-291		12, 11/89 552-555	15, 3/91 304-309	
		8, 4/86 274-279	12, 1/90 123-128		
43, 4/86 335-356	42, 4/85 394-395	43, 10/86 772-776	47, 1/90 136-153		
	64, 1/1/85				
35, 6/7/83					76, 5/21/91
				1, 6/91 177-178	
35, 5/24/83					
	16, 5/14/85				
			9, 1/90 82		
13, 6/83 458	15, 1/85 144-146	16, 4/86 316			
			72, 1/90 147-149	73, 9/91 838-839	
					53, 9/17/91
42, 6/83 553-554	44, 5/85 450	45, 3/86 249-263			
			9, 12/89 375-376		
			3, 12/19/89 2002-2003		
4, 10/83 874-876	6, 9/85 562-564	7, 4/86 398-400		2, 6/91 481-494	
	32, 10/85 543-544		37, 1/90 133-134		
	23, 1/85 87-91	25, 5/86 443-462			
	25, 2/86 157-172				
		17, 3/13/86			

b *Presbyterian Review* (1880-1889), *Presbyterian and Reformed Review* (1890-1902).

B. Reviews of selected liberal works in representative journals and newspapers, 1891-1908

	Stearns, *Present-Day Theology* (1891)	Abbott, *Evolution of Christianity* (1892)	Smyth, *Christian Ethics* (1892)	Beach, *Newer Religious Thinking* (1893)
American Journal of Theology				
Andover Review	19, 5/93 364-366	18, 8/92 188-190	19, 1/93 116-118	19, 11/93 772-773
Atlantic Monthly				
Biblical World				
Bibliotheca Sacra				53, 10/96 767-768
Christian Register			71, 10/27/92	
Congregationalist				
Dial				
Hartford Seminary Record	3, 8/93 310-311		3, 10/92 63-64	
Harvard Theological Review				
Hibbert Journal				
Independent				
Interior	1893 20			1894 54
Literary World				
Lutheran Church Review				
Lutheran Quarterly		22, 7/92 443-444		
Methodist Review		74, 11/92 990-991		
Nation		54, 6/9/92		
New World		1, 9/92 573-575	2, 1/93 196-197	
Outlook				
Presbyterian and Reformed Review	5, 10/94 730-740		5, 4/94 350-354	5, 1/94 187-188
Reformed Quarterly Review [a]			40, 1/93 176	
Religious Education				
Review and Expositor				

[a] After 1898, *Reformed Church Review*.

Gordon, Gospel for Humanity (1895)	Gordon, Christ of To-Day (1895)	Harris, Moral Evolution (1896)	Gordon, Immortality and the New Theodicy (1897)	Clarke, Outline of Christian Theology (1898)	Gladden, How Much Is Left (1899)
		1, 4/97 503-508		3, 1/99 203-206	4, 7/00 638-640
	77, 1/96 124-126				
	53, 1/96 195-196	54, 4/97 396	54, 4/97 398-399	55, 7/98 579-580	
	74, 12/5/95	75, 5/14/96		77, 6/30/98	
80, 11/14/95	80, 11/21/95				
	81, 2/13/96				
	20, 5/1/96				
	6, 12/95 86-88	6, 6/96 263-267	7, 5/97 270-271	8, 8/98 302-304	
				44, 4/06 673-680	
47, 10/24/95					
		1896 858	1897 1442		
	26, 12/14/95				
				28, 10/98 591-594	
		79, 1/97 159-161	79, 5/97 500		
	5, 3/96 150-152	5, 6/96 354-357	6, 6/97 357-359	8, 9/99 588-592	9, 4/00 142-145
52, 10/26/95	52, 11/23/95	53, 3/21/96		59, 6/18/98	
		8, 7/97 531-541	8, 10/97 763-770	9, 4/98 354-356	
	18, 10/96 541-542				4, 10/00 555

(continued)

B. Reviews of selected liberal works in representative journals and newspapers, 1891-1908 (continued)

	Peabody, *Jesus Christ and the Social Question* (1900)	Gordon, *New Epoch* (1901)	King, *Reconstruction in Theology* (1901)	Smyth, *Through Science to Faith* (1902)	Gordon, *Ultimate Conceptions* (1904)
American Journal of Theology	5, 10/01 831-832	6, 4/02 372-374	5, 10/01 813-814	6, 7/02 608-609	8, 4/04 343-349
Andover Review					
Atlantic Monthly					
Biblical World	17, 6/01 469-470		18, 12/01 495-496	20, 12/02 487-489	23, 6/04 474-475
Bibliotheca Sacra	58, 7/01 600-601	58, 10/01 791	58, 10/01 783-787		61, 1/04 201-203
Christian Register					
Congregationalist					
Dial					
Hartford Seminary Record	11, 2/01 134-135	11, 5/01 229-230		12, 5/02 239-240	14, 2/04 154-155
Harvard Theological Review					
Hibbert Journal					
Independent		53, 2/28/01			
Interior			1901 1664		
Literary World					
Lutheran Church Review					
Lutheran Quarterly					
Methodist Review	83, 4/01 328-330				
Nation	73, 8/1/01				
New World	9, 12/00 788-789				
Outlook		67, 3/2/01			75, 11/28/03
Presbyterian and Reformed Review					2, 10/04 670-672
Reformed Quarterly Review[a]	5, 4/01 262-265			9, 1/05 125-128	
Religious Education					
Review and Expositor				2, 1/05 108-112	

[a]After 1898, *Reformed Church Review*.

Coe, Education in Religion and Morals (1904)	Foster, Finality of the Christian Religion (1906)	Mathews, Church and the Changing Order (1907)	Rauschenbusch, Christianity and the Social Crisis (1907)	Smyth, Passing Protestantism (1908)	Bowne, Personalism (1908)
9, 4/05 388	10, 7/06 529-535	12, 10/08 665-667	12, 1/08 172-174		
25, 2/05 154-156	29, 4/07 315-317	31, 3/08 230	31, 3/08 231-232		
	64, 4/07 383-389	65, 1/08 186-187	65, 1/08 185-186		66, 1/09 188
			43, 10/16/07		
		17, 10/07 353-354	17, 7/07 262-263		
					1, 10/08 514
	60, 4/19/06 1906 860				
				28, 7/09 508-509	
		38, 1/08 152-154	38, 7/08 446-448	38, 10/08 590-591	
		90, 1/08 156-157			
		85, 8/15/07	85, 7/11/07	87, 7/30/08	86, 6/18/08
79, 4/22/05	83, 5/12/06		87, 10/5/07	89, 5/30/08	90, 9/5/08
3, 4/05 306-309	4, 7/06 395-400	6, 1/08 169-171	5, 10/07 697-702		
		12, 4/08 290-291	11, 10/07 578-580		3, 10/08 157
	3, 7/06 439-443	5, 1/08 99-102	4, 10/07 669-670	5, 10/08 617-618	5, 10/08 618-620

C. Reviews of selected neo-orthodox works in representative journals and newspapers, 1928-1935

	Barth, *Word of God and Word of Man* (1928)	Pauck, *Karl Barth: Prophet of a New Christianity?* (1931)	Macintosh, *Religious Realism* (1931)	Lowrie, *Our Concern with the Theology of Crisis* (1932)
Anglican Theological Review	11, 4/29 396-397	14, Sp/32 199		15, 4/33 167-170
Biblical Review	14, 4/29 283-287			
Bibliotheca Sacra				
Chicago Theological Seminary Register		22, 6/32 52-54		
Christendom				
Christian Century	45, 12/13/28 1523-1524	49, 1/6/32 19-20	49, 2/3/32 156-157	49, 12/7/32 1506
Christian Century Pulpit				
Crozer Quarterly	6, 4/29 247-248			
Drew Gateway				
Journal of Religion	9, 7/29 498-499		12, 10/32 578-580	13, 1/33 120
Lutheran Church Quarterly			5, 4/32 227-228	
Methodist Review	112, 5/29 469-470			
New Humanist		5, 11-12/32 38-41		
Personalist			13, 7/32 218	
Presbyterian Advance (Tribune)			44, 11/12/31 30-31	
Religion in Life		1, W/32 151-152		
Religious Education			28, 6/33 309-310	
Review and Expositor	26, 10/29 466-467	29, 1/32 116-120	30, 7/33 341-344	30, 1/33 75-77
Union Seminary Review		43, 1/32 258-259		
World Tomorrow				

Tillich, Religious Situation (1932)	Niebuhr, Moral Man and Immoral Society (1932)	Niebuhr, Reflections on the End of an Era (1934)	Richards, Beyond Fundamentalism and Modernism (1934)	Horton, Realistic Theology (1934)	Niebuhr, Pauck, Miller, Church Against the World (1935)
	17, 1/35 60	16, 10/34 313-315	16, 10/34 309-310	17, 1/35 59	18, 4/36 116-118
		90, 4/33 247-248			
				1, 10/35 179-181	
	50, 1/4/33 18-19	51, 3/7/34 323-324			52, 11/13/35 1457-1458
					6, 12/35 287
	10, 10/33 495-496	11, 7/34 365-366	11, 7/34 366-367	12, 4/35 191-192	12, 10/35 52
					7, 10/35 7-8
13, 7/33 348-349	13, 7/33 359-361	15, 1/35 98-100	15, 1/35 80-81	15, 7/35 333-335	
				8, 1/35 111-112	
15, 1/34 81					
	46, 2/23/33 30				
2, W/33 146-147	2, Sp/33 305-307	3, Aut/34 623-624		4, Sp/35 311-312	5, W/36 154-155
28-9, 33-34 415		28-9, 33-34 179-180			31, 4/36 148-149
	30, 4/33 218-221	31, 10/34 521-522	31, 7/34 402-403		33, 10/36 465-466
					47, 1/36 155-156
15, 12/21/32 596	15, 12/14/32 565-567				

Selected Bibliography

Index

Selected Bibliography

The following is a list of the books, articles, dissertations, and other materials that bear most directly upon the subject of this book. It is alphabetized strictly, in order that the reader seeking full citations can find them here instead of looking back through the book for first references. Two kinds of material have been omitted from this select list. (1) Reviews in the religious and theological journals are either designated in the three tables that appear in the Appendix or are cited fully in the appropriate footnotes. (2) Much of the primary and secondary literature on topics not central to liberalism and modernism, but closely related to them, is cited only in the footnotes, particularly in the many cases in which the book or article has been mentioned only once. The entries in the select list have been annotated in accord with the system indicated in the following key. Many items, of course, could properly be identified with several of these genres.

A	Autobiography
Bib	Biblical studies
Biog	Biography
CH	Church history
D	Denominational histories
E	Ecumenicity
F	Fundamentalist opposition
I	Influences upon the American liberal movement
L	Liberalism, primary statements not otherwise categorized in this listing
M	Missions
N	Neo-orthodoxy, works of or on
O	Opposition other than fundamentalist or neo-orthodox
P	Philosophy of religion
Psych	Psychology of religion
RE	Religious education
Sci	Science and religion
Sec	Secondary treatments of liberalism
Soc	Social gospel
T	Theology
U	Unitarianism
W	World War I

U   Abbot, Francis E. "The Intuitional and Scientific Schools of Free Reli-
         gion," *Index*, 2 (April 15, 1871), 113-115.

Soc   Abbott, Lyman. *Christianity and Social Problems*. Boston, Houghton,
         Mifflin and Co., 1896.

Sci   ———— *The Evolution of Christianity*. Boston, Houghton, Mifflin and
         Co., 1892.

Bib   ———— *The Life and Letters of Paul the Apostle*. Boston, Houghton,
         Mifflin and Co., 1898.

Bib   ———— *Life of Christ*. Boston, The Bible Study Publishing Co., 1895.

L   ———— *The Life That Really Is*. New York, W. B. Ketcham, 1899.

A   ———— *Reminiscences*. Boston, Houghton, Mifflin and Co., 1915.

Sci   ———— *The Theology of an Evolutionist*. Boston, Houghton, Mifflin
         and Co., 1897.

W   ———— *Twentieth Century Crusade*. New York, The Macmillan Co.,
         1918.

L   ———— and others. *The New Puritanism*. New York, Fords, Howard,
         and Hulbert, 1898.

W   Abrams, Ray H. *Preachers Present Arms*. New York, Round Table
         Press, 1933.

Sec   Adams, James Luther. "The Changing Reputation of Human Nature,"
         Journal of Liberal Religion, 4 (Autumn 1942 and Winter 1943),
         59-79 and 137-160.

Biog   ———— "William Wallace Fenn as Critic of Liberal Christianity," *The
         Unitarian Universalist Christian*, 29 (Winter 1974-75), 13-17.

M   Ahlstrom, Sydney E. *The American Protestant Encounter with World
         Religions*. Beloit, Wisconsin, 1962.

N   ———— "Continental Influence on American Christian Thought Since
         World War I," *Church History*, 27 (September 1958), 256-272.

Sec   ———— *A Religious History of the American People*. New Haven, Yale
         University Press, 1972.

T   ———— "Theology in America: A Historical Survey," in James Ward
         Smith and Leland Jamison, eds., *The Shaping of American Reli-
         gion*. Princeton, Princeton University Press, 1961.

Biog   Albright, Raymond W. *Focus on Infinity: A Life of Phillips Brooks*.
         New York, The Macmillan Co., 1961.

CH   Allen, A. V. G. *The Continuity of Christian Thought: A Study of Mod-
         ern Theology in the Light of Its History*. Boston, Houghton, Mif-
         lin and Co., 1884.

Biog   ———— *Phillips Brooks, 1885-1893*. New York, E. P. Dutton and Co.,
         1907.

T   ———— The Theological Renaissance of the Nineteenth Century,"
         Princeton Review, 58 (November 1882), 263-282, and 59 (January
         1883), 67-90.

A   Ames, Edward Scribner. *Beyond Theology: The Autobiography of
         Edward Scribner Ames*. Chicago, University of Chicago Press, 1959.

A   ———— "Liberalism Confirmed," *Christian Century*, 56 (March 22,
         1939), 380-382.

Sec   Arnold, Harvey. "The Death of God—'06," *Foundations*, 10 (October–December 1967), 331-353.

Sec   Averill, Lloyd J. *American Theology in the Liberal Tradition*. Philadelphia, Westminster Press, 1967.

O   Ayres, C. E. *Science: The False Messiah*. Indianapolis, Bobbs-Merrill Co., 1927.

Biog   Bacon, Benjamin W. *Theodore Thornton Munger*. New Haven, Yale University Press, 1913.

Sec   Barth, Karl. *Protestant Thought: From Rousseau to Ritschl*. New York, Harper and Row, 1959 (originally published 1952).

N   —————— *The Word of God and the Word of Man*, trans. Douglas Horton. Boston, Pilgrim Press, 1928.

U   Bartol, Cyrus A. *A Discourse Preached in the West Church on Theodore Parker*. Boston, Crosby, Nichols, Lee and Co., 1860.

U   —————— *Discourses on the Christian Body and Form*. Boston, Crosby, Nichols and Co., 1853.

U   —————— *Radical Problems*. Boston, Roberts Bros., 1872.

U   —————— *The Rising Faith*. Boston, Roberts Bros., 1874.

U   —————— *The Word of the Spirit to the Church*. Boston, Walker, Wise, and Co., 1859.

L   Bascom, John. *The New Theology*. New York, G. P. Putnam's Sons, 1891.

L   Beach, David N. *The Newer Religious Thinking*. Boston, Little, Brown and Co., 1893.

A   Beaven, Albert C. "Facing the Generation Ahead," *Christian Century*, 56 (June 28, 1939), 820-822.

L   Beecher, Henry Ward. "Progress of Thought in the Church," *North American Review*, 135 (August 1882), 99-117.

L   —————— *Statement Before The Congregational Association of New York and Brooklyn, in which He Resigns His Membership* . . . New York, Funk and Wagnalls, 1882.

N   Bennett, John C. "After Liberalism—What?" *Christian Century*, 50 (November 8, 1933), 1403-1406.

A   —————— "A Changed Liberal—But Still a Liberal," *Christian Century*, 56 (February 8, 1939), 179-181.

U   Boller, Paul F., Jr. *American Transcendentalism, 1830-1860: An Intellectual Inquiry*. New York, G. P. Putnam's Sons, 1974.

CH
Sci   Bowden, Henry Warner. *Church History in the Age of Science: Historiographical Patterns in the United States, 1876-1918*. Chapel Hill, University of North Carolina Press, 1971.

P   Bowne, Borden Parker. *Metaphysics*, rev. ed. New York, Harper and Bros., 1898.

P   —————— *Personalism*. Boston, Houghton, Mifflin and Co., 1908.

L   —————— *The Principles of Ethics*. New York, Harper and Bros., 1892.

RE
Psych   Bremer, David H. "George Albert Coe's Contribution to the Psychology of Religion." Ph.D. dissertation, Boston University, 1949.

Bib   Briggs, Charles A. *The Authority of Holy Scripture: An Inaugural*

Address. New York, Charles Scribner's Sons, 1891.

Bib   _____ *Biblical Study: Its Principles, Methods and History*. New York, Charles Scribner's Sons, 1883.

Ecum   _____ *Church Unity: Studies of Its Most Important Problems*. New York, Charles Scribner's Sons, 1909.

L   _____ *Whither? A Theological Question for the Times*. New York, Charles Scribner's Sons, 1889.

A   Brightman, Edgar S. "From Rationalism to Empiricism," *Christian*
P   *Century*, 56 (March 1, 1939), 276-279.

Biog   Brose, Olive J. *Frederick Denison Maurice: Rebellious Conformist*.
I   Athens, Ohio University Press, 1971.

D   Brown, Colin G. "Christocentric Liberalism in the Episcopal Church," *Historical Magazine of the Protestant Episcopal Church*, 37 (March 1968), 5-38.

Biog   Brown, Ira V. *Lyman Abbott, Christian Evolutionist: A Study in Religious Liberalism*. Cambridge, Mass., Harvard University Press, 1953.

Bib   Brown, Jerry Wayne. *The Rise of Biblical Criticism in America, 1800-*
U   *1870: The New England Scholars*. Middletown, Conn., Wesleyan University Press, 1969.

T   Brown, William Adams. *Christian Theology in Outline*. New York, Charles Scribner's Sons, 1906.

T   _____ *The Essence of Christianity: A Study in the History of Definition*. New York, Charles Scribner's Sons, 1902.

L   _____ *Is Christianity Practicable?* New York, Charles Scribner's Sons, 1916.

A   _____ *A Teacher and His Times: A Story of Two Worlds*. New York, Charles Scribner's Sons, 1940.

U   Brownson, Orestes A. *A Discourse on the Wants of the Times*. Boston, James Munroe and Co., 1836.

U   _____ *New Views of Christianity, Society and the Church*. Boston, James Munroe and Co., 1836.

D   Bucke, Emory S., ed. *The History of American Methodism*. 3 vols. New York, Abingdon Press, 1964.

W   Buckham, John W. "The Christian Platonism of Dean Inge," *Journal of*
P   *Religion*, 4 (January 1924), 77-83.

W   _____ "Good-Will *Versus* Non-Resistance," *Biblical World*, 47 (January 1916), 33-35.

W   _____ "The Principles of Pacifism," *Biblical World*, 48 (August 1916), 88-90.

Sec   _____ *Progressive Religious Thought in America: A Survey of the*
T   *Enlarging Pilgrim Faith*. Boston, Houghton, Mifflin and Co., 1919.

U   Buell, Lawrence. *Literary Transcendentalism: Style and Vision in the American Renaissance*. Ithaca, Cornell University Press, 1973.

U   _____ "The Unitarian Movement and the Art of Preaching in 19th Century America," *American Quarterly*, 24 (May 1972), 166-190.

Biog   Bultmann, Rudolf. Introduction to paperback edition of Harnack, *What*

	is Christianity? trans. Thomas B. Saunders. New York, Harper and Bros., 1957.

Biog Burnett, Charles T. *Hyde of Bowdoin: A Biography of William DeWitt Hyde.* Boston, Houghton, Mifflin and Co., 1931.

T Bushnell, Horace. *God in Christ.* Hartford, Brown and Parsons, 1849.

T _____ *Nature and the Supernatural, as Together Constituting the One System of God.* New York, Charles Scribner, 1858.

Sci _____ "Science and Religion,"*Putnam's Magazine,* 1 (March 1868), 265-275.

L _____ *Views of Christian Nurture and of Subjects Adjacent Thereto.*
RE Hartford, Edwin Hunt, 1847. Published revised as *Christian Nurture.* New York, Charles Scribner, 1861.

A Calhoun, Robert L. "A Liberal Bandaged but Unbowed," *Christian Century,* 56 (May 31, 1939), 701-704.

F Carter, Paul A. "The Fundamentalist Defense of the Faith," in John Braeman, Robert H. Bremner, and David Brody, eds., *Change and Continuity in Twentieth-Century America: The 1920's.* Columbus, Ohio State University Press, 1968.

Sec _____ *The Spiritual Crisis of the Gilded Age.* DeKalb, Ill., Northern Illinois University Press, 1971.

W Case, Shirley Jackson. "Religion and War in the Graeco-Roman World," *American Journal of Theology,* 19 (April 1915), 179-199.

Sec Cauthen, Kenneth. *The Impact of American Religious Liberalism.* New York, Harper and Row, 1962.

U *The Works of William E. Channing, D.D.* 6 vols. Boston, James Munroe and Co., 1843.

Biog Cheney, Mary Bushnell. *Life and Letters of Horace Bushnell.* New York, Harper and Bros., 1880.

T Chiles, Robert E. *Theological Transition in American Methodism: 1790-*
D *1935.* New York, Abingdon Press, 1965.

T Clarke, William Newton. *An Outline of Christian Theology.* New York, Charles Scribner's Sons, 1898.

A _____ *Sixty Years With the Bible: A Record of Experience.* New York, Charles Scribner's Sons, 1912.

M _____ *A Study of Christian Missions.* New York, Charles Scribner's Sons, 1900.

W Coe, George A. "Contemporary Ideals in Religion," *Religious Education,* 11 (October 1916), 377-387.

RE _____ *The Core of Good Teaching.* New York, Charles Scribner's Sons, 1912.

RE _____ *Education in Religion and Morals.* New York, Fleming H. Revell Co., 1904.

Psych _____ "A Study in the Dynamics of Personal Religion," *Psychological Review,* 6 (September 1899), 484-505.

Sec Coffin, Henry Sloane. *A Half Century of Union Theological Seminary, 1896-1945: An Informal History.* New York, Charles Scribner's Sons, 1954.

W   ———— *In A Day of Social Rebuilding*: *Lectures on the Ministry of the*
Soc   *Church*. New Haven, Yale University Press, 1918.
W   ———— *The Preparedness of a Christian Nation*. New York, Madison
       Avenue Presbyterian Church, 1916.
I   Coleridge, Samuel T. *Aids to Reflection in the Formation of a Manly*
       Character. Burlington, Vt., Chauncey Goodrich, 1829.
D   Corey, Stephen J. *Fifty Years of Attack and Controversy*. St. Louis,
       Christian Board of Publication, 1953.
W   Dieffenbach, A. C. "The Failure of the Religious Press," *Christian*
       Register, 97 (August 1, 1918), 727.
D   Deitz, Reginald W. "Eastern Lutheranism in American Society and
       American Christianity, 1870-1914." Ph.D. dissertation, University
       of Pennsylvania, 1958.
Biog   Dorn, Jacob Henry. *Washington Gladden*: *Prophet of the Social Gospel*.
       Columbus, Ohio State University Press, 1966.
I   Dorner, Isaac A. *History of the Development of the Doctrine of the*
       Person of Christ, trans. W. L. Alexander. Edinburgh, T. and T.
       Clark, 1868.
I   Duffy, John J., ed. *Coleridge's American Disciples: The Selected Cor-*
       respondence of James Marsh. Amherst, University of Massachusetts
       Press, 1973.
I   Easton, Loyd D. *Hegel's First American Followers. The Ohio Hegelians*:
U   *John B. Stallo, Peter Kaufman, Moncure Conway, and August*
       Willich, with Key Writings. Athens, Ohio University Press, 1966.
D   Eighmy, John Lee. *Churches in Cultural Captivity*: *A History of the*
Soc   *Social Attitudes of Southern Baptists*. Knoxville, University of
       Tennessee Press, 1972.
I   Elliott-Binns, L. E. *English Thought, 1860-1900: The Theological*
       Aspect. London, Longmans, Green, and Co., 1956.
D   Farish, Hunter D. *The Circuit Rider Dismounts: A Social History of*
       Southern Methodism, 1865-1900. Richmond, Va., Dietz Press, 1938.
Biog   Fenn, Dan Huntington. "Willaim Wallace Fenn: A Living Influence,"
       The Unitarian Universalist Christian, 29 (Winter 1974-75), 25-31.
L   Fenn, William Wallace. "The Meaning of the Christian Religion,"
       lecture to the Theological Club, Cambridge, Mass., March 24, 1913.
       Fenn Papers, Harvard University Library.
L   ———— "Modern Liberalism," *American Journal of Theology*, 17
       (October 1913), 509-519.
Biog   ———— Untitled memorial article on George B. Foster, *University*
       Record, 5 (Chicago, April 1919), 172-185.
A   Ferm, Vergilius, ed. *Contemporary American Theology*. 2 vols. New
       York, Round Table Press, 1932-1933.
A   ———— *Religion in Transition*. New York, The Macmillan Co., 1937.
F   "The Flood Tide of Liberalism," *Ministers' Monthly*, 2 (September
       1923), 5-6, and (October 1923), 2-3.
L   Fosdick, Harry Emerson. *Adventurous Religion and Other Essays*. New
       York, Harper and Bros., 1926.
N   ———— "Beyond Modernism," *Christian Century*, 52 (December 4, 1935),
       1549-1552.

L   —— *Christianity and Progress*. New York, Fleming H. Revell Co., 1922.

A   —— *The Living of These Days: An Autobiography*, 2d ed. New York, Harper and Row, 1967.

Sec   Foster, Frank Hugh. *The Modern Movement in American Theology:*
T   *Sketches in the History of American Protestant Thought from the Civil War to the World War*. New York, Fleming H. Revell Co., 1939.

T   Foster, George B. *The Finality of the Christian Religion*. Chicago, University of Chicago Press, 1906.

L   —— *The Function of Religion in Man's Struggle for Existence*. Chicago, University of Chicago Press, 1909.

I   Fremantle, Canon William. *The World as the Subject of Redemption*, 2d ed. New York, Longmans, Green, and Co., 1895.

U   Frothingham, Octavius B. *The Religion of Humanity*. Boston, David G. Francis, 1873.

I   —— *Transcendentalism in New England*. New York, 1876.
U

F   *The Fundamentals: A Testimony to the Truth*. Chicago, Testimony Publishing Co., [1910-1915].

D   Garrison, Winfred E., and Alfred T. De Groot. *The Disciples of Christ: A History*. St. Louis, Christian Board of Education, 1948.

W   Garvie, Alfred E. "The Danger of Reaction, Theological and Ethical," *American Journal of Theology*, 21 (July 1917), 325-338

N   Gilkey, Langdon. *Naming the Whirlwind: The Renewal of God-Language*. Indianapolis, The Bobbs-Merrill Co., 1969.

Soc   Gladden, Washington. *Applied Christianity: Moral Aspects of Social Questions*. Boston, Houghton, Mifflin and Co., 1886.

W   —— *The Great War: Six Sermons*. Columbus, Ohio, McClelland and Co., 1915.

Bib   —— *How Much Is Left of the Old Doctrines?* Boston, Houghton, Mifflin and Co., 1899.

A   —— *Recollections*. Boston, Houghton, Mifflin and Co., 1909.

L   —— *Ruling Ideas of the Present Age*. Boston, Houghton, Mifflin and Co., 1895.

Bib   —— *Seven Puzzling Bible Books*. Boston, Houghton, Mifflin and Co., 1897.

Soc   —— *Social Facts and Forces: The Factory, the Labor Union, the Corporation, the Railway, the City, the Church*. New York, G. P. Putnam's Sons, 1897.

Soc   —— *Tools and the Man: Property and Industry under the Christian Law*. Boston, Houghton, Mifflin and Co., 1893.

Bib   —— *Who Wrote the Bible? A Book for the People*. Boston, Houghton, Mifflin and Co., 1891.

W   Gordon, George A. *The Appeal of the Nation*. Boston, The Pilgrim Press, 1917.

L   —— *Aspects of the Infinite Mystery*. Boston, Houghton, Mifflin and Co., 1916.

T   _____ *The Christ of To-day*. Boston, Houghton, Mifflin and Co., 1895.

M   _____ *The Gospel for Humanity: Annual Sermon Before the American Board of Commissioners for Foreign Missions, delivered at Brooklyn, New York, October 15, 1895*. Boston, ABCFM, 1895.

T   _____ *Immortality and the New Theodicy*. Boston, Houghton, Mifflin and Co., 1897.

L   _____ *Jesus and the Individual. Is Human Progress a Delusion? Two Addresses Delivered in the Old South Church, Boston, Massachusetts, at the Morning Services, January 18 and 25, 1925*. Boston, Old South Church, 1925.

M   _____ "The Missionary Motive and the American Board," *Christian Union*, 35 (January 13, 1887), 17-19.

A   _____ *My Education and Religion: An Autobiography*. Boston, Houghton, Mifflin and Co., 1925.

T   _____ *The New Epoch for Faith*. Boston, Houghton, Mifflin and Co., 1901.

T   _____ *Ultimate Conceptions of Faith*. Boston, Houghton, Mifflin and Co., 1903.

L   _____ *The Witness to Immortality in Literature, Philosophy and Life*. Boston, Houghton, Mifflin and Co., 1893.

Biog   Gowing, Peter Gordon. "Newman Smyth: New England Ecumenist." Th.D. dissertation, Boston University, 1960.

Sci   Gulliver, John P. *Christianity and Science*. Andover, Trustees of Andover Seminary, 1880.

O   Hamlin, Cyrus. "The New Departure and Missions," *Bibliotheca Sacra*, 43 (October 1886), 763-771.

I   Harnack, Adolf von. *What is Christianity?* trans. Thomas B. Saunders. New York, G. P. Putnam's Sons, 1901.

L   Harris, George. *A Century's Change in Religion*. Boston, Houghton,
Sec   Mifflin and Co., 1914.

L   _____ *Inequality and Progress*. Boston, Houghton, Mifflin and Co., 1897.

Sci   _____ *Moral Evolution*. Boston, Houghton, Mifflin and Co., 1896.

L   _____ "The Rational and Spiritual Verification of Christian Doctrine," *Christian Union*, 27 (June 14, 1883), 469-473.

Soc   Herron, George D. *The Larger Christ*. Chicago, Fleming H. Revell Co., 1891.

W   Hicks, Granville. "The Parsons and the War," *American Mercury*, 10 (Feburary 1927), 129-142.

U   *The Writings of Thomas Wentworth Higginson*. 7 vols. Cambridge, Mass., Riverside Press, 1900.

O   Hodge, Charles. *Systematic Theology*. Vol. I. New York, Charles Scribner, 1872.

Sec   Hofstadter, Richard. *Social Darwinism in American Thought*, 2d ed.
Sci   Boston, Beacon Press, 1955 (originally published 1944).

N   Homrighausen, Elmer G. "Barthianism and the Kingdom," *Christian Century*, 48 (July 15, 1931), 922-925.

N   _____ "A Young Minister's Counter-Revolt," *Christian Century*, 48 (February 18, 1931), 236-238.

F   Horsch, John. *The Modernist View of Missions*. Scottdale, Pa., 1920.

M

N   Horton, Douglas. "God Lets Loose Karl Barth," *Christian Century*, 45 (Feburary 16, 1928), 204-207.

A   Horton, Walter Marshall. "Between Liberalism and the New Orthodoxy.

N   *Christian Century*, 56 (May 17, 1939), 637-640.

N   _____ *Realistic Theology*. New York, Harper and Bros., 1934.

U   Howe, Daniel Walker. *The Unitarian Conscience: Harvard Moral Philosophy, 1805-1861*. Cambridge, Mass., Harvard University Press, 1970.

Sec   Hudson, Winthrop S. *The Great Tradition of the American Churches*. New York, Harper and Bros., 1953.

E   Hutchison, John A. *We Are Not Divided: A Critical and Historical Study of the Federal Council of the Churches of Christ in America*. New York, Round Table Press, 1941.

L   Hutchison, William R., ed. *American Protestant Thought: The Liberal Era*. New York, Harper and Row, 1968.

Soc   _____ "The Americanness of the Social Gospel: An Inquiry in Comparative History," *Church History*, 44 (September 1975), 367-381.

Biog   _____ "Cultural Strain and Protestant Liberalism," *American Historical Review*, 76 (April 1971), 386-411. © The American Historical Association 1971.

Biog   _____ "Disapproval of Chicago: The Symbolic Trial of David Swing," *Journal of American History*, 59 (June 1972), 30-47. Copyright Organization of American Historians, 1974.

L   _____ "Liberal Protestantism and the 'End of Innocence,'" *American Quarterly*, 15 (Summer 1963), 126-139. Copyright 1963, Trustees of the University of Pennsylvania.

M   _____ "Modernism and Missions: The Liberal Search for an Exportable Christianity, 1875-1935," in John K. Fairbank, ed., *The Missionary Enterprise in China and America* (Cambridge, Mass., Harvard Univeristy Press, 1974), pp. 110-131.

U   _____ "To Heaven in a Swing: The Transcendentalism of Cyrus Bartol," *Harvard Theological Review*, 56 (October 1963), 275-295. Copyright 1963. The President and Fellows of Harvard College.

I I   _____ *The Transcendentalist Ministers: Church Reform in the New England Renaissance*. New Haven, Yale University Press, 1959.

Biog   Hyde, William DeWitt. *Outlines of Social Theology*. New York, The Macmillan Co., 1895.

W   Inge, William R. "The Justice of God in History," *Constructive Quarterly*, 4 (September 1916), 440-457.

W   Jacks, Lawrence Pearsall. "A Theological Holiday—and After," *Hibbert Journal*, 14 (October 1915), 1-5.

W   _____ "England's Experience with 'The Real Thing,'" *Yale Review*, 4 (April 1915), 433-446.

N   Jenkins, F. D. "Germany's New Paradox Theology," *Bibliotheca Sacra*, 83 (October 1926), 427-462.

L   Johnson, David, and others, eds. *The Trial of the Rev. David Swing.* Chicago, Jansen, McClurg and Co., 1874.

N   Kegley, Charles, and Robert W. Bretall, eds. *Reinhold Niebuhr: His Religious, Social, and Political Thought.* New York, The Macmillan Co., 1956.

A   Kern, Paul B. "Hope Sees a Star," *Christian Century,* 56 (May 29, 1939), 412-414.

W   King, Henry Churchill. *Fundamental Questions.* New York, The Macmillan Co., 1917.

P   _____ *The Moral and Religious Challenge of Our Times: The Guiding
M   Principle in Human Development: Reverence for Personality.* New York, The Macmillan Co., 1915.

T   _____ *Reconstruction in Theology.* New York, The Macmillan Co., 1901.

W   _____ *The Way to Life.* New York, The Macmillan Co., 1918.

P   Knudsen, Albert C. *The Philosophy of Personalism: A Study in the Metaphysics of Religion.* New York, Abingdon Press, 1927.

N   Krüger, Gustav. "Theology of Crisis: Remarks on a Recent Movement in German Theology," *Harvard Theological Review,* 19 (July 1926), 227-258.

Biog   Krumbine, Miles H., ed. *The Process of Religion: Essays in Honor of Dean Shailer Mathews.* New York, The Macmillan Co., 1933.

O   Krutch, Joseph Wood. *The Modern Temper.* New York, Harcourt, Brace and Co., 1929.

N   Lewis, Edwin. *A Christian Manifesto.* London, Student Christian Movement Press, 1934.

Soc   Likens, William Henry. "Awareness of Social Problems in the Preaching of George A. Gordon and Frederick M. Meek." Ph.D. dissertation. Boston University, 1961.

O   Lippmann, Walter. *A Preface to Morals.* New York, The Macmillan Co., 1929.

D   Loetscher, Lefferts A. *The Broadening Church: A Study of Theological Issues in the Presbyterian Church Since 1869.* Philadelphia, University of Pennsylvania Press, 1958.

I   Lotze, Hermann. *Microcosmus: An Essay Concerning Man and His Relation to the World,* trans. E. Hamilton and E. E. C. Jones. 2 vols. New York, Scribner and Welford, 1885.

Biog   Love, Donald M. *Henry Churchill King of Oberlin.* New Haven, Yale University Press, 1956.

N   Lowrie, Walter. *Our Concern with the Theology of Crisis.* Boston, Meador Publishing Co., 1932.

A   Luccock, Halford E. "With No Apologies to Barth," *Christian Century,*
N   56 (August 9, 1939), 971-974.

W   Lyman, Eugene. *The Experience of God in Modern Life.* New York, Charles Scribner's Sons, 1918.

W   _____ *The God of the New Age.* Boston, Pilgrim Press, 1918.

W   _____ "The Religion of Democracy," *Union Theological Seminary Bulletin,* 2 (November 1918), 30-54.

P   —————— *Theology and Human Problems: A Comparative Study of Absolute Idealism and Pragmatism as Interpreters of Religion.* New York, Charles Scribner's Sons, 1910.

Biog   McConnell, Francis J. *Borden Parker Bowne: His Life and His Philosophy.* New York, Abingdon Press, 1929.

A   —————— "From Lausanne to Munich," *Christian Century,* 56 (April 19, 1939), 510-512.

W   McGiffert, A. C. *The Seminary and the War: Address Delivered at the Opening of the 82nd Academic Year.* New York, Union Theological Seminary, 1917.

I   McGiffert, A. C., Jr. "James Marsh: Philosophical Theologian, Evangelical Liberal," *Church History,* 38 (December 1969), 437-458.

F   Machen, J. Gresham. *Christianity and Liberalism.* New York, The Macmillan Co., 1923.

F   —————— *Modernism and the Board of Foreign Missions of the Presby-*
M   *terian Church in the U.S.A.* Philadelphia, privately printed, 1933.

P   Macintosh, Douglas C. "Can Pragmatism Furnish a Philosophical Basis for Theology?" *Harvard Theological Review,* 3 (January 1910), 125-135.

M   —————— "The New Christianity and World-Conversion," *American Journal of Theology,* 18 (July and October 1914), 337-354 and 553-570.

P   —————— *The Problem of Knowledge.* New York, The Macmillan Co., 1915.

P   —————— *The Problem of Religious Knowledge.* New York, Harper and Bros., 1940.

T   —————— *Theology as an Empirical Science.* New York, The Macmillan
O   Co., 1919.

N   —————— ed. *Religious Realism.* New York, The Macmillan Co., 1931.

F   McLoughlin, William G. *Billy Sunday Was His Real Name.* Chicago, University of Chicago Press, 1955.

Biog   —————— *The Meaning of Henry Ward Beecher: An Essay on the Shifting Values of Mid-Victorian America, 1840-1870.* New York, Alfred A. Knopf, 1970.

D   Manross, William W. *A History of the American Episcopal Church,* 3d ed. New York, Morehouse-Gorham, 1959.

Soc   Marchand, C. Roland. *The American Peace Movement and Social Re-*
W   *form, 1898-1918.* Princeton, Princeton University Press, 1972.

D   Marsden, George M. *The Evangelical Mind and The New School Presbyterian Experience: A Case Study of Thought and Theology in Nineteenth-Century America.* New Haven, Yale University Press, 1970.

I   Marty, Martin E. *The Modern Schism: Three Paths to the Secular.* New York, Harper and Row, 1969.

I   Marsh, James. "Preliminary Essay" in Samuel T. Coleridge, *Aids to Reflection in the Formation of a Manly Character.* Burlington, Vt., Chauncey Goodrich, 1829.

L   Mathews, Shailer. *The Faith of Modernism.* New York, The Macmillan Co., 1924.

A   ———— *New Faith for Old: An Autobiography.* New York, The Macmillan Co., 1936.

Soc   ———— *The Social Teaching of Jesus: An Essay in Christian Sociology.* New York, The Macmillan Co., 1897.

Sec   May, Henry F. *The End of American Innocence: A Study of the First Years of Our Own Time.* Chicago, Quadrangle Paperbacks, 1964 (originally published 1959).

Sec   ———— *Protestant Churches and Industrial America.* New York, Harper
Soc   and Row, 1967 (originally published 1949).

Sec   Mead, Sidney E. *The Lively Experiment: The Shaping of Christianity in America.* New York, Harper and Row, 1963.

Soc   Meyer, Paul R. "The Fear of Cultural Decline: Josiah Strong's Thought about Reform and Expansion," *Church History,* 42 (September 1973), 396-405.

M   Moore, Edward C. *The Vision of God: Annual Sermon before the ABCFM delivered at St. Louis, Mo., October 10, 1900.* Boston, ABCFM, 1900.

T   Morgan, J. Vyrnwy, and others *Theology at the Dawn of the Twentieth Century.* Boston, Small, Maynard and Co., 1901.

A   Morrison, Charles C. "How Their Minds Have Changed," *Christian*
N   *Century,* 56 (October 4, 11, 18, 25 and November 1, 1939), 1194-1198, 1237-1240, 1271-1275, 1300-1303, and 1332-1335.

Sec   Mott, Frank Luther. *A History of American Magazines.* 5 vols. Cambridge, Mass., Harvard University Press, 1930-1968.

Biog   Muller, Dorothea. "Josiah Strong and American Nationalism: A Re-evaluation," *Journal of American History,* 53 (December 1966), 487-503.

L   Munger, Theodore T. *Essays for the Day.* Boston, Houghton, Mifflin and Co., 1904.

L   ———— *The Freedom of Faith.* Boston, Houghton, Mifflin and Co., 1883.

Sec   Nash, Arnold S., ed. *Protestant Thought in the Twentieth Century:*
N   *Whence and Whither?* New York, The Macmillan Co., 1951.

D   Newman, Albert Henry. *A History of the Baptist Churches in the United States.* New York, Charles Scribner's Sons, 1915.

Biog   Newton, Joseph Fort. *David Swing: Poet-Preacher.* Chicago, Unity Publishing Co., 1909.

N   Niebuhr, Helmut Richard, and others. *The Church Against the World.* Chicago, Willett, Clarke and Co., 1935.

N   Niebuhr, Reinhold. "Barth: Apostle of the Absolute," *Christian Century,* 45 (December 13, 1928), 1523-1524.

N   ———— *An Interpretation of Christian Ethics.* New York, Charles
Soc   Scribner's Sons, 1935.

N   ———— "Let Liberal Churches Stop Fooling Themselves!" *Christian Century,* 48 (March 25, 1931), 402-404.

N   ———— *Moral Man and Immoral Society.* New York, Charles Scribner's
Soc   Sons, 1932.

N   —— *The Nature and Destiny of Man.* 2 vols. New York, Charles Scribner's Sons, 1941-1943.

N   —— *Reflections on the End of an Era.*New York, Charles Scribner's Sons, 1934.

W
N   —— "What the War Did to My Mind," *Christian Century*, 45 (September 27, 1928), 1161-1163.

W   Odell, Joseph H. "Peter Sat by the Fire Warming Himself," *Atlantic Monthly*, 121 (February 1918), 145-154.

N   Offermann, H. "The Theology of Karl Barth: An Orientation," *Lutheran Church Quarterly*, 2 (July 1929), 271-288.

A   Palmer, Albert W. "A Decade's Spiritual Pilgrimage," *Christian Century*, 56 (June 7, 1939), 730-732.

U   Parker, Theodore. *Sermons of Theism, Atheism, and the Popular Theology.* Boston, Little, Brown, and Co., 1853.

N   Pauck, Wilhelm. "Barth's Religious Criticism of Religion," *Journal of Religion*, 8 (July 1928), 453-474.

N   —— *Karl Barth: Prophet of a New Christianity?* New York, Harper and Bros., 1931.

Soc   Peabody, Francis Greenwood. *Jesus Christ and the Social Question.* New York, The Macmillan Co., 1900.

Sec
I   Pfleiderer, Otto. *The Development of Theology in Germany since Kant*, trans. J. F. Smith. London, Swan Sonnenschein and Co., 1890.

W
Soc   Piper, John F., Jr. "The Social Policy of the Federal Council of the Churches of Christ in America During World War I." Ph.D. dissertation, Duke University, 1964.

W   —— "Robert E. Speer: Christian Statesman in War and Peace," *Journal of Presbyterian History*, 47 (September 1969), 201-225.

A   Poteat, Edwin McN. "Searching for Greater Loyalties," *Christian Century*, 56 (February 22, 1939), 244-247.

O   Ransom, John Crowe. *God Without Thunder: An Unorthodox Defense of Orthodoxy.* Hamden, Conn., Archon Books, 1965 (originally published 1930).

Soc   Rauschenbusch, Walter. *Christianity and the Social Crisis.* New York, Harper and Row, 1964 (originally published 1907).

Soc
T   —— *A Theology for the Social Gospel.* New York, The Macmillan Co., 1917.

N   Richards, George W. *Beyond Fundamentalism and Modernism: The Gospel of God.* New York, Charles Scribner's Sons, 1934.

I   Ritschl, Albrecht. *The Christian Doctrine of Justification and Reconciliation*, trans. H. R. Mackintosh and others. Edinburgh, T. and T. Clark, 1900.

T
Sec   Roberts, David E., and Henry P. Van Dusen, eds. *Liberal Theology: An Appraisal: Essays in Honor of Eugene William Lyman.* New York, Charles Scribner's Sons, 1942.

I   *The Life and Letters of Frederick W. Robertson, M.A.*, ed. Stopford A. Brooke. London, Smith, Elder, and Co., 1866.

P   Royce, Josiah. The *Problem of Christianity*, 3 vols. New York, The

Macmillan Co., 1913.

I   Rucker, Darnell. *The Chicago Pragmatists.* Minneapolis, University
Psych   of Minnesota Press, 1969.

F   Sandeen, Ernest R. *The Roots of Fundamentalism: British and American
Millenarianism, 1800-1930.* Chicago, University of Chicago Press,
1970.

I   Schleiermacher, Friedrich. *Sämmtliche Werke.* 10 vols. Berlin, 1835-1862.

Sec   Schneider, Herbert W. *A History of American Philosophy.* New York,
P   Columbia University Press, 1946.

A   Schroeder, John C. "A Deeper Social Gospel," *Christian Century,* 56
(July 26, 1939), 922-925.

Biog   Sharpe, Dores R. *Walter Rauschenbusch.* New York, The Macmillan Co.,
1942.

O   Shaw, Charles G. "Two Types of Liberalism," *American Journal of
Theology,* 20 (July 1916), 360-371.

Sec   Shriver, George H., ed. *American Religious Heretics: Formal and Informal Trials.* Nashville, Abingdon Press, 1966.

T   Smith, Gerald B. "A Quarter Century of Theological Thinking in America," *Journal of Religion,* 5 (November 1925), 576-594.

I   Smith, Henry B. *Faith and Philosophy: Discourses and Essays.* New
York, Charles Scribner's Sons, 1877.

RE   Smith, Hilrie Shelton. *Faith and Nurture.* New York, Charles Scribner's
Sons, 1941.

Biog   ———— "George Albert Coe: Revaluer of Values," *Religion in Life,* 22
RE   (Winter 1952-1953), 46-57.

Sec   Smith, James Ward, and Leland Jamison, eds. *The Shaping of American
Religion.* Princeton, Princeton University Press, 1961.

L   Smyth, Egbert C., and others. "Christianity and Its Modern Competitors," *Andover Review,* 6 (November-December 1886), 510-514, 642-
658, and 7 (January-April 1887), 64-77, 295-308, 391-405.

T   ———— *Progressive Orthodoxy: A Contribution to the Christian Interpretation of Christian Doctrines.* Boston, Houghton, Mifflin and
Co., 1885.

Soc   Smyth, Newman. *Christian Ethics.* New York, Charles Scribner's Sons,
1897.

I   ———— *Dorner on The Future State: Being a Translation of the Section
of his System of Christian Doctrine comprising the Doctrine of the
Last Things, with an Introduction and Notes.* New York, Charles
Scribner's Sons, 1883.

L   ———— *Old Faiths in New Light.* New York, Charles Scribner's Sons,
1879.

T   ———— *The Orthodox Theology of To-Day.* New York, Charles
Scribner's Sons, 1881.

Ecum   ———— *Passing Protestantism and Coming Catholicism.* New York,
Charles Scribner's Sons, 1908.

A   ———— *Recollections and Reflections.* New York, Charles Scribner's
Sons, 1926.

I   _____ *The Religious Feeling*. New York, Scribner, Armstrong, and
           Co., 1877.

Ecum   _____ "Wanted: Church Statesmanship," *North American Review*,
           193 (February 1911), 281-292.

L   Sperry Willard L. *The Disciplines of Liberty: The Faith and Conduct of
W   the Christian Freeman*. New Haven, Yale University Press, 1921.

A   _____ "How My Mind Has Changed in This Decade," *Christian Cen-
           tury*, 56 (January 18, 1939), 82-84.

A   Stafford, Russell H. "Change Without Crisis," *Christian Century*, 56
           (July 5, 1939), 848-851.

T   Stearns, Lewis F. *Present-Day Theology: A Popular Discussion of Lead-
           ing Doctrines of the Christian Faith*. New York, Charles Scribner's
           Sons, 1893.

I   Stoever, William K. B. "Henry Boynton Smith and the German Theology
           of History," *Union Seminary Quarterly Review*, 24 (Fall 1968),
           69-89.

F   Stonehouse, Ned B. *J. Gresham Machen: A Biographical Memoir*. Grand
           Rapids, Wm. B. Eerdmans, 1955.

Biog   Swift, Arthur L. "[Coe] at Union Theological Seminary," *Religious
           Education*, 47 (March–April 1952), 94-95.

I   Swing, Albert T. *Theology of Albrecht Ritschl*. London, Longmans,
           Green and Co., 1901.

L   Swing, David. *David Swing's Sermons*. Chicago, W. B. Keen, Cooke,
           and Co., 1874.

L   _____ *Truths for Today: Spoken in the Past Winter*. Chicago, Jansen,
           McClurg and Co., 1874.

F   Thomas, W. H. Griffith. "Modernism in China," *Princeton Theological
           Review*, 19 (October 1921), 630-671.

N   Tillich, Paul. *The Religious Situation*, trans. H. Richard Niebuhr.
           New York, Henry Holt and Co., 1932.

A   Tittle, Ernest F. "A God-Centered Ministry," *Christian Century*, 56
           (June 21, 1939), 795-797.

A   Tucker, William J. *My Generation: An Autobiographical Interpretation*.
           Boston, Houghton, Mifflin and Co., 1919.

W   _____ *The New Reservation of Time; and Other Articles contributed
           to the Atlantic Monthly during the Occupancy of the Period Des-
           cribed*. Boston, Houghton, Mifflin and Co., 1916.

Biog   Tufts, James H. "George Burman Foster," *University Record*, 5 (Chi-
           cago, April 1919), 180-185.

P   _____ and others, eds. *Studies in Philosophy and Psychology by Former
Psych   Students of Charles Edward Garman*. Boston, Houghton, Mifflin
           and Co., 1906.

I   Valentine, C. W. *The Philosophy of Lotze in Its Theological Aspects*.
           Glasgow, Robt. Maclehose and Co., 1911.

I   Vanderpool, Harold Y. "The Andover Conservatives: Apologetics,
           Biblical Criticism, and Theological Change at the Andover Theo-
           logical Seminary, 1808-80." Ph.D. dissertation, Harvard University,
           1971.

N   Voskuil, Dennis N. "From Liberalism to Neo-Orthodoxy: The History of a Theological Transition, 1925-1935." Ph.D. dissertation, Harvard University, 1974.

Sec   Wagar, W. Warren. *Good Tidings: The Belief in Progress from Darwin to Marcuse.* Bloomington, University of Indiana Press, 1972.

Sec   Welch, Claude. *Protestant Thought in the Nineteenth Century.* New
I   Haven, Yale University Press, 1972.

D   Wentz, Abdel R. *A Basic History of Lutheranism in America.* Philadelphia, Muhlenberg Press, 1955.

Sci   Wieman, Henry Nelson. *Religious Experience and Scientific Method.* New York, The Macmillan Co., 1926.

A   —————— "Some Blind Spots Removed," *Christian Century*, 56 (January 25, 1939), 116-118.

L   —————— *The Wrestle of Religion With Truth.* New York, The Macmillan Co., 1927.

Sec   Williams, Daniel Day. *The Andover Liberals.* New York, Octagon Books, 1970 (originally published 1941).

Sec   —————— "Tradition and Experience in American Theology," in Smith and Jamison, eds., *The Shaping of American Religion.* Princeton, Princeton University Press, 1961.

U   Wright, C. Conrad, ed. *A Stream of Light: A Sesquicentennial History of American Unitarianism.* Boston, Unitarian Universalist Association, 1975.

Biog   Wurster, Stephen H. "The 'Modernism' of Shailer Mathews: A Study in American Religious Progressivism, 1894-1924." Ph.D. dissertation, University of Iowa, 1'72.

Index